Introduction to Critical Thinking

Bruce R. Reichenbach

Boston Burr Ridge, IL Dubuque, IA Madison, WI New York San Francisco St. Louis
Bangkok Bogotá Caracas Lisbon London Madrid
Mexico City Milan New Delhi Seoul Singapore Sydney Taipei Toronto

McGraw-Hill Higher Education

A Division of The **McGraw-Hill** *Companies*

INTRODUCTION TO CRITICAL THINKING

Published by McGraw-Hill, an imprint of The McGraw-Hill Companies, Inc., 1221 Avenue of the Americas, New York, NY 10020. Copyright © 2001 by The McGraw-Hill Companies, Inc. All rights reserved.
No part of this publication may be reproduced or distributed in any form or by any means, or stored in a database or retrieval system, without the prior written consent of The McGraw-Hill Companies, Inc., including, but not limited to, in any network or other electronic storage or transmission, or broadcast for distance learning.

Some ancillaries, including electronic and print components, may not be available to customers outside the United States.

This book is printed on acid-free paper.

1 2 3 4 5 6 7 8 9 0 QPF/QPF 0 9 8 7 6 5 4 3 2 1 0

ISBN 0–07–366027–2

Vice president and editor-in-chief: *Thalia Dorwick*
Editorial director: *Jane E. Vaicunas*
Sponsoring editor: *Monica Eckman*
Editorial coordinator: *Hannah Glover*
Marketing manager: *Daniel M. Loch*
Project manager: *Christine Walker*
Lead media producer: *David Edwards*
Production supervisor: *Enboge Chong*
Coordinator of freelance design: *Rick D. Noel*
Cover designer: *Nathan Bahls*
Cover image: ©*The Stock Illustration Source, Inc., "Future Profile" by Jim Bliss*
Senior photo research coordinator: *Carrie K. Burger*
Photo research: *Mary Reeg Photo Research*
Supplement coordinator: *Sandra M. Schnee*
Compositor: *Shepherd, Inc.*
Typeface: *10/12 Palatino*
Printer: *Quebecor Printing Book Group/Fairfield, PA*

The credits section for this book begins on page 333 and is considered an extension of the copyright page.

Library of Congress Cataloging-in-Publication Data

Reichenbach, Bruce R.
    Introduction to critical thinking / Bruce R. Reichenbach. 1st ed.
      p.   cm.
    Includes bibliographical references and index.
    ISBN 0–07–366027–2
    1. Critical thinking. I. Title.

  B809.2 .R45   2001
  160—dc21   00–021488
                                       CIP

www.mhhe.com

To my students, past and present,
who eagerly debated the issues raised,
pressed the arguments in our socratic dialogues,
responded creatively when challenged,
and energized my teaching with penetrating questions and comments.

Contents

Preface
To the Instructor

You may be asking, "Why another book on critical thinking?" The answer is that the writing level and approach of many of the current books presuppose readers who can read with comprehension and already possess sophisticated critical thinking skills the texts are designed to enhance. For example, critical thinking texts often commence by explaining about and evaluating arguments. But as we will see, analyzing and assessing arguments are higher-level critical thinking skills presupposing prior skills that often need development. Students cannot construct and analyze, let alone evaluate, arguments if they first have difficulty identifying the topic, thesis, and main points of what they read or hear. Many beginning college students who have not developed critical thinking skills flounder in this predicament. Many critical thinking texts also proceed by making numerous fine distinctions that, though important as advanced skill techniques, quickly are lost on beginners who may have trouble enough recognizing the undifferentiated examples in the real world. To teach students who are deficient in critical thinking skills to think critically, the instructor must begin at the beginning.

But how might you be convinced about the level at which some of your students function? Consider the following descriptions of acceptable teaching practices and student responses you may have encountered.

- You presuppose students bring critical thinking skills with them into your course. You assume that they can clearly grasp the theses and arguments developed in the assigned readings, follow the train of argument in your lectures, and find and follow the main points of free-ranging class or group discussions. And yet when you inquire about what they have read or heard, do students give you a multitude of confused ideas with minimal interconnectedness? Do you find students who misidentify the thesis or fail to see how the ideas are developed or defended?
- You assign problems or exercises with the readings to help students test their understanding of what they read. Do you find that students complain

that you expected them to read the material and solve the problems *before* you explained the concepts? Do some students not know how to go about applying what they read or solving the chapter problems or exercises?

- You involve students from the very beginning of your course in evaluative tasks. Perhaps the first questions you ask students about a reading or topic require evaluation of the ideas presented. Do students respond to your questions by saying, "I feel that . . .," thereby suggesting they lack the ability both to ascertain clearly and carefully and to work with the evidence and arguments presented, thus resorting to their feelings?

- On your tests you ask students to compare and contrast. Are you then disappointed when students produce a paragraph on one item and a paragraph on the other, leaving you to perform the integration you expected from them?

- At times you ask students to give the conclusion of the author's argument and to identify the relevant evidence. Do you find many students present a premise as the conclusion and treat the conclusion as evidence for the premise, showing that they confuse these two roles?

- You model critical thinking in your class, looking at several sides of an issue and weighing their respective merits and demerits. Do you find that students who closely follow what you do cannot examine ideas on their own from different points of view in discussion, in papers, and on tests?

One reason for our disappointment with certain student responses lies in the disparity between our academic expectations and student reality. We approach the classroom expecting our students to exercise significant critical thinking abilities. We lecture, conduct discussions, and construct tests at the higher stages of critical thinking—analysis, creative synthesis, and evaluation—for this is where intellectual ferment happens. Here we manipulate, argue for, synthesize, and evaluate ideas. But a number of students have not yet mastered the basic critical thinking skills. They still function at the beginning stages and do not know *how* to access the higher levels that you are demonstrating. Indeed, often they are confused by their instructor's use of these higher-level skills.

It is not that these students lack intelligence. They are bright but need to be taught critical thinking at its beginning. But what is the beginning? My own view of the beginning and how critical thinking proceeds from that point has been influenced by the model developed by Benjamin Bloom in his *Taxonomy of Educational Objectives*. Based on my thirty years of teaching, I believe Bloom has accurately described a realistic set of sequential educational objectives. Indeed, I now incorporate these stages and elements in all my course assignments—study questions, class discussions, papers, and tests—to facilitate students' critical thinking. Bloom's taxonomy, translated into a six-step sequence for developing critical thinking abilities, provides the skeleton for this text.

Those unfamiliar with this taxonomy will find that it provides a very useful way to understand how the skills needed to become a critical thinker can be systematically developed and how they piggyback on each other. By seeing how this model applies to critical thinking, you will be able to assess whether the model will significantly assist your students to become successful critical thinkers. My guess is you will quickly recognize that in large measure Bloom correctly identified the structure of educational objectives and paved the way for students to make significant progress toward the goal of thinking critically.

For those who already are familiar with Bloom's model, this text should prove to be a boon, for it takes seriously his stages of educational objectives and weaves them into a pattern for teaching and learning critical thinking. Intentionally adopting his educational philosophy, I have built this book on the prior themes as it proceeds, while constantly harking back to prior skills. Since learning occurs through reinforcement, students will better learn the skills of critical thinking when provided the opportunity to use repeatedly the same structures in approaching the material to be analyzed.

At the same time, however, I want to stress that no approach to critical thinking should be lockstep. Like us, students function simultaneously in different stages of critical thinking; and critical thinking tasks, which might be relegated theoretically to different stages, are interdependent. Thus, any approach to writing a text about and teaching critical thinking must be flexible and developmental, adjusting to the needs of the context while at the same time recognizing some larger, overarching structure.

CRITICAL THINKING SKILLS AND THE DISCIPLINES

Before we go further, a technical issue must be addressed. Some have suggested that critical thinking texts like this cannot be written because there are no generic critical thinking skills. Such skills, it is argued, are discipline oriented, making it impossible to move among disciplines in such a discussion. Thus, literature has its unique critical thinking skills, biology another set, history another, and so on.

Now it must be admitted that this is true of certain discipline-oriented skills. Literary criticism, for example, is discipline specific, as is historical criticism, though surely the methods of each spill over into other disciplines.

But the skills on which the book focuses cross disciplines. In every discipline readers must be able to recognize topics, issues, themes, theses, main points, premises and conclusions. They must be able to recognize, develop, and evaluate arguments. They must be aware of ambiguity and emotionally laden language that attempts to persuade without reason. They must develop strategies for solving problems. It is these common, basic skills to which we will attend.

Others object that critical thinking skills cannot be taught by themselves. Since skills come embedded in content, instructors must teach content to teach skills.

Again, to a certain extent this is true. If the goal is to teach students to understand the thesis of an argument, the arguments analyzed will have content. Similar things can be said about other skill activities like playing basketball or the piano; no one can develop the skills needed to be a good basketball player or pianist without balls, courts, and nets or pianos and music. So we all learn skills when we work with content. But we can concentrate on the skills themselves as we approach content-laden material. Accordingly, the text will focus only indirectly on the content of the paragraphs and arguments; content will be of concern insofar as it enables students to develop the skills requisite for being good critical thinkers.

AN OVERVIEW OF THE TEXT

Chapter 1 focuses on two case studies that require the application of critical thinking. Its purpose is to motivate students to begin thinking about their assumptions and the need to question what they read, hear, and see.

Chapter 2 lays out the model of critical thinking used to shape this text. By introducing the model early, the book allows students to see how the model functions so that they can operate consciously within its structure.

Chapter 3 attempts to help students become better readers and listeners. Students must be adept at finding the topic, issue, thesis, and main points before they proceed to analyze or critique what they read and hear. Since everything builds on this knowledge, the book emphasizes this basic skill throughout. Several editorials are included to enable students to develop their skills.

Chapters 4 and 5 address comprehension. They focus on language: its value, structure, ambiguity, meaning, and emotive content, with the goal of encouraging students to become aware of how language affects their comprehension. These chapters introduce some basic distinctions that ultimately can prove helpful for making evaluative judgments.

Chapters 6 and 7 consider analysis. Though different kinds of discourse are discussed, emphasis is placed on arguments. The chapters explore what arguments are, the role of premises and conclusions, different types of arguments, and argument recognition. They also instruct on how to diagram arguments, an important skill for discerning argument structure that presents a significant challenge for many students.

Chapter 8 begins the creative synthesis that uses the skills discussed and developed in the book. It emphasizes how to go about writing an essay: how to identify, research, and develop the topic, issue, thesis, and main points. This chapter can be integrated with the earlier chapters, for student writing should be encouraged throughout a critical thinking course.

Chapter 9 addresses problem solving. It focuses on getting students to brainstorm, to see a diversity of problems and relevant solutions, to think about the process of evaluating these solutions, and then to take careful steps to go about resolving the problems. It adapts the method developed by a program called Future Problem Solving, presently used competitively nationwide. Teachers are encouraged to use group work with this chapter. Groups will be directed through seven stages of problem solving and given several scenarios as group problem-solving exercises.

Chapters 10 through 12 concentrate on evaluation. Since successful, rational evaluation cannot occur until the topic, issue, and thesis are identified and the main points developed and explored, these chapters build on the previous ones. Chapter 10 explores methods of evaluating inductive arguments in a way comprehensible to beginning students. Chapter 11 focuses on a limited number of fallacies of content, since these generally are easy for beginning students to understand and master while capturing their interest.

Chapter 12 continues the evaluation process with a brief foray into formal reasoning. Its brevity reflects the view that formal reasoning is a complex, high-level critical thinking skill requiring considerable time, training, and practice to bring students to the level where they can use it in everyday examples. This presents a difficult task for students beginning in critical thinking. Consequently, although this chapter introduces students to some basic reasoning structures they frequently encounter, it is not a substitute for an extended logic course.

TEACHING HINTS

This text grows out of my experience in teaching critical thinking to students who perform below the median on standardized critical thinking and college entrance tests. Hence, it is written intentionally for beginning students who need work in developing reading, writing, and critical thinking skills. These students can become excellent thinkers; they merely need careful guidance in skill development and lots of practice.

I have attempted to avoid needless complexity and endless distinctions, which—though used in higher critical thinking activities—often confuse rather than help the beginning student. One can play with skills only after they are mastered at the basic level. Constant repetition of basic skills will be of more value than making finer discriminations within broad categories.

At the same time, some distinctions are necessary in order to categorize what readers and hearers experience. Labeling items that are different helps keep them distinct in the mind. So the matter of introducing distinctions requires a fine line. Users of the text should feel free to dispense with those distinctions that prove unhelpful or confusing to students. For example, the text distinguishes between ambiguity of meaning and ambiguity of use. This distinction assists students to discover why something is ambiguous and *how* to correct it. At the same time, some beginning students have trouble simply finding the ambiguity. In their case the distinction can be dispensed with until they have developed facility in recognizing ambiguity. Similar things can be said about the section addressing different types of emotive language, like euphemism, innuendo, and hyperbole.

Here are some suggestions for using this text.

- Most of the examples and exercises in this text are not artificial constructions but come from the popular media—newspapers (articles, editorials, letters, cartoons, advertisements) and magazines—that students are more likely to encounter. In choosing examples, I generally tried to avoid those that would date the text (for example, those that appeal to particular historical events, political issues, and current office holders). I encourage you to use this text hand in glove with your local and school newspaper, popular magazines, and television programs. *Find editorials, opinion pieces, letters, advertisements, even cartoons* and give them to your students to practice the skills the book addresses. By choosing issues currently in the news and culture, you can create interesting exercises relevant to current student thinking and reading.

- Integrate Chapter 8, which helps students *write argumentative pieces*, with the other chapters. Students should do a lot of writing on various topics or positions throughout the course. Make sure that students are asked to defend positions in which they do not believe.

- *Videotape television programs* and commercials and analyze them with the class. For example, videotape a *60 Minutes* editorial or a *20/20* segment and have students find the topic, issue, thesis, and main points. Hand out sheets that ask them to record the claims being made, what claims are disputable, and what evidence is being adduced on behalf of those claims. Tape a commercial and have them find any arguments, fallacies, use of emotional language, and the like. Tape a segment of a tabloid-type news show like *Hard Copy* and analyze it for its thesis, the main points used to develop the thesis, the video techniques used to convey points, emotive language, and ways to decode the subtle messages. Such exercises will encourage your students to become active rather than passive observers.

- Have students make a *portfolio* of examples from newspapers, magazines, books, and so on that illustrate ambiguity, vagueness, hyperbole, stereotyping, paragraph diagramming, or the various fallacies. The portfolio can include examples students find in the written or audiovisual media. Students should be asked to give the example (the actual article or a copy of it, or a transcription of it if the source is oral), indicate how it illustrates the critical thinking concept, convince the reader why it illustrates the critical thinking concept, and carefully document their source. Have students periodically bring these examples to class and analyze them in small groups.

- Assign a different student each day to bring in a cartoon or advertisement that illustrates a point made in the chapter being read. She or he might bring it to you ahead of time so you can make an *overhead* of it. Have the student present the cartoon and elicit the class's response to it. This will have the benefits of getting students to look for examples of things they read in the text and of encouraging them to appreciate the complexity of humor or the nature of advertising. Alternatively, make overheads of puzzles (for example, from the card game *Mindtrap*) and have students solve them in class. In the last case, employ the techniques of problem solving developed in Chapter 9 to familiarize your students with those techniques and to help them develop steps to solve problems.

- Many students with weak critical thinking skills have a weak vocabulary because either they rarely read or, when they do, they do not read materials that challenge them with unfamiliar words. In writing this text I struggled with the issue of introducing what students generally would consider to be new words. I have chosen to use a limited number of such words, since the purpose of this book is to encourage students to grow, expand, and develop good learning habits. Have students keep a *vocabulary journal*, entering what they consider to be new words, defining them in their own language (not that of the dictionary), and finding examples from printed material or the media using these new words. This journal could also contain words that the students discover in other courses, thus connecting vocabulary expansion in this course with others they are taking.

- Most of the chapters have a *Collaborative Learning Exercise* for use in the classroom. In addition, many of the exercises can be structured as collaborative learning experiences. Students can work together to compare their work and both identify where they answered the exercises differently from each other and try to resolve those differences in light of the text. While the answers to the odd-numbered examples in the exercises are provided at the end of each chapter, the even-numbered examples can be used in a variety of collaborative learning approaches. The McGraw-Hill philosophy website also offers a number of Critical Thinking Exercises that accompany this text. To utilize these exercises, visit the site at www.mhhe.com/socscience/philosophy.

- Since skills require repetition, *repeat points* made in previous chapters as you go through the exercises. For example, it is important to continue to ask for topic, issue, thesis and main points, even when the particular exercise does not call for identifying them. Or again, comment on how many of the exercise examples start in one direction and then switch theses with contrast words like "but" or "however." Repetition will reinforce important ideas and encourage students to perform basic understanding tasks (like looking for logical or argument-type indicators), even when not specifically directed to do so.

One last item. Our expectations as teachers in using this or any other critical thinking text must not be overblown. The development of skills in any area—athletics, music, driving, cooking—often involves a long process. Only by comparing the beginner with someone who has worked on the skills for a long time is the difference observable. In fact, this contrast exists between the instructor and the student—and often the gap is large. It is easy for us as professional instructors to forget where we once were and hence where many of our students are struggling in their educational pilgrimage. (To get that feeling again, sit in on a course in an area in which you have done no previous work.) Hence, it is important not only to let students in on the model used but also to assure them about the long-term possibilities and advantages of beginning to learn the requisite skills now.

Critical thinking is a skill. So although students will expect immediate results, progress at times in critical thinking, as with other skills, will be glacial. Progress will also plateau periodically. Consequently, students sometimes will be frustrated that they do not get the material or master the skills the first, second, or tenth time. Encourage realistic expectations; help them to understand and accept that their progress at times might be slow and that often they will not attain instantaneous insight into what they read and hear. And as often as possible, try to remove yourself from your own skill level to see how students who are struggling with these skills approach the project of learning them. If they can experience even a little progress through the stages, they can be encouraged to continue.

ACKNOWLEDGMENTS

Thanks are due to people who read part or all of this text and gave me suggestions. These include Vicky Nelson, Tom Morgan, Cass Dalglish, Karen Mateer, Sharon and Rachel Reichenbach, and reviewers for McGraw-Hill: Dr. Jim Fulcher, Lincoln College, Perkin, IL; Dr. Arnold Johanson, Moorhead State University, Moorhead, MN; Dr. Robert Mellert, Brookdale Community College, Lincroft, NJ; Dr. Jill Dieterle, Eastern Michigan State University, Ypsilanti, MI. Many ideas were sharpened in frequent discussions with Milo Shield. The text was class-tested over three years in Critical Thinking classes at Augsburg College and elsewhere; appreciation is extended to the students who made helpful comments and suggestions regarding how the text could flow more smoothly and clearly.

Bruce R. Reichenbach
Augsburg College

CHAPTER 1

Critical Thinking in Real Life

You are about to embark on an adventure in critical thinking. "What is critical thinking?" you may be asking. "How will I be adventuring, and what good will it do me?" You will journey into the lands of questioning, analyzing, and evaluating what you read and hear. You will be challenged to be curious about your world and freed to query. You will be encouraged not to take what you experience, read, or hear at face value, but to look behind the obvious for presuppositions, evidence, and arguments. Your goal will be to strengthen your ability to read more knowledgeably, understand more clearly, analyze more carefully, and assess more accurately.

And what will you gain when the journey is complete? You will have the opportunity to defend your own views and work at solving problems. You will have acquired the knowledge and developed the skills necessary to better engage in the lifelong task of thinking critically so that at the end you will be in a better position to intelligently ask and answer *why*.

But before we turn to the theory guiding the text and to the details of critical thinking, it is worth the effort initially to sample the joys of critical thinking. We do this by looking at two articles that indirectly pose some intriguing questions.

CASE STUDY 1

Take a few minutes to read the following newspaper article.

1 killed when truck hauling cattle trailer crashes into car

Buzz Magnuson/Pioneer Press

A collision Monday evening between a car and a pickup truck pulling a cattle trailer on Interstate 694 east of Silver Lake Road in New Brighton led to one fatality.

One person was killed Monday evening when a pickup truck that was pulling a cattle trailer slammed into the rear of a car and burst into flames on Interstate 694 just east of Silver Lake Road in New Brighton.

The truck driver escaped through the window of his truck and, with his hair smoldering, freed nine steers that were in the trailer. The impact flattened the roof of the car and compressed it into a mass that appeared to be about half the vehicle's normal length.

The accident, which occurred about 7:15 P.M., closed east bound lanes of the freeway for several hours. The identities of the victim—a man—and the truck driver were not available Monday night. The truck was owned by a Monticello man.

Witnesses, who included Dan Johnson of New Brighton, Gordon Raup of Arden Hills and Melanie Neil of Fridley, said the accident was touched off by a car that stopped or stalled in the middle lane. "She (the driver of the stopped car) didn't have her lights on, or flashers or blinkers, nothing," Neil said at the accident scene.

The car was struck from the rear by a small pickup truck, which in turn was struck by the truck towing the cattle trailer. The small truck was pushed aside, and the truck towing the cattle trailer plowed into the rear of a maroon car, and shoved it against the median. The truck went onto the roof of the car and burst into flames. Several other cars collided as vehicles veered around the accident, the witnesses said. The stopped car spun around and ended up facing west in the eastbound lane. Raup said it appeared that the driver was having a seizure when she was helped from her car.

After being released from the trailer, the steers went into the ditch on the south side of the interstate and grazed while wreckers were brought to block the freeway and corral the animals. Charles Gillespie, a salesman from Minar Ford just north of the freeway, was one of several men who helped watch the steers and then herd them into another trailer.

Wayne Wangstad, *St. Paul Pioneer Press*, August 22, 1995

We may ask some questions about this article. In each case, jot down your answers before you proceed to the next question.

1. What is this article about? (We call this the topic of the article.) _____

   _____

2. Using the topic from #1, compose the main question that you think the author tries to answer in this article. (We call this the issue that the author raises. The issue should be in the form of a question.) _____

   _____

3. What answer does the author give to this question? (We call this the thesis. The thesis is the main or primary assertion that the author of the article makes.) _____

   _____

4. What claims does the author provide to support, defend, or develop this assertion? _____

   _____

   _____

   _____

5. Are the thesis and its supporting evidence credible or believable? Why do you think the thesis is or is not believable? _____

   _____

   _____

   _____

Let us return to these questions.

1. Perhaps you said that the topic of this newspaper article is "an automobile crash," but this would not be entirely correct since trucks also were involved. One might more accurately say the topic is "a vehicle crash" or "a fatal vehicle crash."
2. The issue is a bit more difficult to discover, for the newspaper account wanders. The author does not seem to have one question that he wants to address but includes various interesting tidbits about the crash. One student

suggested that the issue is whether the cows were saved. It is true that at the end the article emphasizes rescuing the cows, but it is unlikely that the article focuses on this. A better possibility is "What caused a fatal crash on Interstate 694?" Support for the view that this is the issue can be found in the title, which often clarifies what an article is about.

3. The answer to the third question depends on what we take as the issue. If the issue is as we noted, then the thesis might be that "A stopped, unlighted car caused the fatal crash on Interstate 694."

4. Now for the evidence. The author presents a number of lines of evidence. First, a photo of crushed vehicles accompanies the newspaper account. Second, since the author did not witness the accident, he relies on witnesses (for example, Ms. Neil) to establish that the darkened car was stopped before it was involved in a chain of crashes, first being hit by a small truck and then by a truck pulling a cattle trailer.

    Mr. Raup reported that the female driver of the car appeared to be having a seizure when helped from her car. Does that help us understand the cause of what happened? Maybe, but maybe not. Was she having a seizure (how does a person look when she has a seizure)? Was the seizure the precipitating cause of the crash—was her car stopped because she had a seizure—or did the seizure result from the accident? Sometimes it is difficult to tell whether something is a cause or an effect.

5. Finally, do you believe this newspaper report? Whatever answer you give, it would be appropriate to ask why you do or do not believe it. Adopt the stance of a critical thinker, evaluating the thesis and the evidence to see whether you are justified in thinking that the thesis is true or not.

The first piece of evidence is the photo. Photographs are often very compelling pieces of evidence. They indirectly allow us to be at the scene, to witness the event. We sometimes say, "Seeing is believing," and photographs help us to see. The photo shows several mangled vehicles.

Two questions can be raised about the photo. First, was the photo taken of this accident or was it a file photo? (A file photo is a photograph taken at a previous time, stored in a file, to be used in a relevant situation. Sometimes the newsmedia use file photos to accompany a story when, for example, the person photographed is not accessible or when the event itself cannot be photographed.) Would this be an appropriate situation in which to use a file photo? Why or why not? Second, was the photograph doctored? You might recall O. J. Simpson's famous trial when key photographic evidence showing the accused wearing a certain rare brand of shoe was disputed by the defense on the alleged grounds that someone had doctored the photos. Probably you assumed that the photo in the newspaper crash account was not doctored, but though this seems to be a reasonable view, what evidence would you suggest to support your assumption?

The second piece of evidence involves the witness reports. Witnesses play an important role in building a case when we have not experienced something ourselves. Since we have extremely limited experiences, we rely on witnesses for our information. Two of the alleged witnesses reported how the accident occurred.

How reliable were the witnesses here? Did they actually see the crash, or did they arrive after the crash occurred? Do they have very good visual skills? Who are the witnesses? Do either the reporter or you know them? Are they reliable; are they persons who tell the truth or do they like to create dramatic stories? Note that you probably made a lot of assumptions about these witnesses—whether they saw the event, their reliability—when you read the report.

Perhaps you believe the article because crashes are the sort of thing that regularly happen and you have no reason not to believe it. It is true that thousands of people die in vehicle crashes every year in the United States, so the burden of proof probably lies on those who would want to deny the account.

It was also reported in an apparently credible, large-city newspaper. But one has to be careful. Merely because an article was printed in a newspaper does not establish that the event occurred, or that it occurred as reported. Newspaper reporters are human and make mistakes, as do the newspapers for which they write, though at the same time publication in leading newspapers tends to lend credibility to the account.

The major point here is that in reading this report, we have made very subtle judgments about the reliability of the photo, witnesses, reporter, and newspaper. We have made assumptions that we have not questioned. The assumptions might be correct; we may be justified in holding them. But we need to think about those assumptions.

There is one disquieting fact about the report. Maybe you caught it. If not, read the article again. Who was it that was killed? Note your answer. _____

_____

The article is unclear and somewhat confusing. To see this, first ask yourself, "What was the gender of the person pulled from the wrecked car?" Two witnesses, Ms. Neil and Mr. Raup, reported that she was a female. Yet in the third paragraph the reporter tells us that the fatality was a male. It seems that the article contains a discrepancy.

Before you read on, try to solve the discrepancy for yourself. First, decide how you are going to resolve it. What steps will you take? For example, what do you need to know to resolve the question? _____

_____

_____

_____

Now try to solve the puzzle. _____

_____

_____

_____

We may be able to account for the apparent discrepancy, but it will take some careful reading and some guesswork. Oftentimes we solve problems by elimination: from what we know we eliminate possible answers. Let us adopt this tactic. The fatality does not seem to be the cattle truck driver. It might be the person driving the first small pickup truck to hit the stopped car, but nothing is reported about that vehicle. Maybe the fatality was a passenger in one of the vehicles or in the associated crashes. On closer reading, it appears that there were two cars involved in the main reported accident: the car that was hit because it stopped in the roadway, and a second, maroon car that was shoved against the median. But now we meet another unclarity. The article reports that the trailer-pulling truck landed on the roof of "the car," flattening it. But which car? The words *the car* are ambiguous, for they do not tell us whether they refer to the woman's car or the maroon car. If it is the maroon car, the fatality might be a person from the maroon car shoved into the median.

With this careful reading one might be able to suggest a resolution about what seems to be a discrepancy in the deceased's gender. But the article is confusing, and no clear answer emerges. The point here is that the critical thinker wants to read carefully, to be aware of possible difficulties, to explore reasonable explanations, and when appropriate to think about the credibility of the witnesses. Probably you believe the account is true, though you might be skeptical. Either way, you should reflect on why you believe as you do.

CASE STUDY 2

Here is a second article for you to read carefully.

60-Foot Alligators Sighted in Florida Swamp!

FISHERMAN
Mike Bangor

"The teeth on these 60-foot-long monsters look like cavalry sabers."

Mike Bangor spent four grueling hours paddling his battered airboat back to the launch ramp after it collided with a never-before-seen monster of the Florida Everglades—a 60-foot-long alligator!

"I could have avoided hitting it if I had not been so stunned by its size," the 29-year-old bass fisherman declared. "But I have never seen a gator anywhere near that big in my life.

"When I saw it, I flat couldn't move a muscle. All I could see were its fiery

Reptile Expert Dr. Sidney Broadowski says these giant gators may be survivors from the dinosaur era.

eyes and its incredible teeth—rows and rows of 'em. They looked like cavalry sabers.

"The next thing I knew, 60-footers were popping up all around me. Any one of 'em could have chewed me up and swallowed me in one gulp. They're as long as tractor trailers and the Everglades are full of 'em.

"Thank God I was able to keep my boat running long enough to put a couple of miles between me and them."

Mike, who lives in Homestead, said he believes at least two dozen of the giant gators inhabit the swamp area just west of the Miccosukee Indian reservation.

"I wasn't about to stop and make a head count," Mike said. "As far as I'm concerned, just one of those brutes on the loose is too many. But I could see there was a hell of a lot more than one."

Miami reptile expert Dr. Sidney Broadowski said the giants may be sur-vivors from the dinosaur era that only recently hatched from eggs laid millions of years ago.

"The eggs could have survived if they had been buried in mud by some disaster that occurred after they were laid," Dr. Broadowski explained. "For some reason they worked their way to the surface where the Florida sun hatched them out.

"The gators have been feeding on fish and the deer that inhabit the Everglades. What we have to do now is take them captive so they can be fed and cared for properly.

"If not, they most certainly will die. Then the world will have lost a priceless relic dating back before the dawn of man. We simply cannot allow that to happen."

Tanya Broder, "60-Foot Alligators Sighted in Florida Swamp," *Weekly World News*. August 24, 1999. p. 9. Reproduced with the permission of *Weekly World News*, Inc.

Apply the same questions to this report that you used to think about the newspaper report describing the vehicle crash. Write out your answers before you proceed to the next question.

1. What is this article about? Give the topic. _____
2. Using the topic identified in #1, compose the question that you think the author tries to answer in this article. That is, give the issue in the form of a question. _____
   _____
3. What answer does the author give to this question? That is, give the thesis by identifying the position the author takes on the issue. _____
   _____
   _____
4. What evidence does the author give to support this position? _____
   _____
   _____
   _____
   _____
   _____

5. Are the thesis and its supporting evidence credible or believable? Why do you take the position you do? _____

_____

_____

_____

_____

An answer to #1 is that the article is about alligators.

2. The issue the author raises is, "Were 60-foot alligators sighted in the Florida Everglades?"

3. The author's thesis is that 60-foot alligators were sighted in the Florida Everglades.

4. The article provides several pieces of evidence to support the thesis. First, the article presents a photograph of a 60-foot alligator with sharp teeth. From the caption, "The teeth on these 60-foot-long monsters look like cavalry sabers," it would appear that the author intends her readers to take this photograph as evidence for her thesis. The article also contains photographs of the observer of the reptiles and a reptile expert.

  Second, the author quotes a witness who claims to have seen these gigantic monsters. Mike Bangor, a bass fisherman from Homestead, Florida, recounts his narrow escape after being surrounded by the alligators.

  The third piece of evidence is provided by an alleged reptile expert, Dr. Sidney Broadowski, who, although he did not see the alligators, comments on their origin and feeding habits.

5. The final question is whether the thesis and its supporting evidence are credible or believable. Would anyone be justified in believing that 60-foot-long alligators inhabit the Everglades? A critical thinker must now look at the thesis and its supporting evidence and evaluate this information.

The first pieces of evidence we identified were the photos of the alligator and the witnesses. As we noted in discussing the case of the vehicle crash, generally we believe that photographs provide good evidence. In a way, they make us observers of the scene. In fact, in the case of the truck-auto crash, you probably accepted the authenticity of the photo without any question. Do you also think that the photograph of the alligator is authentic and provides good evidence that 60-foot-long alligators exist in the Florida Everglades? Why do you answer as you do?

Although it appears to be an authentic photo of an alligator, is it of the 60-foot-long monsters reported? Someone may claim that it is a file photograph of a normal alligator; after all, it is difficult to determine size from the photo. Or someone may argue that Mike Bangor did not have time to take nor did he report taking a photo of the alligators that surrounded him. On such grounds, we may question the source and authenticity of the photo. However, the article does not claim that this is the only sighting of monster alligators; maybe other persons have captured their existence on film.

What conclusion can we draw from the photographs of Mike Bangor and Dr. Broadowski? Are these actual photos of these men? You may claim that you have no way to tell. But the same could have been said had photos of Ms. Neil or Mr. Raup been published in the *St. Paul Pioneer Press.*

The second piece of evidence is an eyewitness account of the alligators. In the case of the truck-auto crash, you probably accepted the accounts of the three witnesses, even though you knew nothing about the people. Would you also accept the testimony of Mr. Bangor in the alligator case? Note how the author appeals to ordinary people just as the author of the crash account did. If you believe the first witnesses, will you also believe the witness in the second case? Why or why not?

The writer also appeals to an authority, Dr. Broadowski, to bolster her case. Sometimes titles help lend credence to what people say. At other times we accept testimony from people who lack special credentials while rejecting testimony from people who allegedly have special academic degrees or credentials earned through their experience. What is the significance of credentials like doctor, and in what circumstances are these credentials significant?

If you were a prosecuting attorney, you would want your special witnesses to be authorities with recognizable credentials. Supposedly, such persons would be in a better position to provide credible, knowledgeable testimony. At the same time, the defense is looking for credentialed authorities to give a different and conflicting account. Authorities are aligned on both sides. So although we often listen to people with credentials, it does not follow that they are always to be believed. They too are fallible, have biases, and can be questioned. Critical thinkers think about how to evaluate witnesses, their credentials, and their testimonies.

How could you find out about the reliability of Dr. Broadowski? One action you could take would be to check the telephone books in the Miami area to see whether he is listed, and if so identify the organization he is associated with or even attempt to talk to him personally. Failure to discover his telephone listing may occasion some doubt in your mind about the reliability of the account, although unlisted phone numbers are not uncommon.

Perhaps you rejected the monster alligator account because of its source, *Weekly World News,* which is what is termed a tabloid or sensational newspaper. Critical thinkers evaluate sources to determine their reliability. What experience have you had with the two sources, *The St. Paul Pioneer Press* and *Weekly World News,* so that you are justified in believing the accounts of one and not that of the other? Have you read both, one, or neither? If you haven't read either of them, on what basis can you trust or distrust an account printed in them?

You may suggest that our culture clearly distinguishes the two kinds of papers so that one can immediately determine which is reliable and which not. In American society this may be true, where it is easier to distinguish tabloid newspapers from standard newspapers. But in many other countries the line between them is not so clearly drawn.

You may say that tabloids are not reliable because their purpose is to entertain, whereas this is not the purpose of daily newspapers. But surely there are entertainment aspects in the daily newspaper.

You may reply that although daily papers entertain, their primary function is to present information. A look at other articles in the two newspapers helps confirm this judgment. But interestingly enough, in the same issue of the *Weekly World News,* the paper reports that "In the past 12 months, *Weekly World News* staffers have traveled a distance equal to more than five trips to the moon to report the hottest and most fascinating stories from the four corners of the globe. . . . [They] rang up a budget-busting $1.4 million in long-distance phone calls."

You might say that tabloids present opinion but newspapers give the facts. But what is fact and what is opinion? Can you clearly draw this distinction in practice and claim that standard newspapers and magazines give facts and not opinions? Don't the respective story writers present their opinions and those of any witnesses cited?

Are there any other clues to the reliability of the article? _____

_____

Perhaps you noted that the report is posted from Corkscrew Swamp, Florida. You could research whether there is such a place. The article says that the alligators were sighted just west of the Miccosukee Indian reservation. You could check to see whether such a group of Indians exist and whether they have a reservation in Florida. In addition, you could explore whether it is reasonable to claim that dinosaur eggs could be preserved for millions of years in a state that would allow them to hatch, or whether by now they would have been fossilized. In short, although you yourself cannot check about the alligators (and given their reported size, perhaps you would not want to do so), the article makes other factual claims that provide opportunity for you to assess the accuracy of the account.

These two articles help raise some interesting and important questions about what we are justified in believing and why. Critical thinkers pay attention to what they read and hear and continually ask themselves whether they are justified in believing what they read and hear. They look for evidence to support what is said and for presuppositions that they or the authors bring to the material. Ultimately, they evaluate the evidence to see whether it is strong enough to warrant belief.

The purpose of this text is to help you become a more critical thinker. It will do this by helping you develop certain skills needed to think critically. The text will be successful if you read it, re-read it, and do all the exercises. By the time you are finished with the text, you will see the world and think about what you read and hear in a very different way than when you began.

Discussion Questions

1. What makes someone an authority on a particular subject or area? In what circumstances can the ordinary person's testimony be more readily accepted than that of an authority?

2. Are authorities who have not witnessed the event more reliable than witnesses to the event? When and when not?

3. a. Should you automatically discount writings about things that are extraordinary? Why?
    b. What would be the consequences for science or exploration if you discounted the unusual or extraordinary? (Imagine Columbus talking to Queen Isabella about his discoveries in the New World or Galileo to the Jesuit scholars about the phases of Venus that he saw through his telescope.)
    c. What criteria could we use to decide which accounts about the extraordinary we can or ought to believe?

4. a. What is evidence?
    b. What makes evidence "good" or "credible"? What questions could you ask yourself to try to determine whether alleged evidence is reliable?
    c. Are there times people should ignore evidence in order to come to a conclusion or resolve an issue? Give an example.

5. We greatly rely on vision to determine what we believe. How often have you said, "I'll believe it when I see it?"
    a. Can we believe without seeing? To what sorts of things would this apply, and how else might one establish the credibility of such belief?
    b. Can we see without believing? Give an example.
    c. What is the role of photographs as compared with text in providing evidence for the truth of a claim? Which is more believable, when and why?

Collaborative Learning Exercise

Each student will have a partner with whom to work. With your partner, before class, either (1) find a newspaper article, report, or editorial about whose truth you have some doubt and a tabloid article that you think contains substantial truth, or (2) find two articles or editorials in magazines, newspapers, or books that take two different positions on a topic.

In class, compare these two articles/editorials, giving three reasons why you think the one is probably correct and the other not. Note especially the role of authorities and your own experience in making your decision.

Take your most controversial example to another group and see whether you can convince the group members of your opinion regarding the reliability of this article. What types of reasons did they find most persuasive?

CHAPTER 2

Six Steps of Critical Thinking

Consider the following cartoon.

CITIZEN DOG   **BY MARK O'HARE**

What is the point of the cartoon? _____

_____

The cartoon has something to do with the saying "Getting up on the wrong side of the bed."

- What does that saying mean to you? _____

  _____

  What does the saying mean to the author of the cartoon?_____

_____

- How does an understanding of the saying help us to account for the man's smile in the last box? _____

_____

- Why is the man sitting on the floor? Does the saying help explain why he is sitting on the floor? _____

_____

The author of the cartoon plays with language to get us to think about our ideas. Sometimes we are to take language literally (at face value)—the man actually climbs over the bed to get out on the other side; sometimes we are to interpret language nonliterally (for example, metaphorically). Humor often depends upon the juxtaposition of different uses of language, as in this cartoon. By playing with language the cartoon moves beyond a simple understanding of the common folk expression to poke fun at our language and ideas.

Critical thinking begins first with knowledge and then with comprehension. These activities provide the foundation for all creative and critical thought. Yet knowledge and comprehension form only part of the critical thinking task. Though this book will begin with studying ways to foster attaining knowledge and comprehension, it will go beyond these skills to assist you to develop the intellectual tools needed to *evaluate* properly the information you receive. It will push you to ask why some statement or claim purportedly is true and then help you learn how to assess the reasons given. For example, is the expression "So and so are miserable because they got up on the wrong side of the bed" true in that it helps us explain why some people are grouchy on a particular day?

Since this book proposes to help you become a better critical thinker, you need to know from the outset what we will be doing. *Critical thinking* involves using a cluster or group of interconnected skills to analyze, creatively work with, and evaluate what you read and hear so that you can decide whether or not to believe something or to take a specific action. To become a critical thinker, you need to be able to figure out whether the speaker's or author's opinions are true or false; whether the author has adequately defended those ideas; whether certain recommendations are practical or useful, or impractical and dead ends; and whether particular solutions are likely candidates for solving a problem. This book focuses on helping you develop these skills.

Collaborative Learning Exercise 1

Bring to class a cartoon that pokes fun at a saying or expression or that trades on different meanings of words (contains a pun). Discuss with your partner and then explain to the class how the cartoonist played with language to create the humor.

Collaborative Learning Exercise 2

With your partner, create a cartoon that pokes fun at a saying or expression or that trades on different meanings of words (contains a pun). Explain to the class how you played with language to create the humor. Here is an example to get you started.

Bite off more than one can chew

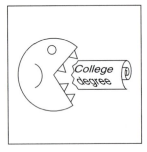

M. J. Reiling

CRITICAL THINKING DISPOSITIONS

Critical thinking involves certain dispositions. A **disposition** is a tendency to act or think in a certain way. For example, as an American driver I have a disposition, or tendency, when I drive around a corner to head to the right side of the road. When I drive in Australia, I must resist that disposition, or tendency; otherwise, I will soon be in a crash.

Dispositions may be thought of as a kind of habit, and habits are very important for success. They enable you to interact with your environment without taking the time to think about how you are going to act. Consider how many accidents you would get into if you had to decide consciously each step to take to stop the car you are driving. Walking, typing, and playing a sport or a musical instrument would be all but impossible if you had to ponder each move or bit of fingering. Habits, or dispositions, are essential to functioning adequately and smoothly in life.

Likewise, forming good critical thinking habits, or dispositions, can help you better cope with your world. They make you a more interesting person, more fulfilled, with richer experiences that take you far beyond what is merely present or apparent to you at any moment. Here is a partial list of dispositions characteristic of many critical thinkers. Critical thinkers

- are curious about the world; they try to be well informed.
- are creative questioners.
- frequently ask *why*, seeking reasons to defend a position.
- use credible sources and mention or refer to them.
- take into account the total situation or context when they interpret something.
- keep their thinking relevant to the main point and avoid going off on tangents.

- look for alternative explanations, positions, or arguments.
- are open-minded and seriously consider points of view other than their own.
- take or change a position when the evidence, grounds, or reasons are sufficient to do so.
- withhold judgment when the evidence, grounds, or reasons are insufficient.
- seek as much precision as the subject permits.
- realize the limits of knowing, and hence look for probabilities rather than proofs.
- realize the role of personal judgments and biases in the knowing process.
- deal in an orderly manner with the parts of a complex whole; they anticipate the next step in the process.
- are sensitive to the feelings, levels of knowledge, and degree of sophistication of others when presenting their findings.
- apply their critical thinking abilities to a wide variety of subjects.[1]

You need not memorize this list, but you might go through it and check off those dispositions that characterize you. Most likely you do not have them all; few people, if any, do. But you already have some of these traits, though probably you never thought much about them. We might say that you have laid the groundwork for being a very good critical thinker. This text aims at helping you to improve. To focus on improving your critical thinking, mark those dispositions that you want to work on during this term. You can turn these characteristics into habits by repeated practice.

CRITICAL THINKING SKILLS

Critical thinking also resembles activities that develop and use skills. Playing a sport or a musical instrument, operating a car or a printing machine, laying bricks or cooking a gourmet meal use a variety of *interconnected skills.* To play basketball well, you must learn to do more than move your arms to shoot the ball. You must learn to dribble, pass, execute plays, rebound, recognize the opponent's moves, and the like. The good basketball player draws on all these skills to succeed in a game.

Skills *build on each other.* To play a Mozart concerto, a pianist must have mastered many elementary skills: using proper fingering, recognizing chords, pedaling properly. After mastery, the pianist no longer thinks about or focuses on the basic skills but uses them automatically when playing.

This means that in all skill areas, a person *begins by concentrating on and practicing the basic skills.* Admittedly, working on basic skills often is not very interesting or exciting. Spending hours dribbling a basketball and shooting can be boring. When I coach youth soccer, the players dislike the repetitive drills; they want to go immediately to scrimmaging. Music students spend hours practicing chords, scales, and runs on the piano or arpeggios on the violin before they ever get to play Mozart. Yet this constant practice of basics eventually pays off when the time comes to play the more difficult pieces. Careful attention to repeating and mastering the basic skills is necessary because success in carrying out the task depends on them.

Skills also are *goal oriented*. You learn skills not for their own sake but as means to some end. You learn to catch and throw a baseball not simply to perfect the task of getting the ball into the leather glove but so that you can play baseball for your own enjoyment, to win games, or to develop baseball into a passionate hobby or career.

Learning to think critically is similar to learning other skills. First, it involves *interconnected skills,* about which this book talks. Here is a sample list that might not be entirely clear now but that will become clearer as you move through the book.

- *Clarification abilities* include the ability to discern the thesis and main points of what you read or hear. You demonstrate your comprehension of the material by your ability to express the material in your own words.
- *Inference-related abilities:* You make an **inference** when you believe that *some true statements provide reasons to think that other statements are true.* For example, from noting that Congress has not passed a balanced budget in twenty years despite the apparent demand from the public to control spending, you might infer or conclude that Congress lacks the will to pass a balanced budget.

Consider the following cartoon.

THE BUCKETS   **BY SCOTT STANTIS**

Source: THE BUCKETS. Reprinted with permission of United Feature Syndicate, Inc.

What evidence does Mrs. Buckets have for her claim that her family had eaten previously at the restaurant? _____

_____

_____

Note that to get this evidence, Mrs. Buckets has to make an inference from the behavior of the man in charge of restaurant seating.

Working with inferences requires you to be able to

- identify and distinguish the evidence (premises) from the conclusion of the reasoning or argument (the point to be proven).

- draw correct conclusions from the information given.
- assess the truth of the evidence.
- dig out the presuppositions of the argument.
- consider the relevance of the information to the conclusion.
- evaluate whether the evidence is strong enough to support the conclusion.

Task

Apply each of these abilities to "The Buckets" cartoon to get a preliminary evaluation of how good Mrs. Buckets's argument is.

You also employ *strategies* to deal with situations in which you find yourself so that you can make wise and carefully reasoned decisions. For example, you develop strategies to cope with too much homework, to work with your teammates to score a goal, to get children to obey you, or to find a job. Some of these strategies succeed, others are inadequate to resolve your problem, and so you revise them. The abilities used to employ strategies enable you to

- decide what is at issue or what is the problem.
- create various options to deal with the problem.
- know where and how to get information.
- identify the criteria for evaluating the options.
- determine how to test various options for dealing with the problem.
- assess or weigh the strengths and weaknesses of the options or proposed solutions.

Strategies can also be used to solve fun puzzles.[2]

Use some of the abilities just listed to reverse the direction that the fish is swimming by moving only three sticks.

```
            /

      / \ /

      \ / \

          \
```

Whether the problem is serious, like solving a social ill, or frivolous, like moving sticks to form a fish, critical thinkers develop strategies that enable them to address the problem in systematic yet creative ways. We will say more about creative problem solving in Chapter 9.

Critical thinking skills are often *interrelated,* so that you develop not only individual reasoning and problem-solving skills but groups of skills that work together to accomplish the task of thinking critically about some problem, issue, or claim.

Second, the skills involved in critical thinking *build on each other.* They are not learned in isolation, and their exercise requires each other. We will say more about this shortly.

Third, critical thinking skills are not learned for their own sake. They are *goal oriented:* to enable you to become a better critical thinker in everyday life. They are means to the ends of enabling you to decide for whom to vote, what product to buy, what position to take on a moral issue, what is wrong with your plumbing, which vacation package gives you the best deal, how to request a pay raise, and so on. Ultimately, your success in what you attempt in life will be measured by how well you are able to creatively synthesize ideas and critically evaluate the claims presented to you.

How do you build skills? The answer is quite simple: *practice.* Practice is necessary to become good at anything. This text will emphasize practice—lots of it so that you can develop the skills needed to become a critical thinker. Since the number of exercises a book can contain is greatly limited and the issues that interest the public change, look for examples from the newspapers, books, and magazines you read. In this way you can improve your critical thinking skills by thinking about topics tailored to your current interests.

THE CHARACTERISTICS OF CRITICAL THINKING

We have spoken about critical thinking in terms of dispositions and skills. Can we give a fuller characterization of it? Two experts in the field of critical thinking define critical thinking as "reasoned and reflective thinking that is focused upon deciding what to believe or do."[3] Critical thinking involves the use of a kind of thinking called *reasoning,* in which we construct and/or evaluate reasons to support beliefs. Critical thinking also involves *reflection,* especially when we examine and evaluate the reasonableness of our own and others' thoughts and ideas. Although as critical thinkers we reflect on others' ideas, we properly employ critical thinking not so much to challenge or correct others as to benefit ourselves: to become self-reflective. Finally, critical thinking is *practical:* we use it both to form our beliefs and to act on them. Our actions will be more rational if they are based on beliefs we take to be justified (having good supporting evidence).

Perhaps this definition sounds too academic. Let's put it another way. Consider this newspaper advertisement.

> Of all the people in the world, if you don't deserve one, who does? You, of all people. You've probably been told that to own a fur is to be pampered and self-indulgent. And so stoic little you have resisted. But your time has come. Because if you're seeking lots of attention in this world, you have to love yourself first. And show it. And what better way than in fur? This winter get all wrapped up in yourself. In fur. You deserve it. You'll love yourself in fur.

Should you purchase a fur coat, as the advertiser suggests? The advertiser gives you several reasons; can you list two of them?

1. _____

2. _____

Now think about those reasons. Does the advertisement give good enough reasons to warrant you laying out big bucks for a fur coat? Fur manufacturers tell you to purchase a fur coat on the grounds that supposedly it will do something for your image and you deserve a fur coat. But does fur contribute to your image? Is it an appropriate symbol in an era when people champion animal rights and question needless killing of animals? Is this a good (moral, practical) way to draw attention to yourself?

Consider a second, political advertisement.

> For treasurer, Bednarczyk. Why Bill Bednarczyk? The present City Treasurer is 76 years old—eleven years past retirement age for most workers. He is drawing a full pension from the Fire Retirement Fund in addition to his salary as Treasurer—a combined income of over $30,000 per year. Whatever his past accomplishments for the city, most people feel he should retire.

Should you follow the advice of this political brochure and vote for Bill Bednarczyk for city treasurer? What reasons does the brochure provide for voting for him?

1. _____

2. _____

You probably noted the appeal to the opposing candidate's age and income. Is a candidate's age or the drawing of additional income from a retirement fund a relevant consideration in making a choice about how to cast your vote for a candidate?

Critical thinking, then, *is the careful, deliberate determination of whether we should accept, reject, or suspend judgment about the truth of a claim or a recommendation to act in a certain way.* It involves being a reflective, persistent questioner, wanting to know *why* you should believe or do something and carefully investigating and evaluating the reasons given. Why should I take biology when I am not sure of my major? Should I marry Steve? Should I invest my money in junk bonds? Should Congress and the individual states pass a balanced budget amendment? Should assisted suicide be legal, and if so, under what circumstances and with what controls? Should women with silicone breast implants be allowed to bring a class action suit against Dow Chemical Company?

Critical thinkers are curious about their world; they do not accept things at face value. They explore the reasons why things are as they are or why people think that things are a particular way. Because they have reasoned and reflected carefully, critical thinkers ultimately have better grounds than most people for deciding what to believe and how to act reasonably.

In a sense, critical thinkers are skeptics. They analyze and criticize; they constantly question why, looking for grounds and evidence behind claims that are made. They tend to doubt, question, and suspend judgment, to postpone affirming statements to be true or taking action. But critical thinkers need not become complete skeptics, that is, people who cannot believe anything. They need not wait indefinitely to make a decision until all the information is in, for they realize that we never have all the information. Indubitable certainty is unattainable. Knowledge is limited and often at best probable, yet we must have beliefs and take action. So critical thinkers creatively put what they have considered and analyzed back together so that they can act.

As you can see, critical thinking has a practical end—to act reasonably. The goal of this text is practical. By the time you have completed it, you should be better able to understand, analyze, solve problems, and evaluate than you did before. Maybe not a lot better at first, but better. It is best at the outset to be realistic about your and the teacher's expectations. The development and mastery of skills require a long and at times slow and painful process. Michael Jordan and Isaac Stern did not master their respective trades of playing basketball and the violin overnight. So you should not be discouraged if your papers do not move immediately from average to excellent quality after you have read and employed the insights of Chapter 8. Again, *skill development and mastery take time.* Don't get discouraged; be encouraged that with practice you will improve. Eventually, many of the skills considered here will become second nature to you; you will use them without thinking about them. Most important, by developing the skills emphasized in this text you have laid the foundation for a lifetime of intellectual growth and enjoyment.

THE GUIDING MODEL FOR THE TEXT

Good critical thinking does not just happen; carefully considered theory lies behind acquisition of these abilities. This text will follow and adapt the work of Benjamin Bloom, who developed and persuasively argued for a six-stage structure of educational objectives.[4] This text will argue that critical thinking skills can be grouped around six educational objectives and their assorted tasks.

1. Acquiring knowledge or information
2. Comprehending or understanding what you read and hear
3. Applying what you understand to given situations
4. Analyzing the information that you understand
5. Synthesizing and creatively using what you understand and have analyzed
6. Critically evaluating what you understand and have analyzed or created

These objectives can be divided into two sets of three. The first three objectives form the foundation for the second three: analyzing, synthesizing, and critically evaluating. The second three involve doing something with the material you have understood.

We will discuss this model in terms of *steps* or *stages* involved in critical thinking. Each of the first four steps presupposes and builds upon the previous step. Steps 5 and 6 build on the first four. (Step 6 can also build on step 5 when you evaluate what you created.) Thus, the steps are sequentially ordered. For each step specific *task words* help you identify the level being addressed. Though you need not memorize these words, the more you are familiar with the words and the level at which they function, the clearer you will be about what is expected of you on tests, assignments, papers, and task assignments. For example, by identifying key task words, you can anticipate the type of answer the instructor wants on a test question. If the instructor asks you to compare and contrast, you know that the instructor wants more than a demonstration of knowledge and comprehension of different views; the instructor wants you to analyze what you know and to interrelate it. We will italicize these task words to help you identify them in our discussion of the six steps.

Step 1: Knowledge

The first step in learning is acquiring facts or discovering information, whether specific data, methods, patterns, or ideas. When you first learn material, you are asked to store it in your mind. Later, you may be asked to recall, repeat, or reproduce that material—for example, on a test, in a discussion, in a job interview, or in a sales pitch to a prospective customer. Sometimes we forget critical information, as the following cartoon illustrates. But when we do, it reduces our effectiveness.

Source: THE DUPLEX. © 1997 Glenn McCoy. Reprinted with permission of Universal Press Syndicate. All rights reserved.

This first step, then, involves acquiring knowledge: knowledge of what is said, written, heard, or seen. This kind of knowledge is foundational to everything we do; it forms the data base from which we operate. The bigger our base of information, the better we can function in society and the more valuable an employee or successful an employer we will be. It also is essential to further learning, for learning occurs when we relate new material to what we already know. To learn, we make connections between the old and the new so that the new can be integrated into the familiar.

Throughout your education you have been asked to demonstrate this kind of knowledge by performing a variety of tasks.

- On multiple choice or matching tests you have been asked to *identify* and *match* persons with dates, places, or events.
- You have also been asked to *list* things: the battles of the American Civil War, the presidents of the United States, the rivers of Asia, the parts of a plant, the Top Ten songs of the year, the specials of the day or types of wine served in the restaurant where you work.
- You have been asked to *define* terms (which you usually accomplish by looking up the terms in a dictionary) and *record* them or to *find* things like the topic, thesis, or supporting evidence in material you read, hear, or see.

- Perhaps you were asked to *sort* or *rearrange* events by the year in which they took place.
- In a class you may have been asked to *repeat* a poem or a speech, like a Shakespearean sonnet or Lincoln's Gettysburg Address.

Adequately performing these tasks requires developing certain relevant skills. In terms of critical thinking, this basic level of knowledge involves the skill of being able to identify what is being said: the topic, the issue, the thesis, and the main points. Accurate identification of *what* is said or written is fundamental to everything else you are going to do with what is spoken, written, or shown in the media. Accordingly, we begin our study of critical thinking in the next chapter by focusing on the skills needed to obtain accurate knowledge of what is being communicated.

Step 2: Comprehension

The kind of knowledge described in step 1 is not the same as comprehension. A person might be able to list the first five rights in the Bill of Rights without understanding what they mean. Similarly, a person might be able to repeat Lincoln's Gettysburg Address without comprehending what Lincoln was conveying in that important speech. Or a person might list the U.S. presidents without understanding anything about the executive branch of our government.

So what is comprehension? **Comprehension** means understanding the material read, heard, or seen. In comprehension you make the new information your own by relating it to what you already know. There are degrees of comprehension. The better you can relate the information to your other knowledge and see its meaning, the better you comprehend it.

The primary test of comprehension is being able to put what you have read or heard into your own words. By substituting your own language, structure of ideas, or arrangement of evidence for that given by the author or speaker, you gain control over the information. This is one reason why many teachers discourage you from giving many quotations in what you write. Being able to quote leaves you at the level of knowledge (in that you can recognize what was valuable or important in what you read), but quoting does not show that you comprehend what you read. The information remains in the language and thought patterns of the author or speaker.

As I walk by the exercise room in the college gym, I see students with books in hand, trying to mark them with a highlighter as they walk on treadmills or climb the stairmaster. I admire their diligence but wonder about what they retain and comprehend. What is wrong with simply underlining or using a highlighter? There are three strikes against relying solely on this method. First, students have a tendency to highlight most of the text, thus saving little time during review. Second, this method does not identify levels of importance. Some of what you read is more germane to the thesis; other material relates to the subtheses rather than the main thesis; some is simply expository or provides examples, while other material is extraneous or contains asides. Simply using a highlighter does not indicate these differences unless you go to great lengths to color code. Third, and most important, merely marking the material does not force you to put it in your own words.

Comprehension requires you to make the material your own. If you merely mark or underline the text, the words remain the author's; you have not processed what the author has written. Only when you translate the thesis and main points into your own words, either in the margin or in a separate notebook, does the material become yours. And when it becomes yours, you retain it longer.

We associate many tasks with comprehension. Key words help you identify this stage of critical thinking.

- You may be asked to *discuss, express,* or *explain* what you have read, heard, or seen. This task requires you to use your own language to communicate what you know.
- Someone may ask you to *restate, rearrange, summarize* or *interpret* the material.
- You may be requested to *infer* or *draw a conclusion* from what you have read, seen or heard.

In each case, you are asked to go beyond mere reiteration of what was stated to interpret the material and give it your own meaning. Note that none of this is possible without your having a basic knowledge of the material. If you cannot find the topic, issue, or thesis of the author, if you cannot identify the basic facts, or if you confuse the main point the author makes with the evidence given to support that point, you will not be able to accurately interpret or comprehend what was communicated. Thus, knowledge rightly precedes comprehension.

Step 3: Application

You know that you know something when you are able to do something with it—for example, to apply it to an actual situation. Several years ago I installed a new garage door opener. The forty-page manual was very detailed, and I carefully followed all the instructions—sometimes wondering whether I understood them correctly. How, then, was I to know whether I really understood the manual? The answer is simple: did the garage door go up when I pushed the button? If it did, I understood the manual; if it did not, I needed to reread and reapply what was written.

Application of the material involves a number of tasks.

- *Apply* what you have learned to an actual situation.
- *Illustrate* or *give an example* of what was said.
- *Prepare* a dish to show you understood the recipe.
- *Predict* what will happen when the teacher mixes these two beakers of chemicals.
- *Demonstrate* that the thesis is true, or *develop a scenario* that shows how what you have read will work out.
- *Dramatize* the moral that you just discussed.

What ties these tasks together is that first, each requires you to know what you have read, heard, or seen, and requires you to comprehend it. Second, each requires you to carry out some task to apply what you comprehend to an actual situation. This is the level at which your employers initially will evaluate your performance. They will assess whether you can accurately carry out their instructions and perform the prescribed occupational tasks. If you cannot, no matter how much you protest that you understand your responsibilities, they will not continue to employ you.

Throughout, this book asks you to use the skill of application. Hence, no special chapter will be devoted to it. The text asks you to read and comprehend what is written and then presents you with exercises that give you the opportunity to demonstrate your comprehension. Successful completion of the exercises, preferably without paging back to the section of the text you already read dealing with that topic, shows that you know and comprehend what you have read; failure to correctly complete the exercises often means that you need to go back and reread the text to acquire the comprehension necessary to successfully answer the exercises.

My students sometimes comment that it is unfair to expect them to do the exercises before I discuss or explain in class the material they are to read. But consider. The purpose of the exercises is to let you know for yourself whether you understood what you read. Hence, you should complete the exercises to the best of your ability before you get to class, so that you can spend the class time asking questions about and discussing what you did not understand (as revealed by your not being able to answer specific exercises). Indeed, in the world outside of school, your employers do not explain everything you are to do. Often they give you a project and then ask you to apply what you understand by carrying out tasks not demonstrated for you ahead of time. So that you may check your work, the odd numbered exercise examples are answered at the end of each chapter.

These first three ability levels—knowledge, comprehension, application—prepare critical thinkers for the three higher stages. They are prerequisites to being able to analyze, synthesize, and evaluate what you read or hear.

Step 4: Analysis

Analysis involves breaking what you read or hear into its component parts in order to make clear how the ideas are ordered, related, or connected to other ideas. By seeing the organization and structure of the communication, you can discern the relationships between the ideas and perhaps the basis for the positions taken.

Bloom notes that analysis deals both with form and with content. Analysis of the *form* concerns the structure of what you read or hear.

- Critical thinkers *look for organizational patterns or principles* in what others present to them.
- They *observe the relationships* between the ideas, noting their temporal relation and their logical order.
- They are able to *break down* the material into its components.

Just as, if not more, important is the analysis of the *content* of the communication. Critical thinkers develop the ability to

- *order* the material, to *distinguish dominant from subordinate ideas* or themes.
- *distinguish statements of evidence from hypotheses.*
- *see* what *assumptions* or presuppositions the author makes.

- *find evidence* of the author's purposes.
- note how one idea *relates* to another.
- *categorize* information received.
- set up *comparisons* among things.

Since analysis can involve identifying the evidence for a thesis, it often will involve working with arguments. Hence, critical thinkers

- accurately *distinguish conclusions from the evidence that supports them.*
- *see how the premises connect* and are relevant to the conclusion.

Developing your analytical skills allows you to assess the strength of arguments better than you were previously able.

Step 5: Synthesis

Synthesis involves the ability of putting together the parts you analyzed with other information to create something original. You reach out for data or ideas derived from a variety of sources to produce an object, paper, solution, pattern, or organization not evident in the beginning. Your creativity plays a key role as you reconfigure the information and ideas.

Perhaps at some stage of your life you enjoyed working with Legos. Constructing the object pictured on the box would be an example of step 3, application: taking the pieces and connecting them according to the instructions on the box show you understand and can follow instructions. But at some point you probably tired of building and rebuilding the same pictured object and began to combine Legos from several boxes to make novel objects. At that point you moved beyond application to the creativity of synthesis.

Similarly, at some point in your education you probably were asked to write a paper telling what so-and-so said about some subject. You were asked to apply your understanding of what you read. But perhaps your teacher went beyond this to ask you to stake out your own position. Your challenge was to integrate material from various sources to create or defend your view. At this point you went beyond application to synthesis.

Synthesis task words clearly invoke creativity.

- *Compose* an essay that ties the ideas of several short stories together.
- *Invent* or *imagine* something new.
- *Revise* or *transform* something; *modify* a current plan to take account of other requirements (redesign a kitchen).
- *Show* how you might solve the problem a different way than you or someone else did.

Each of these activities involves the skill of synthesis applied to some area of communication or learning. In particular, this book applies the relevant skills of synthesis to help you write argumentative essays defending some point of view and solve problems.

It is easy to see how synthesis involves the preceding four steps. To create, you must know and comprehend what you work with, and you must be well aware of the elements or parts that you synthesize—how they relate to each other and how they function.

Step 6: Evaluation

The final stage of critical thinking is evaluation. Once we have understood and analyzed what is said or written and the reasons offered to support it, we can proceed more effectively to evaluate the strength of the position. Many terms indicate the evaluative task. *Appraise, assess, evaluate, judge, weigh, rate,* and *grade* are just some of these terms. Each asks you to evaluate the information presented so that you can decide whether you ought to give assent or withhold belief, or whether you ought to take or refrain from taking action.

Critical thinkers especially look at connections between the evidence and the conclusion the evidence allegedly supports. They ask, How strong is the evidence? If the evidence is true, is it strong enough to warrant my belief? Is there contrary evidence that is either presented or suppressed? What are the presuppositions? Are the presuppositions defensible, or are they hidden because they are indefensible?

Critical thinkers often delay judgment until they have time to evaluate the reasons given by the author for his or her claim. However, judgment is not always postponed until enough evidence is present. Sometimes the matter is important enough to require action apart from sufficient evidence. If someone yells for you to leave the building because a fire is burning in the basement, carefully investigating the evidence might cost you your life. But critical thinkers do not make it a general practice to act or believe without first considering the relevant evidence.

It is important not to put evaluation ahead of the other critical thinking steps and, in particular, not to put it first. Sometimes we tend to respond to what we hear or read by first making an evaluative judgment, even before we have attended to the reasons given to support the view. This response is called "a rush to judgment." Instead of identifying and analyzing the reasons, we note whether the view agrees or disagrees with what we already believe. If it agrees, the view is true, right, or beautiful; if not, it is false, wrong, or ugly. Sometimes our response invokes affective behaviors; the view is true, right, or beautiful if we like or enjoy the ideas; it is false, wrong, or ugly if we dislike them. Because we have not looked at the reasoning, we have no idea how the person actually argued for his or her thesis and little awareness of other reasons that might be presented to support the view. Our evaluation consists of saying, "I *feel* that . . ." Feelings substitute for reasons when evaluation precedes analysis.

Critical thinking does not dispense with feelings, but neither does it make judgments solely or primarily upon such. Reliance upon the emotive or affective aspect of our lives must be coupled with careful, rational evaluation of the evidence or reasons that might be presented for the positions considered.

Exercise 1

For each of the following test questions, use our six-step model of critical thinking to determine at what stage of critical thinking the question asks you to perform. Some questions have several parts and use different critical thinking skills.

1. What is one example of a symbol in Hemingway's *Hills Like White Elephants?*

2. The federal government recently started requiring that all colleges and universities report key information like graduation rates. This is an example of (a) a problem, (b) an opportunity, (c) a directive, (d) all of the above, (e) none of the above.

3. Based on our discussion of those factors that inhibit prosocial behavior, explain what we as individuals might do to increase appropriate helping behavior.

4. Define and place in context two of the following: Donatism, penance, Luther's view of baptism.

5. Modify the computer program so that it prints the sequence of numbers backwards rather than forwards.

6. Why do you think Mrs. May, in Flannery O'Connor's *Greenleaf,* wants to kill the Greenleaf's bull?

7. Explain in your own words the two competing theories in urban sociology: "metropolitan division of labor/urban ecology" and the "new international division of labor/political economy."

8. Sell me a can of any spray deodorant using "Monroe's motivated sequence." (Label the five steps involved in correct order; then briefly illustrate each.)

9. In a carefully reasoned essay, describe and explain the underlying and immediate causes of the I and II Punic Wars, as described in the readings and class lecture.

10. Considering what we have studied about scientific thought and the possible flaws in nonscientific thinking, describe how some therapists and clients may come to believe in repressed memories that are not in fact true.

11. The author of the text observes that "millions of Americans voted with their cars between 1950 and 1990, moving from the urban core to the suburbs." Discuss how this has affected the racial, ethnic, and social class housing patterns typical of most U.S. cities and your own neighborhood.

12. Comedy and tragedy are often treated as generic opposites. What are comedy and tragedy? Show how Shakespeare combined elements of both in his plays.

13. Define "micro" and "macro" analysis. Then explain why both types of analysis are necessary for an adequate understanding of the present condition and future possibilities for your neighborhood.

14. The Legal Aid Society has filed a class-action lawsuit stating that it is unconstitutional to limit the benefits allowed to newcomers to the level of benefits they would have received in the state from which they are moving. Which vestige of the Elizabethan Poor Laws and Settlement Act of 1662 is this lawsuit attempting to override?

15. Most people listen with an efficiency rate of about 70 percent. True or false?

$$\bigcirc \xrightarrow{\text{?}} \bigcirc \text{CH}_2\text{CH}_2\text{CH}_2\text{CH}_3$$
$$\text{Cl}$$

16. Explain Weber's concept of ideal type and bureaucracy.

17. Compare the arguments that Fried and Sade give to show that we do or do not have a right to adequate health care. Be sure to show *why* they differ on this issue.

18. Devise a reasonable synthesis for 3-chlorobutylbenzene from benzene. There will be more than one right answer.

19. How does the Muslim understanding of the Quran differ from the Christian understanding of the Bible as an inspired text?

20. List five different things the Windows 95 operating system allows you to do.

21. Describe an ethical dilemma you have faced. **a.** Why is this an ethical dilemma? **b.** Which values or duties or whose interests are in conflict? **c.** Construct the arguments that a teleologist or utilitarian might use to evaluate this situation. **d.** How would you resolve this dilemma using Gewirth's Principles Hierarchy?

22. What two factors or variables are the basis of understanding environmental uncertainty? Briefly explain.

23. Suppose you are a leader of a group that is making an important and urgent decision. To avoid a groupthink bias, which of the following instructions to the group might be best? **a.** Stick together to find the best decision, **b.** Be as objective as possible, **c.** Consider the opposite point of view, **d.** Each of the above would be equally effective.

24. a. What is a teleological (utilitarian) ethical theory? What is a deontological ethical theory? **b.** How are these two theories similar and different? **c.** Using the case study that follows, show *how* Mill and Kant, as representatives of the respective theories, would go about resolving the moral dilemma. (Make sure you show *what* the dilemma is and *how* they would go about resolving it.) **d.** Develop one major criticism of each theory.

25. Design two good organizational questions that demonstrate what you have learned so far but have not been asked in other questions in this test.

Collaborative Learning Exercise 3

Bring to class two assignments or test instructions from other classes you are taking or have taken. With your partner, analyze the words used in the questions or instructions found in the assignment. Use these words to identify the levels of critical thinking you are asked to demonstrate in the assignments. Then discuss how understanding the critical thinking skill you are asked to demonstrate might help you better answer the question or carry out the assignment.

The remainder of this book focuses on these six task-oriented skills.

- Attaining knowledge
- Comprehending what is said or written
- Applying what is comprehended to some situation
- Analyzing the ideas and the reasons behind them
- Creatively synthesizing ideas
- Evaluating the ideas or claims made

With the exception of application, which is incorporated throughout in the form of exercises, this book develops the six steps sequentially. Chapter 3 deals with skills related to attaining knowledge. Chapters 4 and 5 address comprehension by attending specifically to skills needed to work effectively with language. Chapters 6 and 7 emphasize analysis by concentrating on the skills of recognizing and constructing explanations and arguments. Chapter 8 addresses synthesis by helping you construct an argumentative paper in favor of some thesis, while Chapter 9 works with your skills in creative problem solving. Chapters 10–12 focus on skills needed to evaluate the truth of claim or arguments.

Whether and to what extent you develop these skills will depend on how much you practice using them. The more you work with this six-step structure in all your reading and listening, the more you will become comfortable with critical thinking. If you are careful in the earlier stages, your syntheses and evaluations will be more fruitful and much better. You will be more creative because you more clearly understand what you are working with. Your evaluations will go beyond, "I feel that . . ."; you will be able to give good reasons why a claim is worthy or unworthy of belief or action.

So much for the introduction of our theoretical model. Now it is time to get to work on developing the skills themselves.

Collaborative Learning Exercise 4

You are already an expert in some area that interests you. That is, there is something that you can do so well so that you can evaluate whether someone else's performance is good, accurate, or correctly done. Your task is to find a partner who knows nothing about this area and to teach that person some relevant basic information or elementary skills. In doing so you will bring that person through the six stages of critical thinking. Here is a procedure to follow.

1. Identify an area about which you have an interest and feel somewhat qualified to make evaluative judgments about another's performance.
2. List ten basic items of knowledge that someone needs to know in order to perform well in the area you identified.
3. Find a partner who does not know much about this area and explain these ten items to

that person in your own words; then have that person tell you in his or her own words these ten basic items.
4. Discuss some way you can determine whether your partner understands this basic information.
5. Have your partner compare the skills needed to succeed in your area with those needed to succeed in the area of her or his expertise.
6. Work with your partner to sketch out a creative project using the information and skills pertinent to your area. What might this project look like, and how would you both go about carrying it out?
7. Develop with your partner a list of criteria you would use to evaluate whether someone had performed well in the area on which you chose to work.

Notes

1 Adapted from Stephen P. Norris and Robert H. Ennis, *Evaluating Critical Thinking* (Pacific Grove, CA: Midwest Publications, 1989), 12.

2 SOLUTION TO THE PROBLEM: 1. The problem is how to accomplish the goal in only three moves. 2. One might construct various ways to move the sticks. The solution involves raising the fish's body line. 3. One tests the options by seeing whether the picture of the reversed fish is created in only three moves.

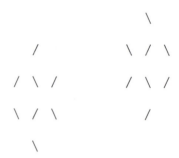

3 Norris and Ennis, 3.

4 Benjamin Bloom et al. *Taxonomy of Educational Objectives* (New York: Longmans, Green and Co., 1956).

ANSWERS TO THE EXERCISES

Exercise 1.

1. Knowledge—a what question
3. Comprehension—explain
5. Application or Synthesis—modify
7. Comprehension—explain
9. Comprehension—describe and explain
11. Comprehension and Synthesis
13. Knowledge and Comprehension
15. Knowledge
17. Analysis—compare
19. Analysis—compare
21. Comprehension (a & b); analysis; synthesis
23. Knowledge or comprehension
25. Synthesis—design

CHAPTER 3

Knowledge

Acquiring Information

Have you ever left a lecture or talk, looked at your friend and said, "What did that speaker say?" Perhaps your friend replied, "I don't know. I didn't understand a thing." It is possible that the speaker did not really say much and that the talk was a waste of time. Successful communication requires that the speaker say something to listeners in a comprehensible way. But maybe you found the talk difficult to follow for other reasons. Maybe you were puzzled because you did not know what topic the speaker addressed. The topic was strange, foreign, or something you never "got into." Or perhaps you got the topic but had no idea of what the speaker was saying about that topic. You could not repeat or apply what the speaker said. Neither could you critique it. If so, you realized that you knew little more coming out of the talk than when you entered. Probably from your perspective, attending the lecture was a waste of time.

Without knowledge of what the speaker said, you cannot critically think about what you heard. The same applies to your reading. Knowledge underlies all critical thinking. Critical thinking without knowledge is like a carpenter without any wood: you have nothing with which to work. To acquire knowledge of what is communicated, you must identify the *topic* the writer or speaker is discussing, what the writer or speaker takes to be the *issue* or problem with respect to that topic, what *position* the author or speaker takes on the issue, and finally, where appropriate, the *main points* the author or speaker

Collaborative Learning Exercise

Watch with your class a videotape of a television editorial, a short talk given on campus, or some commercial lecture. With a partner decide the speaker's topic, thesis, and the main points given to develop or defend the thesis. Evaluate how successfully the speaker communicated and note the reasons why the speaker was or was not a successful communicator.

uses to support or develop the position he or she takes on the issue. Helping you recognize these four elements is this chapter's task.

THE TOPIC

We begin with the **topic,** which is what a sentence, paragraph, series of paragraphs, chapter, book, video, or speech is primarily about. In effect, it is the main or central *subject* of the communication. The topic might be a thing, event, person, or idea. Generally it is expressed by a word or two or three, at most a phrase. You should *not* express it by a complete sentence, because by then you are moving on to state some claim or thesis about the topic.

One way of thinking about the topic is that the topic provides the *category* under which you or the writer would classify the paragraph or group of paragraphs. Think about how you research using the subject index of the library computer. The computer asks you to type in a word or two that will identify what you want to find information about. These words constitute the topic of your research.

Consider the following example from the beginning of an editorial.

> There are as many reasons to support the proposed balanced-budget amendment to the Constitution as there are families in the United States. The American family will benefit the most if Congress passes the amendment and it is ratified by the states. (John Kasich, "Do We Need a Balanced Budget Amendment?" *Denver Post,* February 9, 1997)

What is this paragraph's topic? That is, what is the paragraph about? _____

_____

The topic here is easy to find, for it is mentioned in both sentences; it is "the balanced-budget amendment to the Constitution."

Consider a second example, a letter to the editor.

> In recent blizzards in Minnesota and the Dakotas, stranded motorists were rescued through acts of providence and/or by heroes only after being lost for frightening and threatening periods of time. Cellular phones and headlights were undependable as means of locating them. A suggestion: Add some Roman candles or a modern version of a Very pistol (used to fire multi-colored flares high into the air at sea) to the usual "survival supplies." The pistol has demonstrated its effectiveness in locating lost, inoperative ships and/or survivors. Directions with the car kit could specify that stranded motorists fire the Roman candles or the Very pistol every hour on the hour until they were located. (John R. Thurston, letter, *St. Paul Pioneer Press,* February 5, 1997)

What is the topic of this letter? _____

One possibility is "winter survival supplies." Another view is that the topic is "Roman candles and the Very pistol." For some the first is too broad, for others the second is too narrow a topic. In any case, note that people might legitimately differ about their understanding of the topic.

Sometimes topics are more difficult to find, as in this third example.

> After winning his 400 semifinal last Monday, Michael Johnson threw his shoes into the stands, then belatedly and sheepishly realized that the shoes had *spikes*. Johnson's only real competition in the 400, world-record holder Butch Reynolds, pulled a hamstring in his semifinal, so the thrill of the final lay in the widening distance between Johnson and his rivals—it was like watching Secretariat in the Belmont. Unpressed, he won his 55th straight 400 in 43.39, an Olympic record just 0.2 sec. off Reynolds' world record. "I'll get that record eventually," said Johnson. . . . (Steve Wulf, "Double Fast," *Time,* August 12, 1996, p. 46)

What did you take to be this paragraph's topic? _____

_____

Perhaps you suggested that the topic of this report from the 1996 Summer Olympic Games is a person, Michael Johnson. The paragraph is *about* him. At the same time you could also say that it is about an Olympic race or world records.

Sometimes the topic is not mentioned directly. Consider this fourth example.

> The ocean stubbornly held on to its mysteries for most of last week. It was especially uncooperative on Thursday for the men and women investigating the crash of TWA Flight 800. Rain and strong winds disrupted and eventually interrupted search operations. But on Friday there was a breakthrough. Deep Drone 7200, a remotely operated robot outfitted with cameras that can explore ocean depths without divers, located part of the cockpit, "The nerve center of the aircraft," as Robert Francis, vice chairman of the National Transportation Safety Board described it. . . . (Christopher John Farley, "If It Was a Bomb, Then Whodunit?" *Time,* August 12, 1996, p. 26)

What do you think is the topic? _____

Its topic is an event, namely, the search for the wreckage of TWA Flight 800. Though the search is not mentioned directly, this is what the paragraph is about.

To *find the topic,* ask yourself, "What is the author or speaker talking about?" Here are two clues.

- Sometimes communication comes with titles.

Titles often give the topic of the piece. This is particularly true of newspaper and magazine articles or editorials.

> Banned Freon Now Favorite of Smugglers
>
> Freon, the now-banned refrigerant used in car air conditioners, has emerged as the No. 2 smuggling problem, behind drugs, for U.S. customs agents along the Mexican border. "If you look at contraband crossing the U.S.-Mexican border, we're looking at cocaine, marijuana, heroin, prescription drugs, and then Freon," agent Steve Hooper said. Scientists believe Freon, used in the air conditioners of most automobiles built before 1993, is eating away Earth's ozone layer. The black market for the gas has flourished since Jan. 1, when it became illegal to manufacture or import it in the United States. U.S. motorists can still buy Freon made before 1996 or recycled Freon, but a dwindling supply and excise taxes have sent the price soaring. (*Charlotte Observer,* August 13, 1996)

Here the topic is _____

Another way to find the topic in a paragraph is to

- Locate the grammatical subject of either the first or last sentence in the paragraph.

This strategy works provided these sentences contain the main thesis of the piece you are reading. (We will say more about the thesis shortly.) This approach provides no sure cure to the problem of identifying the topic, but it sometimes provides a start. The previous example about the Olympics, in which Michael Johnson is the subject of the *topic or lead sentence* (the first sentence in the paragraph), illustrates this approach.

To reiterate, different people may identify different topics for a paragraph, article, chapter, or speech. You will discover this if you do Exercise 1 with a group. Identification of different topics does not necessarily mean that someone who disagrees is wrong; it shows that people can categorize or organize material differently. *What is important is that the topic you identify be contained in the issue and thesis* (about which we will speak shortly).

To summarize, the first thing to discover in written or oral communication is its topic. The topic is what the communication is about, the subject or category under which you would place it.

Exercise 1

Give the topic for each of the following paragraphs. [In this and the other exercises in this chapter you might legitimately differ from others. However, since not every answer proposed is equally satisfactory, be prepared to tell why you differ.]

1. A charter school is a semi-public school funded by both state and educational funds and private grants and contributions. Charter schools are free to create their own curricular guidelines and school policies which may differ from those set by the local school district. (School brochure)

2. Dr. Kevorkian has become a caricature of his own cause. He stokes the fires of debate, generating heat but not light. (*Akron Beacon Journal*, August 21, 1996)

3. They guzzle water and nutrients while hastening wind erosion. But scientists at the Central Great Plains Research Station in Akron, Colo., found that planting winter wheat where sunflowers had just bloomed can reap 12 bushel more per acre. Still, the best sunflower is a dead sunflower: The stalks keep moisture and nutrients in the soil. (Charles Fenyvesi, "They're Not All that Bad," *U.S. News and World Report*, January 27, 1997)

4. You're born, you go to school, then one day things begin to get interesting. NAVY: let the journey begin. (Advertisement)

5. It's no surprise that only the smartest, most aggressive Sport Utility Vehicles are able to climb their way to the top of the automotive food chain. What's also no surprise, is that's where you find the new Toyota 4Runner. To begin with, its more powerful 183-horsepower V6 engine declares this is an off-road vehicle with some teeth to it. Yet no matter how far into the wilderness these horses carry you, you're never far from civilization.

The new 4Runner has a more spacious interior. Leather-trimmed seats. (Advertisement)

6. The Chinese Government is not creating unemployment in America; it is the multinational corporations that are responsible for cutting jobs and exporting them to China. When labor costs rise in China, these corporations will maximize profits by moving their manufacturing operations again to another country with even cheaper labor. (David Chiang, letter, *Time*, August 12, 1996, p. 8)

7. I wish to object to the manner in which the name of SGS Société Générale de Surveillance was mentioned in "The Last Mystery of World War II," leading your readers to suspect that SGS would retain assets of Holocaust victims. The accounts mentioned in your article do not relate to hidden Holocaust cash but to funds mostly arising from business transactions which were kept by SGS during the war. These funds were returned to their beneficial owners as far as we can ascertain from files still available from that time. Indeed, these names were disclosed on a confidential basis to U.S. authorities by the company itself in order to help them trace Nazi assets in Switzerland in the context of "Operation Safehaven." The OSS report dated July 1945 describes our company as being "very cooperative" in this context. The company at the time was run by my grandfather, Jacques Salmanowitz. Born in Latvia from a Jewish family, he gave immense and continuous support and help to friends and business acquaintances whose lives and assets were threatened by the Nazis in occupied Europe. SGS therefore cannot be associated with the accusations mentioned. (Elisabeth Salina Amorini, letter, *U.S. News & World Report*, August 5, 1996, p. 11) Reprinted by permission.

8. Judge Lawrence E. Kahn ruled that New York State can order auto manufacturers to sell thousands of electrically powered vehicles in the state beginning this fall [1997]. But the real question is whether he can order customers to buy the cars. I am old enough to recall the Ward Baking Company electric vehicles delivering their products to grocers in the 1930's. It had nothing to do with environmentalism; it was simply more economical for a truck that did short-haul, stop-and-go driving to be powered by electricity. The effort should be made to electrify this class of trucks. They contribute a disproportionate amount of pollution with their mode of operation. Why California and New York try to promote the electric vehicle for use by the average motorist defies all reason. (Morton Sobell, letter, *New York Times*, August 10, 1997).

9. Kids tend to fall into two groups: those who follow and those who rebel. By rebel logic, when everyone else is using drugs and alcohol, the only choice is to reject that form of indulgence. Meet the Straight Edgers, a hermetic movement of mostly white, male, suburban teenagers who swear to forgo drugs, drink, and tobacco. Some are vegetarians. Some even practice celibacy. Like many of their less disciplined brethren, they favor tattoos, baggy pants, and body piercing. But the conformity stops there. . . . Disgusted by wasted friends, more and more kids are embracing the

movement. They get their buzz from their all-important music and from Straight Edge "beer"—Snapple. . . . (Excerpted from Brendan I. Koerner, "Walking on the Strait Edge," *U.S. News & World Report*, February 10, 1997, p. 16. Copyright. 1997. U.S. News & World Report. Visit us at our website at www.usnews.com for additional information.)

10. To appreciate how relatively well the immigration service's criminal deportation program is working now is to appreciate how poorly it functioned before. In 1986 the agency was deporting 1,000 criminal aliens a year. This year the number could be 50 times that. . . . The easiest place to find criminal aliens is behind bars, and the most expedient way to deport them is to bring them before an immigration judge so they can be released from prison directly onto a plane or bus. (Deborah Sontag, "U.S. Deports Felons but Can't Keep Them Out," *New York Times*, August 11, 1997, p. A8)

11. Sure, there's the U.S. Open. But the USTA Tennis Teacher's Conference is where tennis professionals and enthusiasts meet to stay on top of their game. There is no better place to make connections, trade tips and keep up with cutting edge technology. And if you sign up by August 2nd, you have an option to buy U.S. Open tickets. So don't miss out—you only get one shot each year! (Advertisement)

12. For the first time there is a consensus of the world's scientists that the earth is warming and this is caused by human activity. This warming will continue at an accelerated pace in the 21st century and lead to substantial interference with the earth's climate system. A major reduction in carbon-based energy consumption, in excess of 50 percent, is needed to prevent this, as well as to allow ecosystems to naturally adapt to the climate changes and to protect world food production. These are the conclusions of over 1,500 of the top scientists published in the 1996 Intergovernmental Panel on Climate Change (IPCC) report. (*The North Star Journal*, June/July 1997)

13. There are encouraging signs that soaring rates of juvenile crime may be tapering off. Still "the number of teenagers in the United States [is expected to] increase by about one percent a year for the next 15 years. This means that even if the juvenile crime rate held steady, the total number of crimes committed by young people would rise." That makes it imperative to pursue more aggressive efforts to divert juveniles from a life of crime. (Fox Butterfield, "After Decade, Juvenile Crime Begins to Drop," *New York Times*, August 9, 1996, pp. A1, A25)

14. Porsche works hard to build the world's finest sports cars, and they want people to keep them that way. So, every new Porsche now comes filled with 12 quarts of Mobil 1. Porsche believes that no other oil performs better. They use it for developing new engines, too, and in all of their racing cars. They also work with Mobil people . . . Mobil's name now appears in a place of honor—on a plaque in Porsche engine compartments. It recommends that you keep using Mobil 1 for as long as your Porsche exists. (Advertisement)

15. Violent behavior has multiple—and interlocking—causes, of course. They include poverty, hopelessness, abuse, poor parenting, illegal drugs, mental illness, alcohol, racism, distorted values, gangs, the absence of fathers and the influence of violence in movies and TV. Of these, the easiest and quickest to change may be television and movies. (Joan Beck, "A Call to Tone Down Violence," *Chicago Tribune*, August 8, 1996)

16. Yes, Major League Baseball is boring. . . . Two simple changes will return action to major-league ball: (1) Move the pitcher's mound back 5 to 10 feet, and (2) soften the baseball. Moving the mound means pitchers will have a better position from which to play defense and pick off runners but will have to work harder for strikes. Each pitch will take longer to get to the catcher, encouraging the runners to take off. Every strike thrown will cross the plate at a reduced speed, giving the batter more time to adjust his swing, resulting in more hits. However, the softer ball will fly on a shorter trajectory, falling sooner into the infield or outfield, resulting in more defense. Net result: more action, restored balance between pitching and hitting—and I won't fall asleep face down in my peanuts and Cracker Jack. (Bill Sharp, letter, *U.S. News & World Report*, January 27, 1997, p. 7.)

17. I agree that umpires in both leagues need to apply the entire strike zone to the game. In addition, allowing for a Bob Gibson-style brushback would sure bring back pitching power. Let's not get into sudden death, clocks, and all those things that would turn the sport into football or basketball. If you want baseball excitement, spend your time teaching your kids the nuances of the game and why it is important that it change little. Let baseball remain consistent. It is meant to be this way, a modern-day religion without a single God and no pretension of salvation for any of us. (Philip Guercio, letter, *U.S. News & World Report*, January 27, 1997, p. 7.)

18. When your dog bites someone, common sense tells you that there's a problem to deal with. But if it bites again and again, common sense says the dog is not working out and must be euthanized, rather than putting the problem onto someone else's lap.

    I work with animal control, but in reality the *pet owner* is supposed to control the dog. Yet, I have witnessed pet owners throw themselves on the mercy of judges, city attorneys and police departments, begging them to spare the dog, which they'll send to live "in the country." . . .

    Dog bites contribute to higher medical and homeowners' insurance, loss of limb and/or life, and in children, on whom most bites are afflicted, medical visits, nightmares and fear of dogs. . . . The basic responsibility is up to the pet owner. All it takes is common sense. (Diane Ganzer, letter, *St. Paul Pioneer Press*, August 13, 1996)

19. Watching the Olympics, it was disconcerting to realize that the body I had slouched across the couch contained the same basic parts as those of the adolescent waifs hurtling through their gymnastic routines. I couldn't even enjoy my ice cream until the coverage moved on to sumo wrestling. Then I mused about there being no fat-lady venue in the village.

Even in obesity, the scales are weighted in favor of the men. Nobody would watch, or even tolerate, fat folds on the fairer sex. . . . From 20 years of working with them, the clinical psychologist is convinced that young women are products of a look-obsessed, media-saturated, girl-poisoning culture. (Rosemary Falls, "Look-Obsession Hurts Our Girls," *Waco Tribune Herald,* August 11, 1996)

20. Kenya's Lake Nakuru used to turn pink every year, not from toxic chemicals or rogue algae but from a dazzling carpet of flamingos—up to 2 million of them, settling into the lake's shallow waters to feed on its rich supply of small aquatic plants, mollusks and crustaceans. The dramatic spectacle, and the abundance of rhinos, leopards and other animals around the lake, prompted the Kenya government in 1968 to make Lake Nakuru a national park. Tourists followed, as many as 200,000 a year, boosting the nearby town of Nakuru's economy and its pride in the lake's flamingo show.

    Yet today, Lake Nakuru is mostly brown, the color the cracked mud left behind by its slowly receding waters. Desultory groups of flamingos break the monotony, but the mass migration has receded too. . . . Yet despite the concerted efforts of an imposing international coalition, no one knows for sure why the lake is drying up, why the flamingos are leaving—or what to do about it . . .

    Explanatory theories—from global warming to flamingo fickleness—abound. But the prime suspect in the avian drama is Nakuru's booming growth. . . . Yet growth has brought troubling environmental side effects. The town's already inadequate water supply is pumped mainly from underground boreholes, which could be taxing groundwater supplies to the lake. . . . (Excerpted from Tim Zimmermann, "The Mystery of Lake Nakuru," *U.S. News & World Report,* August 5, 1996, pp. 46–7. Copyright, 1996, U.S. News & World Report. Visit us at our website at www.usnews. com for additional information.)

THE ISSUE

Once you have found the topic, the next step is to identify the issue the author or speaker raises. The **issue** is the main or primary *question* the author asks and then goes on to answer. The question should contain the topic, preferably (but not always) as the subject of the question.

Return to the first example under "The Topic" (on page 32). The topic is the balanced budget amendment to the Constitution. The issue the author raises is presented in the first sentence, where he promises reasons for his view that Congress should pass the balanced budget amendment to the Constitution. If we *turn this statement into a question,* we get the issue "Should the balanced budget amendment to the Constitution be passed?" The issue is not, "Will the American family benefit if the amendment passes?" That the family will benefit is given as a reason for adopting the amendment and is what we later term a main point.

In the second example (page 32) under "The Topic," which dealt with winter survival, the first sentence sets the stage for the author's suggestion in the third sentence. If you turn this suggestion (which is his thesis) into a question, you get the issue: "Should Roman candles and the Very pistol be part of a vehicle's winter survival supplies?" Note that the topic, winter survival supplies, is part of the question the letter writer raises and answers. *The issue contains the topic.*

The topic in the third example (page 33) was Michael Johnson. What issue is raised? _____

_____

It is harder to get an issue out of this paragraph, for the paragraph lacks a unifying or topic sentence. Neither the opening nor the closing sentence in the paragraph provides the issue. The question the author seems to be raising is, "Did Michael Johnson win the Olympic 400 meters impressively?" The first sentence is tangential to his winning, while the last sentence quotes Johnson's affirmation that he will break the world record. In this case you have to see toward what point the middle part of the paragraph is directed.

The topic of the fourth example on page 33 was the search operations for the wreckage of TWA Flight 800. What issue is raised? _____

_____

The issue can be derived from the first or topic sentence. Turn this into a question: "Were the search operations for the wreckage of TWA Flight 800 successful?"

The topic the fifth example on page 33 is Freon, and the issue is _____

_____

To find the issue in this paragraph, turn the title into a question: "Why is Freon being smuggled into the United States" or "Why are smugglers turning to Freon?" Often by manipulating the title in this way, you can formulate the issue the author raises.

Questions can be posed either directly or indirectly. To formulate the issue directly, you can use words like *do, can, how, should,* or *why.* You can also introduce the issue as an *indirect question* by using the word "whether," for example, "Whether Michael Johnson won the Olympic 400 meters impressively" or "Whether the search operations for Flight 800 were successful." The important thing is that you correctly identify the issue. The issue

- must contain the topic.
- should be the main question that the author is trying to answer, the question that gives rise to what is written or said. Put another way, it should capture why the person is writing or speaking on the topic.
- should be a question that can be given an answer, though not necessarily a simple one.
- should be a question that can be answered in at least two different ways in cases where the question occurs in the context of an argument. Otherwise

there is little sense in writing or talking about it. Simply put, the issue should be *disputable.*

Issues are the hardest element to find because often they are not stated explicitly. You might first have to find the main conclusion and then turn it into a direct or indirect question in order to find the issue. That is, sometimes it is easier to find the thesis (the main point the author is making) and then turn the thesis into the issue. At other times the issue is easier to identify than the thesis, especially when the author directly introduces the question he or she addresses. In either case, *the main conclusion of the piece is the thesis* (about which we will talk in a moment), *and this thesis or conclusion is the answer to the question—the issue—the author or speaker poses.*

Often by reading the first and last lines of a paragraph, or by reading the first and last paragraphs of a longer piece, or by reading the title if there is one, you can get an idea of what issue the author raises. But this is not always true; there is no easy formula that governs how people write. The author might start out with an interesting sidelight or an attention getter. But by reading the beginning and the end, you at least have a fair shot at finding the issue.

One key for finding the issue is to look for the word *should.* If you find a statement containing the word *should,* you can latch on to it as a candidate for an issue because to say that something should be done is to answer the question, Should something be done? More than likely the author is taking a stand in response to the should-question. *Should* indicates an obligation, and obligations are often debatable. Since issues should be interesting and debatable, allowing for different sides that might generate important points worthy of discussion, *should* is an almost perfect identifier of an issue.

One final point. A good test for checking if you have correctly identified the issue is whether you can find the answer to your question in the text you are reading. If you cannot, use the topic to pose another issue and see whether the author answers this question in the text. *If the author does not directly answer the question you have chosen as the issue, more than likely you have not correctly identified the author's issue.*

Exercise 2

Read the paragraphs in Exercise 1 and give the issue raised in each.

Exercise 3

Give the topic and issue of each of the following paragraphs.

1. Love began with motherhood. For mammalian young to survive, mothers must invest considerable time and energy in them. Of course, the varying growth rates of mammalian species require some mothers to invest more time and energy than others. An elephant seal suckles her pup for only a few weeks before abandoning it; other species, including elephants, some primates, and especially people, lavish attention on their young for years. (Shannon Brownlee, "Can't Do without Love," *U.S. News & World Report,* February 17, 1997, p. 58)

2. Buying a satellite dish to see the football you want can leave you just as flat. With PRIMESTAR, you can get all the football you want without tak-

ing a hit for a ton of money. Because we don't make you buy the dish. You'll see over 100 NFL games and more college football than you ever dreamed. And since we've added more of the sports channels you want, you'll have more sports action than ever. But here's the best part. All the sports channels are grouped together. So you can watch as many games as you want, and you'll always know where they are. In fact, we've grouped all 160 of our channels. Making Primestar as easy to watch as it is to get. No wonder we're the best value in satellite TV. Call Primestar. (Advertisement)

3. I live in a senior high-rise where roughly a third of the tenants are émigrés from Russia. For the most part, we welcome these new arrivals. But there is a growing resentment about the largess that our government bestows on these people. Unlike our ancestors—who come here not expecting any benefits or help and who either took any kind of work available until they were on their feet or settled outside the cities to grub the land until they could afford to buy their own,—this country has seen fit to heap benefits immediately. Can you imagine the frustration some of us, who live on a rigidly fixed Social Security check, feel when we see newcomers flock to this country and receive immediate unrestricted benefits . . . I can barely hear my neighbors speak to me, but I cannot afford a twin hearing-aid set, as the audiologist says I need, or purchase a new pair of eyeglasses, all because my total income is $635 a month, which makes me ineligible for medical assistance or any other kind of help. It is humiliating to watch people who have never paid a dime in taxes line up to collect SSI benefits, food stamps, free medical help, glasses, etc. Whatever happened to the sponsors of these people who promised to keep them off the welfare rolls for five years? It's not fair. (Mary Rogers, letter, *St. Paul Pioneer Press*, January 25, 1997)

4. A primary reason why women fare so poorly in old age is because the pension system, which rewards employment longevity and consistency, was not designed with women's employment patterns in mind. Women spend fewer years in the job market and less time at each job than men do. Not to mention that they earn less while they are working and tend to cluster in the kinds of employment—low-wage, part-time, and service-oriented— with the fewest pension options. . . . (Celia Moore, "Pensions Made Woman-Friendly," *Ms.,* July/August, 1997, p. 34)

5. With all the talk about the Consumer Price Index (CPI) overstating inflation, and proposals to revise it to reduce governmental expenditures, nobody points out the obvious: Inflation does not raise all prices equally. The cost of living does not go up much for some people, but it goes up more than the CPI indicates for other people, especially for aged retirees who spend much more for medical expenses than the average person. And as everyone knows, medical prices have risen far faster than the CPI and will likely do so again. For us aged retirees, the CPI should be increased so we can keep up to our rising cost of living. That means that the Social Security cost of living increase should be bigger each year than the present CPI indicates. (Harlan Smith, economics professor emeritus, University of Minnesota, letter, *St. Paul Pioneer Press*, January 25, 1997.)

6. AT&T is not in league with porn providers. Nor does AT&T do business with information providers of adult content when it is not required to do so. A decade ago, AT&T adopted stringent guidelines for domestic calling that establish standards for responsible use of premium-billed 900 pay-per-call service. We did this voluntarily and were the first carrier to set such guidelines. We specifically refuse to provide 900 premium billing for any pay-per-call providers whose program contains explicit sexual content. (Robert Aquilina, vice president, production management, AT&T, Bedminster, NJ, letter, *U.S. News & World Report,* March 3, 1997, p. 6)

7. Analysis of whale harvesting records suggests that there was a large and rapid decrease in Antarctic summertime sea-ice between the 1950s and 1970s. Such a change in sea-ice extent would have global significance, because ice cover of the polar oceans is an important component of the Earth's climate system. It exerts strong controls on the exchanges of energy between atmosphere and oceans at high latitudes. Sea ice has a higher albedo than the open ocean and thus modifies the energy balance of polar regions. It also acts as an insulating blanket, reducing the transfer of heat from the underlying oceans to the cold polar atmosphere. These processes introduce a positive feedback into the climate system, making the climate naturally variable in polar regions and, potentially, making them particularly sensitive to changes in forcing such as those caused by increasing anthropogenic emissions of greenhouse gases. . . . (Eugene Murphy and John King, "Icy Message from the Antarctic," *Nature,* September 4, 1997, p. 20)

8. Apart from one or two lamentable lapses, the Clinton Administration has been a more responsible steward of the American landscape than its Republican predecessors. It has resisted Congressional efforts to enrich local and commercial interests at the expense of America's national resources, and has embarked on ambitious efforts, as in the Everglades, to correct misguided policies of the past. Yet each day brings another test, and in some instances the Administration can be found wanting.

   That is certainly the case with its decision . . . to approve exploratory oil drilling on Federal land in the red-rock country of Utah, where . . . President Clinton established a national monument to protect up to 1.7 million acres from development. . . . Environmentalists believe that if the well yields substantial amounts of oil, more wells are sure to follow, destroying the wilderness values that Mr. Clinton vowed to protect. (Excerpted from "A Monument, or an Oilfield," *New York Times,* September 18, 1997, p. A34)

9. In species where the only thing that a male contributes to his offspring is his sperm, he is usually . . . more or less indiscriminate in his courting. But a male stickleback invests more than just sperm in his progeny. He has to build the nest in the first place, defend the eggs from predators, and keep them oxygenated by fanning them with fresh water. He therefore has something to lose if he spends his time looking after suboptimal eggs. He also has something to trade, which should allow him to be choosy about which females he allows to lay their eggs in his nest. And the more desir-

able (and therefore the more courted) a male is himself, the choosier he can afford to be.

Sarah Kraak . . . set out to prove this point experimentally. First, she showed that having extra eggs in a nest does indeed reduce hatching success. This means that a male has a real interest in limiting the size of his clutch (which is normally contributed to by several females). She also showed that the size of a female correlates with the weight of her eggs, and that heavier eggs produce more successful fry. So, if males are being choosy at all, they should probably choose large females. . . . ("Birds Do It, Bees Do It," *The Economist*, August 30, 1997, pp. 59–60)

10. Recapture the glorious days of "Camelot" with America's most beloved first lady. The Jackie Doll. Young and beautiful, she was the closest thing America ever had to a Queen. Yet her intelligence and vitality represented every American woman. And her style and elegance inspired women the world over. Now the Franklin Mint proudly joins forces with Jackie's own designer, world-renowned Oleg Cassini, to present the Jackie Doll. Crafted in poseable, lifelike vinyl. Dressed in the shimmering white double satin gown she wore on her historic state visit. Completely accessorized with famous faux pearl necklace, matching stole, gloves, shoes and clutch—all authenticated by Cassini in every detail. Individually hand-numbered. Just $90. (Advertisement)

11. Regarding Nicholas Lemann's suggestion that teaching eight one-semester college courses per year would be "hardly oppressive" for "Fantasy College" professors: Lemann is living in his own fantasy world. . . . If our hypothetical superprofessor teaches four three-credit courses per semester, that's 12 contact hours per week. Doesn't sound bad, right? What Lemann and many other critics of higher education seem to overlook is the time required to adequately prepare for this "light" teaching load. If a conservative figure of three hours' preparation time per hour of classroom teaching is used, superprofessor is now devoting 48 hours per week to teaching. Of course, since the professor is teaching at a college that doesn't believe in research, he won't have any graduate students to help with the time-consuming tasks of composing and grading exams. Time for meeting with students? If he teaches four courses per semester, he'll have more students lined up outside his office than he knows how to handle. Throw in the requisite committee responsibilities, and it's easy to see that superprof is going to be putting in 60-plus hours per week. Of course, if Lemann has any interest in research or writing, he graciously allows that these tasks can be performed on his own time. (Robert D. Garrison, letter, *U.S. News & World Report*, January 27, 1997, p. 7)

12. According to a report by the Human Rights Watch arms project, American land mines were picked up in the field or stolen from stockpiles and used against our troops in Korea and Vietnam. . . . They also killed American soldiers returning through their own minefields. Therefore, the report says, we should reduce the risk to our forces. The history is accurate, but the conclusion is nonsense.

Mines used in Korea and Vietnam were laid by hand. They were armed by removing a pin and could be disarmed by replacing the pin. Most of today's United States mines are dropped by aircraft or otherwise remotely delivered; they are sealed and cannot be disarmed once laid. Enemy troops foolish enough to try to pick up an active mine for re-use will be killed. Moreover, to let our soldiers move back through the areas we have mined, our mines self-destruct at a preset time after being laid. Thus the mines don't injure or kill civilians after the battle.

Yes, our mines could be stolen, as could any other weapon. Rifles, for example, are easier to steal and to use than remotely delivered mines. Presumably we will next be told that our troops will be safer if we take away their rifles. (Enid McKitrick, letter, *New York Times,* August 5, 1997, p. A18. Reprinted by permission.)

13. The Supreme Court's refusal to recognize physician-assisted suicide as a constitutional right for all Americans obviously is a crucial decision that will affect thousands of people in this country. But the court's decision must be viewed separately from an equally important question: What will we as a society demand as a standard for good care at the end of life? Properly given, such care might substantially reduce the number of patients considering physician-assisted suicide.

The overwhelming evidence from the largest clinical study ever conducted with dying people shows that Americans too often face death in pain and attached to machines. That study, published in the Journal of the American Medical Association in 1995, was a wake-up call to many who are concerned about improving care at the end of life. This goal is attainable and should be a much higher priority for medical schools, hospitals, insurance companies, the clergy and other groups. And if these professionals are to help us, as a society and as individuals, we must overcome our fears about discussing death.

I helped care for my father and grandfather, who, like many people, died from prolonged illnesses. My experiences taught me that the unpleasant prospect of our deaths does not preclude meaningful experiences at the end of our lives. Although some people may be sad and physically compromised during their last months and years, these days also can be an opportunity to appreciate life's last chapter and to reach out again to loved ones.

We must focus not on whether we have the right to ask a doctor to end our lives prematurely, but on the changes that need to take place to ensure that systems exist to help us die with dignity. (Rosalynn Carter, "All of Us Must Face Hard Facts of Death," *Atlanta Constitution,* July 2, 1997)

14. Our military has one central responsibility, and it performs that superbly: to protect the security of the nation. In the bloodiest century ever, this country hasn't engaged in a major war for over 20 years and appears safe as far as the eye can see.

Far from a frolic in bed, life in the Army these days can be lonely and tough. Since the end of the cold war, the Army has cut its forces by a third while the White House has tripled the number of its overseas missions. As a result, the average soldier now spends 180 days a year deployed away from home, more than double the number of a decade ago. Late last month [May 1997], the Army announced that American soldiers are serving in 100 countries, the largest number in its history.

. . . In the 19 months since deploying to Bosnia, U.S. forces haven't had a single untoward incident with a civilian there, and not one American soldier has been killed in combat. Whatever else they have accomplished for the long term, our troops have helped give people there a year and a half without slaughter and mass rapes.

Those who say that soldiers must also learn to behave themselves are absolutely right. Throughout the services, the military should crack down hard on cases of sexual harassment and abuses of power. Everyone must be an officer *and* a gentleman.

But we should not expect our fighting forces to be warriors on the field and saints off it. Rules of common sense should prevail. Just as the military should apply the same rules to men and women, and to officers and enlisted personnel, it should call off witch hunts looking into behavior of 15 or 20 years ago. The issue shouldn't be whether a military person has sex off base but whether he or she abuses a position of authority and causes disorder in the ranks.

In the meantime, we should remember that thousands of fine men and women are out there at this very moment, sentries standing watch around the world. They don't do it for the money; most could earn significantly more in the private sector. They do it because they find pride and satisfaction in preserving freedom. It's time their commanders rallied the troops and told them during this period of stress that the nation salutes their honor and service. . . . (Excepted from David Gergen, "Saluting Those Who Serve," *U.S. News & World Report,* June 23, 1997, p. 64B. Copyright, 1997, U.S. News & World Report. Visit us at our website at www.usnews.com for additional information.)

15. The author claimed that "quitting smoking isn't monstrously difficult; deciding to quit is." It is true that some smokers quit easily, throw their smokes into the toilet and never think about it again. However, research verifies what most smokers have long known: Nicotine is powerfully addictive.

Most smokers have unsuccessfully tried quitting a number of times. Their failure is not due to lack of character or willpower. Relapse rates for those who try to stop using heroin, alcohol and tobacco are identical. Yes, some are able to quit, but most relapse into life endangering use again and again.

Rules must be appropriate to the product or activity they regulate, whether they be safety rules for motor vehicles or controls on the sale and manufacture of prescription drugs. The FDA rules are appropriate. They bring the method of sale and promotion under the control of someone other than the industry which profits from the sale of an addictive drug. And, they treat tobacco similarly to other products. (Jeanne Weigum, letter, *St. Paul Pioneer Press,* September 4, 1996. Reprinted by permission.)

Changing the Topic or Issue

Not every piece of writing has just one topic. A chapter in a book is often unified around some broad topic that serves as the central topic. But within books or chapters authors can have several topics that they wish to cover. In a book, for example, each chapter might treat a different topic that relates to the overall topic of the book. In good book writing, authors move from one topic to the next in an orderly fashion. Critical readers pay attention to the structure of what they are reading.

Similar things can be said about issues. Sometimes in the book, chapter, or section the topic remains the same, but the author switches among different issues related to that topic. The author may be taking a multifaceted look at the topic. At other times, when the book contains different topics, the author raises different issues. Critical readers note when an author raises a new issue.

A problem can occur when authors or speakers raise a new topic or issue in a way that does not further the discussion but rather obscures the issue and confuses the reader or listener by moving off in a new direction. This especially characterizes speakers when they speak without the benefit of notes; they tend to move by train of thought from one topic or issue to another until what they consider at the end bears only a distant or little resemblance to the issue with which they began. Perhaps they return to the original issue; sometimes they do not.

You might compare this shift in issue to what happens when a group of people get together to talk. Have you ever charted a party conversation? Someone starts the conversation on one topic. Gradually it moves to a related topic, then to another, and soon the conversation has moved a great distance from the original topic. You might not even be able to recall what the original topic was. This is acceptable in freely moving party conversation but not when you are writing a paper or giving a speech.

Here is an example of getting off the issue in one paragraph. The author begins by dealing with the idea of fate.

> Mo Tzu's philosophy on fate is very different from Confucius's. He thought men's action determines their fate, while Confucius thought one's fate is predetermined so one can only accept it but not try to change it. This thought is reflected deeply in his approach to one's social position. People should stay in their position and not rebel. This is why Confucianism was accepted by almost all the rulers in Chinese history. Confucius himself was born into a noble family. So his philosophy represents the ruling class a lot. But Mo Tzu had a very different point of view from Confucius. He thought people can always change their fate by their action. For him, one's poverty or wealth is not predetermined; it is decided by one's effort. So people should control their fate themselves. Mo Tzu also might be the first philosopher in Chinese history who argued the equality of human beings. In his view, a farmer could become a ruler if he is wise enough and can do useful things. Not like Confucius, Mo Tzu praises physical work. He thought everything that can produce wealth is good and useful to society.

Though the author of this paragraph begins by considering two Chinese thinkers' views of fate and whether one should accept or try to change one's fate, at the end she has moved to the question of whether human beings are equal and whether people's work benefits society. The author has moved by train of thought from the notion of effort to be employed in changing one's fate to the role of physical effort in producing wealth in society. Thus, the paragraph ends by considering an issue that was not raised at the outset.

Here is a longer and clearer example of the same problem.

> After a Doleless week, a week dominated by Bill Clinton's almost ethereal balm and fluidity, the Republican candidate reappeared on Labor Day before an enormous crowd in St. Louis—and seemed, by contrast, harsh and constricted, an awkward figure, a retiree: an old man with a great tan. There isn't much Dole can do about this; it is who he is. Yes, it's still early. A lot can happen between now and November. The electorate is volatile. Bill Clinton is neither loved nor admired. And . . . Bob Dole might just *dominate* in the debates. You don't think so? Well, maybe Clinton will stumble. . . .
>
> Anyway, back to awful. Good crowds, like St. Louis, mean nothing in a fall campaign; bad crowds mean a lot. The crowds I saw were thin at best. The Dole staff tried to combat their candidate's ancient, distant image by staging "Listening to America" seances, in which the nominee fielded marshmallowy encomiums from carefully selected audiences. . . . [A]n old Russell High School classmate named Ray Leonard asked what he'd do about Social Security. Dole reminisced about the Social Security deal he made in 1983, said it would keep the system solvent until 2012. . . .
>
> Afterward Leonard wanted to give his old friend the benefit of the doubt. "I felt he answered it," he said. Really? I asked. "Well, he didn't give any specifics. I'm not worried about Social Security being there for me. I'm worried about my son. But that's hard, I guess. No one's talking about that."
>
> No one at all. . . . The press, which usually harps on the entitlement monster, has pretty much given both candidates a pass—in part, no doubt, because it's futile to ask. . . .
>
> Both Clinton and Dole . . . have made value noises in support of [a bipartisan commission]. But will it actually happen?
>
> "Oh, it's got to happen," says Nebraska Sen. Bob Kerrey, who cochaired the *last* bipartisan entitlements commission. Kerrey makes a compelling case: both the Clinton and Republican "balanced" budget schemes are phonies. Both have $60 to $80 billion in unspecified discretionary spending cuts. . . .
>
> Kerrey knows where the money is. He's been liberated by his commission's report. He can say what his colleagues can't: that we won't be able to run even the crudest, bare-bones government—and worse, we'll tax our children into poverty—unless we get control of Medicare and Social Security. . . .
>
> (Joe Klein, "Pretty Close to Awful," *Newsweek,* September 16, 1996, p. 51)

Can you spot the shift in topic and issues? _____

_____

_____

The editorial begins with a discussion of Bob Dole's 1996 presidential campaign and whether his campaign was going well. Then it moves to a question an old friend posed to Dole about Social Security, and finally proceeds to consider Social Security's role in balancing the budget and whether Congress will pass Social Security and Medicare reform. One thing leads to another in this editorial until before long the topic has shifted and the editorial ends up talking about the chances of Social Security reform in Congress.

In short, you have to be aware when an author moves gradually by train of thought from one topic to another. Sometimes the shifts are subtle, as in the fate example, but eventually, with enough shifts, the author has moved to address a different topic or issue. Critical readers and listeners are aware of possible shifts, note the place where that shift occurs, and consider the implications of these shifts for understanding the entire piece.

Watching for this problem is an important part of your writing. When you write, it is good practice to jot down your topic and issue in some obvious place in front of you. Then every so often pause in your writing, reread what you have written, and ask yourself whether you still are addressing the original topic and issue. If so, fine. If not, find where your train of thought led you astray and begin again from that point.

Exercise 4

In the following paragraphs first identify what you take to be the topic and issue the author addresses. Then indicate where the author has gotten off the topic or issue and note the new topic or issue.

1. Children who have been given no values will continue in destructive behavior. Simplistic punishment does nothing to dissuade negative behavior. For example, Johnny breaks into the video store and is arrested. Brought home, he is punished by taking away his car keys and telephone for a week and canceling his weekend ski trip. Mom and Dad don't know that Johnny's girlfriend has a car and a cell phone and is sneaking out for the weekend. There is no real punishment or consequences for his actions. The media has been charged with the duty of baby-sitting today's children. One cannot hold them responsible for the rise in crime when they had no idea that they were babysitters.

2. One type of testing done on animals is for cosmetics. More people today argue that this should be stopped and scientists should find alternative ways to test cosmetics. The problem with testing cosmetics with animals is always the issue that animals' skin types, etc., are not identical to human skin types. With all cosmetic research we are not 100 percent sure that the cosmetic will not affect us. You will find a lot of companies printing "not tested on animals" because cosmetic industries realize that people are buying those products. Most cosmetic industries are now doing dermatological testing in place of animal testing. The European Union is waiting for a decision to see if it will be illegal to sell cosmetics that are tested on animals. If this does pass, it will take place in the beginning of the year 1998. With this decision more people and companies will realize how pointless this type of testing on animals is.

3. Many pro-choice people are for abortion simply because the constitution guarantees everyone the freedom of choice. To deny women their right to decide whether or not they want to abort will be denying them their Constitutional Right. Whether pro-choice people believe that abortion is morally wrong or not, they believe that it would be unconstitutional not to give a mother the right to choose to abort. Even convicted criminals sentenced to death have, to some extent, the freedom of choice. They are not

put to death before their numerous appeals run out. The purpose of these appeals is to help preserve the life of the criminal for as long as possible. If for some reason all of their appeals are denied, they were at least given the opportunity to go on living.

4. Since the large majority of the children enrolled in bilingual programs are Spanish-speakers, most bilingual education programs are directed toward this group. Promoters of bilingual education are just a small part of a political movement supporting their favorite party candidate. They do not support the movement for Latino equality, power, and influence in American society.

5. If teens are worried about what their parents think about having sex, they should at least try to talk to their parents about those subjects. Most teens today are stubborn and refuse to talk to their parents, so they put themselves through all the heartache and pain about their decision to have an abortion. If they do decide to have an abortion, then the parents should be notified. Parents are still responsible for their teen, so they should know if their teen is thinking about an abortion. Teens need their parents' consent if they wish to have an abortion anyway. Parents should always know everything about their teen.

THE THESIS

The third element in obtaining knowledge of what is being communicated is the discovery of the author's thesis. The **thesis** is the main point the author or speaker wants to make. Each paragraph should have its thesis, as should the entire piece. *The thesis should be the author's response to the issue raised, expressed in a complete sentence.* If the author has asked whether something is the case, the author should go on to say whether it is or is not the case. If the author asked how something happens or what caused something to happen, the author should go on to say how it happened or what caused it. *In argumentative writing, the thesis is the main conclusion.*

Sometimes the thesis is a simple affirmation or denial in response to the question posed in the issue. For example, if the author asks whether workers should join a union, his or her thesis might be, "Yes, workers should join the union," or "No, workers should not join the union." At other times the thesis is more complex, with the emphasis on "maybe something is the case" or "perhaps it ought to be done," or "it is the case in part." For example, the author might reply to the issue about unions by saying that workers should join a union only in particular circumstances or for particular reasons.

Finding the thesis should be easy once you have identified the topic and issue. In a well-written paragraph, the thesis generally resides either at the beginning as a topic sentence or at the end as a concluding sentence. That is, the *topic sentence* tells what the author intends to establish, while the *conclusion* asserts that the author established it. In longer articles, the thesis may be either at the beginning or end of the article or in both places.

Though this is the common structure, it is not a set rule. You will find many exceptions. Let me note two related kinds.

First, some authors use an opening paragraph as an *attention getter* before they get down to the issue at hand. For example,

> [Revoking] the driver's licenses of fathers who aren't paying child support seems to have been working well—not only to reimburse the system for supporting so many children, but also to force a lot of fathers to take responsibility for their children.
>
> Now my question: what punishment goes to mothers who do everything they can to prevent fathers to see—much less to have an active part in parenting—their children? Time and time again, despite these fathers' desire and insistence to be as much a part of their children's life as the mother, the courts favor the mothers, granting limited visitations. The visitations are then further limited when Dad isn't allowed to call his child on the days he doesn't have him/her. (Cathleen Jorissen, letter, *St. Paul Pioneer Press,* August 23, 1996)

This letter starts off by addressing whether the program revoking the drivers' licenses of fathers negligent of child support is successful. But the issue changes in the second paragraph to whether mothers who prevent contact between fathers and their children should be punished. It is easy for a casual reader to be misled into thinking that the first thesis presented is the author's main thesis.

A *second* kind of writing, similar to the first, can also be misleading. The author begins with what seems to be the key thesis and perhaps even develops or supports it. Then midstream the author switches to his or her real position, which *opposes* the thesis or position with which he or she began. For example,

> A press that went to war on [Right to Know] now censors itself on a false rape allegation. Not the first time, either. We've been doing this number for years and patting ourselves on the back for making our "conscience" run our newsrooms. But conscience has nothing to do with it. This is political correctness. . . . (Sidney Zion, "Should Media Start Reporting Names of Rape Victims? Yes: Not All 'Victims' Are Telling the Truth," *St. Paul Pioneer Press,* February 20, 1997)

Here the original or beginning thesis *sets up* the author's thesis, which has to do with political correctness.

Consider the following.

> One of the most unkillable human instincts is the urge to learn, and C-SPAN is the place to satisfy that itch. In some ways, C-SPAN is the fulfillment of an old journalistic dream—great newspaper editors have always tried to get their reporters to write stories that would let the reader see what happened. C-SPAN DOES IT. This is the answer for those who believe the media are biased. You don't have to take Dan Rather's word for what happened or what was said—you can watch it for yourself. It's enough to make you wonder whether journalism has any function left, except to synopsize for those who haven't the time to spend hours listening. But "objective journalism," which is, of course, never truly objective, is so unsatisfactory. To present facts without their context is to leave facts meaningless. Anyone can listen to a Congressional debate on C-SPAN, but it turns out only the knowledgeable can appreciate one. (Molly Ivins, "You Don't Have to Rely on the Brokaw/Jennings/Rather Versions," *TV Guide,* December 3, 1985)

The topic of this paragraph is "objective journalism," that is, allowing viewers to witness the event for themselves. The issue is whether objective journalism is desirable. The beginning of the paragraph seems to indicate that objective journalism is desirable, a modern journalistic advance. Viewers no longer need reporters or commentators; they can witness and understand the event for themselves.

However, notice the crucial word *but* about two-thirds of the way through the paragraph. *But* here indicates a change in the thesis. The topic is the same, as is the issue. But the author wants to take the position opposite to that with which she started the paragraph. She argues that objective journalism is unsatisfactory.

Here is another example. Pick out the place where the thesis appears to reverse.

> The argument has been made that to cut down on teenage drunk driving we should increase the federal excise tax on beer. Such a measure, however, would almost certainly fail to achieve its intended result. Teenagers are notoriously insensitive to cost. They gladly accept premium prices for the latest style in clothes or the most popular record albums. And then, those who drink and drive already risk arrest and loss of driving privileges. They would not think twice about paying a little more for a six-pack. (Patrick Hurley, *A Concise Introduction to Logic*, 6th ed., Belmont, CA: Wadsworth, 1996.)

Probably you picked up on *however,* which in this paragraph sets a reversal in the thesis. Words like *but, however,* and *nevertheless* set contrasts between what goes before and what comes after. They often indicate that the author wants to make a switch in the ideas presented, that what the author started the paragraph or article with is not the point he or she wishes to make. Critical thinkers watch for such signals of contrast.

One final point. *It is important that the critical thinker not confuse the thesis with the supporting evidence for the thesis.* Consider the following from a brochure.

> By the time you add the costs all up, driving your car to work can be very expensive. But if you want to cut that figure in half, all you have to do is contact Rideshare and add a passenger. You'll both save money and the more passengers you add, the more money you save. To figure out your current commuting costs and the potential savings, call Rideshare for an easy-to-use worksheet.

What are the issue and the thesis? _____

_____

_____

Someone might say that the issue is "Can we can save money driving to work?" But the matter of saving money has to do with the reasons for something else, namely, using Rideshare to commute to work. Note the concluding sentence, which tells the reader to "call Rideshare." Turning this concluding sentence into a question, you get the issue: "Should I contact Rideshare for commuting?" The thesis is that you should, while the matter of saving money comes in as the author's main reason for contacting Rideshare. In short, it is important not to confuse the point of the paragraph or paragraphs with the supporting material, which we call main points.

Consider one more example.

> Our college provides some excellent opportunities for students to enhance their education and develop new skills outside the classroom. Involvement in a student organization or activity can heighten your college experience in a number of ways. Some of the benefits include social, educational, values, and skills experience.

What are the issue and the thesis? _____

_____

_____

Here you might have written that the issue is "Can extracurricular activities benefit students?" But this example is similar to the previous example, except that it does not overtly ask the reader to participate in the activities. The request is implied in the paragraph so that we might say the thesis is that students should participate in extracurricular activities. That these activities are beneficial is presented as the reason students should participate and hence constitutes a main point. What can be learned from comparing these last two examples is that sometimes authors actually present their issue and thesis, and sometimes they do not. In the latter case, readers need to derive it from what else is said.

We have spoken about distinguishing theses from main points. It is time to move on to discuss main points.

Exercise 5

Find the thesis in the examples in Exercise 1.

Exercise 6

Find the thesis in the examples in Exercise 3.

Exercise 7

Find the thesis in the following examples.

1. For more than a century, the American Association of University Women (AAUW) has promoted education and equity for women and girls. In communities across the country, 135,000 AAUW members take the lead today to ensure women a place among the leaders of tomorrow. Your action today will make the difference. Join AAUW. (Brochure)

2. More than 90 percent of American women who want to avoid pregnancy report using a birth control method. Still, the reality is that nearly 6 in 10 U.S. pregnancies are unplanned. As a result, a quarter of the 6 million pregnancies in the United States each year are terminated.

   The U.S. market for a new abortion method is huge, and one probably will be available by year's end [1997]. After years of controversy, the abortion pill RU-486 moved closer to final approval with the settlement last month [February 1997] of a lawsuit involving its former distributor. . . .

The drug is likely to make pregnancy termination more accessible in areas lacking surgical-abortion providers. . . . (Excerpted from Rita Rubin, "Birth Control Failure," *U.S. News & World Report*, March 3, 1997, p. 66. Copyright, 1997, U.S. News & World Report. Visit us at our web site at www.usnews.com for additional information.)

3. I moved to this area years ago to raise my children in an environment with strong family values, good work ethic, and a dedication to community. The Aug. 4 article depicting Lawrence Coss as a rags-to-riches, solid Midwest businessman just showed me how wrong I was.

   How could so many pages be dedicated to a man who carries so little family values that he allows his mother to live in a one-bedroom apartment? From the picture it looked as if the woman may not even be blessed with a window to look out of. Couldn't he even spare a mobile home in one of the parks he owns?

   Why does this man leave in his path a trail of laid-off executives? What has happened to all the top executives, many of whom gave years of their lives to build Green Tree, who were handed their last paycheck long before planned retirement? Are there not any successful people to write about who have a reputation of honesty and integrity? . . .

   I wonder if the reason Coss refuses interviews is because he feels great guilt in looking back on what he has done. Or is he a man who lives with a cold heart? I hope that in the future you could dedicate more space to people who have less in their back pockets and more in their hearts. (Kendra Lear, letter, *St. Paul Pioneer Press*, August 11, 1996)

4. A recent poll by the Public Agenda Foundation found that 80 percent of all Americans believe young people today have little chance for success without a college education. But while many recognize the value of a college diploma, few know its cost.

   For millions of families, college expenses are a growing cause of anxiety—an anxiety that is often fueled by media coverage. College costs have become a regular feature in magazines and newspapers and on the nightly news. Frequently these stories focus on the highest-priced colleges and universities attended by fewer than 2 percent of the nation's students.

   Unfortunately, this type of sensationalized, slanted coverage generates more heat than light and only perpetuates the sense of unease that families feel regarding the affordability of a college education. The story that needs to be told is that we have a strong and diverse system of higher education in this country. And this diversity—from our community colleges to our research universities—ensures that quality education abounds in all price ranges. . . . (E. Gordon Gee, "Cost of College Education Remains One of America's Great Bargains Despite Tuition Increases," *The Phoenix Gazette*, August 19, 1996)

5. Psychiatrists who defend the diagnosis of MPD [multiple personality disorders] say cases are now rising because, until recently, most MPD sufferers were misdiagnosed with illnesses like schizophrenia. But even proponents concede that it is overdiagnosed. National Institute of Mental Health psychiatrist Frank Putnam, for example, a leading MPD researcher, has found in studies that some 20 percent of MPD diagnoses are incorrect. He

blames criteria that are too vague, requiring little more than the appearance of distinct personalities and extensive amnesia. "Sometimes therapists fall in love with the diagnosis, " he warns. . . . (Excerpted from Joannie M. Schrop, "Questioning Sybil," *U.S. News & World Report*, January 27, 1997, p. 66. Copyright, 1997, U.S. News & World Report. Visit us at our web site www.usnews.com for additional information.)

6. There are an estimated 3,200 children under 13 living with AIDS in the United States, and thousands more are infected with the virus that causes the disease, according to the Centers for Disease Control and Prevention in Atlanta. But these youngsters account for just 1 percent of the nation's AIDs cases, and as a result they have long been an afterthought in the epidemic. AZT, the first antiretroviral medication for AIDS, was approved by the Food and Drug Administration in 1987 for adults; it was three years before the drug was available for children. . . . The problem goes beyond a simple lack of approved medications. Some adults have trouble with the combination therapy, and the same is true of children. For some, the drugs do not work at all, and for others they stop working after a time. And although doctors are free to prescribe any adult-approved medication for children, many are reluctant to do so with protease inhibitors because less is known about the way children respond to them. . . . (Sheryl Gay Stolberg, "A Revolution in AIDs Drugs Excludes the Tiniest Patients," *New York Times*, September 8, 1997, p. A14)

7. It is ironic that the possibility of life having once existed on Mars would raise doubts about the existence of an omnipotent Creator. Christians have always accepted that other sentient beings exist in the universe besides humans. Angels are mentioned throughout the Bible.

   Rather, it is the Darwinists who should be rethinking their theories. Darwinian evolution and its successor theories hold that life evolved from a series of random chance occurrences or mutations. The Earth, therefore, is the one out of billions of possible planets where all of the elements necessary for life to occur came together at the exact right moment—under the precisely correct conditions.

   Life on Mars means that a random occurrence, the odds against which are measured in the billions, happened not once, but twice, and in the same solar system. Now, what are the odds of that happening? (Robert Bode, letter, *St. Paul Pioneer Press*, August 24, 1996. Reprinted by permission.)

8. NASA's announcement that a team of scientists may have discovered evidence of previous life on Mars has aroused intense public interest. But why so much hubbub about organic molecules and some bacteria-like organisms that passed their prime millions of years ago? The answer lies not in what was found, but in the chasm of knowledge the findings uncovered.

   Daniel Goldin, the administrator of the National Aeronautics and Space Administration, is correct in calling this a "startling discovery," and it is impossible not to marvel at it. But what these scientists mainly have proved is how little we know and how little effort we are putting into solving one of mankind's greatest mysteries: Are we alone?

Humans have always suspected there was life on Mars because of its distance from the sun and the ancient water channels visible through telescopes on Earth. . . . When the Viking missions 20 years ago failed to find evidence of life there, that was generally assumed to be the end of the story. But thanks to advanced space technology the story has a new exciting chapter. We got lucky this time. Having stumbled upon a Martian meteorite in the Antarctic, we used our best scientific equipment—and information we had about Martian conditions because of the earlier Viking missions—to theorize that there once was life on Mars.

But we shouldn't have to wait for breathtaking scientific discoveries just to drop into our lap—or at least onto our polar cap. Technology is at a stage now where it's feasible to bring surface samples of Mars back to Earth and prove conclusively whether at least rudimentary life ever developed on the red planet.

No matter what the search of Mars reveals, though, it would be naive of us to think that we are alone in the universe. With billions—trillions?—of stars and planets out there, there is undoubtedly not only life but intelligent life. Discovering such life is simply a matter of priorities. . . . If we are willing to commit the necessary resources, we can look not just at Mars but far beyond. NASA has made the search for other life in the universe one of its key programs as we enter the next century. . . .

Who or what is out there? Millions of years ago, interplanetary explorers to Earth would have found large reptiles ruling our planet. We don't know what we'll find out there; but there is no question that we must look. (James A. Lovell and Brian Kyhos, "Continue Our Quest in Space," *Denver Post*, August 10, 1996)

9. I believe there are some fundamental structural problems . . . with putting a balanced budget requirement in the Constitution. This addition would change the balance of power among the three branches of government, and some of the proposals would even change the balance of power within the legislative branch. On a more practical level, it would increase the cost of government well above what is needed for a given level of service and have a potentially harmful effect on long term interest rates. . . .

I believe it will either prove to be an unenforceable promise, or its enforcement will shift unprecedented budgetary powers to the courts and the president. One concern is that a president could assert broad powers to withhold spending or modify programs and benefits using the balanced budget amendment as justification. This could occur even if Congress, acting in good faith, had passed a balanced budget but the president did not believe it was balanced. This shift of power is in direct contradiction to the basic plan of the Constitution, which assigns primary power over the purse to the people's elected representatives in Congress.

Secondly, a balanced budget amendment would give rise to a flood of litigation. And if the courts do have to enter this area, they could find themselves embroiled in matters of spending and taxes that have always been the province of elected branches of government. . . . (Martin Olav Sabo, "Is Constitutional Change Needed to Slay Deficit Dragon?" *St. Paul Pioneer Press*, February 5, 1997)

10. Water vapour is scarce in planetary stratospheres because it freezes out at the cold tropopause, which marks the lower boundary of the stratosphere. In spite of this, there have been some hints of water in the stratospheres of Jupiter, Titan and Uranus, and we have direct measurements of its presence on Saturn, Uranus and Neptune. . . . What might be supplying water to these upper atmospheres? The three main possibilities are interplanetary dust, large comet nuclei, and circumplanetary material such as ring particles. . . .

The cometary source seems the least likely, however, because the water vapour from each impact would disappear in a decade or so, and in any case would probably be converted to CO by reacting with atmospheric methane in the high temperatures of a large impact. Influx from rings is likely to be confined to low latitudes, and although the rate at which material spreads to higher latitudes is poorly known, this characteristic could discriminate between rings and interplanetary dust. Unfortunately, the new ISO measurements are of too low resolution to tell us whether the water vapour is uniformly distributed or confined to equatorial regions.

The main conclusion to be drawn from these detections of water vapour on the outer planets may be that our expectations of the flux of icy particles in this part of the interplanetary medium were correct. (Donald M. Hunten, "Pipelines to the Planets," *Nature*, September 11, 1997, pp. 125–6)

THE MAIN POINTS

Once you have identified the topic, issue, and thesis, what remain to be discovered are the main points used to support or develop the thesis. These constitute the body of the communication. If you have only one paragraph, the main points are found in its contents. If you are working with a longer piece, you have to proceed paragraph by paragraph, hunting for the main points relevant to the thesis.

If the communication is *argumentative*, the main points provide the *evidence* for the thesis. As you read material that you think argues for the truth of the thesis, you should ask, "Why does the author think the thesis is true?" With this question in the background, you then search for the answer to this question. You are a detective, investigating for the author's clues or actual statements of evidence or support. As with the thesis, the main points should be *expressed in complete sentences,* not with sentence fragments.

You can find an argument in the first example under "The Topic" (page 32). We have noted that this example's thesis is that the proposed balanced budget amendment to the Constitution should be passed. The author goes on to give a reason for his position: it will benefit the American family. Similarly in the second example about winter survival supplies on page 32, the thesis that some Roman candles or a Very pistol should be part of a vehicle's winter survival supplies is supported by appealing to past experience: the pistol has been shown to be effective in locating lost inoperative ships and/or survivors.

Note that we are not evaluating the main points or reasons given. We are not questioning whether it is true that the balanced budget amendment will actually benefit the American family or that the Very pistol has been successful in the past. At this point we merely want to know what the author is arguing; we are after knowledge, not assessment.

Sometimes the author presents the evidence in an obvious way; at other times the evidence is hidden. And sometimes the evidence is misleading, pointing in another direction. In the last type of case the author seems to present contrary evidence. Here the critical thinker looks to see whether the author introduces an objection to the position and then responds to that objection. We will say more about this type of writing shortly.

If the writing is *informative* or *descriptive,* the main points provide the description that develops the thesis. Here the difficulty is to isolate the main developing features from less significant features. Since not every feature is equally important, you need to decide judiciously what you think the author considers most important in the thesis development. This decision involves making an informed judgment that you can support from the text.

Examples 2 and 3 under "The Topic" (pages 32 and 33) illustrate a descriptive approach. In Example 3, the author develops his thesis that Michael Johnson won impressively by relating how Michael Johnson threw his spiked shoes into the stands after his victory and presenting the time of his victory. Example 4 develops the thesis by describing how rain and wind disrupted the search operations and how Deep Drone later located part of the cockpit.

If you are reading a simple paragraph, the *main points* are the reasons supporting or ideas developing the thesis in that paragraph. For example,

> There is little reason to vote for Mary Smith for mayor. For one thing, she will be 66 next month, which means that she would be the oldest mayor we have ever had. For another, she will be drawing retirement benefits from her teacher's pension at the same time as she gets paid for being mayor; no one should get two salaries for doing one job. Finally, she has lived in this community only four years. She is not a native of our city and hence cannot understand how we think about things. No, don't waste your vote in November on Ms. Smith.

In this paragraph, the topic is Mary Smith, the issue is "Should you vote for her?" and the thesis is that you should not vote for Mary Smith. Immediately, critical thinkers wonder why we should not vote for her. The author helps us by providing reasons for not doing so. You should be able to pick out the three reasons or main points.

1. _____

   _____

2. _____

   _____

3. _____

   _____

If the piece is longer, the main points are spread throughout it, often in separate paragraphs. This makes it harder to understand but richer in content and development. Consider this example.

We have now recognized the necessity to the mental well-being of mankind of freedom of opinion, and freedom of the expression of opinion, on four distinct grounds. . . .

First, if any opinion is compelled to silence, that opinion may, for aught we can certainly know, be true. To deny this is to assume our own infallibility.

Secondly, though the silenced opinion be an error, it may and very commonly does, contain a portion of truth; and since the general or prevailing opinion on any subject is rarely or never the whole truth, it is only by the collision of adverse opinions that the remainder of the truth has any chance of being supplied.

Thirdly, even if the received opinion be not only true, but the whole truth; unless it is suffered to be, and actually is, vigorously and earnestly contested, it will, by most of those who receive it, be held in the manner of a prejudice, with little comprehension or feeling of its rational grounds. And not only this, but, fourthly, the meaning of the doctrine itself will be in danger of being lost or enfeebled, and deprived of its vital effect on the character and conduct; the dogma becoming a mere formal profession, ineffacious for good. (John S. Mill, *On Liberty*)

Before you go on, identify Mill's topic, issue, thesis, and main points.

Topic: _____

Issue: _____

Thesis: _____

Main points: _____

_____

_____

_____

Mill's topic is individual liberty, his issue is whether persons should be given freedom of opinion, and his thesis is that they should. He then proceeds to give four reasons for granting people freedom of their opinion. They are the following:

1. The opinion expressed might be true.
2. It might contain some truth and help bring out the rest of the truth.
3. The truth needs to be challenged, lest we hold it merely because it was passed down and not for a good reason.
4. Truth unchallenged loses its vitality for doing good.

To find the main points in a longer piece, carefully go through each paragraph, noting the main point of the paragraph and asking how each point relates to the overall thesis. Some paragraphs might contain several arguments or important descriptive elements relating to the main point. Also, some paragraphs might repeat main points already made.

This is the ideal: each paragraph's main point has some relation, direct or indirect, to the main thesis. It may be a main point, a subpoint, or an illustration or expansion of the thesis. In practice, however, this is not always the case. So you must decide which of the paragraphs' main points are critical to defending or developing the thesis and which are not. Making this call takes sleuthing and selectivity.

As you can see, no easy formula exists for finding the main points. You are the detective and have to search them out. As you read,

- Read actively, with the question "Why is the thesis true?" or "How is it developed?" in mind.
- Constantly ask how what you are reading is connected to the thesis of the piece.
- Express the main points in complete sentences so that complete ideas are presented.
- Look for apparent disparities between what you are reading and what you take to be the author's thesis. Sometimes authors introduce an objection to their position and then proceed to answer it. This can be misleading, for you might take the objection as one of the author's main points, whereas the author introduces the objection in order to answer it. The answer given is a main point of the author.

Exercise 8

Identify the main points in the examples given in Exercise 1.

Exercise 9

Identify the main points in the examples given in Exercise 3.

Exercise 10

Identify the main points in the examples given in Exercise 7.

ACTIVE READING

By now you should have a good idea of what to look for when you read or listen. Identifying these four elements provides the basis for everything else you do as a critical thinker when you read or hear.

One final question remains: how do you implement this strategy in your reading and listening? The answer is that you need to be an *active questioner* as you read or listen. You should read or listen asking, "What are the topic, issue, thesis, and main points?" writing each down as you proceed, either in the book margins or on a separate piece of paper. *Active readers and listeners* not only get more out of the material; they retain what they have learned for a longer period of time than those who read passively.

When you pick up something to read, *first* skim through it to find the topic. Look at the headings, if there are any. If there are no headings, read the first and last paragraphs of the section to see what the topic is. Doing this gives you some idea of what to look for as you read. If you are listening, attempt to quickly identify the topic. Does the talk have a title? Is it part of a larger program? Use any clues you can pick up to assist you.

The *second* task is to identify the question or issue that the author is addressing. This helps identify why the author is writing or the speaker talking. As we have noted, this is perhaps the hardest step. You need to turn the topic into the question or questions about which the author or presenter is interested. *In a good piece of writing or in a good presentation the issue should be presented early on.*

Task *three* is to identify the author's thesis. What position is the author or speaker taking on the issue? To be an active reader, you should note this thesis and then continually relate whatever you read or hear to that thesis. The thesis provides the unifying idea.

Task *four* is to identify the author's main points. As you read, write down the main points, preferably in complete sentences using your own words. These probably are located in one or two paragraphs in a shorter piece and in separate paragraphs in longer pieces of writing. Eventually, as you write down the thesis, main points, and their supporting subpoints, you create a workable, detailed outline of the presentation that improves your knowledge of what is communicated.

One method is to write these points in the margin of the text. The advantage of this is that the main points are directly connected with the textual material; the disadvantage is that book margins are often too narrow to write a sentence stating the main point of the paragraph. Another method is to write the outline on a separate sheet of paper; this allows you to see more directly the development of the author's main points. Whichever method you use, active involvement with the ideas helps you retain what you have read or heard.

A great practical advantage of outlining awaits you: if you follow this pattern, when you review for your tests you will not have to do much rereading. A review of your marginal or notebook outline should reveal the main points and the developing or supporting arguments for the thesis. By reviewing this material, you will have a good idea of how the author developed the main points to support the thesis without having to reread the text.

Task *five* involves review. Once you have read the material, do not simply close the book and head off to do something else. Close the book and try to recall the topic, issue, thesis, and main points. If you cannot do this immediately after reading, you need to go back and reread sections of the material so that you can. Thorough review requires you to engage the text more than once. To further cement the material in your mind, go back the next day and try to recall the elements we have stressed. Or before you read the next section or chapter, review what you read the previous time or in the previous section. Doing so substantially increases your retention and ultimate recall.

Task *six* goes beyond reading and writing to actually making use of the material in some way. You may recall our stress on application in Chapter 2. You retain things when you both make them your own *and* find a way to use them. Think, for example, of the vocabulary lists you memorized in school. If you simply memorized the word and its meaning or synonym, you may have known it for the test, but probably you soon forgot it. However, if you find ways to use these new words,—for example, by creating sentences for them— you retain them longer. They can actually become part of your vocabulary.

So here is a suggested way to read carefully and critically. (Some of you will recognize in this the basic elements of what is often referred to as the SQR^3 method.)

- Skim to find the topic.
- Question to find the issue(s).
- As you read, identify the thesis or theses.
- Write down the main points.
- Review the thesis and main points.
- Use the material in some way.

As you perform these six tasks, your knowledge increases because you put what you read and hear into your mind's memory bank. If you merely read the material, you remember less than 10 percent the following day. If you read actively and use what you read, the amount you can recall increases dramatically.

Before you close the book on this chapter—and possibly forget what we have talked about—recall that the development of skills takes great practice. This chapter will stick with you only if you persist in reading in the fashion indicated here. This should become your pattern of reading, not only in this course but in all your courses.

Exercise 11

Identify the topic, issue, thesis, and main points in the following paragraphs.

1. Anybody can have a few flakes from time to time . . . happens to the best of us. Fortunately, there is something you can do. It's called Head and Shoulders. Regular shampoos just rinse away flakes that you already have (so they can come back). Head and Shoulders actually helps prevent flakes before they even get started. The only thing that might give you away is that great looking head of hair. (Advertisement)

2. A second distinction has been attempted in terms of experience. A being who has had experience, has lived and suffered, who possesses memories, is more human than one who has not. Humanity depends on formation by experience. The fetus is thus "unformed" in the most basic human sense.

   This distinction is not serviceable for the embryo which is already experiencing and reacting. The embryo is responsive to touch after eight weeks and at least at that point is experiencing. At an earlier stage the zygote is certainly alive and responding to its environment. The distinction may also be challenged by the rare case where aphasia has erased adult memory: has it erased humanity? More fundamentally, this distinction leaves even the older fetus or the younger child to be treated as an unformed inhuman thing. Finally, it is not clear why experience as such confers humanity. (John T. Noonan, Jr., "An Almost Absolute Value in History," in Ronald Munson, *Intervention and Reflection* (Belmont, CA: Wadsworth, Inc.)

3. Supply-side economics is just plain wrongheaded. Given great market demand for goods and services, business will operate at high capacity levels, yielding significantly improved profits. That will stimulate new investment from all over the world. Putting the money into the hands of the poorest half of the population, who spend essentially all of their income, will rapidly generate demand. Giving the bulk of the money to

the top 10 percent of earners, which is what the flat 15 percent tax cut and the reduction in capital-gains taxes will do, will merely stimulate stock-market speculation. This leads to a disorderly market, certainly not good for the nation's economy. The Republican program is, as previously reported, really misguided economics! (Martin H. Wohl, letter, *U.S. News & World Report*, September 9, 1996, p. 4. Reprinted by permission.)

4. The House National Security Committee confirmed the earlier reports that the tragic deaths of the 19 American servicemen in Saudi Arabia were caused by the fact that we "asked" the Saudis for additional security prior to the incident, and they refused.

   Common sense should tell you that you don't ask the Saudis for anything, where American lives are at stake. You *tell* them what to do. And when they don't do it, you pull a gun on them.

   Defense Secretary Perry should be fired forthwith. (Walter G. Perry, letter, *St. Paul Pioneer Press*, September 4, 1996, p. 4).

5. Those of us old enough to remember the civil rights revolution of the '60s and the profound social transformations that preceded it may find it hard to realize that most Americans today were not yet born when all this happened. This lack of personal knowledge is, for the unscrupulous, a golden opportunity to create a history that serves their own purposes. One of the key self-serving myths to emerge is that blacks owe their economic and social advancement to the civil rights victories of the '60s. Incessant repetition of myths does not, of course, make them true . . . That does not mean that the civil rights revolution was unnecessary. There were injustices that needed to be redressed and resistance to doing so. . . . But it also paints a vision of racial progress in America that we have seldom seen. Blacks have not advanced by being passive recipients of government largesse or by high-decibel rhetoric. Most have made money the old-fashioned way: they have *earned* it. As of 1940, the average black adult had only a grossly inferior elementary school education. But as more blacks became better educated and left the South, incomes of black males rose faster than incomes of white males—all well before the civil rights revolution. More blacks rose into professional ranks in the years immediately before the Civil Rights Act of 1964 than in the years immediately afterward. Too many black "leaders" today have a vested interest in the application of old myths. They are like Moses in reverse—leading their people back into the welfare state, to a self-imposed isolation from the growing opportunities all around them. (Thomas Sowell, "Yes, Blacks Can Make It on Their Own," *Time*, September 8, 1997, p. 62)

6. Congress can do the strapped National Park System and its 80 million annual visitors a service. Lawmakers should pass pending legislation that allows more corporate money to augment public money in the system, while adequately ensuring that increased commercialism will not intrude on the integrity of the 369 park sites.

   Under the legislation the National Parks Foundation, the official not-for-profit organization that supports the park system, would be allowed to establish business relationships with a selective number of private partners to raise revenue.

Except for the ideological opponents of public lands, this legislation should have no natural enemies. It is written carefully enough to avoid conflicts of interest or commercial exploitation of parks or sites, while giving potential private partners a value for their investment in a National Park System sponsorship through advertising their good citizenship. . . .

If you have visited a park recently where the biffy wasn't spiffy, more private revenue could help the park service do deferred work on plumbing and other critical infrastructure.

The National Park Foundation has kept in proportion the changes it seeks as an agent for fund-raising. The potential from well-chosen corporate sponsorships directed at the park system is pegged at a market of $50 million to $100 million a year. Under current operation, the foundation raises only $3 million to $4 million a year for the parks. The increase would be substantial but not overwhelming. The National Park System runs on a $2 billion budget. More corporate revenue and in-kind contributions are intended to augment—not buy out—the public nature of a park system that has become a victim of its own popularity in lean times.

Of course, changes in the executive branch could result in an interior secretary more like Jim Watt than Bruce Babbitt. In that case, the National Park Foundation's role as a reliable steward to balance interests might require Congress to keep an eye out as a safeguard against abuse.

But for now, and with obvious needs in the National Park System, legislation to increase public-private partnership for the parks is a good deal. ("Let Private Partners Assist National Parks," *St. Paul Pioneer Press,* August 20, 1996)

7. . . . With Steve Spurrier and Peyton Manning on the same field, most would think the best offense would win Saturday's matchup between No. 3 Florida and No. 4 Tennessee at Gainsville, Fla. Further proof of that point: in the past four meetings between the Volunteers and Gators, the winning team, in each case Florida, has scored at least 31 points.

But the majority of talk leading up to the highly anticipated game at The Swamp is not of Manning's arm or Spurrier's strategy. Instead, both sides believe the winning team must do a very simple thing: hold on to the football. "The winner of this game the last four seasons has had the least amount of turnovers," Tennessee coach Phillip Fulmer said. "They have beaten us because we have not taken care of the football."

In the past four meetings, Tennessee has had 15 turnovers, Florida six. Last season, the Volunteers had five in the first half; two seasons ago, the Gators had 20 points off turnovers. That is why Fulmer has called Tennessee's inability to hold on to the ball two games into this season (seven fumbles, three interceptions) a "big concern." . . . (George Dohrmann, "Turnovers Tell Tennessee's Tale," *St. Paul Pioneer Press,* September 18, 1997)

8. Millions of Americans will honor the American worker this Labor Day weekend when they travel on one of his proudest achievements: the nation's interstate highway system.

Begun nearly 40 years ago, the interstates now stretch more than 45,000 miles, reaching every state and serving nearly every citizen and business. They represent one of the most successful federal programs ever. They have helped make America the most mobile and prosperous civilization in history. Indeed, mobility and the personal freedom it provides are important American values.

But as important as the interstates are, they're in trouble. They're in growing disrepair and increasingly congested because we aren't maintaining, modernizing or extending them fast enough.

According to the Federal Highway Administration, only about 40 percent of our interstates are in good to very good condition. More than one-third are in poor to mediocre shape. And about one quarter of the interstate bridges are substandard. Nearly half of the interstates are congested.

Keeping 45,000 miles of highways, bridges and cloverleaves in top condition is costly, but that's not the problem. The money's there.

Americans pay some $114 billion a year in taxes, tolls and fees related to automobiles, fuels and roads—with the expectation that the money will be used to build and maintain a first-class system of highways. The problem is that only about two-thirds of this—some $76 billion—is spent on roads. The government uses the rest to reduce the deficit, fund mass transit and pay for other federal, state and local programs.

In at least one state, Maryland, the government spends more on mass transit than on highways, despite the fact that highways meet 98 percent of the state's transportation needs.

We're diverting money from highways when highways need it—and the tradeoff is a bad one. The interstates move about 80 percent of all freight and support a $350 billion a year tourist industry. Our economy—and the jobs of millions of Americans—depend on them.

Reducing the deficit is important. Mass transit makes sense when it moves people as economically as highways, which is rarely true. But we can't afford to let the condition of our interstates worsen by the diversion of taxpayer money collected for their maintenance.

Roads that are congested and in poor repair result in more accidents, causing additional deaths and injuries and requiring expensive medical services. They increase fuel consumption and produce more pollution. They slow traffic and increase shipping costs. And they increase the cost of vehicle maintenance. According to the American Highway Users Alliance, the average motorist today is paying an extra $122 a year because of rough pavement that increases vibration and damages tires.

Today, the interstates must accommodate the growth and problems of the '90s—a quadrupling in road travel not anticipated at their birth, tighter budgets, heavier trucks and higher speeds. And although Congress has committed more money for highways in the next few years, we're not spending at the rate necessary to solve today's future problems and meet the needs necessary to solve today's problems and meet the needs of the future.

For example, in the Washington D.C. area where I live, official forecasts show the region growing some 40 percent in population, 50 percent in jobs, and 75 percent in highway travel by 2020. Yet current transportation plans call for only 20 percent more highway capacity.

Highways help make America run. They make us richer and freer. They expand economic and lifestyle choices. Moreover, the problems associated with them are being solved: the highway death toll has generally been decreasing; and thanks to cleaner cars and fuels, pollution is steadily declining even though we're driving more.

We need our highways, but they won't continue to serve us well if we don't invest in them adequately. The fact that that's not happening isn't fair to the American workers who built them—or to the millions of Americans who now depend on them and who pay taxes for their expansion and maintenance. The Highway Trust Fund has the money to do a better job. All that is needed is the government to meet its obligation to the taxpayers. (William F. O'Keefe, "Spend Road Taxes on America's Roads," *Tallahassee Democrat*, September 2, 1996)

9. Perhaps more than any other ecological no-no out there, dams enrage environmental activists. Legend has it that John Muir, founder of the Sierra Club, died of a broken heart after the O'Shaughnessy Dam in Yosemite National Park was built despite his group's protests. These activists argue that you can't redirect millions of gallons of water—even for such worthy causes as flood control or renewable-energy projects—without having at least some deleterious effect on the local environment. But documenting long-term changes to ecosystems along rivers is complex, so such conclusions have been difficult to test.

A recent study of Swedish rivers . . . has succeeded in quantifying the extent to which biodiversity can be choked off by dams. Researchers at Umea University counted different species of trees, shrubs and herbs at some 90 sites along rivers that had been dammed. Some of the Swedish dams are nearly 70 years old, which enabled the team to examine how ecosystems change over decades. In addition, the group surveyed species along pristine rivers in Sweden. . . .

Christer Nilsson, who led the Umea team, . . . and his colleagues . . . demonstrated that in some areas, certain types of trees and shrubs did recover, especially along small, so-called run-of-river impoundments. But in total, the number of plant species fell by 15 percent, and the size of the habitat along the riverbank also decreased. Near larger storage reservoirs, the researchers found that the number of species within a given area dropped by about 50 percent.

More surprising to Nilsson were the long-term trends in these ecosystems. After a dam was built, the diversity of plant species rebounded only during the first 20 or 30 years before tapering off. Nilsson attributes the subsequent scarcity of new species to either a gradual depletion of seeds over the decades or a slow deterioration of the habitat.

Studies such as this one should figure prominently in the ongoing debate about whether and how to maintain aging networks of dams throughout the world. One option being considered in the United States is the periodic opening of certain dams. Last year's uncorking of the Glen Canyon Dam and the resulting flood in the Grand Canyon, intended to revitalize riverbanks and wildlife, were ecologically "trivial," according to Jack Stanford of the University of Montana's Flathead Lake Biological Station.

"But from a sociological standpoint, it was huge," he says. That brief flood could be the first drop in a very large bucket to restore the ecology of dammed rivers, in which the primary concern is endangered animals, particularly fish. . . .

The U.S. Army corps of Engineers is studying the possibility of breaching four dams along the Snake River and lowering the reservoir behind the John Day Dam on the Columbia River as part of a play to protect salmon runs. . . .

Opponents of such plans protest that dams are vital to the livelihood of the West. Lewiston, Idaho, for example, is an inland port along the Snake River. Without the current system of dams, jobs in the area shipping goods to market would dry up.

Dismantling dams would take years of construction work. And the payoff could take decades or more, even with extension environmental rehabilitation. Dutch Meier of the U.S. Army corps of Engineers points out that the removal of the dams on the Snake River could very likely reveal "scoured, denuded hillsides with entirely changed ecosystems." Meier adds: "Just because you pull the plug on the tub and make the water go away doesn't mean you won't leave a bathtub ring." (Sasha Nemecek, "Frankly, My Dear, I Don't Want a Dam: How Dams Affect Biodiversity," *Scientific American,* August 1997, pp. 20, 22)

10. It was Friday afternoon and the traffic gods whizzing overhead in helicopters were warning of the bumper to bumper, creep and beep, weekend exodus. I was crawling over the city line when a young man in an old Toyota cut in front of me and, in the style for which Boston drivers have become famous, threw me the finger.

Thank you and have a nice day.

I was somewhere near the New Hampshire border doing penance for my early escape from the office by listening to talk radio. John from Boise was making his feelings about gay marriage as explicit as you can without using expletives. Paul from Bismarck, or was it Carl from Potsdam?, was talking about the president and first lady in ways that do not reflect well on his upbringing.

So kind of you to call.

Halfway up the sea coast, my Thank God It's Friday Mood had darkened considerably. As I crossed the Maine border, I pushed Patti Smith into my tape deck. But my internal track was playing a second tape entitled: What on Earth is Wrong With People?

I am no double for Miss Manners. More than one unkind phrase has tripped off my tongue or fingertips. But if I was happy to be leaving civilization that late summer weekend, it may have been because civility had already departed.

The previous night, exploring the vast mansion of the Internet, I wandered into several unfamiliar chat rooms. Some of the visitors were people who change nicknames more often than they change socks. These are people who checked their courtesy along with their identity at the door. A main method of communication in these chambers seems to be flaming.

What they have in common with the digit-wagging driver, with the talk show-callers, is not just their aerobic exercise of the "freedom of speech"—a freedom that leaves even this First Amendment junkie grimacing. They belong, rather, to the growing uncommunity of people who now act with the protection of anonymity.

Would that driver have expressed his opinion if he thought I knew his mother or his boss? Is the man from Bismarck equally nasty at his local market? Have any of the flamethrowers singed someone under their own name?

The rap on America is that we live today in a disunited state where, in the near-cliché phrase of Robert Putnam, we even "bowl alone." There are fewer communities to which we belong these days, fewer places where we are known.

At the same time, there are far more opportunities for being anonymous. We have become as unaccountable to each other, as unaccountable for what we say, as unnamed sources. . . .

These thoughts follow me onto the ferry to one of the islands that dot this Maine coast. This floating community hall, where islanders check on the cork bulletin board and on each other's children, traverses the short haul and long psychic distance to a place where people wave to each other along the country roads. Not just because it is an island custom but because we know each other.

If I have learned anything in my 15 years here as a summer person, it's the delicate ecology of island life where people are both away and together. It's the sense of community that comes from independence and mutual dependence.

I have learned that civility—not always intimacy and rarely hostility—sustains a community. That civility only rules when people understand that they must abide each other and abide together. . . .

On a mainland of individualists it's no surprise that many value the liberation that comes from being unknown. No surprise that many change identities as if life were a masquerade ball, or as if there were an endless supply of fresh starts.

But as a nation we suffer more from a lack of cohesion than a lack of independence. If the center isn't holding, it's because there simply aren't enough stakeholders.

So, on a later summer weekend, I look back at the coast of America. From here, it seems as if the contentious, fractured story of this country is now being written by American Anonymous. (Excerpted from Ellen Goodman, "Anonymity Provides Cover for Mushrooming Incivility," *Boston Globe*, September 5, 1996. © 1996, The Boston Globe Newspaper Co./Washington Post Writers Group. Reprinted with permission.)

Exercise 12

Cut out or copy articles, letters, or editorials from newspapers, magazines, or sections of texts that you use for other courses. For each, write out the topic, thesis, issue, and main points.

ANSWERS TO THE EXERCISES

Answers to Exercise 1

1. Charter schools
3. Sunflowers
5. Toyota 4Runner
7. SGS; assets withheld by SGS from Holocaust victims
9. Straight Edgers
11. USTA Tennis Teacher's Conference
13. Juvenile crime
15. Violent behavior
17. Improving major-league baseball
19. Thinness in young women; the media

Answers to Exercise 2

1. What are Charter schools?
3. Are sunflowers a beneficial crop?
5. Is the Toyota 4Runner a top Sport Utility Van?
7. Did SGS withhold funds from Holocaust victims?
9. Who is the new rebel group called Straight Edgers?
11. Should you attend the USTA Tennis Teacher's conference?
13. Should we take action to divert juveniles from committing crime?
15. Can we affect the causes of violent behavior?
17. Should we change the rules of baseball?
19. Are young women victims of a media that encourages them to be unnaturally thin?

Answers to Exercise 3

1. Topic: motherhood
   Issue: Does love begin with motherhood?
3. Topic: (Russian) émigrés
   Issue: Should recent émigrés get social benefits without having paid prior taxes?
5. Topic: Social Security cost of living index
   Issue: Should the Social Security cost of living index be tied directly to the Consumer Price Index?
7. Topic: Antarctic sea-ice
   Issue: Would a large and rapid decrease in Antarctic summertime sea-ice have global significance?
9. Topic: Male stickleback
   Issue: Is the male stickleback choosy about the females he allows to lay eggs in his nest?
11. Topic: Teaching loads; professors
    Issue: Should college professors have a heavier teaching load?
13. Topic: Care for the dying
    Issue: Should we provide a standard for good care at the end of life?
15. Topic: FDA rules
    Issue: Are FDA rules appropriate?

Answers to Exercise 4

1. Topic: destructive behavior. Are parents responsible for the rise in the destructive behavior of youth? The author moves from the role of parents in failing to commu-

nicate values to their children to denying that the media is a cause of the rise in destructive behavior.

3. Topic: abortion. Do women have the right to choose to have an abortion? The author moves from a consideration of the right to choose an abortion to the right of criminals to appeal their sentence. One might consider this an analogy; however, the paragraph never comes back to the topic of abortion.

5. Topic: communication between parents and their teens. Issue: Should teens try to communicate with their parents? The author moves from the view that teens should talk to their parents about problems to find out the parents' perspective, to the view that parents should know everything about their teens.

Answers to Exercise 5

1. A charter school is a semipublic school funded by both state and private funds.
3. Sunflowers are a beneficial crop.
5. The Toyota 4Runner is a top Sport Utility Van.
7. SGS did not withhold funds from Holocaust victims.
9. The Straight Edgers are a counter-culture group that avoids alcohol, drugs and often sex.
11. You should attend the USTA Tennis Teacher's Conference.
13. Flamingos have departed from Lake Nakuru because of the city's growth.
15. We can affect the causes of violent behavior.
17. Instead of changing the rules of baseball, we should spend our time teaching our kids the nuances of the game and why it is important that baseball change little.
19. Young women are victims of a media that encourages them to be unnaturally thin.

Answers to Exercise 6

1. Motherhood in mammals requires a significant investment in time and energy.
3. Recent émigrés should not get social benefits without having paid prior taxes.
5. The Social Security cost of living index should not be tied directly to the Consumer Price Index.
7. A large and rapid decrease in Antarctic summertime sea-ice would have global significance.
9. The male stickleback is choosy about the females he allows to lay eggs in his nest.
11. College professors ought not to have a heavier teaching load.
13. We can provide care for dying people rather than use physician-assisted suicide.
15. The FDA rules are appropriate.

Answers to Exercise 7

1. Topic: AAUW
   Issue: Should a woman join AAUW?
   Thesis: A woman should join AAUW.
3. Topic: Lawrence Coss
   Issue: Does Lawrence Coss exemplify solid values in his rags-to-riches story?
   Thesis: Lawrence Coss does not exemplify solid values in his rags-to-riches story.
5. Topic: Multipersonality disorders
   Issue: Are multiple personality disorders really increasing?
   Thesis: Some psychiatrists say multiple personality disorders are not really increasing.
7. Topic: Life on Mars
   Issue: Does the possibility of life on Mars pose a problem for the Darwinian theory of evolution?

Thesis: The possibility of life on Mars poses such a problem. Note that *rather* in paragraph 2 changes the paragraph's direction.

9. Topic: Balanced budged amendment

Issue: Should Congress enact a balanced budget amendment to the Constitution?

Thesis: Congress should not enact a balanced budget amendment to the Constitution.

Answers to Exercise 8

1. The paragraph gives two descriptive characteristics of charter schools: they are funded by a mixture of public and private funds and they are free to create their own curricular guidelines and school policies.
3. Sunflowers guzzle water and nutrients and hasten wind erosion. Yet they also increase fertility for winter wheat and keep moisture and nutrients in the soil if not removed.
5. It has a more powerful engine, a more spacious interior, and leather-trimmed seats.
7. The funds referred to did not belong to Holocaust victims and were returned to their proper owners. The OSS report indicated that SGS was cooperative in this matter.
9. The author describes various characteristics of these individuals who conform and do not conform with young drug and alcohol users.
11. By attending you can make connections with other tennis professionals and enthusiasts, trade tips, keep up with cutting edge technology, and buy U.S. Open tickets.
13. Since the number of teenagers will increase 1 percent each year for the next fifteen years, the number of crimes will increase.
15. We can change television and movies.
17. Baseball is meant to be played the way it is.
19. The Olympics are provided as evidence to support the thesis that young women are victims of the media's concentration on thinness.

Answers to Exercise 9

1. Mammalian mothers spend a lot of time nurturing their young.
3. Our ancestors worked when they emigrated. I cannot meet my medical needs on my Social Security check. It is humiliating to watch these émigrés collect.
5. Certain parts—medical care—of the CPI increase faster than others, and this particularly affects older people living off of Social Security.
7. Sea-ice is an important component of the Earth's climate system. A number of subpoints—that it exerts strong controls on the exchanges of energy between atmosphere and oceans at high latitudes, that it has a higher albedo than open ocean, and that it acts as an insulating blanket—defends this.
9. A male has a real interest in limiting the size of his clutch. Heavier eggs laid by larger females produced more successful fry.
11. Professors would not have adequate time to prepare, to conduct research, to meet with students, or to do committee work.
13. The author identifies a study reported in the *Journal of the American Medical Association*. She reports her own experience with her father and grandfather.
15. 1. Nicotine is addictive a. Many smokers tried to quit and failed. This was not due to character faults or lack of willpower. b. The relapse of smokers is similar to that found with other addictive drugs. It treats tobacco like other addictive drugs.

Answers to Exercise 10

1. AAUW has promoted education and equity for women and girls. AAUW women are leaders across the country.

3. He has few family values, as shown by allowing his mother to live in a one-bedroom apartment. He left a trail of laid-off executives.

. Multiple personality disorders are overdiagnosed. The reason for this is that the criteria for diagnosing disorders are too vague.

. Darwinists hold that life evolved from random chance occurrences. But if Mars has life as well, this unlikely event occurred not once but twice in the same solar system, and that is very unlikely.

. The amendment would change the balance of power among the three branches of government and within the legislative branch. The amendment would increase the cost of government. The amendment would either be unenforceable or shift budgetary powers to the courts. It would give rise to a flood of litigation.

Answers to Exercise 11

1. Topic: Head and Shoulders shampoo
Issue: Should you use Head and Shoulders shampoo?
Thesis: You should use Head and Shoulders shampoo.
Main points: Head and Shoulders helps prevent flakes before they get started.
3. Topic: Supply-side economics
Issue: Is supply-side economics wrongheaded?
Thesis: Supply-side economics is wrongheaded.
Main points: 1. Supply and demand business yields improved profits. These profits stimulate investment, which puts the poor to work. The poor spend their income and stimulate the economy. 2. Tax cuts to stimulate the economy only stimulate stock market speculation. This leads to disorderly markets.
5. Topic: Progress of Blacks
Issue: Is the civil rights movement responsible for Black economic progress?
Thesis: Black economic progress is not due to the civil rights movement, but to hard work.
Main points: 1. Incomes of Black males rose faster than those of white males between 1940 and 1964. 2. More Blacks became professionals before than after the Civil Rights Act of 1964. 3. Those who tell us otherwise have a vested interest in maintaining the welfare state (special privileges for Blacks).
7. Topic: Football game between Tennessee and Florida
Issue: Will turnovers be the key to deciding the football game between Tennessee and Florida?
Thesis: Turnovers will be the key to deciding the football game between Tennessee and Florida
Main points: 1. The winner of this game the last four seasons has had the least amount of turnovers. 2. Tennessee has a lot of turnovers already this season.
9. Topic: damns, ecosystems
Issue: Should we dismantle dams?
Thesis: The author does not give a clear response to the issue posed.
Main points: 1. A study is presented to show that ecosystems are seriously affected in areas near dams. 2. Periodic opening of dams has a minor effect on ecology. 3. Dismantling dams can affect shipping and port cities. 4. Dismantling dams might not restore the ecosystem.

CHAPTER 4

Comprehension

Making Information Your Own

Undoubtedly you encountered several new words in Chapter 3. Perhaps you noticed how not knowing these words affected your understanding of the sentences or paragraphs where they occurred. Several years ago my critical thinking class worked through one of the paragraphs in Exercise 1 in Chapter 3: "Dr. Kevorkian has become a caricature of his own cause. He stokes the fires of debate, generating heat but not light." One student was able to pick out and repeat correctly the author's thesis in this brief paragraph. When I asked her to put the thesis in her own words, there was a long pause. Finally she looked at me and asked, "What is *caricature?*" Though this student was able to recognize the thesis in the example, she could do nothing more with it because she did not comprehend what the sentence said.

Comprehending what we read or hear means making the ideas our own. To make it our own we need to be able to put what is written or said into our own words. Understanding—the ability to make something our own—comes in degrees. Sometimes we fully comprehend what we read and can clearly explain it to someone else. Sometimes we have a partial idea of the material and can explain only some of it to another person. At other times, when our understanding is vague, we do not know how to explain the ideas expressed. Yet in each case translating what is written or said from someone else's language into our own is the first step toward comprehension.

This and the following chapter attend to comprehension and language, emphasizing not only our attempts to put others' ideas into our own language, but also noting various ways in which language can be confusing and misleading. Because language is rich and complex, in using it we can go astray in diverse ways. We examine ways language can be used and misused, with the ultimate goal of helping you become aware of how you can employ language more effectively to express your ideas more clearly and be more fully aware of how others use language.

Language makes comprehension possible. We use language in speaking, writing, signing, and thinking. When we read what others have written or listen to them speak, we actually are involved with two languages: the other person's and our own.

We generally understand *our own language.* We have a pretty good idea of what we mean when we say something. We put our meaning into language; our language expresses what we mean. However, there are exceptions. Sometimes we misspeak or say things that we think we understand, but when pressed we are not so sure that what we said clearly expressed what we meant to say. Several years ago someone questioned me about a paragraph in a book I had written. When I reread the paragraph, I also could not make sense of what I had written. Presumably when I wrote the paragraph I knew what I was writing, but I did not communicate clearly enough for a reader, including myself at a later time, to comprehend it.

Perhaps you have had a similar experience. You said something, but when someone asked you what you meant, you were not so sure. It sounded good at the time. The words were familiar. But you might not have paid sufficient attention to what the words actually communicated. Maybe it was because you used words that were familiar but which you never clearly defined. Or perhaps what you said was so vague or the grammatical structure of the sentence was so unclear that your comments could be interpreted in different ways.

In short, familiarity with our own language provides no guarantee that we fully comprehend what we say or that we can communicate effectively. We need to think carefully about our own language, in particular about what the words, phrases, sentences, and paragraphs mean.

At the same time, your inability to express what you think you understand is a sign that you really do not understand. Generally, the ability to put the information into words is a sign of understanding. The clearer you can express yourself, the more clearly you have understood.

When we consider the *language of others,* comprehension becomes more difficult. Sometimes the other person's language is familiar, invoking ordinary words and sentence structures. At other times it appears to be a strange language. In these cases we struggle to understand what someone else is saying.

Failure to comprehend what others say or write can result from several factors. Let us note five of them.

- The language of others contains the unfamiliar.

Others' language can be filled with words whose meanings are unknown to the reader or listener, either because the words are novel or because they are technical terms requiring specialized knowledge. My daughter's science teacher once asked her to memorize a list of words related to chemistry: *ions, colloids, solvents, solutes.* She memorized the list and their definitions so that she could pass the matching test. But when I asked her what ions and colloids were, she had no idea. Because she memorized the words in the language of the textbook author, which was not her own language, the words had little if any meaning for her. The result was that she was unable to use them in meaningful sentences. Her case is not unique. The meaning of what others say or write sometimes presents a mystery. If we want to understand it, we need to penetrate their language.

Education often acquaints us with unfamiliar language. Think of your first day in a class with a brand new subject matter, like biology, economics, or philosophy. Think how your head began to spin as new words were spoken (*enzyme, codons, vacuole, countervailing power, induced disinvestment, laissez faire, metaphysics, epistemology*), or words with which you were familiar (*cell, market, demand, competitor, person*) were given new twists and connections. These words function in specific ways in those disciplines; to understand these words you have to think like a biologist, economist, or philosopher. Only after you begin to think in these ways do you feel comfortable with the class and comprehend the teacher and the text.

- The word order may be different or some of the sentences may be intolerably long.

Unfortunately, this is often a feature of academic writing. In some books a single sentence may encompass half a page.

- The communication is incomplete.

Often our communication is cryptic. [Do you know what I mean by this word? To comprehend this sentence you need to understand the word *cryptic.* If you are unfamiliar with the word, look it up and write its definition *in your own words* in the margin of the text.] One day when my teenage daughter and I drove onto the freeway after returning from a visit to the surgeon, she said from the back seat, "Isn't it surprising that this one doesn't have a light thing." I was quiet for a while as I attempted to decipher what she said. She wore a heavy leg brace from her recent surgery, so my first thought was that "light thing" stood in contrast to the "heavy thing" she was wearing. After that idea led nowhere, I attempted to interpret "light" as in "light bulb." Where in this car should there be a light bulb where there is none? That too led me nowhere. She finally broke the silence, "You didn't understand what I said, did you?" "No," I replied. "What I meant," she said, "was that this entrance ramp, unlike others on the freeway, has no traffic light to control traffic getting onto the freeway." Now I understood. Her original statement was so incomplete that I had no idea what she was talking about, though she knew what she was saying because she could rephrase it.

Necessarily, all our descriptions are to some extent incomplete. For example, suppose I tell someone in a conversation about what happened when I went cross-country skiing yesterday. When I describe my skiing, I leave out most of the story. I cannot and do not want to provide every detail or say everything that happened in the two hours of skiing—the condition of the snow on all parts of the courses, the slope of each hill, the depth of the snow on the hills, what happened and how I felt when my skis went out from under me on the curve at the bottom of the first hill, the winter clothes I was wearing at the time, my body temperature, the types and shapes of trees I saw. If I reported every detail, the reporting would take longer than the actual skiing. Conversation would cease because others would never get the chance to speak in turn. So we speak cryptically to convey our message and to allow others to respond with their story. We intentionally or unintentionally omit or ignore most of the details and make assumptions about what the other person may already know.

But now the mystery begins as the listener attempts to search out and fill in what is missing from what we said. Some details the listener does not need to fill in because they are unessential to the story. Other details, however, are essential for the story to make sense. Consequently, when we listen we "read into" what the other says. On one hand, if we can add what is missing or assumed, our comprehension can be increased. On the other hand, if we contribute the wrong material, we run the danger of misunderstanding what is said. Making up for incompleteness is both necessary and dangerous for our mutual understanding.

- Our language has connotations.

Each person to some extent has his or her own language. Though we frequently use words that have common meanings for both communicator and listener, we also use words that for us have special **connotations**—that is, words with specific associations, connections or emotional attachments that play a significant role in our communication but with which others might be unfamiliar. A fuller communication would let others in on how we use our language.

For example, consider how people use the words "conservative" and "liberal." One summer I was in Chile, listening to a professor describe former President Ronald Reagan as a liberal. This description did not sit right with me, for Reagan is known as a conservative. The use of the term so affected my understanding that I could not follow her points. Finally, I found the opportunity to question her about her use of the term "liberal," and she explained that she was using it to refer specifically to Reagan's free trade policies. Reducing tariffs and barriers to free trade between nations was a liberal position on trade. Only when I understood how she was using the word *liberal* and the connotations the word had for her could I begin to make sense of what she said.

- Language comes couched in a conceptual framework.

That framework we might call our **worldview.** It expresses our larger perspective from which we interpret our experience. Our worldview includes our fundamental conceptual categories, beliefs, the way we know things, and our outlook on the world. It arises from the influence of our parents, teachers, peers, cultural and ethnic heritage, and community. Thus, to understand other persons, it is important to understand where they are coming from and their biases, culture, emotional make-up, and beliefs. Comprehension takes account of that larger framework.

Consider, for example, how different people use the word *creation* as applied to nature. A person who believes that God brought everything into existence means something very different by this word than someone who does not believe in God at all. Both persons might use the terms *creation* and *creature,* but each brings to it a different set of connotations that the hearer or reader must penetrate.

Our language is *context sensitive.* Its meaning relates to the situation in which the discourse occurs. Suppose, for example, someone said, "He ran home." What does this mean? Well, it depends on the context. If the person said this at a baseball park, it would probably mean something very different than if it were said in the street outside your house in the presence of some bullies.

As we already noted, one consequence of these differences between your language and that of others is that once you translate what others have communicated into your own language, you may have altered what they said. You may have understood only part of their communication or, more seriously, have taken them to mean something they really did not mean. You may have misinterpreted the communication in terms of your own desires or conceptual categories.

A classic example is found in a story about Croesus, king of ancient Lydia. The great Persian army of King Cyrus had Croesus's sizable army under siege. Croesus was in a quandary about whether to concede to his enemy's demands or resist. He sent his emissary to the oracle at Delphi in Greece to inquire about what course of action would be most auspicious. On receiving the inquiry, the oracle replied that if Croesus attacked the Persians, he would destroy a mighty army. The king received the news with joy, thinking that the oracle foresaw his destruction of the Persians, and set about attacking the enemy. His forces soon were completely routed. His life spared, Croesus inquired from Delphi—possibly to get his consulting fee returned—about how his losses squared with the oracle's message, for he had attacked the Persians but had not destroyed the mighty Persian army. The oracle replied that its prediction had been correct after all; Croesus had destroyed a mighty army—his own. His misunderstanding cost him his throne.

There is no easy way to guard against miscommunication or misunderstanding, but some steps can be taken to help minimize the danger.

♦ Inquire how other people have understood the communication.

If what you think the person said agrees with what others understand, you probably have heard or read the person correctly. Of course, everyone could have missed the point, but that is a less likely outcome than that one person missed the point. Consulting with groups helps us arrive at a common consensus of understanding.

♦ Try to explain back to the other person what he or she said. This is one way to test whether both of you are operating on the "same wavelength."
♦ Note what you think might be some important assumptions that the speaker or author is making and inquire of the speaker, if possible, about those assumptions.
♦ Always give the other person the benefit of the doubt if there are problems like contradictions or inconsistencies in the communication. Try to interpret the communication in ways that minimize these difficulties.

In effect, we function in a world filled with different languages, our own and that of others. Comprehension occurs when we are able to bring these languages closer together. The more they coincide, the better we comprehend what is communicated. This chapter is dedicated to overcoming obstacles to bringing the two languages closer together.

Collaborative Learning Exercise

1. Write a page describing in some detail a person, place, thing, or event that interests you.
2. Exchange paragraphs and read your partner's paragraph. Write down
   a. your partner's viewpoint (his or her interests, relation to what he or she wrote about, or assumptions).

   b. things your partner left out of the description you would like to know.
   c. language that you find unclear.

3. Share these observations and rewrite your page so that the description is clearer.

Exercise 1

Readers often are invited to comment on articles published in magazines and journals. A number of readers wrote letters responding to an article by David Miller published in *Science.* A subsequent letter writer wrote concerning these letters and Miller's response to them that "the writings of some scientists and philosophers appear as overwhelming semantic gobbledygook." Two of those letters are reprinted here. First give the topic, issue, thesis, and main points of the letters. Then decide whether the charge leveled against these letters has merit, telling why you decide as you do.

Letter A

> Miller says, "Skepticism is correct." Does he detect no tingling sense of warning that the mountain top on which he stands is slippery with oil and beginning to shake? As he ably states it, skepticism denies that any opinion, even when applied only to the level of common sense, is more likely than another, on the basis of experience or evidence. I agree only insofar as Miller's position is unsupported by evidence. Actually it is a self-nullifying paradox. His calling Hume's opinion a 'discovery' is another. Philosophers are struggling to hold on to science as simply one subdomain of their province of knowledge through reason. Quite to the contrary, I have felt for some time now that science has left philosophy behind, having found and held tightly the simple idea that one can ask certain questions in ways that increase our ability to predict nature's behavior. It is no more or less than that, and so it has escaped from philosophy's grasp. Science's core principle of falsification is a harsh master—one, in my opinion, that philosophers prefer to evade. The postmodernist-deconstructionist emperor had no clothes, only arcane verbosity signifying nothing. (*Source:* Paul Odgren, letter, *Science,* July 9, 1999, p. 199. Used by permission)

Letter B

> Miller appears to confuse logic and intellectual authority and how Karl Popper resolved the problem of scientific knowledge with the critical search for errors. The assumption of philosophy is that, because the authority created by scientific

arguments depends on deduction, the authority created in turn by such arguments must arise also from a parallel kind of deduction. Philosophers call this justification. But Popper shows that this is a false parallelism because the authority of scientific argument is created by logic in regard to our pursuit of truth as a goal. Miller ignores this and so asserts rather than explains Popper's key insight that the rational authority of science comes from its search for errors.

This point about rational authority coming from goals rather than justification may seem obtuse, but consider the case of aircraft safety. Here an intense process of error detection occurs based on logical and empirical argument, yet the authority created by such deductions about airworthiness does not link to any ultimate justification, as it comes entirely from the pursuit of safety as a goal. The same process in regard to truth backs the authority of science. (*Source:* John R. Skoyles, letter, *Science*, July 9, 1999, p. 200. Used by permission)

Exercise 2

Carefully read this editorial written during the 1996 presidential campaign.

For peddling his books, route might lead to White House

Maureen Dowd

I was sitting in my office, feeling left out. Was I the only person in the country who had not been slipped an advance copy of Colin Powell's book? Then I heard a hum.

Mirabile faxu! Someone at Random House remembered me. And they were leaking me something even more valuable than the book—a confidential memo about the book, typed on the poohbah's stationery:

Date: Aug. 1, 1995
From: Harry Evans
To: Collin Powell
Re: The campaign

Now that your presidential campaign is about to go into hard covers, I would like to review our strategy.

If my orchestration of your book tour goes as planned, in the course of a single breathless week you will be transformed from a self-promoting bureaucrat who left Saddam in power to an overwhelming favorite to win the White House. Remember, "Crusade in Europe" helped get Eisenhower the Republican nomination, and that was back before Larry King invented the fawn-o-rama.

I understand your distaste for the traditional political process. It's grubby and demeaning for a man such as yourself to bother with pig roasts, position papers and small-time reporters. That is the beauty of our plan: You float above the fray, a generalizing general. Merchandising transcends politics. No, merchandising is politics. With a first printing of 950,000, who needs a vision?

I'm pretty certain you can be bigger than the pope. (He works with our people, too. He'll be here next month. Let's do lunch.) You can bypass New Hampshire and Iowa and go straight to the Kirkus primary. Don't worry about those books by Lamar Alexander and Ross Perot. They'll only get Sally Jessy.

Stay on message as you crisscross the country: "I'm not campaigning at the moment," "I don't know if I'll ever campaign" and "I'm not an expert on these matters yet." Rehearse these lines as often as you did that brilliant. "Cut it off and kill it" line about the Iraqi army. (Maybe you should have rehearsed the "kill it" a little more. Ha, ha!)

You have a gift for elusiveness rare in this confessional age. The book is a slippery masterpiece, eliding your role in various world travesties. From My Lai to

continued

For peddling his books, route might lead to White House *continued*

Iran-contra to Desert Storm, you had a bad feeling but by the time things blew up your had moved on, and *it was not your fault.* Don't mention your pals Woodward and Bradlee at the Wal-Marts. If people realize what a total Beltway animal you are, we won't be able to protect you from pork rinds. And try not to sound so defensive when you talk about Saddam. Remember, you were not the president or secretary of defense. *It was not your fault.*

Our marketing strategy is a dynamic mix of access and the denial of access. This will whip everyone into a frenzy. We kick off the campaign with a party at I Trulli on the East Side. Tina and I will round up the usual elites. Eat fruit tart enigmatically and offer some Reaganesque remarks about how there is no limit to how far this country can go. Liz Smith will rave about the bound asparagus. Wait until she sees the bound book!

We've also arranged a conglomerate tease. We sell excerpts to Time, and then shriek when Newsweek purloins the book, giving us double exposure. Time will be mad, but they'll still pony up a party in Washington.

We'll give an exclusive—I know you prefer to be inclusive, ha, ha!—on the "issues" to Barbara Walters. The papers will have to run excerpts from an ABC press release hyping the Walters interview because we'll bar them from writing about the book for several more days! This will be part of an elaborate series of cascading embargoes. If reporters whine that they feel exploited, just murmur: "I'm sorry, Random House has my hands tied." *It isn't your fault.*

Then you move on to Katie-Tom-Larry-David-Jay, never letting yourself be pinned down. Say it would be easiest to run as a Republican. Also say that the time has arrived for a third party. Also say that you haven't ruled out challenging Bill Clinton. (Note: Don't get the Larrys confused. Sanders is not a real talk show host.)

Don't worry about a conflict of interest. I'll be available for more image consulting once you're in the Oval Office. What's good for Random House is good for the United States.

Source: Maureen Dowd, "Candidate from Random House," *New York Times,* September 14, 1995, p. A26. Copyright © 1995 by The New York Times. Reprinted by permission.

1. What are the topic, issue, thesis, and main points of this editorial?

2. Do you think that the writer received this memo from Random House? Why or why not?

3. How does your answer to question 2 affect the way you understand this editorial?

FACT AND OPINION

Perhaps in your class discussion you debated the authenticity of the alleged memo in Exercise 2. If your class is like the ones I teach, debate rages on both sides. Some students say that the memo was genuine; otherwise the author would not have cited the memo and it would not have been published in a reputable newspaper. Other students see the memo as a literary device. For evidence they point to the negative tone and the critical statements made about Colin Powell in the alleged memo to him. Perhaps in the end you decided that whether the memo was genuine or not was just a matter of opinion.

How often have you heard it said or said yourself, "That's just your opinion"? Frequently, the words "just an opinion" are used to dismiss another's viewpoint quickly and easily. "Just opinions" allegedly are not worth much because they are subjective: they simply reflect the view of the holder of the opinion. They are also not worth much because in a culture that emphasizes relativity, all "just opinions" are equal. You have a right to your opinions and I to mine. Since we cannot judge among opinions, they have little market value.

What we really want are the facts, and by facts we usually mean the opposite of opinions. Facts report objective things that one can see, hear, smell, or feel, the sorts of things about which everyone can agree. They are supported by common experience.

The result is that in common discussion we presuppose a conflict between fact and opinion. A person consults horoscopes for opinions, a doctor for facts. The two are supposedly on opposite sides of the same coin: the one lacks authority and possesses only personal value, the other has authority and hence plays a legitimate role in forming beliefs.

Although this portrays the common view, I think it is mistaken in a way that can have serious consequences. In particular, it tends to reinforce a common attitude toward opinion, leading to failure to pay attention to and take seriously people's opinions. We cease to be listeners, comprehenders, and critical thinkers. Instead we become dismissers—that is "just their opinion." Perhaps you have seen it in your classes: when professors talk, students take notes because they have the facts to make their opinion count (especially on tests). But when students talk, it is merely their opinion and the pencils and pens are silent.

People's opinions *do* matter. Your opinions matter. What we need to discover is whether your and others' opinions are true and worthy of being believed. Do they accord with the facts? Are they supported by evidence and good reasoning, do they contradict established evidence, or is the matter currently undecidable because reliable, relevant evidence is absent? Critical thinkers undertake to answer these questions about opinions.

What is opinion and what is fact? Let me begin with facts. Facts are the way things are, the way the world is. Thus, investigators like the TV detective Colombo want to discover the facts. They want to know what really is the case—"just the facts, ma'am; just the facts."

A fact makes a statement true. For example, the statement "The Earth is the third planet from the sun" is true and the statement "The Earth is the fifth planet from the sun" is false because of the fact that the Earth is the third planet from the sun. What makes the first statement true is not that you learned it, that some textbook says this is the case, or that somebody observed it. These are ways by which people *come to know* the truth about how the Earth relates to the sun, but this is not what makes the statement that the Earth is the third planet from the sun true. That is, *we should not confuse what makes a statement true with how we come to know its truth.*

Indeed, whether something is a fact, and hence whether the statement that reports or expresses it is true, is independent of anyone's knowledge of that fact (except in cases where the facts have to do with your knowledge, as in "I know she is at the dentist.") For example, does the statement "The Moche were a Pre-Incan culture" express a fact? You probably don't know the answer to this question. But whether you do or do not affects neither the facts in this case nor the truth of the statement. If the Moche were a Pre-Incan culture (as they were), then the statement is true regardless of your beliefs.

This understanding of facts has some interesting implications. For example, the statement "Dinosaurs existed" expresses a fact *if* dinosaurs existed. What about the statement "God exists"? The normal reaction is that this expresses not a fact but an opinion because people disagree about this claim. But the claim that dinosaurs existed is also an opinion that people hold. That dinosaurs existed is a fact if they did exist. Similarly with "God exists"; this statement reports a fact *if* God exists. Thus, the issue of whether God (or dinosaurs, elm trees, or your mother) exists has nothing to do with opinion but everything to do with whether it is a fact that God (or dinosaurs, elm trees, or your mother) really exists.

A fact, then, is what actually is the case, and the task of our investigative skills is to discover the facts. The problem is that getting to the "way things really are" is often very difficult. Part of the problem has to do with the world itself. While some facts are easier to discern (that dinosaurs existed and that elm trees and your mother exist), other facts are more difficult (such as whether or not God exists or O. J. Simpson committed murder). In the cases of God, crimes, causes of diseases, life elsewhere in the solar system, and the like, much investigation of available evidence is needed to decide the case. Perhaps you encountered this debate about opinion and evidence in the previous exercise when you tried to decide whether the memo was actually from the editor of Random House or whether it was a literary device employed by the author, Maureen Dowd.

The other part of the problem of getting to know the facts has to do with us as knowers or discoverers. Each of us approaches the world with our own *sensory limitations.* Some sensory limitations are common to us all. Some sounds extend beyond our range of hearing; you can't hear the dog whistle but Rover can. Ultraviolet colors extend beyond our range of sight, while objects like atoms and electrons are too small or fast to be seen with the naked eye. When we focus on something, we tend to miss other features that are present. (Perhaps you have been in an auto accident where you were blind-sided at a traffic light because you focused on the traffic light or approaching traffic and ignored the input of your peripheral vision). Some people possess keener sight or hearing than others; some have sensory disorders (color blindness) or deficits (loss of hearing or blindness).

We also experience *sensory distortions.* Our minds compensate for what the senses present us so that we see things the way they ought to be rather than as exact sensory reports. For example, look at the door or window across the room from you. If you are at an angle to it, your sensory data should present you with a trapezoid. Yet if I ask you about the shape of the door or window that you see, you would unhesitatingly say that it is rectangular. Our minds adjust the trapezoidal sensory data based on what they "know" to be the case.

However, at times our senses fool us when they make adjustments. In the photograph of people standing in a room, note how our senses present us information that the mind adjusts, giving us a very distorted view of the reality of the room.

Ames Room: Sensory distortions. Changes in perspective and size give a distorted view of reality.

In this example called the Ames Room, we are more willing to put up with the anomaly of people being of different sizes than with certain facts about the room: that the floor is radically sloped, that the doors and walls are trapezoidal rather than square, that the floor tiles are not square but diamond-shaped. We perceive the room as a normal room when in fact it is not.

Perhaps more serious are our *conceptual distortions.* We view the world from a particular cultural, social, historical, and value bias. This bias can effectively distort the way we perceive things, leading to false or mistaken judgments about the way things really are. In one intriguing experiment, people from two social classes were asked to put their hand in a bag and report on the size of the coins it contained. Those from a wealthy background said that the coins were small; those from economically deprived backgrounds reported they were large. More than likely, social conditioning helped influence their tactile perceptions.

Not so long ago (and still somewhat today) this conceptual bias was manifested in how boys and girls were treated. Girls were weak and had to be protected from overexertion. When they played basketball they were not allowed to run up and down the court like the boys but could only dribble twice before passing. Only when these conceptual biases were erased could girls' basketball be played with the same rules as governed boys' basketball.

What this means is that we all face a challenge in attempting to get to the facts of the case, to discern the way things really are. When we do this, we form opinions about the way things really are. **Opinions** are our own beliefs about the world.

We all have opinions. In fact, every idea we express or judgment we make communicates our opinion about the way things are. Even if we report someone else's opinion, it is our opinion that this is his or her opinion. What we work with, then, are our opinions. Consequently, to dismiss an opinion as "just opinion" leaves us empty, for all that each of us has to work with are opinions.

Facts are not the opposite of opinions. Facts and opinions are not at two ends of the same scale; rather, they are two very different things. Facts are the ways things really are in the world; opinions are our beliefs about the facts. Hence, there are no true or false facts; facts simply *are.* But there are true or false opinions, depending on whether these opinions correspond with the facts.

So what might the phrase "just opinion" mean? Often it means that someone holds an opinion without considering or having evidence or reasons for or against it. It is belief without warrant or basis. This lack of basis does not make "just opinions" false or unworthy of consideration; they could be true opinions. It merely means that those who hold such opinions have not considered or lack the evidence needed to help them to determine whether their opinions represent the facts and hence are true. Critical thinkers want to know what reasons or grounds a person might give in support of an opinion. In effect, they move from "just opinions" to substantiated or supported opinions, opinions they might be justified in holding.

Indeed, the point of critical thinking is to have true opinions—that is, opinions that report or accord with the facts. We do this by investigating ours and others' opinions to the best of our ability to see whether these opinions can be justified. Philosophers appeal to a variety of criteria to establish opinions. Opinions are justified when they are reliable; my belief that this food is not poisonous reports the facts if when I eat it I don't get sick. Opinions are also justified when they are supported by evidence of various sorts: from experience, reasoning, or authorities. My belief that the approaching clouds will bring torrential rain is justified by my past experiences with similar looking clouds. The better and stronger the evidence, the more we are justified in thinking that our opinions or beliefs are true.

In Chapters 10 through 12 we will consider the role evidence plays in justifying our own or others' opinions. We will study ways of evaluating that evidence to help us better determine when our or others' opinions are true and when they are not. For now it is important to remember that facts are not the opposite of opinions. The goal of critical thinkers is to identify which opinions report the facts and which do not—which opinions are true and which are false.

STATEMENTS

We just argued that one of the goals of a critical thinker is to determine whether opinions are true or false. We express our opinions in *statements.* For example, scientists may express their opinion that life came to planet Earth aboard icy asteroids by making a statement to that effect. So if we are going to comprehend what other persons say, we have to understand the statements they make.

Statements and Sentences

Statements are *assertions*, expressed by complete or incomplete sentences, *that are either true or false.* The following express statements because what they express is either true or false.

1. Mary loves John.
2. John is loved by Mary.
3. While the teacher was peering over her shoulder, Susanne was trying to figure out the answer to the geometry problem.
4. that the book was interesting to read

We might note some interesting features of these examples.

♦   While sentences 1 and 2 are different, they make the same statement or assertion. Put another way, the two sentences make only one statement.

♦   Sentence 3 contains only one sentence but makes two statements: "the teacher was peering over her shoulder" and "Susanne was trying to figure out the answer to the geometry problem." We know the sentence contains two statements because we can ask concerning each whether it is true or false. It is true or false that the teacher was peering over her shoulder and true or false that Susanne was trying to figure out the answer to the geometry problem.

♦   We could claim that sentence 3 contains only one statement, for the claim that "Susanne was trying to figure out the answer to the geometry problem while the teacher was peering over her shoulder" is true or false. Hence, the division of sentences into statements is somewhat (but not entirely) arbitrary, depending on how the writer or reader wishes to structure the statements.

♦   Number 4, which is a sentence fragment and not a sentence, expresses a statement—the book was interesting to read—that is either true or false.

What these examples show is that it is important not to confuse **sentences,** which are groups of words that make statements, questions, requests, commands, or exclamations, with statements. The sentence is the vehicle that conveys the statement; the statement is what the sentence conveys. Since sentences often do not correlate one-to-one with statements, a sentence may contain one or many statements. *Often sentences have to be divided in order to clarify further the respective statements the sentence makes.*

So how do you know what the statements are in a sentence? One clue is to

•   ask whether a group of words expressing a claim is true or false.

In the example "As he rode to the bank, his bicycle was struck by a speeding car," you can ask whether "he rode to the bank" is true or false; likewise, you can ask whether "his bicycle was struck by a speeding car" is true or false. Both of these are claims and hence make statements.

A second clue is to

•   look for the main verbs in the sentence and use these to construct your statements.

For example, in the sentence "For two and a half hours the scientists collected blood and fat samples, extracted a vestigial tooth to determine the bears' ages, attached ear tags, and recorded the bears' temperature, length, girth, and weight" (*National Geographic,* January 1998, p. 58), there are four main verbs: collected, extracted, attached, and recorded. Though you may treat the entire sentence as a statement, you may also treat it as making four statements: "for two and a half hours the scientists collected blood and fat samples"; "the scientists extracted a vestigial tooth to determine the bears' ages"; "the scientists attached ear tags"; "the scientists recorded the bears' temperature, length, girth, and weight." Each main verb takes *the scientists* as the subject but expresses a different claim that is either true or false.

Third,

- clauses either may or may not be treated as statements.

Whether one treats them as separate statements depends on the one who analyzes the claim. It also depends on what else is said, especially if the claim is part of an argument. For example, in the statement "As the helicopter swooped low and made several passes over the fleeing bears, a .32-gauge rifle poked out and fired twice, sending a tranquilizer dart into each bear's shoulder," you can treat this entire sentence as making one statement. But you can also analyze the sentence into four statements: "the helicopter swooped low over the fleeing bears"; "the helicopter made several passes over the fleeing bears"; "a .32-gauge rifle poked out and fired twice"; "the rifle sent a tranquilizer dart into each bear's shoulder." As we already noted, how you divide the sentences can vary. Precisely how you divide the sentences matters less at this point than your seeing that statements are either true or false. In working with deductive arguments, the division becomes much more significant.

Consider the following paragraph, in which the various statements are indicated by brackets.

[At 16 Walter attended St. Mark's Mission in Nenana,] [where his outdoor skills and pleasant personality attracted the attention of the explorer, Episcopal missionary and later Archdeacon of Alaska, Hudson Stuck,] [who adopted him as his travel companion and camp assistant.] [In 1912, (Walter) accompanied Stuck on one of the explorer's greatest expeditions,] [during which Walter became the first person to set foot on the summit of Mount McKinley.] (Claire Rudolf Murphy and Jane G. Haigh, "Gold Rush Women," *Alaska,* October 1997, p. 49)

This paragraph well illustrates how sentences can convey more than one statement, each of which can be true or false.

The important points are that sentences are not the same as statements, statements are what interest us because we desire to discover the truth or falsity of claims, and only statements can be true or false.

Exercise 3

1. In the following paragraphs, identify statements by putting brackets around each statement. Sometimes you may have to add words to help the statement make sense.

Unlike most hunters, I came to the sport relatively late in life. I first went hunting in my late 20s. I got my chance courtesy of a new friend, a longtime hunter who introduced me to the mysteries and rituals of the sport and drilled into me his own highly evolved commitment to hunting ethics. Those were singular gifts—both the hunting skills and the ethics—and ones that can be repaid only by passing them on to another generation of hunters.

I've been hunting for about 20 years now, mostly for deer, but recently for ducks. The land I hunt is private, and I hunt there by permission. Access and competition are not problems, but poaching, trespassing, and road hunting are highly visible to everyone who hunts in the region.

My views on hunting, my sense of ethics, my sense of hunter behavior problems, and my expectations of myself and of those I hunt with are all products of my experiences in the field—with a measure of reading, discussion, and fireside debate thrown in for seasoning. I was taught to hunt for the joy of hunting and for the deep satisfaction of having hunted well, not for the bag; to take pride in my outdoor skills more than in my kill; to savor wild game; to know the land where I hunt; to study the critters, learn to read the woods, and work with my hands to improve habitat; and to expect other hunters to do pretty much the same. . . . (Maitland Sharpe, "Taking a Stand," *Outdoor Ethics Newsletter,* 12, no. 2 (Winter 1993), p. 7)

2. Find two paragraphs from a newspaper or magazine article and identify the statements that are being made by putting brackets around each statement. Where necessary, add words to help the statements make sense.

Diverse Functions of Sentences

Our first point was that statements are assertions, expressed by complete or incomplete sentences, that are either true or false. A second important point is that not all sentences make statements or assertions; they do other things instead. We communicate with each other for many reasons: for friendship, to get basic necessities, to navigate from place to place, to find out what happened, to understand the world better, to pass judgment in law courts, and so on. To comprehend, we must note how the language is being used—that is, we must discover its purpose or function. Here is a partial list of types of sentences that do not make statements because they are neither true nor false; yet they serve other functions.

- *Ordinary questions:* What time is it? How do you get to the dining hall from here?

Ordinary questions serve an *interrogative function:* because we want some information, we ask a question.

What time are you coming to dinner?

How many people were at the ball game?

Why won't this wrench turn this nut?

- *Commands:* Don't block my driveway when you park!

When we want someone to do something, we may give a command. Commands have a *directive function.* Their point is to obtain a behavioral response from someone.

Shut that window.

Chew with your mouth closed.

- *Requests:* Will you marry me?

Sometimes we want people not to give us information but to perform a certain action. But since it is inappropriate to issue a command to them in that context, we make a request. Such sentences have a *request function*.

Please pass the sugar?

Will you write a letter of recommendation to graduate school for me?

- *Rhetorical questions:* What would we do without good first grade teachers?

Sometimes we want someone to agree with us but we don't want to get that person's agreement by being blunt, so we ask a rhetorical question. When we ask rhetorical questions, we do not expect people to disagree with us; we assume that they will accept the position the question rhetorically asserts as true. For example,

Will Congress ever pass effective legislation to control the excesses of the IRS?

The person is probably not asking for information or making a request but affirms his or her frustration and belief that Congress will not act to curb the IRS. Whether this is actually a rhetorical question can be determined only by looking at the context in which this sentence appears.

Note how the author effectively uses rhetorical questions in the next paragraph to get the readers to agree with him.

> The proposed amendment is merely to initiate dialogue. Does the reader agree that American children should be protected? Are these protections and entitlements generally palatable? If so, let the dialogue (on having a children's rights amendment) begin. (Charles Gill, "Essay on the Status of the American Child, 2000 A.D.: Chattel or Constitutionally Protected Child-Citizen?" *Ohio Northern University Law Review*, p. 17)

- *Expressive utterances:* Damn it!

Sometimes we use language to express our emotions or feelings. We are not trying to convey information so much as to express our mood or pleasure/displeasure at what is happening.

I love you very much.

This sentence might look like an assertion that could be either true or false. But think how you would react if, when you told your friend that you loved him or her, your friend responded, "True." This response would be inappropriate because you are expressing how you feel—for example, in a way equivalent to giving that person a hug or kiss.

- *Performative utterances:* I nominate Janet for president.

Some of our language functions in place of an action. The words have a function that could just as well be carried out by doing some prescribed action. The umpire yells to the batter,

"You're out."

A hand and arm gesture can serve the same function as what he utters. Or again, you walk down the hall and see someone you know. You ask,

"How are you?"

The question, How are you? generally is posed not to acquire information about another's health but is part of a ritual greeting. You could just as easily have stuck out your hand or hugged the person. Note how surprised (and perhaps irritated) you are when someone responds by stopping and telling you all about his or her physical ills that day; you probably think the person missed the ritual nature of the greeting.

You may enter the theater.

The usher is not making a statement that is either true or false but rather is granting you permission to act in a certain way.

One way to see that sentences performing the various functions we just described do not make statements is to note that "true" or "false" would be an inappropriate response to these sentences. If, when you give the command, "Don't block my driveway," your neighbor looks at you and says, "False," his response is inappropriate. You wanted him not to park where he did, not to give a response of "True" or "False." Asking whether what is written or said can be true or false is a good test to determine whether it makes a statement or not.

Although this distinction between sentences that make statements and those that do not seems straightforward, matters are more complex than they seem at first. Some sentences of the types we just described can convey statements.

Consider *commands*. Though commands are not statements, they can be translated into statements. That is, underneath the command element of the sentence lurks a statement. For example, the command "Don't block my driveway," contains the statement, "You should not block my driveway," which can be considered as true or false. Of course, the translation from the command "Don't block my driveway" to the statement "You should not block my driveway" loses something—namely, the command element that demands a behavioral response from your neighbor. But the command contains within it a statement as an important element.

Similar things can be said about certain kinds of *questions*. Consider, for example, the *negative question*, "Why didn't you tell me that you were out of printer cartridges when I spoke to you on the phone?" This negative question might be rephrased in terms of a statement, "You didn't tell me that you were out of printer cartridges when I spoke to you on the phone," and a question, "Why not?" Note that the first sentence conveys a statement that is either true or false, while the second sentence utters a question that asks for a response.

Another kind of question is the *rhetorical question*. Rhetorical questions do not look for answers; they are rather a cloaked way of making a statement. Rhetorical questions are effective because the speaker does not appear to make a claim but solicits the opinion of the listener; in fact, however, the speaker does make a claim with which the listener is expected to agree. For example, "Amelia Earhart was the real American girl, as modest as she was courageous. What more could one want in a heroine?" The question posed in the second sentence does not look for information but makes a statement that the author takes as true. The statement is "Amelia Earhart was a true heroine."

Critical thinkers are aware of the diverse functions of language and are able to discern when sentences make statements and when they do not. Thinkers with more advanced skills can look at sentences and identify the different functions they serve. Our interest is in sentences that make statements, for since these are either true or false, they are appropriate objects of evaluation.

Exercise 4

Identify the functions of the following sentences. Where the sentences make statements, put brackets around those statements.

1. Shut the door.

2. As Sheila entered the room, her mother said, "Shut the door."

3. Take your elbows off the table. It is impolite to eat with them on the table.

4. Why didn't the CEO just fire the incompetent accountant rather than trying to hide what he did?

5. The rain pelted the soccer players, turning the field into a quagmire.

6. I now pronounce you man and wife.

7. That was a dirty, lousy trick you played on your sister, hiding a mousetrap in her bed.

8. The butler couldn't have stolen the bridal gown because he was out in the kitchen cutting up the wedding cake at the time.

9. What do you get when you cross a goat with a sheep?

10. Well, don't you think that lawyers are like politicians, just out for the money?

11. The street was slippery because it had just rained and this was the first rain of the season.

12. Won't you please contribute to the firefighter's unemployment fund this year?

13. I believe that one ought to do what one is told.

14. One ought to do what one is told.

15. Welcome, guests.

Compound Statements

There is a kind of statement that can be confusing. These are called **compound statements** because they are composed of simple statements, but they cannot be treated as a mere conjunction of simple statements because *their truth depends on the relationship between the individual statements.*

Consider the sentence, "If I leave the front door unlocked, a burglar can enter." How many statements do we have here? You may have said, "Two": "I leave the front door unlocked" is one; "A burglar can enter" is the other. Although the sentence contains these component statements, this analysis ignores the *if* part of the sentence. This kind of statement is called a *conditional.* It talks about neither leaving the front door unlocked nor burglars entering but about the *relationship* between leaving the door unlocked and burglars entering. It says that if one thing happens, then the other will happen. Hence, this sentence makes one compound statement, not two statements. In short, *if . . . then, or conditional, sentences make one statement, not two.*

The same analysis applies to either/or statements (what we later term *disjunctive statements*). "Either we get a new car or I am not going to work at that new job across town" has two component statements. But the either/or statement is not a conjunction of these components; it is one statement that talks about the relationship between the component statements. In effect, statements connected by *either-or* contain one compound statement, not two.

One more complication. Suppose that I replace the word *if* with *since:* "Since I left the front door unlocked, the burglar entered." Here we have a sentence with two statements, for it claims both that I left the front door unlocked and that the burglar entered. It also contains an implicit or hidden third statement, namely, that the two events are connected: if I leave the front door unlocked, a burglar can enter. In short, *since . . . then sentences can be interpreted as containing two explicit statements plus an implicit statement connecting the two.*

What all this means is that we have to be careful with sentences and statements. Sentences are complex vehicles, doing many things. One thing they do is convey statements. Critical thinkers seek within sentences the statements that help them understand what is being communicated.

One last aside about our complex language. Sometimes the word *proposition* is used in place of *statement.* Some people (mainly philosophers) make a distinction between *proposition* and *statement*, but for our purposes we use *statement, proposition, assertion,* and *claim* synonymously in this book.

Exercise 5

Identify the statements in each of the following sentences by putting brackets around each one.

1. To decrease tension in the region, the Pentagon delayed its latest war games.

2. The fastest computer on the market is not an IBM or its clone, but an Apple clone.

3. If computer prices drop much lower, the manufacturers will start losing money on their product.

4. What would we do if we didn't have the convenience gas stations to get snacks after midnight?

5. As Apple Computer attempts to turn the company around, it will be interesting to see what happens with the clone manufacturers licensed by Apple.

6. When the stock market is down, John is upbeat; when the market is up, John is depressed.

7. He would be much happier if he did not play the stock market.

8. Please pass me the jelly doughnuts.

9. People are always ready to lend a helping hand when they see that the need is genuine.

10. Sex is popular on the Web today, but its hot sales could be a fading phenomenon.

11. The microbiologists placed the clay mixture into a heavy acid concentrate so that they could test its reproductive capacity.

12. Can't the makers of computer software make it more user friendly?

13. Either Los Angeles will get a new football franchise or else the National Football League will place a struggling, small market team there.

14. Other researchers have begun to doubt that earth's ancient atmosphere looked like the mix of gases in Miller's flasks, and they are searching for evidence that amino acids and other organics, which litter the skies, were ferried to Earth by comets, meteorites and dust. (Shannon Brownlee, "A Cosmic Imperative: Make Life," *U.S. News & World Report*, August 19, 1996, p. 50)

15. At the height of summer, silence becomes relative. The background noise is a ceaseless whine and whir of billions of flying insects, a mist of particulate life rising from moss-level to the tops of the trees. Because the sound is so steady, . . . the effect is like that which any "white noise" machine creates. (Richard Leo, "Silence," *Alaska*, October 1997, p. 22)

16. It's always fun to find an interesting, little-known corner of the [stock] market to write about. But occasionally something happens to make me turn to a well-known . . . subject.

    Recently, two co-workers confided that with the stock market so crazy, . . . they had decided to switch money from growth . . . mutual funds into an S&P 500 "index" fund. Since index funds aim only to match the market rather than beat it, their managers can't make big mistakes; in fact, they can't make any mistakes. Each day, they use investors' money to buy or sell whatever stocks are in the index at the stocks' closing prices. So my co-workers figured that while the market keeps up its wild ways, their money will be safer. . . . (Excerpted from Steven D. Kaye, "The S&P's Surprising Fangs," *U.S. News & World Report*, August 5, 1996, p. 63. Copyright, 1996, U.S. News & World Report. Visit us at our website at www.usnews.com for additional information.)

17. $125 million dollars over six years just for one person to play basketball. How does Glen Taylor justify this? What executive decisions does this basketball person have to make? Does he decide how to defend our country? Does he decide how to help survivors of war-torn countries? Does he decide how to help the poor starving people in our own country? Does he decide how to stretch the classroom budget to meet the needs of students? Does he decide how to keep open clinics and hospitals throughout the state, the country? Kevin Garnett, I hope you will decide to help not only your family, but also your local, state and adopted community organizations, schools and churches. (Gale Belk, letter to the editor, *St. Paul Pioneer Press*, October 7, 1997. Reprinted by permission.)

18. Unlike many other studies that use one-time snapshots of the poor, both books rely on new research that tracks poor families over years, even decades. Mayer calculates that even if policy makers miraculously managed

to double the income of the poorest 20 percent of families, the national teen-child-bearing rate would drop only from 20 percent to 18 percent, the high school dropout rate would go from 17.3 percent to 16.1 percent, and the mean number of years people were in school would rise from 12.80 to 12.83. She concludes, too, that doubling poor families' income would hardly change the proportion of young women who become single mothers and might actually increase idleness among young men by reducing their incentive to work. . . . (Excerpted from David Whitman, "Is Lack of Money the Reason Kids Stay Poor?" *U.S. News & World Report,* June 2, 1997, p. 33. Copyright, 1997, *U.S. News & World Report.* Visit us at our website at www.usnews.com for additional information.)

OUR KNOWLEDGE OF TRUTH AND FALSITY

We started this chapter by noting that we need to put others' communication into our own language if we are to comprehend what they communicate. The opinions or beliefs of others are expressed in statements. We have noted that statements must be distinguished from sentences and that statements are assertions that are either true or false. It is time now to attend to the question of truth.

Consider the following claims:

1. J. F. Kennedy was the thirty-fourth president of the United States.
2. Abraham Lincoln was the fifteenth president of the United States.
3. Pachelbel wrote the Canon in D.
4. Pluto has a solid core.
5. The first person to walk on the moon was really a Russian cosmonaut, not the American Neal Armstrong.
6. Michael Jordan has scored more than 15,000 points in his career with the Chicago Bulls.
7. DNA is necessary to make proteins.
8. UFOs exist.
9. They believe that UFOs exist.

Next to each statement, write whether it is true or false.

What you wrote for each of these statements reflects your personal knowledge and beliefs. Certainly not everyone in your class gave the same response to this list. Why is this so? Several important points arise from considering this question.

First, what makes these statements true or false? Statements are actually **true** when they correspond to reality (the facts) and false when they fail to correspond. For example, what makes number 6 true is the fact that Michael Jordan actually scored more than 15,000 points. If he did not score that many points for the Bulls, number 6 is false. In our list, number 1 is true because of the sequence of U.S. presidents; number 2 is false because of that same sequence; number 3 is true because of Pachelbel. The truth of number 4 depends upon how Pluto is structured. It was true or false even before Pluto was discovered or scientists had the equipment to ascertain its core.

You might wonder about numbers 8 and 9. They differ in an important way. On one hand, you might think that the truth of number 8 depends on who states number 8, but that is not so. Its truth or falsity does not depend on anyone's belief but on whether or not UFOs actually exist. Number 9, on the other hand, depends for its truth not upon the existence of UFOs but on what the persons for whom *they* stands believe. If the persons to whom *they* refers believe in UFOs, the statement is true regardless of whether UFOs exist; if the persons do not believe in UFOs, the statement is false. In short, whereas number 8 is about UFOs, number 9 is about persons and those persons' beliefs.

This leads to the *second* point, namely, that with the exception of number 9, the truth of the statements in our list does not depend on anyone's beliefs about their truth; their truth depends on the way the world is or was. Of course, the truth of number 9 also depends on the way the world is. What makes it unique from numbers 1–8 is that it is about persons and their beliefs and hence is made true or false by whether the persons hold that belief.

The *third* point is that although the truth or falsity of a statement depends on reality and not on the believer (unless the statement is about the believer), what the statement means depends on persons—either the speaker or the reader/hearer. Since different people may understand the terms in a statement in different ways and hence take a statement to mean different things, what *counts as* the reality that makes the statement true or false may differ from person to person. Hence, in effect, the *truth* of a statement depends both on the meaning of the statement (in that this determines what counts to make the statement true) and on the reality that will satisfy the truth demands of the statement.

Return to number 8. Whether number 8 is true depends on whether there are UFOs. But the matter is not that simple, for it also depends on what a person means by the word *UFO*. Different persons have different conceptions of UFOs. Strictly speaking, number 8 means that some flying objects have not been identified. Since even the hardiest skeptic will admit this, number 8 understood in this sense is true. But some people have richer notions of *UFO*, taking *UFO* to mean flying objects piloted by aliens. This claim differs substantially from the claim about mere unidentified objects and is much more disputable. So whether number 8 is true depends, on one hand, on reality itself; but on the other hand, which reality is spoken about is determined by how the language of number 8 is understood. This shows that *we must first determine the meaning of a statement before we can proceed to determine its truth.*

This important principle is often forgotten. We sometimes plunge into evaluation without first understanding what the person says. We quickly impose our meanings or understandings of terms on what the other person has written or said and make an evaluative judgment about its truth. But we must first understand what the other person says and means before making a judgment of truth or falsity. Only then can we be sure that we are adequately communicating and evaluating that person's idea and not our own.

Fourth, the truth of some statements is easier to discover than that of others. Though each statement is true or false because of some fact about the world, how we *know* or determine whether the statement is true or false is quite another matter. Each of us has limited knowledge; our backgrounds differ, exposing us to diverse experiences and sources of knowledge. Though I would be in a position to determine the truth of numbers 1 and 2, for me to discover for myself the truth of numbers 4 and 7 would pose quite a challenge. Given the secrecy of the former Soviet Union's space program in the 1960s, we might have a hard time showing that number 5 is not true, though it seems likely that it is not true. What this shows is that our *knowledge of the truth* of a statement is contextual, relative to such things as our experience, our background knowledge, and what else we accept as true.

Consequently, it is important to distinguish between a statement as being *actually* true and our *knowing* that it is true. Statements can be true quite apart from our knowing them to be true. But we cannot escape our limited and fallible apparatus for knowing. Hence, what we know of truth and what we claim for the truth of statements admit of degrees. Sometimes we are certain or almost certain that something is the case; other times we are less than certain or even dubious about the claim. We can distinguish various strengths that we might assign to beliefs or claims, using various qualifiers like *possibly, probably,* or *certainly.*

- *Possibly true:* A statement is possibly true when there is no reason to think it necessarily false.

For example, it is possibly true that there is life in other galaxies, for there is no reason to think that life on other galaxies is impossible.

This, however, is a very weak sense of *true,* for anything that is not logically contradictory is possibly true. For example, an advertisement for bananas goes, "Possibly the world's most perfect food." Since no reason is given to support this claim, the claim is possibly true in that there is no reason to think the claim is necessarily false. But this is a very weak sense of true, providing no ground for purchasing and eating a banana rather than another food, since the same might be said of other foods like grapefruit or potatoes.

Given this, we might suggest a little stronger version of *true.*

- *Possibly true$_1$:* A statement is possibly true when there is some evidence to think it true, but not enough evidence to decide.

Continuing the previous example, we might say that it is possibly true$_1$ that there is life in other galaxies because observations from the Hubble telescope have given us reasons to think that other galaxies house planets circling suns and that their distances from their own suns are compatible with the existence of life forms. But we have no evidence one way or another sufficient to say that these planets harbor life.

To take another example, the author of a recent book suggests that President Kennedy actually was shot by the accidental discharge of a rifle used by one of the Secret Service agents riding in his car. The author proceeds to present evidence for this. After reading the book, if one concludes that the evidence is weak one might say that this is at best a possible truth. It is possible that the bullet that entered JFK's head came from an agent's rifle, but the evidence is not strong enough to persuade one to come to a decision that this hypothesis is probable.

To say that a statement is possibly true in either of the preceding ways is to say that the truth of the statement is *unknown.* That is, there is not enough evidence to decide one way or the other regarding its truth. We know it is not necessarily true or necessarily false, and in the case of Possibly True$_1$ there is some evidence relevant to its truth, but not enough evidence exists for us to think that the statement is probably true.

- *Probably true:* A statement is probably true when there is more reason to think that it is true than false.

Even here we think of degrees of probability. Some statements or claims are better supported than others so that their probability of being true is high, whereas other claims have good reasons, but either the reasons are weak or else contravening reasons leave significant doubt, in which case the probability is lower. In the last case we might still think that the claim is probably true (that is, more likely true than not) but would not bank very heavily on it.

For example, the statement that the moon plays a significant role in the tidal action of the ocean has a very high degree of probability, whereas the claim that life once existed on Mars is believed to be probably true by some who think they have relevant evidence from Martian rocks found in Antarctica, though it does not have anywhere near the probability that the claim about the tides has.

> Whether statements about the future are probably true depends not only on our confidence in the information we have and on our belief that the future will be like the past but also on our cultural world view. For example, in Hispanic or Islamic cultures, statements about the future are qualified with the phrase, "If God wills" ("si Dios quiere" or "insha Allah"). In these cultures the confidence a person has about the outcome of specific events may be proportional to the degree to which that person thinks that God intervenes in earthly affairs.

When there is no doubt about the truth of a statement, we say that the statement is certainly true.

- *Certainly true:* A statement is certainly true when there can be no doubt about its truth.

There are few statements that satisfy this requirement in the strictest sense. One kind of statement that does is a necessarily true statement.

- *Necessarily True:* A statement is necessarily true when to deny it would yield some sort of contradiction.

For example, "A triangle has three angles," "A mule results from breeding a horse with a donkey," and "the vice-president of the United States is the presiding officer of the Senate" are examples of necessary truths. We know they are true because to deny them results in a contradiction.

While we might restrict certainty to such a high level, this view is not very reasonable. There are many things I have no doubt about, though they are not necessarily true. For example, I have no reasonable doubt that there is a tree outside my window, even though the denial of this claim would not yield a contradiction. Thus, one might modify the definition of *Certainly true* to read reasonable doubt in place of doubt. Thus we have

- *Certainly true$_1$:* A statement is certainly true when there is no reasonable doubt about its truth.

Of course, what constitutes reasonable doubt is a matter of disagreement. Philosophers have disputed this point for over two thousand years. Though the dispute is interesting and important, for ordinary purposes we can rely on an intuitive understanding of what constitutes reasonable doubt, noting that people might legitimately differ over this.

Similar things can be said about falsity. A statement is false when it fails to correspond with reality. However, determining falsity can be as difficult as determining truth. As with truth, there are degrees of falsity. We can make a parallel listing for falsity.

- *Possibly false:* A statement is possibly false when there is no reason to think it necessarily true.
- *Possibly false$_1$:* A statement is possibly false when there is some evidence to think it false, but not enough evidence to decide.

In both these cases, we can say that the truth or falsity of the statement is *unknown.* We lack sufficient information to make a reasonable judgment about truth and falsity.

- *Probably false:* A statement is probably false when there is more reason to think that it is false than true.
- *Certainly false:* A statement is certainly false when there can be no doubt about its falsity.

One way a statement can be certainly false is for it to be necessarily false.

- *Necessarily false:* A statement is necessarily false when it asserts some sort of contradiction.

Finally, paralleling our discussion about certainty in truth, we can revise our definition of certainly false statements to include the absence of *reasonable* doubt about its falsity. Hence,

- *Certainly false$_1$:* A statement is certainly false when there is no reasonable doubt about its falsity.

To *summarize,* statements are true or false insofar as they do or do not correspond with reality, with the facts. Our human difficulty lies in discerning when statements correspond, and this correspondence in part depends upon the meanings assigned to the statements. Finally, our knowledge of the truth of statements comes in degrees, obliging us to qualify our statements, using qualifiers such as *possibly, probably,* or *certainly.*

We can chart what we have said about our knowledge of truth coming in degrees with the following.

A statement is TRUE when it corresponds with reality	A statement is FALSE when it fails to correspond with reality
UNKNOWN *Possibly true:* no reason to think it is necessarily false, or some evidence for its truth exists, but not enough to decide	UNKNOWN *Possibly false:* no reason to think it is nessarily true, or some evidence for its falsity exists, but not enough to decide
PROBABLE *Probably true:* more reason to think it is true than false	PROBABLE *Probably false:* more reason to think it is false than true
CERTAIN *Certainly true$_1$:* no reasonable doubt about its truth *Necessarily true:* denial yields some sort of contradiction	CERTAIN *Certainly false$_1$:* no reasonable doubt about its falsity *Necessarily false:* asserts some sort of contradiction

Collaborative Learning Exercise

With your partner, determine whether the following statement is true or false.

> The statement inside this box is false.

Explain why this statement presents a problem.

Exercise 6

Determine which of the following statements is certainly true or false, probably true or false, or unknown (possibly true or false).

1. The moon is made of green cheese.

2. Carl was quite excited when he found a four leafed clover.

3. Sally found a picture of a four angled triangle in her geometry text.

4. Primitive bacteria inhabited Mars billions of years ago.

5. The next president of the United States will be a female.

6. The clarity of water depends upon the number of particles suspended in it.

7. The Titanic will never be raised from its grave in the North Atlantic.

8. Bach wrote the *Moonlight Sonata* for the prince of Brandenburg.

9. If the Palestinians and Israelis could solve the land problem, the violence in their country would significantly decrease.

10. One specific gene is responsible for most cases of acute alcoholism.

QUALIFYING AND QUANTIFYING WHAT WE SAY

Since our knowledge of truth and falsity comes in degrees, we have seen that it is often appropriate to qualify what we say. When we might not be certain that our opinion is true, we reflect this hesitancy in our language. In fact, this is what we have done in the previous section when we spoke about statements being possibly, probably, or certainly true or false.

Qualifiers

Qualifiers are words that function to strengthen or weaken what is said. *They show the degree of certainty or confidence we have in what we assert.* That is, qualifiers are about us because they communicate how strongly or weakly we believe a statement to be true or false. To express weak confidence in what we say or to suggest some hesitancy on our part, we use words like *seems, perhaps, maybe,* and *possibly.*

Maybe it will rain today.

Perhaps the Democratic candidate will win the election this fall.

It seems like the salesperson was telling the truth about the lawn mower.

Possibly the train left the tracks just after the highway crossing.

To *strengthen* what we want to say, we use words like *is likely, probably, is the case that, of course, in fact, surely,* and *certainly* that express our confidence in the truth of our assertion. The last five terms in this list are very strong because they remove any hesitancy regarding the communication. Consider the examples just given with a change in the qualifier and note the different feeling you get about the assurance with which the statement is asserted.

Surely it will rain today.

The Democratic candidate certainly will win the election this fall.

Of course the salesperson was telling the truth about the lawn mower.

Probably the train left the tracks just after the highway crossing.

Not all strengthening words convey the same certainty. While the first two—*is likely* and *probably*—leave room for doubt, the last five—*is the case that, of course, in fact, surely,* and *certainly*—assert certitude.

These words, then, provide clues about the author's confidence in his or her opinions. When you read, you need to look for these terms so that you can distinguish what the author is confident about from what the author is less confident about.

When you use weakening or strengthening terms, you should be aware of how they affect the reader or listener. On one hand, the use of weaker terms shows your humility about what you claim. It suggests that you are careful not to claim more than is warranted. However, continued use of weakening terms can lead the reader or listener to wonder why you are communicating about the topic at all if you are so unsure of anything you say. Consider the following letter.

> From what I've read, it doesn't seem that our current leadership has expressed indignation nor made contrition for leaving servicemen in Korea. But maybe we can't expect much from those who would allow such a betrayal to take place or go unpunished for these past four decades. Perhaps we must look to ourselves and thank God for our abandoned comrades and for the lives they gave for us. We might also ask our God to be just with those in our government responsible for this travesty—damn just. (Guy Glover, letter, *St. Paul Pioneer Press*, October 1, 1996)

Notice all the words of hesitancy: *seem, maybe, perhaps, might.* They weaken the force of the author's argument. Informative or persuasive communication works best in a context where a person has something worthwhile to say. Continued hesitancy puts that worth in doubt.

On the other hand, continued use of strengthening words may lead your reader or listener to begin to wonder whether things really are so certain as you make out. Are you aware of your assumptions? Have you thought about other options? Are there differing opinions you might attend to? These questions suggest that terms of certainty work best when you have shown your reader or listener that you have carefully considered other perspectives, opinions, or options and that you have very good, if not decisive, reasons to think that they are inadequate, reasons that you are willing to share.

One other thing to watch for is that qualifiers can be misleading. They can lead you to think that there are more opportunities for you than actually exist. For example, consider the following advertisement.

> THANK YOU NUMBER ONE: A FULL RANGE BELL CORDLESS TELE-PHONE. If you are one of the fastest to reply to this survey by first class mail, phone or fax, you could receive a FREE Cordless Phone.

The operative word here is *could*. The authors of the ad do not know and hence cannot assert that you will receive a free phone; they only know that it is possible. At the same time, the ad's bold print suggests that the advertiser will give you a phone for replying to the survey. If you focus on the bold print, you miss the uncertainty which, in effect, frees the company distributing this advertisement from being obligated to do anything. By printing *FREE* in bold letters, they have distracted from the *could*.

Quantifiers

Quantifiers are terms that function to indicate *how many of the subject* are being talked or written about. If you have confidence that all of the group about which you speak are the way you describe them, you can use words like *all* or *each*. For example, "Each member of the team came prepared to play hard to win the big soccer match." But if you think there might be exceptions, weakening terms might be introduced: *most, many, some, a few, several*. "Some members of the team came prepared to play hard to win the big soccer match." Events might also be quantified in terms of times: strong words include *always, every time*; weak terms are *occasionally*, and *rarely*. "It always rains on my vacation." "It sometimes rains on my vacation." Words like *all, every*, and *each* in the subject indicate statements that are called **universal statements.** Statements with words in the subject like *most, many, some, a few*, and *several*, which indicate that not everyone or everything was involved, are called **particular statements.**

- Universal: All (Every, Without exception) cars imported into the United States are inspected for safety.
- Particular (Less than all): Some (Most, Several, Many, 100,000, Ten, One) cars imported into the United States are inspected for safety.

We have a tendency to speak in universal terms, often without evidence that our statement is true in every case. Have you ever heard someone say, "That happens all the time," or "He is always doing that," or "Everybody else wears jeans to concerts"? However, rarely (note the quantifier) can we speak about all of something being the case or something happening all the time. The world is very diverse. Consequently, it is often better to couch your language in terms that reveal some hesitancy about how many of something have the features you are ascribing to them, unless you have good evidence to think that your statement applies to all of those you are discussing.

Sometimes it is difficult to tell whether the statement is universal or particular. This occurs when no quantifying term is provided. For example, in the statement "Whales are mammals," our background knowledge tells us that being a mammal applies to all whales, making the statement universal. However, "Rose blossoms last for four days" is not a truth that would apply to all rose blossoms but only to the average blossom. So we have two types of cases: one where each member of the class has the property (each whale is a mammal) and one where the property applies to the average thing (the average rose blossom lasts for four days). When what is referred to is the case of the average thing, the statement is best understood as particular, referring to most blossoms or the average blossom. In each case, we have to look at the context and introduce our background knowledge to determine whether the statement is particular or universal.

This ambiguity is important for critical thinkers. Consider the following ad.

Patients who take our brand of capsule improve within twenty-four hours.

Is this statement universal or particular? If it is universal, it provides a good guarantee that you will improve by using this product. But that would be a very strong claim. If the claim is true at all, it is probably talking about the average patient recovery time, in which case it may or may not apply to you. But note that the company leaves the statement vague, perhaps intentionally. You as the consumer need to determine whether it is a universal or a particular statement, and if particular, to how many patients the statement applies.

Groups

There is another complexity about statements that we need to address. Consider two statements:

The cat finished all the milk in her bowl.

The Boy Scout troop ate all its food supplies on the canoe trip.

The subject of both of these statements begins with the word *the*. Does *the* indicate that the word is particular or universal? It depends. In the example of the cat, *the* indicates a particular cat and hence the statement is particular. In the example of the troop, however, *the* refers not to an individual but to a group of individuals. Statements about groups are to be treated as universals.

Groups often are introduced by the word *the* (or some functionally equivalent term like *our*, as in our Girl Scout Troop) and have some sort of organization. The organization might be very organized or formal—the soccer team, the climbing party, the executive committee, the Student Senate—or loose—the crowd on the beach, the union, the voters in district eleven, the physician's patients. When we speak about groups, we need to determine whether we are speaking about the group as an entity or whole, or whether we are speaking about the individual members of the group.

On one hand, sometimes the language refers to the *group as a whole* rather than to its individual members. For example,

Our football team is the fastest in the league.

The predicate *the fastest in the league* applies to our team as a whole and not to every member. Some of the team members may be slower than the fastest runners of other teams, but the claim is that our average team speed exceeds the other team's average speed. Or again, a trucking firm might advertise,

Our trucks log millions of miles to deliver your goods on time.

Not every truck logs millions of miles; this characteristic applies to the group of trucks (the trucking firm) rather than to each truck individually.

> The people voted for a Democratic President and a Republican Congress in 1996.

Not every person in the country voted in the pattern indicated. Hence, this statement is best understood as referring to the group of voters, not to the individual voters.

On the other hand, there are times when the language refers to *every member of the group.*

> The tour will stay in a 5-star hotel while the ship is docked.

In this case, each member of the tour will stay in the 5-star hotel. If you are a tour group member and are refused such lodging on the grounds that it only applies to the group, you would be outraged. Or again, think about the trucking firm's advertisement,

> Our delivery trucks are inspected annually for safety.

The characteristic of being inspected annually would apply to every truck in the firm.

Confusing characteristics of groups with those of the members of the groups can be misleading and, at times, humorous. For example,

> The freshmen class drank twenty cases of soft drinks at the Homecoming dance.

The subject—freshman class—refers to a group. When it says that the class drank twenty cases of soft drinks, it does not refer to each group member—otherwise all the freshman would be very sick—but to the group as a whole. Or again,

> The faculty is gradually aging.

Gradual aging characterizes each of my colleagues as we move through life. But consider the claim,

> The faculty is getting younger.

This claim specifies a property that applies to the group and not to the individuals. The apparent paradox in this statement is explained by the fact that the average age of the faculty is declining as younger people are hired to replace retirees.

To determine whether the characteristic spoken about applies to the group or to the individual group members, you need to ask, *first,* whether each member could actually have the characteristic described. If each member could have it, then the characteristic should be interpreted as applying to the individual group members; if each member cannot have it, then the characteristic must be applied to the group as a whole. *Second,* you should inquire whether every member of the group has the characteristic ascribed. If there is reason to think this is not the case, give the benefit of the doubt to the author or speaker by interpreting the statement as being about the whole group and not about each and every group member.

We classify statements about groups as universal statements. Statements about the *individual members* of the group are universal in that all the group members have the characteristic in question. Statements about the *group as a whole* are universal in that the group is treated as a single person or entity to which the characteristic applies, though the characteristic does not apply to each group member.

Exercise 7

Indicate whether the following statements are universal or particular.

1. Many senior citizens from the Frost Belt winter in the Sunshine States.

2. Cooked eel is quite tasty, once you get used to the idea.

3. Rarely does anyone break par on this course, with all its traps and bunkers.

4. The whole family turned out for the reunion party at Grandpa's cabin.

5. The family ate five buckets of Kentucky Fried Chicken.

6. College students head back to the books when Labor Day rolls around.

7. What goes around comes around.

8. The President's Cabinet differed with him over his foreign policy.

9. Geese fly south in the winter when the temperatures plummet.

10. The mountain climbers passed twenty-six herds of goats on their ascent to the glacier.

11. Many are called, but few are chosen.

12. The executives of the company make twenty-six million dollars annually.

13. Twenty-six herds of goats were spotted by the mountain climbers on their ascent to the glacier.

14. The union picketed the General Motors plant in Dearborn.

15. The union went on strike against General Motors in July.

Exercise 8

Indicate whether the statement is qualified, quantified, or both, and identify the terms that accomplish this.

1. Surely most of the people enjoyed the concert.

2. If he only completed his homework, he would probably improve his grade in the class.

3. More often than not your peers drag you down rather than inspire you to greater heights of accomplishment.

4. She thought it was more likely that he was at the hospital visiting his ill sister than that he was in a board meeting.

5. The whole class was acting disruptively when the three teachers walked in the room.

6. One never knows when one's time is up; so one should always plan ahead by drawing up a will.

7. Three of the candidates debated before the audience; when the entire audience was polled, 57 percent said they would vote for the most conservative candidate.

8. Frequently he cannot find where he laid his tools, but he always knows where he set down his last cup of coffee.

9. About 55 percent of students in the urban public school failed the eighth grade competency test. Of course, one would expect this, given the fact that many of these students come from homes where English is not spoken as the primary language.

10. For two of the teams this was a successful year because they made it into the finals for the first time.

Exercise 9

For the following, indicate whether the statements are universal or particular. Then indicate the words that affect the quantity or quality of the claim.

1. Be among the fastest responses we receive for the survey and you could be eligible to qualify for this superior example of communication, a cordless telephone. (Advertisement)

2. All of the state's school districts offer voluntary early childhood programs for their children.

3. Surely many of the accounts of what happened at the riot were greatly exaggerated. Only five of the residents of the apartment were injured in the melee, and all of these injuries resulted from their own acts. It seems that the reporters were biased in their accounts.

4. A lot of the people who recently immigrated into our community remain unemployed. Many of them are walking around the town during the day, which demonstrates the problem. The city council should work with the local industries to try to find meaningful jobs for these people.

5. Hunters want wildlife managers to "make more moose" by enhancing habitat, but that's neither cheap nor easy. . . . "Moose habitat covers more than 3 million acres in the Mat-Su Valley, . . . [b]ut only 15 percent of the area [is] available for habitat enhancement." Of this 15 percent, most is inaccessible, and some has little or no enhancement potential. . . . About 17,000 moose live in the Mat-Su Valley. On average, one moose needs 56 acres of browse to get through a winter. A 10 percent increase in moose would cost between $2.6 and $26 million, depending on which enhancement method is used. . . . (Les Palmer, "Expensive Meat," *Alaska*, April 1997, p. 54)

CAN, OUGHT, AND IS

When we begin to pay attention to language, we discover important differences between words that we often mistakenly use synonymously. Let us note three of these words.

- *Is*

Is talks about what really happens and comes in three tenses. *Was* addresses what happened in the past; *is* addresses what is happening now: *will be* addresses what will happen in the future. *Is* language is generally not problematic, but sometimes it can be confused with

- *Ought*

Oughts do not tell us what is, has been, or will happen. Rather, oughts address the ideal: what would be good *if* it happened.

> The company ought to raise his salary above minimum wage.

Because oughts address the ideal rather than the real, it is generally a mistake to move from ought to is or vice versa. What is the case cannot tell us what ought to be the case; and the fact that something ought to be the case does not inform us that it is the case.

A third word is

- *Can*

Can indicates what is possible.

> She can swim twenty-five laps of the pool in under ten minutes.

This statement does not say that swimming these many laps is what she is actually doing or even desirable (ought to be done), only that it is something that she is able to perform. Swimming twenty-five laps is within her ability.

It is important that these three different realms—the actual, the desirable, and the possible—be carefully distinguished in discourse and that one not confuse or move illicitly between them. Consider the following:

> Everybody deserves a second chance in life. When someone murders another person, instead of being sentenced to death, they can be sentenced to many years of rehabilitation.

This paragraph from a student paper illustrates the confusion. The writer has moved from considerations of oughts—"deserves a second chance"—to consideration of cans—"can be sentenced to a prison term where they will undergo rehabilitation." That some action ought to be undertaken (for example, reforming Medicare) does not imply that it can be done (given certain political realities). Similarly, that some action can be taken (polluting our rivers) does not imply that it ought to be taken. Critical thinkers carefully monitor their use of these three verbs.

Choosing the most appropriate verb depends on the context. When deciding if I should run the Boston Marathon, I consider whether "I *can* complete the marathon in this heat." Once I am running, I show my determination by affirming that "I *will* complete the marathon in this heat." But if I get cramps along the way, I might wonder whether "I *ought* to complete the marathon in this heat," for doing so might cause me serious physical damage. Critical thinkers pay close attention to the context when they decide which of these verbs is most appropriate, recognizing that each conveys a unique meaning.

For each of the following, indicate which is the most appropriate term: *is (was, will be), can (could),* or *ought (should).* You may have to add helping words for the sentence to make sense. In some cases, different answers are possible, with the result that you may disagree with other students about which words fit best, depending on how you see the context.

1. When the couple went to the counselor, they discussed whether they _____ have genetic testing done for Huntingdon's disease.

2. When the couple contacted their insurance agent, they asked whether they _____ have genetic testing done for Huntingdon's disease.

3. When the sulfuric acid is added to the liquid, you _____ smell a distinct odor.

4. My hands are tied; I have no choice; what else _____ I do?

5. I did not know that that is what _____ happen.

6. The opinion poll showed that 65 percent of the respondents were in favor of modifying Social Security. Clearly this gives Congress a mandate: it _____ change the Social Security system.

7. That politicians _____ serve the people who elect them does not mean that they _____ .

8. That the Dodgers _____ win the World Series does not mean that they_____ .

9. That gangs _____ in control of the drug traffic in the neighborhood does not mean that they _____ .

10. I would if I _____ , but I _____ not, so I _____ not.

SUMMING-UP

This chapter has focused on the role language plays in our comprehension. It has distinguished statements from sentences and has addressed some of the complexity that we can find in statements. Complexity can result not merely from the structure of the sentence or the addition of certain qualifying or quantifying words but also from the very ambiguity of the language used. To the matter of ambiguity we turn in the next chapter, where we continue our discussion of comprehension.

ANSWERS TO THE EXERCISES

Answers to Exercise 3
[Unlike most hunters, I came to the sport relatively late in life.] [I first went hunting in my late 20s.] [I got my chance courtesy of a new friend,] [(my friend is) a longtime hunter who introduced me to the mysteries and rituals of the sport] and [(my friend) drilled into me his own highly evolved commitment to hunting ethics. [Those were

singular gifts—both the hunting skills and the ethics]—and [one that can be repaid only by passing them on to another generation of hunters.]

[I've been hunting for about 20 years now, mostly for deer,] but [recently (I hunt) for ducks.] [The land I hunt is private,] and [I hunt there by permission.] [Access and competition are not problems,] but [poaching, trespassing, and road hunting are highly visible to everyone who hunts in the region.]

[My views on hunting, my sense of ethics, my sense of hunter behavior problems, and my expectations of myself and of those I hunt with are all products of my experiences in the field—with a measure of reading, discussion, and fireside debate thrown in for seasoning.] [I was taught to hunt for the joy of hunting and for the deep satisfaction of having hunted well, not for the bag;] [(I was taught) to take pride in my outdoor skills more than in my kill;] [(I was taught) to savor wild game;] [(I was taught) to know the land where I hunt;] [(I was taught) to study the critters,] [(I was taught) to learn to read the woods, and [(I was taught) to work with my hands to improve habitat;] and [(I was taught) to expect other hunters to do pretty much the same.]

Answers to Exercise 4

1. Command
3. Command and statement
5. One or two statements: The rain pelted the soccer players, turning the field into a quagmire. Or, The rain pelted the soccer players. The rain turned the field into a quagmire.
7. Expressive function. In this case, the writer is probably expressing his emotions about what the person did to his or her sister.
9. Ordinary question. The answer is a geep.
11. Three statements: the street was slippery; it had just rained; this was the first rain of the season.
13. Expressive function, here expressing a belief
15. Performative or expressive function

Answers to Exercise 5

1. [To decrease tension in the region, the Pentagon delayed its latest war games.]
3. [If computer prices drop much lower, the manufacturers will start losing money on their product.]
5. As [Apple Computer attempts to turn the company around,] [it will be interesting to see what happens with the clone manufacturers licensed by Apple.]
7. [He would be much happier if he did not play the stock market.]
9. [People are always ready to lend a helping hand when they see that the need is genuine].
11. [The microbiologists placed the clay mixture into a heavy acid concentrate] so that [they could test its reproductive capacity.]
13. [Either Los Angeles will get a new football franchise or else the National Football League will place a struggling, small market team there.]
15. [At the height of summer, silence becomes relative.] [The background noise is a ceaseless whine and whir of billions of flying insects,] [(insects become) a mist of particulate life rising from moss-level to the tops of the trees.] Because [the sound is so steady,] [the effect is like that which any "white noise" machine creates.] ("Silence," *Alaska*, October 1997)
17. [$125 million dollars over six years just for one person to play basketball.] How does Glen Taylor justify this? (question, possibly rhetorical) There follows a series of rhetorical questions. [This basketball person does not have to make executive

decisions.] [He does not decide how to defend our country.] [He does not decide how to help survivors of war-torn countries.] [He does not decide how to help the poor starving people in our own country] [He does not decide how to stretch the classroom budget to meet the needs of students.] [He does not decide how to keep open clinics and hospitals throughout the state, the country.] Kevin Garnett, I hope you will decide to help not only your family, but also your local, state and adopted community organizations, schools and churches. (expressive utterance)

Answers to Exercise 6

1. Certainly false, though not necessarily false
3. Certainly false because necessarily false
5. Possibly true
7. Probably true
9. Probably true

Answers to Exercise 7

1. Particular
3. Particular
5. Universal, applying to the group
7. Universal
9. Universal
11. Two statements, each particular
13. Particular
15. Universal; unclear whether it applies to the entire group or to each individual

Answers to Exercise 8

1. Qualifier: surely
   Quantifier: most
3. Qualifier: More often than not
5. Quantifier: The whole
7. Quantifier: Three, the entire, 57 percent
9. Quantifier: about 55 percent, many
   Qualifier: Of course

Answers to Exercise 9

1. Universal. Qualifier: could
3. 4 statements:
   Particular: Quantifier: many; qualifier: surely
   Particular: Quantifier: Five
   Universal: Quantifier: all
   Universal: Qualifier: it seems
5. First three statements [Hunters want . . .; that's neither cheap nor easy; moose habitat covers . . .] are universal; the rest are particular. Quantifiers: 15 percent, most, some, about 17,000, one, 10 percent

CHAPTER 5

Comprehension

Clarifying Your Language

Not everything we say or write is clear. We may believe it is clear because it is clear to us, but others may not understand what we are saying or writing. Sometimes our communication is ambiguous or vague, open to a variety of interpretations. One newspaper columnist wrote that Joe Paterno gave "a $3.5 million gift, together with his wife Sue, to the school's library and scholarship foundation." The reader may think that the library is grateful for the money but may puzzle over what the library will do with Paterno's wife. Critical thinkers know that language can be ambiguous and attempt to avoid ambiguity as much as possible in informative and argumentative discourse.

At the same time, however, ambiguity has its place. Poetry, for example, reaches into human depths because the words used have different layers of meanings. Using the treasure stored in words, poets give added dimension to what they write. In the last stanza of "Stopping by Woods on a Snowy Evening," Robert Frost writes:

The woods are lovely, dark and deep,
But I have promises to keep,
And miles to go before I sleep,
And miles to go before I sleep.

From "Stopping by Woods on a Snowy Evening" from *The Poetry of Robert Frost,* edited by Edward Connery Lathem. Copyright 1951 by Robert Frost. Copyright 1923, © 1969 by Henry Holt and Company, LLC. Reprinted by permission of Henry Holt and Company, LLC.

If we consider only the obvious words of the poem, Frost writes about a rider pausing by some woods on a New England winter sleigh ride. On a deeper level, however, Frost seems to be speaking about life in general, about the attractiveness of death (sleep), and about the need to go on with life (promises to keep) before yielding to death. Here words like *sleep* and *promises to keep* hold a richer meaning than what might appear on the surface. So in some contexts, like poetry, ambiguity is valued and encouraged.

But we focus not on poetry but on argumentative or persuasive discourse, where we attempt to avoid ambiguous language. So this chapter continues our discussion of comprehension and language. It aims to enable you to better understand the points others make and to present your points clearly. To accomplish this, we focus on ambiguity arising from four circumstances: the careless use of language, confusion between different meanings of terms, grammatical misuse of words, and vague language. We end the chapter by focusing on emotive language.

AMBIGUITY RESULTING FROM CARELESS USE OF LANGUAGE

The first type of ambiguity stems from not saying what you really want to say. It arises from sloppy or careless use of language. Consider the following report of how two words got confused.

> My friends and I went to the Festival of Nations. We were walking through the Bazaar when my friend turned to the rest of us and asked, "Were you here last year when they had the Confederate $20 bills going around?" We all just kind of looked at each other, wondering how someone managed to get ahold of Confederate money, and why they would spend it.
>
> She went on, "Yeah, they even made an announcement saying that this Confederate money had been found, and vendors shouldn't take bills with a certain number."
>
> I started laughing and said, "You mean counterfeit money." (*St. Paul Pioneer Press*, May 23, 1997)

One form of the careless use of words is called **malapropism.** This term is applied particularly when words that sound alike are confused, as in the cartoon on page 110.

Careless use of language can lead to humorous results. Here is an example constructed from various student papers.

> Ancient Egypt was inhabited by mummies, and they all wrote in hydraulic. They lived in the Sarah Dessert and traveled by Camelot. . . . Certain areas of the dessert are cultivated by irritation. . . .
>
> The Bible is full of interesting caricatures. In the first book of the Bible, Guinesses, Adam and Eve were created from an apple tree. One of their children, Cain, asked, "Am I my brother's son?" . . .
>
> Moses led the Hebrews to the Red Sea, where they made unleavened bread, which is bread made without any ingredients. Afterwards, Moses went up on Mount Cyanide to get the Ten Amendments. . . . David was a Hebrew king skilled at playing the liar. . . . Solomon, one of David's sons, had 300 wives and 700 porcupines.
>
> The Greeks were a highly sculptured people, and without them we wouldn't have history. . . . Socrates was a famous Greek teacher who went around giving people advice. They killed him. Socrates died from an overdose of wedlock. After his death, his career suffered a dramatic decline. [Richard Lederer, *Anguished English* (New York: Bantam Doubleday, 1987) pp. 10–11.]

Source: FRANK & ERNEST. Reprinted with permission of Newspaper Enterprise Association, Inc.

Words can be used carelessly in other ways as well. Consider these examples allegedly from newspaper headlines. Can you identify the careless use of language?

War dims hope for peace

If strike isn't settled quickly, it may last awhile

Cold wave linked to temperatures

Couple slain; police suspect homicide

Careless use of language becomes serious when it occurs in contexts that create significant misunderstanding. Consider the following sentences that a student presented as the basis for the paper he intended to write.

Issue: Do people agree that abortion should be done?

Thesis: Abortions should not be performed.

The student believed that these two sentences were related as issue and thesis. But clearly they are not. The subject of the first is "people" and the verb is "agree." It expresses a noncontroversial question about people's attitudes, easily answered by finding people who agree and some who disagree that abortions should be performed. Since the question can be resolved quickly by experience, it is not a worthy paper thesis. The second—that abortions should not be performed—is very different. The subject is not *people* but *abortions,* and the verb is *should not be performed.* This thesis cannot be established by empirical research on people's attitudes about abortion but must be addressed by careful arguments directed toward determining the morality of abortion.

Consider another example also from a student paper.

> The smoking industry could agree not to target kids. That would include taking signs down around public places and stopping with the free shirt promotions.

The writer here fails to understand the difference between "stopping" free shirt promotions (not doing the promotions) and "stopping with" them (which means they still can be employed, but nothing more will be done). Or again, consider the following sentence from a book.

> Experimental replications of these accounts have failed to produce unqualified, collaborative results.

What the author really meant was "corroborative." This is either a typographical error (which can occur easily in printed materials) or else a confusion of two different words by the author. The difference between "corroborative" and "collaborative" radically alters the meaning of the sentence.

Or again:

> Male mortality patterns are more variable than female patterns; that is, many more men die in early and middle age than women, who tend to die in more of a concentrated clump toward the end of life. (Malcolm Gladwell, "The Sports Taboo," *The New Yorker*, May 19, 1997, p. 52)

Whereas we would think that everybody dies at the end of life, the author has women tending to die toward the end of life, leaving one bemused about a possible gap between *toward the end of life* and *at the end of life*. Furthermore, what does it mean to "die in a concentrated clump"? Do women get together to die all at one time?

Our point is that critical thinkers pay close attention to the words and phrases they use. As one cartoon character puts it, "You should mean what you say and say what you mean."

AMBIGUITY RESULTING FROM CONFUSION OF DIFFERENT MEANINGS

A second kind of ambiguity results from confusion about the *meanings of words*. It is termed **semantic ambiguity**. A word has ambiguity of meaning or semantic ambiguity when it could mean two different things and the context fails to make clear which meaning is intended.

> She put her glasses on the table.

Glasses here could refer to the objects you use to improve your vision or to an object from which you drink. To clarify which kind of glasses is meant, the writer might add the word *reading* or *water* to *glasses* (reading glasses or water glasses).

> The soccer team was upset.

Upset could mean that the team was expected to win but was beaten, or it could mean that the team members were extremely unhappy.

Speakers and writers sometimes intentionally employ this kind of ambiguity in **puns**—humor that invokes a play on words. What makes puns possible, let alone interesting, is that they trade on ambiguities of language to create their double meaning. For example:

> When the head waiter at the restaurant asked whether she had reservations, the lady said, "Yes, but I will eat here anyway."

The ambiguous word is *reservation*. Can you give its two meanings? _____

_____

Consider two other examples.

> When the veterinarian pronounced the dog dead, the client asked for a second opinion. The vet let a cat out of its cage; the cat promptly sniffed the dog from head to foot and when there was no reaction, went back into its cage. The client received a bill from the vet for his services and for a cat-scan.

> Line in an old movie. "How dare you belch in front of my wife!" "Sorry, old man. I didn't know it was her turn."

Can you identify the semantically ambiguous words in each? _____

_____

The suspect words respectively are *cat-scan* (taken literally or in terms of a machine) and *in front of* (meaning actually in front of or before).

Puns or ambiguities of meaning not only play a role in a particular kind of humor, they also are used to attract consumer attention in advertisements. Consider an advertisement showing a cow standing over a Pepsi sign:

> "Meet over a Pepsi."

The ambiguous word is *meet*. Written, it is not ambiguous; its ambiguity appears when it is spoken, for *meet* can also be understood (as the picture suggests) as *meat*. (*Meet* and *meat* are **homonyms**, that is, words that have the same pronunciation but have different meanings and spellings.)

> Billboard, with a picture of a person driving a convertible: "Get the rays you deserve."

Can you find the homonyms suggested by this advertisement and give the

meanings of the two words? _____

_____

Another advertisement

> A better world. Only $9.95

seems to promise a cheap way to solve the world's problems, until you learn that it is an advertisement for a world map.

Ambiguity of meaning (semantic ambiguity) becomes more serious when people use ambiguous words in ways that create confusion and misunderstanding in serious arguments. We will say more about this when we discuss equivocation in Chapter 11.

AMBIGUITY RESULTING FROM UNCLARITY
OF USE

113

CHAPTER 5
*Clarifying Your
Language*

A third kind of ambiguity has to do with the *grammar* or *syntax* of the sentence. When for one reason or another the grammatical structure is unclear so that what is communicated is ambiguous, the result is **syntactic ambiguity.** Let us look at a variety of ways grammar can create ambiguity.

Ambiguous Referent

Pronouns like *he, she,* or *it* are used frequently in speech and writing. When you use pronouns, you should make very clear exactly to whom or to what they refer. That is, *you should always be able to point to the exact word or words to which these pronouns refer.* If you cannot do so, your pronouns have an **ambiguous referent.** Failure to be clear about referents can lead to confusion and misunderstanding. For example,

Susan read the letter Yvonne wrote while she was on the bus.

What is unclear here is to whom the pronoun *she* refers. Does it refer to *Susan* (in which case Susan was on the bus), or does it refer to *Yvonne* (in which case Yvonne was on the bus)? This type of ambiguity occurs frequently in student writing. Here is one such example.

When I see the cartoon camel smoking it is no big deal.

To what does *it* refer: *smoking* (in general) or the *cartoon camel smoking*?

To reiterate, it is essential that when you write or speak, you make clear to what other word or words the pronouns you use refer. If you cannot do this, you cannot expect your reader or listener to be able to do it.

Ambiguous Modifier

Sometimes we use modifiers without giving a clear indication of what word or words they modify. For example,

Sign in a hotel: NO SMOKING ROOMS AVAILABLE

What does the word *no* modify? Does it modify *smoking,* so that you could get a room specifically set aside for nonsmokers, or does it modify *smoking rooms,* so that there are no rooms available where you can smoke?

Another way modifiers can be ambiguous is when the dependent clause with which the sentence opens fails to properly modify the subject of the sentence. For example,

Covered with a cloth, the kids won't see the cookies on the counter.

The dependent clause *covered with a cloth* is meant to modify *cookies,* whereas the writer has mispositioned it to refer grammatically to *kids.* To eliminate the ambiguity, the sentence should be rewritten to say, "Because cookies on the counter are covered with a cloth, the kids won't see them."

Problems with modifiers can occur in other ways as well. Consider:

Elizabeth had a big piece of cake and dish of ice cream at her birthday party.

Does *big* modify *dish* as well as *piece,* so that she had a big piece of cake and a big dish of ice cream, or does it only modify *piece,* so that she had a big piece of cake and a regular sized dish of ice cream? When you use adjectives to modify one noun in a series, you should make it clear whether the adjectives modify only one noun or all the nouns in the series. If the dish of ice cream was of normal size, you might write, "Elizabeth had a big piece of cake and a dish with one scoop of ice cream at her birthday party."

In short, it is essential that when you write or speak, you make clear the relation between modifiers and the words that they modify. This can be accomplished by proper positioning of the words or by using various grammatical constructions like clauses or prepositional phrases.

Ambiguous Grammar

Instances of **ambiguous grammar** occur when one or several words in a sentence can function grammatically as more than one part of speech. Consider the alleged newspaper headline,

Eye drops off shelf

If *drops* is a noun, we are told that a certain kind of medicine was removed from the store shelves. If, however, *drops* is a verb, then we are told that an eye fell off a shelf. The meaning shifts, depending on the grammatical function of the words *eye* and *drops.*

Bumper sticker: Did you wake up grouchy this morning, or did you let him sleep?

Grouchy here could be an adverb, modifying *wake up,* or it could be a noun, referring to a particular person. The second part of the sentence interprets *grouchy* the second way. When words can function in different grammatical ways in a sentence, it is important to rewrite the sentence so that it is clear precisely how each word functions.

It should be noted that oftentimes ambiguity in grammatical function is accompanied by semantic ambiguity. For example, in the previous example, *drops* is semantically ambiguous: *eye drops* refer to a liquid; *eye drops* means that the eye fell.

Ambiguous Comparison

Ambiguous comparison occurs when it is unclear precisely what is being compared. For example,

Susan enjoys playing with her dolls more than Mary.

It is unclear whether Susan enjoys playing with her dolls more than Mary enjoys playing with her dolls, or whether Susan enjoys playing with dolls more than playing with Mary.

Mike wants to see the Grand Canyon more than Tom.

One way of addressing ambiguity of comparison is to add more words to the comparison. For example, Susan enjoys playing with dolls more than Mary does. [You might note that the sentence does not say *her dolls*; the word *her* is omitted. If the word *her* were left in, the sentence—Susan enjoys playing with her dolls more than Mary does—would still be ambiguous, for it would be unclear whether Mary enjoys playing with Susan's dolls or with Mary's dolls.]

You might wonder why we have given so much attention to ambiguities of use. One reason is that they are prevalent in student writing: sometimes because the writing has not been proof read, other times because writers have not paid careful attention to their grammar. Yet grammar is very important, for unclear grammar affects meaning, making it more difficult to understand what is written or said.

Exercise 1

Here are some alleged newspaper headlines. Determine whether the headline is ambiguous because of the meanings of the terms (semantic ambiguity), because of how the terms are used (syntactic ambiguity), or both. Then identify the terms that create the ambiguity.

1. Include your children when baking cookies

2. Police begin campaign to run down jaywalkers

3. Safety experts say school bus passengers should be belted

4. Pope's guard, wife shot

5. Survivor of Siamese twins joins parents

6. Farmer bill dies in house

7. Teacher strikes idle kids

8. Prostitutes appeal to Pope

9. British left waffles on Falkland Islands

10. Lung cancer in women mushrooms

11. Drunk gets nine months in violin case

12. Iraqi head seeks arms

13. Reagan wins on budget, but more lies ahead

14. Squad helps dog bite victim

15. Shot off woman's leg helps Nicklaus to 66

16. Enraged cow injures farmer with ax

17. Miners refuse to work after death

18. Juvenile court to try shooting defendant

19. Stolen painting found by tree

20. Two Soviet ships collide; one dies

21. Killer sentenced to die for second time in 10 years

22. Drunken drivers paid $1000 in '84

23. Red tape holds up new bridge

24. Deer kill 17,000

25. New study of obesity looks for larger test group

26. Chef throws his heart into helping feed needy

27. Ban on soliciting dead in Trotwood

28. Lansing residents can drop off trees

29. Local high school dropouts cut in half

30. New vaccine may contain rabies

31. Air head fired

32. Old school pillars are replaced by alumni

33. Bank drive-in window blocked by board

34. Hospitals are sued by 7 foot doctors

35. Some pieces of Rock Hudson sold at auction

AMBIGUITY RESULTING FROM VAGUE LANGUAGE

The fourth kind of ambiguity to watch for is **vague language.** A term is vague when it is imprecise. The imprecision generally stems from the fact that the term or phrase admits of degrees and the context is not clear enough to enable the reader to determine those degrees. For example:

> My mother is old.

The vague term is *old;* at what age does one become old?

> The commencement speaker's talk was long.

The vague term is *long;* for how much time must something take for it to take a long time?

> They sell big ice cream cones at the dairy down the street.

Big here is vague; what might be big for a 5-year-old might not be big for a teenager.

> The stewardess makes over $30,000 a year.

Here we are given the base figure, but we have no idea how much the salary exceeds the base figure.

The skies are not cloudy all day.

The vague terms are *not . . . all.* Does it mean that the skies are never cloudy, or that there is at least some sunshine during each day?

Vagueness is not always bad or to be avoided. Sometimes we just do not know how many people were at the park, how much money we spent, how cold it was, or how far we traveled. In cases where we do not know or the precise figure does not matter, we can still convey some idea of the range of options by using vague terms like *about 50 people, several dollars, colder than yesterday,* and *over 30 miles.*

At the same time, critical thinkers are not misled by vague terms, particularly when they are asked to take some specific action based on the vagueness. This means that you must read carefully and ask what is really being said. Here are some examples where you are asked to make some purchases based on vagueness.

> Everyone runs the risk of being a flood victim. In fact, between 25 percent and 30 percent of flood insurance claims come from "low risk" areas. It could happen to you.

The term *risk* here is vague. Does it mean that it is possible (which is true) or that it is probable (which is not true) that everyone (note the universal) will experience a flood? Further, note that the first use of *risk* differs from the second use, where the term stands in contrast to high-risk or flood prone areas (note the quotation marks around *low risk*). The fact that between 25 percent and 30 percent of flood insurance claims come from low-risk areas does not show that everyone runs a risk of being flooded.

> Call today and save up to 45 percent on Northwest Airlines.

Up to can mean anything from 0 to 45 percent. Since that is a large spread, it is difficult to know precisely how much you will save on any given flight, if you save anything. In fact, if you pay attention to airline fares, you know that since airlines put severe restrictions on which tickets they discount and the conditions under which they are discounted, it is very possible that the flight you want may not qualify for any savings.

> We have made our chocolate 25 percent richer than before.

This advertisement contains two vague terms. First, 25 percent of what? You have no idea how rich the chocolate was before. If it was only 2 percent rich to begin with, it is still less than 3 percent rich with the improvement and maybe not worth purchasing. Second, what is it for chocolate to be richer? The ad is vague on this critical point, for it gives no definition of *richness* nor any way to determine richness.

Vagueness both cannot and should not be avoided entirely. Critical thinkers look to see if they have enough information to make the appropriate decision.

- Is information missing that is essential to determining the truth of the claim?
- If a comparison is being made, do you know the terms of the comparison. Twenty-five percent greater than what?
- If a range of figures is supplied, is the range narrow enough to allow you to know the best course of action? "Up to 40 percent off regular price" might be too large a range.

- If a comparison is being made, are the same things being compared, or is the author comparing apples and oranges? For example, "The federal deficit is less than it was during WW II." Maybe so, but the fact that we were at war then and not now and that inflation has altered standards of comparison might be important factors in deciding whether the two figures are comparable.

In effect, how vague an author should be in any given piece of writing depends on a variety of things: the type of writing, the purpose for writing, how much the author knows, and how essential the exact information is to the presentation. At the same time, readers want to be aware lest vagueness leads them to take unreasonable actions.

Exercise 2

Determine whether the following are ambiguous because of careless use of words, unclear meaning (semantic), unclear use (syntactic), or vagueness. If ambiguous because of *careless use* of specific words, note the words. If ambiguous because of unclear *meaning,* note what term is ambiguous and give the two meanings of the term. If ambiguous because of unclear *use,* note what it is about the grammar that makes it ambiguous. If *vague,* note which terms are vague and tell why they are vague.

1. The wind-up, the pitch, you're outta here. (Advertisement for Northwest Airlines showing a grandmother batting a baseball)

2. 1996 Luxury Car savings rebates up to $3,600. Interest rates from 2.9 percent. Total savings up to $10,000.

3. Adam

Source: ADAM © 1995 Universal Press Syndicate. Reprinted with permission. All rights reserved.

4. Rush (Limbaugh) is right. (Bumper sticker)

5. Turn down your radio. It is too loud.

6. She told us about going to see her grandmother yesterday.

7. Advertisement showing a shiny car in the driveway. "It should look beautiful. Our engineers have spent the last 28 years polishing it."

8. Mothers very rarely need abortions to save their lives. Many women are diagnosed with mental or physical altercations, but nothing that will hinder their lives in any way after having a baby. (Student paper)

9. Frank and Ernest

Source: FRANK & ERNEST. Reprinted by permission of Newspaper Enterprise Association, Inc.

10. Anthropology: the science of man embracing women (College catalog)

11. We're going to look at lots during the Parade of Homes.

12. Mid-America Dairymen buys Borden cheese units.

13. The two United States Senators from our state are conservative.

14. A Fair of the heart (Sign at the food building of a State Fair)

15. "It's wonderful that we have eight-year-old boys filling sandbags with old women." (Larry King on the sandbagging efforts to prevent flooding on the Mississippi River)

16. Cadillac Catera: Born to zig. (Advertisement)

17. She was heading downtown to her office but got held up.

18. With Tide, my kids have a very bright future. (Advertisement showing a mom next to her daughter, who is wearing a graduation hat)

19. Even though numerous studies have shown the benefits of small school systems, they do not always do so. (Student paper)

20. It would be extremely difficult because a woman would be carrying her baby for nine months and then give it up after they conceive birth. (Student paper)

21. In cases of incest and rape, sympathizers are often quick to suggest abortion to end an unfortunate pregnancy. I propose that those abortions will create more destruction, whether the mother had a normal conception or was a victim of rape or incest. (Student paper)

22. Although some studies show the percentage of violence on the television today, there are other studies that have shown the opposite. (Student paper)

23. People who go shopping often spend a lot of money.

24. All snakes are not poisonous.

25. America's biggest doughnut company (Advertisement)

26. Chemists have solutions (Bumper sticker)

27. Notice on office wall: All employees who are not fired with enthusiasm soon will be.

28. Not allowing women who have been raped to have an abortion is the best example of a waist of tax payers' money. (Student paper)

29. John plays with toys more than Linda.

30. He said that he was a thief.

31. Tammy can't come to the phone. She's out.

32. Because of capital punishment, some criminals will kill less innocent people.

33. Three times more fudge (Advertisement)

34. Lee's answer to dress codes: Jeans you can check at the door. (Advertisement)

35. Every one needs a little comfort. (Advertisement for Comfort Liquor showing a man in a reclining chair on a beach, accompanied by a pretty woman in a bathing suit)

36. Receive the lowest prices than ever before on our biggest and best selection of magazines read by educators—up to 87 percent off. (Magazine order advertisement)

37. With the Capitol in the background, Sandra Stasenke of Fairfield, CA, holds a photo of her son Alex, who died of gunshot wounds, during a gun-control rally Monday. (*Associated Press,* October 1, 1996)

38. Let us offer this book to God triune, the effort of many hands, the fruit of artists' work, a product of ink and paper. (A church litany)

39. The IRS is correct: filing a federal income tax return does not violate your rights. However, being forced to file does. Since taxes are revolting, why aren't you? (Letter, *Minnesota Daily*)

40. If out too long, my son won't eat the cold chicken.

LAYERS OF MEANING

When attending to language, it is important to realize that language has multi-layered meanings. That is, words or phrases might have meaning in different ways. Note the different senses of the word *mean* in the following:

> Having to get up early for my class tomorrow means (implies) that I cannot stay up late tonight partying.

> A red sky in the morning means (is a sign) that we will have bad weather today.

> She did not mean (intend) to pull the chair out from under you when you sat down.

> *Rachel* means (has the etymology of, its original meaning was) *ewe*.

Although each of these is an important meaning of *mean*, here we focus on three other senses: designation, denotation, and connotation. Because a word may have meaning in all three senses and because each is different, being able to distinguish and recognize which kind of meaning is intended is important

1. Meaning as **denotation.** What a word denotes is the thing, person, characteristic, or action to which the word points or refers. The denotation of proper names is clear: it is the particular object that is named. The denotation of *thirty-fifth president of the United States* is the person John F. Kennedy. The denotation of *Sears Tower* is the tallest building in downtown Chicago. The denotation of general terms is broader; it includes all the objects or events to which the word properly applies. Whereas the denotation of *thirty-fifth president of the United States* is one person, the denotation of *president of the United States* includes all the presidents up through the most recent. *Ball* denotes many round things; *blue* denotes a particular color had by many objects. *Mowing* refers to the action of reducing the length of grass in a lawn or field. Perhaps the simplest and easiest way to understand denotation is to think about pointing. Words understood denotatively point to things, characteristics, or actions. That to which they point is their *referent*. Proper names, like *Statue of Liberty*, point or refer to specific objects; general nouns like *tree* can denote many objects; verbs like *running, thinking,* and *building* denote actions.

2. Meaning as the **designation** of the word. Designation is the sort of meaning you find in the dictionary. It is the definition of the word in terms of its essential characteristics—that is, the characteristics that something must have to be properly denoted by a specific word. For example, a brougham has the essential characteristics of being a closed, four-wheeled carriage with the driver's seat outside. This is the designation of *brougham*. If an object were not a carriage or were not enclosed, it could not be a brougham. The word *brougham,* therefore, designates those characteristics that an object must have to belong to the class of things called broughams.

The designation of a word does not refer to all the characteristics of a thing, only to those that are essential. For example, broughams have many characteristics: a particular color, a particular state of cleanliness, having a driver today, or a construction of wood or metal. These are interesting and perhaps important features of the one you may consider purchasing or riding in, but they are not relevant to the designation of the word *brougham,* for they are not essential to the object being a brougham. Hence, they do not function as part of the designation or definition of *brougham.*

3. Meaning as **connotation.** The third layer of meaning concerns the emotional content we as individuals or a community associate with the word or phrase. The connotation of a word is the characteristics that are not part of the designation but that come along with or are associated with the word. For example, what characteristics do you associate with the word *rat?* If this question were posed to a group of people, most would probably think of words like *dirty, found in garbage, carries rabies,* and the like. But suppose you had a rat for a pet. The connotations of the word *rat* would be very different: perhaps *inquisitive, has soft fur, tickler,* and so on. None of these characteristics is part of the designation of *rat,* for they are not essential for something being a rat. But they may be among the characteristics emotionally conjured up by the word. Often the connotations depend upon the experiences we have had with an object.

   The role of experiences becomes interesting when we encounter words that might be unfamiliar. Think of the connotations of *brougham.* Perhaps the word is unfamiliar to you and has no connotations. Several years ago the Chrysler Corporation bet that the word had good connotations when they named one of their car models "Chrysler Brougham." They hoped it would connote class and style and entice a certain kind of customer to purchase the car. You might think of other car and truck names—Mustang, Pinto, Seville, Sierra, Ranger, Ram, Taurus, Spirit, Breeze—and ponder what connotations these words have that would cause automobile manufacturers to give these names to vehicles to increase their marketability. Or consider the names given to fragrances—Avatar ("fragrance of possibilities"), Safari, Gravity ("the force that pulls you closer"), XS ("sensation to excess"), Curve ("see where it takes you"), Tabu, Obsession, and Vanilla Musk ("what innocence does for sensuality"). These names tell you nothing about the product but make various implicit promises for its performance.

   Connotations are important because they add richness to our language. But they are also problematic because the connotations I give to a word may differ from those you give. For me, a word may have negative connotations, while for you it may have positive connotations. So when we share words, we need to be aware of their connotations. We say more about this in the next section.

Exercise 3

Note whether each of the following statements expresses the designation, denotation, or connotation. (You may also note instances when *mean* has other meanings.)

1. planet: Mars

2. planet: a heavenly object that shines by reflected light and orbits around a sun

3. dictator: Joseph Stalin

4. dictator: a ruler possessing absolute power and authority

5. dictator: a very disagreeable and egocentric person

6. A free country is a place like the United States, Canada, Japan, or France.

7. A widow is a woman whose husband has died.

8. What I mean by setting a good example is not putting your feet on the furniture.

9. Watch her run. Then you'll know what I mean by *fast*.

10. To honor someone is to hold her or him in high regard.

11. The color red is the sexy color.

12. Caviar is a very disagreeable dish.

13. A government worker is a bureaucrat.

14. An educator is someone who preserves and transmits knowledge and culture to succeeding generations.

15. By a civil rights activist I mean someone like Martin Luther King, Jr.

16. By toothpick I mean a slender piece of wood that is used to remove food from between the teeth.

17. Happiness means having your own car.

18. A phrase is a sequence of a few words that, though not a sentence, conveys a single thought or idea.

19. Towering clouds means that it is going to rain.

20. Cumulus clouds are thick, towering clouds with a flat base.

21. By cumulus clouds I mean those to the south, over Johansen's farm.

22. A roommate is someone who is always sticking her or his nose into your affairs.

23. A hunter is someone who murders animals.

24. I mean what I say and I say what I mean.

25. An immoral act is torturing puppies for amusement.

EMOTIVE LANGUAGE

Though the designation and denotation of words are important, it is the connotations that often play a special role in communication. They can influence readers and listeners in nonrational ways, appealing to their emotions in place of reason. This special role frequently goes unnoticed, for while we concentrate on the first two senses of *meaning*, we miss the connotations because they are more subtle. Consequently, connotations deserve special attention by the critical thinker.

Consider the word *mistress*. A mistress is a woman who has power, authority, or ownership; traditionally, the mistress was the head of a house. The abbreviation Mrs. stands for mistress and connotes respect for a married woman. The word *mistress*, however, has a second meaning or designation; it can also designate a woman who is maintained by a man primarily for sexual purposes. But note the change in the connotations of *mistress*, from positive respect to looking askance at the woman's sexual role. Interestingly enough, the word *mister* does not have such dual connotations.

This illustrates how connotations can be affected by gender. A tramp is someone who is homeless; but when applied to a woman, *tramp* connotes a woman of loose morals. *Loose* applied to a man is positive—he hangs loose, is easy going, casual; but applied to a woman the term *loose* connotes the undesirable characteristic of having low sexual morals. "If a man is untrustworthy and adventurous, or if he takes sexual advantage of a woman, he is a dog; a woman who is a dog is sexually unattractive, unsuitable for dating."[1] In effect, the connotations of some words reflect a gender bias that can underlie our discourse without our being overtly aware of it.

Connotations can reflect other biases as well. Note the various terms that have been applied to and by African Americans: Negroes, Colored people, Blacks, African Americans, persons of color. Some of these convey positive connotations; others neutral or negative connotations. And many connotations are culturally based. For example, whereas for many African Americans, *Blacks* is an acceptable term, Africans would consider such a term derogatory.

Or again, note the emotive content of *bastard*. To see its emotive value, consider how different it would be to yell an epithet like "born out of wedlock" at someone rather than calling her or him a bastard; all the emotive punch is gone.

Consider the following groups of words. Note next to each word whether it has a positive, negative, or neutral connotation for you. You might think of a sentence for each row and then substitute in turn each of the words to see whether the sentence changes emotional content when you substitute different words.

smart	nerd		intelligent
woman	lady	dame	girl
adolescent	young adult	teen	minor
teacher	professor	instructor	co-learner
child	kid	youth	juvenile
borrow without asking	steal	shoplift	loot
denomination	sect	cult	
senator	politician	public servant	
nude	naked	pornographic	
patriot	nationalist	rebel	
cop	policeman	peace officer	

Although the words in the rows are not synonymous, they can at times be substituted for each other. Why, then, use one word rather than another? We often choose the word based on the emotional content we wish to convey. In doing so we recognize that language is not emotively neutral and that emotive language is a powerful communication tool.

Sometimes the appeal to emotionally laden connotations can be quite blatant. Consider the words used in this perfume advertisement.

> There is an air of insatiable desire about Shalimar. . . . Shalimar, the most exquisitely voluptuous perfume on Earth.

The words *insatiable desire* and *most exquisitely voluptuous* are used to convey emotion rather than any specific content about the perfume. Note how you would feel about purchasing the perfume if the advertisement read

> There is a funny odor about *Pungent*. . . . *Pungent*, the cheapest scent you can get in your local discount store.

The following letter to the editor dates from the Vietnam War era, but emotive language still rings throughout.

> I heard on the radio that a poll had been taken at the University of Minnesota, and that most of the votes had been given to George McGovern. It doesn't take a smart person to figure that out. A pretty good percentage at the university at both Minneapolis and Duluth are dirty-looking, long-haired kids who speak of policemen as pigs, while they themselves fit the description better. McGovern wants to grant amnesty to the slackers who turned their backs on their country, and that is why these kooks are for him.

In this letter the author uses emotive language in place of reason to explain why most university students were pro-McGovern in the 1972 presidential election.

Task

Underline the words in the previous letter that are chosen for their emotive content rather than for their strict designation. Then see if you can supply more neutral language for those underlined words. How does supplying more neutral language change the letter? Does the letter still have any "bite"?

Though some authors do not hide their emotive language, other authors and speakers use emotive language very subtly. Skilled authors can use it to convey their message without the reader really being aware of it. Consider the following effective piece.

> Five crows appeared on the lawn this morning just at the first daylight hour. Swaggering, broad shouldered fellows they were—glossy, vain, independent.
>   I went out to fetch the paper from the walk. With an indignant croak, the crows levitated onto a branch of the neighbor's maple tree, waited until the nuisance of me had disappeared, then flapped down to continue their prospecting. . . .

Why those five would stop off to spend most of an hour in a city yard I can't guess. But there they strutted, and sometimes spoke. And the coarseness of their voices alarmed the tuxedo cat who, when I came back with the paper, was waiting nervously, to be let inside . . .

Common they may be. But they are intelligent, as birds go. Handsome and able in flight, even on the ground they have a kind of sleek elegance about them.

I can never see crows near at hand without feeling a little twinge of sorrow—regret about something remembered, something that happened more than 30 years ago. Only once in a lifetime of hunting have I even aimed a gun at something I did not intend to eat.

It happened one frigid twilight during a winter I was spending alone in a woodland cabin. I'd tromped a cold hour or two looking for a squirrel for supper, but squirrels were scarce that year and I was coming back with nothing for the pan. A solitary crow, no doubt a laggard from his group, came over the trees ahead of me, black against the last lemon light. For no reason I could afterward explain, even to myself—simply with that carelessness of someone who hadn't yet had enough losses to know the value of anything—I swung the gun and fired.

It was a random, utterly purposeless thing. And I was startled when the bird spun awkwardly down almost at my feet. I remember the guilt I felt in that moment, and in the day afterward as I tried, without success, to splint and heal the broken wing and thereby earn some kind of absolution. The crow would have none of my clumsy penitence. He fixed me furiously with his amber eye. And each night, while I slept, he tore the bandage off again.

It ended badly, as such things generally do. Some wrongs are without remedy, some cruelties past mending. I buried the poor feathered thing at the edge of the cabin clearing. Even now, half a life later, I know the exact place. And while there's no redeeming so sad and pointless an affair, I believe I learned from it a young man's first lesson in the certainty of consequences.

The crows that came to my lawn this morning do not know, of course, what happened at that woods edge on an evening 30-some years ago. But I know. The past never can be entirely put behind. What we have done is part of what we are, and will be with us always—as this memory has stayed with me.

How much accumulated weight of deliberate or careless wrong is one prepared to carry? In the end, that calculation governs the decisions of life. (Charles W. Gusewelle, "The Weight of Remembrance Extends the Half-Life of a Life of Regret," *The Kansas City Star,* August 24, 1996)

What is the topic of this piece? _____

What issue does it raise? _____

What is its thesis? _____

_____

What are the main points? _____

_____

_____

As a reader, I would suggest that the topic is not crows, since the author goes beyond discoursing about crows to make a larger point. Drawing from the piece's final paragraph, the topic seems to be careless wrongs. The issue likewise is not about crows. Rather, the author generalizes from an incident that he had with a crow. The issue thus is "Do careless wrongs stay with and affect us?" Evidence that this is the issue comes from both the title and the final two paragraphs. The thesis is that careless wrongs remain with us. The author makes one main supporting point, which is to be found in the story of the senseless shooting of the crow and the regret the author feels about it. From this incident he infers a general conclusion about careless wrongs.

But where is the emotive language? It is present, but very subtly. First, consider how you feel about crows. What words do you associate with crows?

_____

_____

You might think about ugly black birds, scavengers that live off road kills, make raucous calls, dive bomb you, and raid other bird nests. Surely these are negative connotations.

But note the description of crows given by the author. Write down the

words the author uses. _____

_____

Soon you see that the author uses words that convey only positive connotations. He writes about the crows' strength, handsomeness, elegance, and independence. This subtle shift in language helps the author convey his message of regret over killing something that we might normally dismiss as being of little worth but which the author now treats as of great value. He accomplishes this change through his use of emotive, descriptive language.

Critical thinkers also realize that the emotional content attached to any particular word might not be the same for the speaker or writer as for the hearer or reader. For example, for many Germans in the 1930s, the name Hitler evoked the rise of German nationalism from the ignominious defeat of World War I; for others it brought terror and loathing. Or again, East Africans do not like the term Black applied to them, yet it is an appropriate and desired term for African Americans in the United States. It also can matter who uses the term. *Baby* used by a coach can have different connotations than when used by a boyfriend. Hence, you need to be sensitive not only to what you want to convey but also to how the hearer or reader will take what you said. It is often difficult to determine ahead of time what impact your words will have on your readers or listeners. It takes extreme sensitivity and the ability to put yourself in another's shoes. And even then, unless you receive some kind of direct and immediate feedback, the influence of your words can remain unclear.

Exercise 4

Edit the following advertisement for hair color by single underlining the word or phrase in the brackets that provides the best positive connotations and by double underlining the word or phrase in the brackets that provides the worst negative connotations.

[The absolute end of flat colors; The chance to change your hair color; Do your hair again]. Introducing the new hair color [Color-Wash; Vibrant Colors; Down-Home Color; Reuben's Colora]. Color so [multifaceted it shimmers; usual no one will notice; different it will stand out]. Crystal pure colorants. [Dark in the bottle; Undiluted and clean; Coloring that requires gloves to apply.] [Has flecks of other colors; Slightly streaked; Filled with double highlights.] For shimmering highs and lows. [Doesn't wreck or ravage hair; Easy on dried out hair; Takes your hair to the max.] For first-timers or nth timers. [Lots of different colors to choose from; A different color every week; Brilliant diversity.] The new [language; rumor; discussion] of color.

SIX WAYS TO MISUSE EMOTIVE LANGUAGE

Emotive language can be misused in a variety of ways to affect the reader or listener. We focus on six ways.

Stereotyping

To **stereotype** is to treat a person as if he or she comes out of a mold. Stereotypes are frequently used to get the reader or listener to believe that someone has a particular characteristic because he or she belongs to a particular group that allegedly has this characteristic. For example, Robinson Jefferson must be rich: after all he plays professional baseball. In this example, baseball players are assigned the characteristic of being rich, perhaps on the basis that some have very lucrative contracts, and then this characteristic is transferred to one or a specific baseball player. Or again, Sheila is just another of those crooked politicians. Here the stereotype is that politicians are crooked, and since Sheila participates in that group, the author has applied to her the same characteristic. We have a tendency to stereotype people—nerds, saggers, jocks, long hairs, teenagers, Ivy Leaguers, Italians, Mexicans, Japanese, Midwesterners, Californians, salespersons, CEOs, secretaries—and thereby fail to treat them as individuals unique in their own right.

Note that stereotypes rely upon the connotations of terms like *baseball player*, *student*, and *politician*. Only some members of the group might have the designated feature, making it grossly inaccurate to apply this feature either to the majority of people in the group or to any one person without more evidence that it is appropriate or applicable. Put another way, stereotyping involves making hasty generalizations about entire groups from small samples. This generalization is then applied to particular individuals.

Euphemism

Euphemism is the substitution of a word that has positive connotations for a word with neutral or negative connotations. Euphemisms can be used for several purposes. First, we try to avoid offending people by using words with a positive ring. For example, we euphemize bathroom functions. When a child has to defecate, we say that it has to *go potty;* for adults, we say that they have to go to the *bathroom, restroom, lavatory, powder room, little girls' room,* or *John.* (Interestingly enough, we have no neutral word for the "toilet room" where we go not to bathe, rest, wash, or powder. Even *water closet* is a euphemism). Or again, it is not polite to say that people are fat; we say they are *stout, hefty* or *husky* (if male). Clothes for big women come in *women's sizes* (as opposed to misses or junior sizes) or *half-sizes.* More humorously, we might say that people are not stupid; rather, they are a *few fries short of a Happy Meal, have too much yardage between the goal posts,* or *forgot to pay their brain bill.*

Second, we also use euphemisms when we talk about bad situations or when we want our audience to think positively about a situation that is neutral or bad. Instead of saying a person died, we say the person *passed away, passed on to his eternal rest, went to the other side,* or *kicked the bucket.* When someone dies we *lose* our friend. Persons are *laid up* when they are sick. Instead of saying that a person did something morally wrong, we say that the person *made a mistake* (thereby removing the moral dimension of the action). Instead of saying they swore, we note they used *selected choice words.* We speak about *armed conflict* rather than war, *liberation* rather than invasion, *police action* rather than military deployment, *engage the enemy* rather than fight and kill, *casualties* rather than killed and wounded.

In each case, the situation is "bettered" by providing a word or phrase with positive connotations. At times by using euphemisms we avoid saying what some may consider as offensive; at other times, as in war, it hides the grim realities and horror of the situation.

Dysphemism

In contrast with euphemisms are **dysphemisms,** which are the substitution of a word that has negative connotations for a word with neutral or positive connotations. For example, one *wastes* rather than kills. A political candidate or religious evangelist *peddles* his beliefs. A person born with a disformity is called a *freak* rather than disfigured. Dysphemisms are used to influence people to think negatively about a person, situation, or event.

Note the dysphemisms in the following paragraph on Indian casinos.

> That green-eyed monster known as jealousy and greed sat back on its haunches on the banks of the Potomac, surveyed what it perceives as its kingdom, rested those beady eyes on the Indian nations of this land, thought they would be easy pickins, and started to introduce legislation to divest these nations of their gambling dollars by adding a big (34 percent) federal tax on them. . . . (Tim Giago, "Congress Should View Indian Nations as Sovereign Peers," *St. Paul Pioneer Press,* June 23, 1997)

The author uses "green-eyed monster . . . sitting on the Potomac" in place of "Congress"; he uses "fixed its beady eyes" in place of "took note of."

Innuendo

With **innuendo,** a person makes a veiled assertion (usually negative) without directly saying what is meant. In fact, an innuendo might literally express the opposite of what is meant. The *way* it is said suggests that the meaning is other than what is stated—though the negative is not necessarily present at all. It provides the speaker with a kind of self-protection even when the meaning is clear. For example:

> It was announced recently that federal grants would help hire 14 new police officers for our city. A batch were approved for the suburban communities where I live. I'm so relieved that my garage will be less likely to get burgled if I'm stupid enough to leave it open.

The second statement is an innuendo, suggesting exactly the opposite of what it says. The author uses this language to indicate she does not feel that adding new police officers in the suburbs is a good deployment of them. We discover this fact by reading further in the editorial. "Although their needs pale in comparison to those in Detroit or St. Paul, suburban police departments have fallen all over each other to dip into the presidential pork barrel. Federal money, which might be expected to be targeted to problems too big they can't be handled with local or state dollars, is being passed out to the relatively trouble-free 'burbs.' " . . . (Debra O'Connor, "Sending More Cops to the Suburbs May Be Misguided," *St. Paul Pioneer Press*, February 19, 1995)

Here is a second example.

> [R. J. Reynolds says] it doesn't want kids to smoke. "If we believed for a minute that the camel ad induces children to smoke," a spokesperson said, "we wouldn't wait for the FTC or anyone else to act. We would immediately change the campaign."
>
> Sure.
>
> . . . The messages are not merely subliminal, they are overt. Smoking will make you all the things you want to be. But the companies say this is only to promote brand loyalty among people who already smoke.
>
> Right. . . .
>
> (Martin Dyckman, "Breaking the Camel's Back," *St. Petersburg Times,* August 15, 1993)

The words *Sure* and *Right* are innuendoes. Though it sounds as if the author is agreeing with the cigarette company spokespersons, in fact the author is very skeptical of what they are saying. The author's skepticism emerges when we recognize that he means the opposite of what he says.

Hyperbole

A **hyperbole** is a statement exaggerated to create a good or bad connotation. Though the truth is stretched beyond what the evidence might allow, the statement leads the reader to the emotional conclusion that the author desires. Perhaps you have heard an ad claiming "the lowest prices ever." If you think about such a claim, you immediately recognize that it is an exaggeration; inflation alone over the last forty years would make such a claim untrue.

Can you find the hyperbole in this example?

> The little kid was screaming at the top of his lungs. The checkout lines at the supermarket were backed up. Every human being in the greater Philadelphia area in need of 10, 15 or 20 items was standing with or next to me in the opti-

mistically named "express" lanes. (Arthur Caplan, "Research Review Finds Spanking Does More Harm than Good," *St. Paul Pioneer Press*, October 30, 1996. Reprinted by permission of the author.)

Persuasive Comparison

Persuasive comparisons compare a person, place, or thing to something else in order to persuade us that the person, place or thing has a certain characteristic. The comparison is simply assumed and given emotive content, rather than argued for. Through such comparison, negative or positive traits are thus transferred from the one thing to another without the use of rational grounds. The author in effect begs the question by assuming that the comparison is correct and banks on the emotive content in the comparison to get away with it. For example:

> Who does Ford think it's fooling? . . . Whoever came up with the idea for that itty-bitty spoiler on the Taurus' trunk should be fired! It's like an overweight woman trying to wear a thong. (Excerpted from Darrell Caraway, letter, *Motor Trend*, January 1997, p. 12. Reprinted by permission.)

Instead of arguing for his view about the spoiler, the author uses an emotionally laden comparison to make his point.

Speakers and writers use devices other than these six to convey their message emotively. There is nothing wrong with conveying a message with emotions; communication would be dull indeed if we dropped its emotive content. If "I love you" were said in a dry, matter-of-fact way, what response would it get? Furthermore, cultures differ in the amount of and manner in which emotion is embodied in communication. Nevertheless, critical thinkers watch especially for times when emotive language *substitutes for good reasons*. At such times it functions illicitly and must be carefully recognized.

Exercise 5

In the following, identify the stereotypes, euphemisms, dysphemisms, innuendoes, hyperboles, and persuasive comparisons. Note what words are responsible for these.

1. It is in the manner of football coaches that they have colorful language and mannerisms. It is also in the nature of football coaches that they have voices that can carry over the width of a football field. A soft-spoken coach would be fairly ineffective in all the noise of a football game. (*The Star News*, October 15, 1997)

2. Your weekly guide to carrion in the Cities. Vultures are birds of prey. Culture vultures are birds of art . . . long creatures hunting for something that feeds the soul. Remember, vultures eat anything, but sometimes there's some indigestion. (A restaurant review, *Pulse*, October 1, 1997)

3. A can't miss movie.

4. The latest news from Wall Street is that your stocks went south.

5. The IRS's abuse of taxpayers is not a phenomenon of recent years. It was initiated in the 1950s, when Harry Truman sicced the IRS on practically every small-business man in the United States of America. Now as then, Congress will huff and puff, but it will not blow the house down. IRS abuses have survived and grown regardless of the party in power in Washington. It is still the only agency besides the Environmental Protection Agency and Occupational Safety and Health Administration in which the burden of proof lies with the accused. To eliminate this Frankenstein monster the creators must be removed. They are members of Congress. (Roy Thatcher, letter, *St. Paul Pioneer Press*, October 16, 1997. Reprinted by permission.)

6. Hefferren says she was nauseated, dehydrated, "shaking uncontrollably" and in shock after being knocked down by a boy and his bicycle. She acknowledges that "her story will strike some readers as very mild"; in fact, it is ludicrous, almost a parody of an effete woman's introduction to reality. This hothouse flower suggests that the criminal justice system's relative unconcern with her case demonstrates society's deranged priorities. The prosecutor who declined to issue a warrant for the 12-year-old's arrest was right to ignore her posturing. (Michael Sloan MacLeod, letter, *Newsweek*, January 28, 1991, p. 8)

7. I can't believe Jack Keebler thinks this car is gonna draw a "horse laugh" from the public. That's one of the silliest things I've ever read, because that car is without a doubt one of the finest looking pieces of automotive equipment I've seen. I think Keebler's been playing with the rest of the elves for way too long. (John Carter, letter, *Motor Trend*, July, 1997, p. 12)

8. Remember growing up in your house back home? Remember walking down the stairs in your pajamas, dragging your blanket behind you. Memories are our common bond, and many of them have to do with growing up at home. Our homes are important to us; they reflect our personalities and outlooks on life. House and home go hand in hand. Yet when referred to as a living environment, a house becomes four walls with a roof on top. In an effort to remove memories, and thus prevent an emotional outburst, the administration uses neutral words like environment or residential space to distance us from the truth. At our college, houses are working environments and offices. The houses become distant and cold—eventually to the point of simply being assets on a bank statement. Since we have been conditioned to see houses as simply buildings that take up space and do not efficiently meet the needs of the college, we no longer care when houses are torn down and demolished. (Stephanie Palmquist, "Home, Shmome," *Echo*, October 10, 1997)

9. Outside of literary circles and academia, I have met no one who reads Pynchon. His notoriety must be the result of the same pretense to artistic sensibility that lets art galleries get away with selling rubbish for $25,000 simply because it's signed by an alleged artist. (Warren T. Taylor, letter, *National Review*, July 28, 1997, p. 2)

10. Norwest's Unbelievable Free Checking. Everyone's Gawking About It. You can see it on their faces. People everywhere are amazed by our brand new Unbelievable Free Checking. (Advertisement)

11. Death is nothing at all. I have only slipped away into the next room. I am I, and you are you: whatever we were to each other, that we are still. Call me by my old familiar name, speak to me in the easy way which you always used. Put no difference into your tone: wear no forced air of solemnity or sorrow. Laugh as we always laughed at the little jokes we enjoyed together. Henry Scott Holland. To place an obituary ad, please call. (*Minneapolis Star-Tribune*, October 24, 1997)

12. *Pulse* wanted to find out for its readers how El Niño might influence the weather this winter, so we approached several well-known TV meteorologists to ask if they would care to explain it in this space. Unfortunately, they scoffed at being limited to 800 words and not having any color weather maps. Plus, they wanted money. So, instead, we were able to get a recent graduate of an influential meteorology college who was willing to talk to us.

    Meteorologist: El Niño will provide recent graduates of meteorology colleges across the country with a great opportunity to find work. Personally, I expect to have an on-camera position by December, and my hair, as nice as it is, will have nothing to do with that. It will simply be because I know how to tell people about the weather. It's a gift. All my teachers told me so. (*Pulse*, October 15, 1997)

13. After a closed door meeting with 20 Black community leaders, the mayor came up with yet another ludicrous and ridiculous idea. The mayor decided to throw yet another bone to the Black community by promising to boost efforts to provide more recreational opportunities for Black youths. (James Krisimini, letter, *St. Paul Pioneer Press*, February 21, 1991)

14. A spine-squeezing mystery. Ashley Judd is irresistible. (Movie advertisement)

15. Young girls and old women, innocent and worldly, virginal and fecund. Within the walls of the kingdom on the flat plains of Texas, David Koresh knew them all—in the Biblical sense. . . . He began a decade ago with Lois Roden. She was 67 and the widowed leader of the Branch Davidians when the 23-year-old Koresh . . . arrived at the Mount Carmel compound. He confessed to the group that he worried about his excessive masturbation. . . . His next lover was at least a little bit closer to his own age. In 1984, he married Rachel Jones, the 14-year-old daughter of two followers; . . . Koresh claimed to be monogamous for two entire years. But then, followers say, God told him to build a new House of David, one with many wives, just as King David had. . . . As the years passed, the "wives" got younger and younger. Michelle Jones, 12, was his wife Rachel's little sister and, an ex-follower says, Koresh's special favorite. At least a dozen other nubile members of the flock succumbed. . . . Former followers say Koresh claimed to pick his wives for their spirituality; it was probably just a coincidence that they were all good-looking. . . . (Barbara Kantrowitz, "The Messiah of Waco," *Newsweek*, March 15, 1993, p. 56).

16. I want to begin to evaluate students at our college by comparing stereotypical examples from other small colleges. Please don't feel offended if you have a friend who attends one of these colleges. They are generalizations and

every generalization has exceptions. Chances are, though, that if they don't fit the description now, they soon will. We will begin our assessment with the neighboring College A. A student must get dressed up to attend class and must bring out the name brands of Tommy Hilfiger and Polo in order not to be shunned by classmates. A student there must drive a nice car which he or she did not pay for, but a car for which daddy paid handsomely. Most importantly, they all must adhere to the same standards and therefore act the same, talk the same and wear the same gel to slick their hair.

College B also has distinct qualities. Although not as fashion oriented, they also have an image to uphold. Their image is an "outdoor" look. Any article of clothing that screams nature is accepted. As a student at college B, you also must travel to a foreign country at least twice during your education, which of course daddy pays for also.

To define the attitude of students at our college, many people would use the term apathetic. Honestly, I agree. Most students have little school spirit, involvement and some even bad-mouth the college's name. I believe that this same apathy makes our students special. Students don't care if you don't wear the correct brand or trend of clothing. Clothing in classes can range from nice to dress pants to sweat pants. Students don't think twice about seeing someone still in their pajamas and unshowered in their morning class. Students also don't care if you drive a 1985 Mercury Topaz or a 1997 Honda Civic. Wheels are wheels at our college, even if they are on your roller-blades. (Tracey Glumich, "In Search for Identity," *Echo*, September 26, 1997).

17. Generations of Americans have been brainwashed with psychological and psychiatric theories that identify the individual as the source of many problems that are basically social in origin. (Harry Specht and Mark E. Courtney, *Unfaithful Angels* (New York: Free Press, 1994))

18. I'm as puzzled as everyone else over here about the American habit of seeking advice on every aspect of one's private life. In England, we thrive on our own inhibitions; they're all we can truly call our own. Among the English, it's considered self-pitying to air difficulties, but Americans are unembarrassable. They tell their whole life story on the air. They'll invite a camera crew into their toilet out of a general feeling of openness. ("Unembarrassable," an interview with Martin Amis, in "How the World Sees Us," *New York Times Magazine*, June 8, 1997, pp. 44–5)

19. The MX-3. Suspension lets it change direction quicker than a politician in an election year. Plus a fold-down rear seat that is widely rumored to be more spacious than some Manhattan studio apartments. (Advertisement)

20. The renovation of University Village is another stop in the Disneyfication of Seattle, where real-life merchants are eliminated to make way for stores that cater to a fantasy life that is enjoyed by only those in a certain economic sector. Just last month I had occasion to visit University Village. It was not a success. I needed a book, socks, a small kitchen knife and a bit

of hardware. The only bookstore to be found is a behemoth that drives locally owned independent stores out of business. I found the clothing stores boutiques lacking the basics. The kitchen store is equipped with expensive gourmet items, and the only hardware store still standing is a bric-a-brac filled Coppery. Real life doesn't resemble this place, indeed. Seattle doesn't need more playpens like University Village for the yuppies and Microsoft millionaires. Seattle needs real-life merchants who are struggling to save for a down-payment on a house, education for their children and maybe (if they are successful) even their retirement. (Name withheld by request, letter, *The Seattle Times*, October 24, 1997. Reprinted by permission.)

Exercise 6

Here are two editorials that exemplify emotive uses of language. First determine the topic, issue, thesis, and main points of the following editorials. Then underline the words chosen specifically because of their emotive content and identify them according to the six types that were explained on pages 128–131. Finally, replace the words with other words that have a more neutral meaning and note what happens to the editorials.

A. Tonya Harding competed to represent the United States in the Olympics as an ice skater. Her husband and bodyguard were convicted of attacking and injuring one of Tonya's competitors; Tonya denied involvement and was not tried. This editorial appeared after Tonya's ex-husband circulated a picture of Tonya, topless in a wedding dress, to the media.

Tonya Flashes Her Fascinating Facets to Media

First of all, it was a pleasure to see the Brat with her clothes on. In fact, I almost didn't recognize Tonya Harding when she appeared fully attired in front of the media Friday. The topless wedding dress must have been at the cleaners.

Her days as the Trailer Park Temptress from Hell apparently behind her, however, the Brat is attempting to undergo a metamorphosis. Or perhaps she simply is molting. In any event, just when we thought we had seen it all, so to speak, Harding is trying to come across as:

A) Tonya the devout Christian;
B) Tonya the devout patriot;
C) Tonya the devout humanitarian. . . .

"I am very upset and I am ashamed," she said of the infamous home video that supposedly was sold to the show by her ex-husband. "I'm embarrassed. If everyone could put themselves in my position, how would you feel?"

Not so good. Especially if I picked up a London Sun and saw naked photos of myself while I was trying to eat eggs in the morning. The British tabloid did not bother to "digitalize" Tonya the way the TV show did. It simply showed her in all her glory. . . .

Tacky, isn't it. Admit it, folks. You can't get enough of the Brat. You know it's true. People are fascinated by the hard-as-nails little ice queen, who now is doing her best Shirley Temple.

The Brat sat in front of the world Friday flanked by her Kewpie doll coach, Diane Rawlinson, and two members of the United States Olympic Committee. Rawlinson was amazing, grinning like an idiot even through the most tragic inquiries.

Asked about the death threats Harding has received, the ever-smiling Rawlinson said, "We really can't worry about death threats. The Lord has a master plan. If it is meant to be, it is meant to be." . . .

"God has helped me take care of half of my problems," Tonya said.

It's a miracle!

One minute she is hanging out with thugs and screwballs, the next she is having out-of-body religious experiences. Amen, sister. You are saved. Go and club no more.

Then there was Tonya the devout patriot, who talked lovingly of all her American Olympic teammates in Lillehammer. "And I'd like to say congratulations to Dan Jensen," she announced, cheerfully.

I'm sure Dan was thrilled. Just a scant two hours after finally shedding his loser image, it seemed unlikely he would want to be associated with the Harding brood. Nothing to be gained there. It would be like winning the top prize and then looking into the TV camera and shouting: "I'm going to Three Mile Island!"

The Brat also let it be known that she agreed to stay away from the opening ceremonies at the request of team officials. Anything for the good of the team. . . .

Well, when an athlete is suspected of plotting to injure her rival, shows up naked on television, fires off pistols in a parking lot and hangs around with all manner of human debris, the media does tend to overreact.

And finally there was Tonya the humanitarian. After mentioning how she has sold her story to another TV tabloid show, . . . the Brat said she really wasn't going to profit from it. After paying legal fees and such, she was going to use the money to do good. . . .

So there you have it. Just another all-American girl getting ready to compete in the Olympics. What's all the fuss about?

"I have a great deal of respect for Nancy (Kerrigan)," Tonya added. "We met briefly and had a positive conversation. It's private."

That nasty little maiming incident seems nearly smoothed over.

"A lot of Americans have their own opinions," the Brat said. "I feel like I'm lucky to be here and I thank God. I just want to be treated fairly. I need to be strong and follow my Olympic dream and win the gold. "When it is over, I can sit down and cry."

It's all so . . . morbidly fascinating. (Tom Powers, "Tonya Flashes Her Fascinating Facets to Media," *St. Paul Pioneer Press,* February 19, 1994)

B. This editorial comes from a college newspaper.

Political Correctness Hindrance to Liberal Arts

Two New York University freshmen from two different small towns in Nebraska experience the huge metropolis for the first time:

Student #1: Hey dude! Look over there by the fountain.

Student #2: Oh sick! Two guys kissing in public! Why I never . . .

Student #1: Know what we call those types back in my town? We call them heaters.

Student #2: Well I just think they are a couple of faggots myself.

A Stranger: Hey, that's rude! Those people are not faggots, nor are they heaters. The term is homosexual, you homophobic jerks. Besides, they are human beings anyway.

Does this situation sound familiar? Who is wrong in this situation, the students or the stranger? For the politically correct pity-providers, the "homophobic" attitudes of the students are at fault. They will tell you that for a long time homosexuals have been oppressed by the "evil" heterosexual community. Such use of derogatory terms like "faggot," "dyke," "homo" and "queer" are the signs of an ignorant and hateful society.

So if words like "faggot" are derogatory, what category do the labels "homophobic" or "bigot" fall under? The pity-providers will tell you that these terms represent the truth of people like the two students. These same people must subscribe to the theory of "two wrongs make a right," so the latter two terms are not considered derogatory . . .

In an article on political correctness in the March 18, 1991, issue of "National Review," University of Chicago professor of sociology James S. Coleman states: "Academics are dedicated to pursuing truth. But not all truths are politically correct." Believe it or not the same type of thinking has infiltrated our college campuses. Is it not the mission of a liberal arts college to give an individual a well-rounded education so they may become well-rounded students? If we are to pursue what we believe to be true, should we do so without reservation or coercion from the new oppressive governing authorities of academia? Do individuals have the right to question professors' views that differ from their own? . . .

A few weeks ago a professor told the class that the term papers should contain inclusive (politically correct) language. For example, the term "man" should not be used when we refer to humanity. I told him that "man" is a general term for referring to human beings and he should not require the class to do this because it would affect our academic freedom and our pursuit of truth. The professor along with a few Lola Granola feminists then tell me that I am not living in the 20th century and that I should wake up and smell the coffee.

After using selected colorful metaphors to get my opinion across, I am disappointed that the rest of the students in the class did not speak out because they are fed with types of milk-fed liberal, narrow minded, idealistic rhetoric. . . .

We should express our beliefs and debate with our professors without fear if we are to pursue what we believe to be true. This is what a liberal arts education is all about. If it is not, the mission we are pursuing will have been in vain. (Matt Mirmak, "Political Correctness Hindrance to Liberal Arts," *Echo*, April 26, 1991)

BIAS-FREE LANGUAGE

We have suggested that language can convey a great deal more than what appears on the surface. Sometimes what it conveys is what is intended, as in the editorials in Exercise 5. The authors there used language to shock, perhaps even to offend. But other language conveys things that we often do not even recognize. In fact, authors might not think that it conveys or connotes anything in particular, while for readers it might signal a great deal. Consider the following letter.

The Aug. 9 paper reported a crime that had taken place. A man had cut through the screen door of a woman's apartment in an apparent attempted burglary. The man stabbed and raped the woman who lived there. The story was tragic enough, but listen to how the investigating sergeant told it: "He confronted her and she was sexually assaulted. She was stabbed and there was some choking."

Why not say, "He confronted her, he sexually assaulted her, he stabbed her and he choked her." That wording has an entirely different sound to it now, doesn't it? It sounds like a man committed a heinous crime against a woman, rather than the weak description that used the passive voice, allowing the subject of the verbs, 'raping and stabbing and choking,' to escape responsibility.

I hope and pray that we catch this man and bring him to trial. And when we try him for this crime, that we will place the responsibility and the spotlight where it belongs, on the subject of the verb, not on the person to whom these horrible things were done. It's bad enough being the victim of a crime without having our language work against us in our call for justice. (Anne Dimock, letter, *St. Paul Pioneer Press,* August 20, 1996. Reprinted by permission.)

From the point of view of the latter writer, the investigating sergeant focused on the woman rather than on the criminal. The letter writer took the sergeant's passive language as subtly suggesting that possibly the woman was at fault, or if not at fault, at least was at a place where she should not have been. To the letter writer, the language spoke volumes, volumes that were probably not intended by the sergeant.

Bias, also often unintentional, can likewise appear in the use of gender-based language. Though traditionally it has been grammatically proper to use *man* in the generic sense to refer to humanity and *he* as a pronoun referring to all persons (whether male or both male and female), in the last two decades women have pointed out that male gender language conveys a subtle bias against women. They have suggested several remedies, all of which are geared to avoiding obvious gender-biased language.

Undoubtedly the best remedy for gender-biased language is to avoid it altogether. Here are several suggestions.

- In place of *man*, use terms like *human, humanity,* or *people.*
- In place of *he* or *she* to refer to all people, put the pronoun and what it modifies in the plural. That is, talk about *they* or *them.*
- If you must use the singular, *one* or *person* often works. If you are really stuck, use *he or she.* Using *she* generically can be as offensive (and misleading) as using *he* generically.

In using the plural you must be careful, for a plural pronoun must refer to a plural noun. So it is not proper to write, "The college student is in a awkward position with their new-found freedom," "If someone is sick, don't bother them," or "Each person has the right to say what they want." The pronouns *their, them,* and *they* have no referent. We could supply *his, him,* or *he* respectively in the sentences, but that introduces gender-biased language. The best way to rewrite these sentences is to use the plural: "College students are in an awkward position with their new-found freedom," "Don't bother people who are sick," or "People have the right to say what they want."

- Use gender-neutral terms when speaking about occupations or positions that could be staffed by members of both genders and whose gender at the time you are speaking is unknown. Chairman→chairperson or chair; fireman→firefighter; policeman→police officer

- Avoid stereotyping your characters, giving men masculine roles and women feminine roles or characteristics. Women can play excellent hockey and men can make good homemakers.

The point is not to introduce new rules and prohibitions, but to be aware of the subtleties of language and its effects on the listener. Though using male or female terms generically may not bother you, it may offend another. Avoiding gender language is, at the very least, a matter of politeness. But more than that, it expresses sensitivity to the changing gender roles in our society.

Collaborative Learning Exercise

The following letter suggests that language can convey subtle biases. How does the author suggest that language can convey a bias? Defend whether or not she is correct. Can you think of a similar example?

> Does sex matter? In science, as perhaps in sex, it is the questions that matter. Thus the question "What contributions have women made in science that a man could not have made?" may be the wrong question. Why not ask, "What contributions have men made in science that a woman could not have made?" It is, of course, the male culture of science that conditioned [the author of the article] to ask the question he did.

In speaking to science students, I often pose the following experiment. Listen carefully as you say, "There is no science problem that has been solved by a man that could not be solved by a woman." Then say, "There is no science problem that has been solved by a woman that could not be solved by a man." Do they mean the same thing? And the students often answer, "No"; the first seems to say that a woman scientist can be as good as a man. In contrast, the second seems to say that women solve only simple problems, which of course a man could solve.

[*Source:* Vera C. Rubin, letter, *Science* (August 13, 1999), p. 1013. Used by permission.]

SUMMING-UP

In these last two chapters we pointed out that comprehension—making the material your own—involves paying close attention to language, which is the foundation for our communication. We have focused on basic constituents of comprehension—statements—and discussed ambiguity and the sensitive use of language. Critical thinkers realize the importance of language and attend closely to it. We now move on to the fourth step of critical thinking, analysis.

Notes

1. Elaine Chaika, *Language: The Social Mirror* (Boston: Heinle & Heinle, 1994), 367.

ANSWERS TO THE EXERCISES

Answers to Exercise 1

1. Syntactically ambiguous on *include*: does it modify *baking* or *cookies?*

3. Semantically ambiguous on *belted:* put in seat belts or beat with a strap

5. Semantically ambiguous on *joins:* goes to live with parents or puts the parents together in Siamese fashion

7. Syntactically and semantically ambiguous on *strikes:* noun (an action of labor union) or verb (hitting)

9. Syntactically and semantically ambiguous on *left:* verb (to leave something) or noun (political position); and *waffles:* noun (a food) or verb (is uncertain in its position)

11. Semantically ambiguous on *case:* where you keep a violin or a legal proceeding

13. Syntactically and semantically ambiguous on *lies:* verb or noun (untruths)

15. Syntactically and semantically ambiguous on *shot off:* noun with preposition (the ball bounced off her leg) or adjective (her leg was shot off her body)

17. Syntactically ambiguous on *after death:* is it their own death or the death of a co-worker?

19. Semantically ambiguous on *by:* an action taken by the tree or indicating a location

21. Syntactically ambiguous on *for second time:* does it modify *sentenced* or *die?*

23. Semantically ambiguous on *holds up:* delays or supports

25. Syntactically ambiguous on *larger:* does larger refer to the size of persons studied or size of group?

27. Syntactically ambiguous on *dead:* noun (dead persons) or verb (failed legislatively)

29. Syntactically ambiguous on *dropouts:* refers to individuals or the rate of departure from school

31. Semantically ambiguous on *Air head:* head of aviation sector or someone who simply does not have it all together

33. Semantically ambiguous on *blocked by board:* the executive board refused to allow the window or wood was put there to restrict access

35. Semantically ambiguous on *of:* parts of the person or belonging to the person

Answers to Exercise 2

1. Semantically ambiguous: the pitch could be as in baseball or as in an advertisement pitch. *You're outta here* can mean that you struck out or that you are flying away (preferably on Northwest).

3. Syntactically ambiguous: The boys misunderstood what *it* referred to: the furniture rather than the game.

5. Vague: How loud is *too loud?*

7. Semantically ambiguous: *Polishing* can mean improving it or making it shiny.

9. Semantically ambiguous: *Alone* can mean by itself or by yourself.

11. Semantically ambiguous: *Lots* can mean much or pieces of real estate.

13. Vague: What is it to be conservative?

15. Semantically ambiguous: *With* can mean along side of or using.

17. Semantically ambiguous: *Held up* means delayed or robbed.

19. Syntactically ambiguous: to what does *they* refer?

21. Syntactically ambiguous: does *conception* refer to the mother's conception or that of the fetus?

23. Syntactically ambiguous: *often* can modify *shopping* or *spend.*

25. Syntactically ambiguous: Does *biggest* modify *doughnut* or *company?*

27. Semantically ambiguous: *fired with enthusiasm* can mean excited or relieved of their job enthusiastically.

29. Syntactically ambiguous: the comparison is unclear—comparing his playing with toys rather than playing with Linda, or his playing toys with Linda's playing toys.

31. Semantically ambiguous: *out* can mean asleep or out of the house.

33. Vague on *three-times.* You do not know what is being compared.

35. Semantically ambiguous: *Comfort* can mean ease or a particular brand of liquor.
37. Syntactically ambiguous: *during a rally* could modify *holds* or *died*.
39. Semantically ambiguous: *revolting* can mean disagreeable or rebelling against authority.

Answers to Exercise 3

1. Denotation
3. Denotation
5. Connotation
7. Designation
9. Denotation
11. Connotation
13. Connotation
15. Denotation
17. Denotation
19. Meaning here is understood in the sense that one thing is a sign for something else (called signification): the clouds are a sign of rain.
21. Denotation
23. Connotation
25. Denotation

Answers to Exercise 5

1. Stereotype of football coaches
3. Hyperbole (*can't miss*)
5. Dysphemism (*sicced*); persuasive comparison (Congress with the Big Bad Wolf; the IRS with Frankenstein)
7. Either dysphemism or persuasive comparison—*living with the elves too long*
9. Persuasive comparison (artistic sensibility of those who appreciate Pynchon with art galleries that sell trash)
11. Euphemism (*slipped away into the next room*)
13. Dysphemism (*throw another bone*)
15. Dysphemism (*nubile, succumbed*); innuendo (*knew them all, worried about his excessive masturbation, a little bit closer to his age, claimed to be monogamous, just a coincidence they were good-looking*)
17. Dysphemism (*brainwashed*)
19. Persuasive comparison (*politician*). Hyperbole (*more spacious than some Manhattan studio apartments*)

Answers to Exercise 6

A. Topic: Tonya Harding
   Issue: Is Tonya Harding a sincerely good person?
   Thesis: No, she is a hypocrite.
   Main points:
   1. She claims to be a devout Christian.
      a. She invokes the name of God.
      b. She says God helps her with her problems.
      c. Then she hangs out with criminals.
   2. She's acting like a devout patriot.
      a. She commends Dan Jensen.
      b. She stays away from the opening ceremony for the good of the team.
      c. Yet she has character flaws.

3. She's acting like a humanitarian.
    a. She uses her money to do good,
    b. yet she smoothes over the clubbing incident.

Innuendo: It was a pleasure to see the Brat with her clothes on; I almost didn't recognize Tonya Harding when she appeared fully attired; The topless dress must have been at the cleaners; metamorphosis (insect); molting (snake), Anything for the good of the team; Just another all-American girl; it's a miracle.

Dysphemism: Brat; Temptress from Hell; Harding brood; grinning coach; human debris; morbidly fascinating

Hyperbole: ever-smiling.

Euphemism: fascinating facets; in all her glory

Persuasive comparison: hard-as-nails little ice queen; Shirley Temple; Kewpie doll; like an idiot; Tonya the devout patriot; nothing like winning the top prize and going to Three Mile Island

Stereotypes: thugs and screwballs; devout Christian; devout patriot; devout humanitarian

CHAPTER 6

Analysis

Distinguishing Types of Discourse

Whatever you read—a paragraph, an editorial, an article, a chapter in a book, or a book—has been written for a specific purpose. The purpose may be to inform the reader about persons, places, things, or events; or it may be to persuade the reader or hearer of the truth of a thesis. To fully understand what is written or said, you need to identify that purpose. Once the purpose is identified, you can proceed to better analyze what the author has written.

Consider the following editorial, whose use of innuendoes we sampled in Chapter 5.

> That green-eyed monster known as jealousy and greed sat back on its haunches on the banks of the Potomac, surveyed what it perceives as its kingdom, rested those beady eyes on the Indian nations of this land, thought they would be easy pickins, and started to introduce legislation to divest these nations of their gambling dollars by adding a big (34 percent) federal tax on them. The federal government (the House of Representatives and the Senate), in its infinite stupidity, often tries to find easy solutions to difficult problems by placing unfair burdens upon those least able to defend themselves.
>
> Yes, there are several tribes making huge profits from their casinos, but these tribes make up only 5 percent of the total and this 5 percent takes in 80 percent of all casino dollars. Most tribes use the profits from their casinos to fund social programs on their reservations. They use the money to build homes, schools, businesses, hospitals, provide retirement benefits and scholarships and more.
>
> Does the federal government levy a 34 percent tax upon the casinos in Las Vegas or New Jersey? These casinos are for-profit enterprises that turn most of their profits over to stockholders and individual owners. Their profits are not used to fund social programs that would benefit their state governments.
>
> Is the federal government considering levying a 34 percent tax on the state lotteries? Most of the answers are "no," because the government considers state governments to be sovereign. If the lawmakers would read the Constitution, they would find that the men who drafted that document considered the Indian nations to be sovereign as well.

Congress cannot continue to stomp upon the rights of the sovereign Indian nations of this continent with impunity. The National Indian Gaming Regulatory Act was a congressional mess from the word "go" and continues to be the fly in the ointment of the Indian nations. It was passed without the full approval of the Indian nations and was thrown together without a lot of input from the very people who would most be affected by it. But then, that's the way Congress has always acted and reacted to the problems and solutions of the Indian nations. I would venture to say that no more than 15 percent of the Congress have even a smidgen of knowledge as regards the Indian people. They learned about the Indians from the non-history books written by non-Indians using their own image as a guideline. As the old saying goes, history is written by the victors. . . .

It is high time every member of Congress took out a copy of the Constitution and read Article I, Section 8. It reads, "Congress shall have the power to regulate commerce with foreign nations and among the several states, and with the Indian tribes," which points out that Indian tribes enjoy the same rights and protection of foreign nations and state governments. When Congress decides to enact laws affecting Indian nations, it should do so with full cooperation and input of the tribal presidents, councils, governors and chairpersons. Indian nations should be accorded the respect and consideration offered to state governments.

With this tool in hand, it is time for the leaders of the Indian nations to challenge the Indian Gaming Regulatory Act, an act passed without full consideration and input of the Indian nations, and have it rewritten with their full cooperation. Congress must stop looking at Indian nations as helpless wards and victims, and consider them equal partners as sovereign nations. (Tim Giago, "Congress Should View Indian Nations as Sovereign Peers," *St. Paul Pioneer Press,* June 23, 1997)

What is Giago's

Topic? _____

Issue? _____

Thesis? _____

Main Points? _____

_____

_____

Giago wrote this editorial for a particular purpose. Is that purpose to inform or to persuade? _____

His article contains a carefully crafted argument to persuade the reader to accept his thesis. Thus, to understand what he is saying, you need to see that he is writing an extended argument and find that argument.

In this chapter we look at different ways authors attempt to inform or to persuade. Our emphasis is on persuasion and the arguments constructed for that purpose. We focus on arguments because since critical thinkers want to discover whether what is said is true, they need to identify the evidence or grounds someone has for thinking it is true. This evidence allegedly supports the conclusion, and, as we shall see in Chapters 10 through 12, is what we attend to when we evaluate the claims people make.

THREE TYPES OF INFORMATIVE DISCOURSE

Sometimes the author or speaker intends to *inform* the readers or listeners about something. In the following sections we look at three types of informative discourse: description, comparison, and explanation.

Description

Often the informative purpose is realized by giving a description. For example,

> The band of Hutu rebels stormed into a Tutsi refugee camp, chased down screaming women and children and butchered more than 300 of them with guns, machetes, spears and clubs. Their work done, the marauders set fire to the camp. Last week, stunned survivors rummaged through the ruins in a miserable attempt to recover charred remains of still-smoldering bodies. . . . (Excerpted from Stefan Lovgren, "Burundi's Trail of Fear," *U.S. News & World Report,* August 5, 1996, p. 44B. Copyright, 1996, U.S. News & World Report. Visit us at our web site at www.usnews.com for additional information.)

Descriptions tell us what things are like around us. In one sense, they reside at Bloom's first step, knowledge, because they provide basic information to the reader or listener. However, more sophisticated descriptions can push us to the higher step of analysis, where authors or speakers analyze something with the intent to inform. For example, they might break down a scene or situation into its component parts, classifying the parts in a way that fits the point they are making or that leads the reader or listener to observe the scene or situation in a specific way. Since descriptions are always selective, focusing on some items while ignoring others, they can reflect some conscious or unconscious communicative purpose or view of things that critical thinkers want to discern.

Descriptions, however, do *not* present reasons in favor of the truth of the statements made; rather, what they describe is presented as a given—something for the reader or hearer to accept that does not need defense.

> Raskolnikov did not sit down, but he felt unwilling to leave her, and stood facing her in perplexity. This boulevard was never much frequented; and now, at two o'clock, in the stifling heat, it was quite deserted. And yet on the further side of the boulevard, about fifteen paces away, a gentleman was standing on the edge of the pavement; he too would apparently have liked to approach the girl with some object of his own. (Fyodor Dostoyevsky, *Crime and Punishment*)

In this passage Dostoyevsky describes a scene in which the novel's hero figures. Though the statements in the paragraph relate to each other, *none of them depends on another for its truth.* Each stands on its own merits.

Descriptions play an important role in our lives. Specifically, they provide background data that critical thinkers can use in evaluation. There is one feature of descriptions, however, that merits attention, and that is the use of emotive language to get the reader or listener to go beyond comprehension to make a value judgment about what is described. We looked at emotive language at the end of Chapter 5, but its importance in affecting readers is worth reemphasizing.

Note the words used in the Hutu example: *screaming women, butchered, marauders, charred remains, still-smoldering bodies.* The writer of this description has not only analyzed the scene for readers but has carefully chosen language that leads readers to evaluate the alleged actions of the Hutu and perhaps the character of the Hutu themselves.

Here is a second example of the way emotive language functions in a description.

> Readers inclined to take [Eric von Däniken's] gospel with a grain of salt as large as Lot's wife will fly in the face of some 14 million other readers who have harkened to the intriguing theories of a 38-year-old Swiss hotelier, iconoclast, school dropout and ex-convict named Eric von Däniken. . . . Von Däniken, whose style and method combine elements of Carlos Castaneda, Ripley's "Believe It or Not" and "Star Trek," followed up with "Gods From Outer Space" and is ringing up more sales on another mind-boggling book, "The Gold of the Gods." . . . (S.K. Oberbeck, "Deus ex Machina," *Newsweek,* October 8, 1973, p. 104).

In this review of von Däniken's books, what seems like a mere description is heavily loaded with emotive language. Note the persuasive comparison—*grain of salt as large as*—and the emotive language used in the description of the author—*hotelier, iconoclast, school dropout, ex-convict.* Note also the persuasive comparisons with Carlos Castaneda (who wrote books dealing with drug induced experience), Ripley (who wrote *Believe It or Not*), and the space fantasy *Star Trek.* The language of the description is designed to bring the reader to a negative evaluation of von Däniken's books without providing a reason for this evaluation. Thus, to repeat a theme from Chapter 5, critical thinkers should be aware of the emotive content of what they read and hear, even when it appears to be only a description, so that they are not misled into giving evaluations where the author has strictly given only descriptions and no arguments.

Comparison

A second kind of informative discourse that more directly involves Bloom's step of analysis is comparison. How was President Lyndon Johnson similar to President Franklin Roosevelt? Compare the situation of African Americans in the South before the Civil War with that of Africans in South Africa before the end of apartheid. Note the similarities and differences between union and nonunion shops. Contrast RNA with DNA. Show why Willie Mays was a better center fielder than Mickey Mantle. In responding to these instructions, you are asked to conduct a careful analysis of two or more things, noting the ways in which they are similar and different.

Perhaps from tests you have taken or papers you have written you are familiar with questions asking you to compare. Directives to compare require you to go beyond mere knowledge, which identifies what you have learned. They ask you to go beyond comprehension, where you put things in your own words. They push you into analysis, asking you to take what you comprehend and rework it to show the relationships that hold between the items being compared. Some might argue that comparison can even push you on to synthesis, where you are forced to see new and creative relationships that were not evident when you learned the information you are now asked to integrate.

How should you go about responding to a question or directive that asks you to compare things? Since comparison requires you to go beyond simple comprehension, you need to do more than merely present a paragraph on topic X (President Lyndon Johnson) and another paragraph on topic Y (President Franklin Roosevelt). Giving separate paragraphs on each topic shows that you have some comprehension of X and Y. But as yet you have not done what was asked: to compare. You left that task for your reader.

The important thing to note about comparing X and Y is that your topic is less about X and Y directly than about the *characteristics* of X and Y. That is, X and Y are being compared *in terms of their features,* not simply in and of themselves. This is another reason why writing separate paragraphs about X and about Y is a mistake.

You can do a comparison in several ways. One way is to write one paragraph on the similarities between X and Y and another on their differences. This process allows you to integrate X and Y, but it is rather uninteresting. It simply lumps together all the similar characteristics in one paragraph and all the different characteristics in another, much like pouring salad ingredients into a bowl and mixing them.

A more interesting and effective way of writing a comparison is first to list the characteristics that X or Y possesses and then to note whether both X and Y have these characteristics and whether they have them in similar or different ways. To carry this out,

- Make a chart with the persons, things, or events to be compared in a row across the top.
- Down the left column list the characteristics of these persons, things, or events you might want to consider.
- Group the characteristics according to the features they have in common. This will make your subsequent writing task easier, for you can then write separate paragraphs on each of these groups.
- Note how the items compare with respect to these characteristics. Do they have them, not have them, have them somewhat, or have them in different ways?

Here is an example comparing two sports.

Characteristics	Football	Baseball
The equipment:		
ball:	oblong	round
uniforms:	helmet, pads, cleats	batting helmet, cleats, gloves
other:	goal posts	bases
The field:		
size:	100 × 300 ft.	about 350 × 350 ft.
shape:	rectangle	fan-shaped with an inner diamond
Rules for play:		
for scoring:	1, 2, 3, 6 points	individual runs
moving the ball:	thrown, carried, kicked	thrown, batted
player motion:	after ball is snapped	after ball is batted

Undoubtedly you can think of many other similarities and differences between football and baseball. No matter how many you identify, the first task is to list the characteristics and note their presence, absence, or adaptations in the various sports. After this is accomplished, you can write several paragraphs, organizing each paragraph around one of the groups of characteristics you identified: a paragraph on equipment, one on the fields, and a third on the rules. You as the author of the comparison can now note what is *significantly* similar or different about the two sports; you do not leave the task for your reader. Actually doing the comparison demonstrates that you know more than each sport individually; you actually see *relationships* between the sports, relationships that were probably not spelled out originally but that you have now made explicit through your comparative analysis.

Indeed, to turn implicit relationships into explicit relationships is the very function of comparisons. To make the relationships explicit, you need to analyze the things being compared so that you can choose those items or characteristics worthy of comparison. Again, however, comparison does not involve arguing; you present or describe the items but do not contend for the truth of the comparisons. To contend for the truth, you would have to construct an argument.

Exercise 1

1. Compare two things, persons, or events. Begin by constructing a list of their relevant characteristics. Then write a page noting how these characteristics are similar or different in the two things you are comparing.

2. The following exercise presents the nutritional value of various fast food meals. First note what meals you want to write about and construct a list of their relevant characteristics. You have to be selective in the information you use. Then write a two-page paper as a report for this magazine, presenting an informative comparison of fast food meals. ("Fast Food: Eating Fast, Eating Healthy." Copyright, 1997, by Consumers Union of U.S., Inc., Yonkers, NY 10703-1057. Reprinted with permission from *Consumer Reports*, December, 1997, p. 14.)

Eating fast, eating healthy
Lessons to help you choose a lean meal

Below are pairs of meal options—what we call a "lean" meal and a "large" meal—from Burger King, McDonald's, Wendy's, and KFC. Each pair contains a mini-lesson in nutrition. To put the numbers of calories, fat, saturated fat, and sodium in perspective, keep in mind these government recommendations: A person who eats 2000 calories a day should aim to limit total fat intake to about 65 grams, saturated fat to 20 grams, and sodium to 2400 milligrams. In parentheses below, we've included the percentage each meal contributes to the daily value (DV), to show you how close each meal gets to that daily target quota.

Less is less (Burger King)

No burger is truly lean, but the *Whopper Jr.* is a good compromise for portion control: It's more of a mouthful than a regular hamburger or cheeseburger, but not as big as Burger King's flagship sandwich. And it even tastes just as good as the *Double Cheeseburger with Bacon,* which has an extra 15 grams of fat. Ask for no mayo and you'll save 9 grams more, reducing the *Whopper Jr.'s* total fat to 15 grams. Choosing a salad as a side dish is a good policy, but only if you watch how you dress it. The reduced-calorie Italian is also fairly low in fat; a packet of ranch or blue cheese dressing, on the other hand, has more fat than an order of onion rings (though fewer calories).

Whopper Jr.: salad, reduced-calorie dressing; orange juice
   635 calories
   28 g. fat (43% DV)
   10 g. saturated fat (50% DV)
   945 mg. sodium (39% DV)

Whopper with Cheese; onion rings; medium vanilla shake
   1340 calories
   66 g. fat (102% DV)
   22 g. saturated fat (110% DV)
   2390 mg. sodium (100% DV)

Go grilled (McDonald's)

Simply by avoiding the fried items in the large meal here, you can get about the same amount of food but less than half the calories and one-fifth the fat. You can shave 12 grams of fat and 240 calories off the large meal choosing a small order of fries. But be aware that you can also add up to 21 grams of fat and 180 calories to the lean meal by substituting a packet of regular salad dressing for the fat-free one. The two sandwiches were served with the same condiments and roll, but the fried coating on the *Crispy Chicken Deluxe* provided an interesting texture to the sandwich—when it was, indeed, crisp. (Half the time, our expert found it soggy). Of course, frying adds fat.

Grilled Chicken Deluxe; salad, fat-free dressing; lowfat milk
   515 calories
   9 g. fat (14% DV)
   3 g. saturated fat (15% DV)
   1435 mg. sodium (60% DV)

Crispy Chicken Deluxe; large french fries; large Coke.
   1290 calories
   48 g. fat (74% DV)
   8 g. saturated fat (40% DV)
   1460 mg. sodium (61% DV)

Watch the toppings (Wendy's)

With this lean option, you can spoon some of the chili onto the baked potato instead of piling on butter or margarine (7 grams of fat per packet) or sour cream (6 grams of fat per packet). Just how important are the toppings you choose? Consider that a *Bacon & Cheese Baked Potato* has nearly as many calories as the *Big Bacon Classic* burger—though the latter has 12 grams more fat. The chili (which isn't included in our Ratings and costs $1 a serving) tasted pleasant, though not terribly special, with a moderately strong tomato flavor and typical chili spices. The beef was dry and without

continued

Eating fast, eating healthy
Lessons to help you choose a lean meal continued

much flavor; the vegetables were almost minced rather than chopped.

Small chili; plain baked potato; iced tea
520 calories
7 g. fat (11% DV)
3 g. saturated fat (15% DV)
825 mg. sodium (34% DV)

Big Bacon Classic; large frosty
1150 calories
47 g. fat (72% DV)
21 g. saturated fat (105% DV)
1790 mg. sodium (75% DV)

Choose light, make it lighter (KFC)
You're already ahead of the game if you start with roasted rather than fried chicken. Strip off the skin, and you'll just about cut the fat in half again. Note also that light meat is somewhat less fatty than dark. Happily, *Tender Roast* is not only more healthful—it tasted better than *Original Recipe,* which had a flavorful but oily coating. (We didn't try *Tender Roast* without the skin.) As for side dishes, any-

thing with a mayonnaise-based dressing—for example, cole slaw or potato salad—will add heavily to the fat total. KFC offers a number of low-fat choices, including collard greens (or "Mean Greens," as the colonel calls them) and Red Beans and Rice.

Tender Roast breast without skin; Mean Greens; Red Beans and Rice; medium Diet Pepsi
369 calories
10 g. fat (15% DV)
3 g. saturated fat (15% DV)
1807 mg. sodium (75% DV)

Original Recipe breast; cole slaw; potato salad; medium Pepsi
1010 calories
47 g. fat (72% DV)
10 g. saturated fat (50% DV)
1983 mg. sodium (83% DV)

(Although this material originally appeared in Consumer Reports, the selective adaptation and resulting conclusions presented are those of the author and are not sanctioned or endorsed in any way by Consumers Union, the publisher of Consumer Reports.)

Explanation

A third kind of informative discourse, which also can involve analysis, is explanation. Consider the following cartoon.

For Better or For Worse® by Lynn Johnston

Source: FOR BETTER OR FOR WORSE. Reprinted by permission of United Features Syndicate, Inc.

In this cartoon El wants an explanation for why she still has the same bulges in her hips despite all the exercise she gets. Connie's explanation for this involves a pun (ambiguity of meaning) on "lard" (Lord): "The lard works in mysterious ways."

Explanations are informative discourse in that they tell us *why* something happened. They provide an *account* for what happened in term of the alleged *causes* of the effect. As with the previous forms of informative discourse, the author analyzes the situation (here in terms of cause and effect) but does not argue for the truth of the claim about the causal relationship. The author merely asserts that something is the cause of some effect.

Here are some other examples of explanations.

- She sued for divorce yesterday because her husband ran off with another woman and the car.
- Skim milk has less fat than whole milk because the fat has been processed out of it.
- Simon got an A on the test because he stayed up all night studying.
- The Yankees will win the World Series because they have so much money from their television market to purchase premium free agents.
- She swerved across the road and ran into the tree because she had a severe heart attack.
- The reason why potato chips aren't good for you is that they have so much fat.
- She explained why she opened the door to the burglar by telling the police that the man showed her what looked like a police badge.

In each of these examples, circle what is *given* (what is known, namely, the effect) and underline the *explanation* presented to account for the given (the suggested cause).

There are different kinds of explanations; let us look at two that are worth mentioning and distinguishing. First, **physical explanations** appeal to some natural cause to account for the event.

- Heat causes the mercury in a thermometer to rise.
- She has difficulty breathing because she has asthma.
- A rock cut a slice in the sidewall, making my front tire go flat.
- His tent collapsed when the bear tripped over the cord and pulled out the stakes.
- After the tornado went through his farm, he no longer had a barn.
- The reason my tomatoes are not growing is that it is so dry.
- The heavy snow pulled down the electrical wires, shutting down my computer.

These examples invoke various physical conditions as causes of the effects: features of the weather like snow and wind, physical objects like rocks, and health conditions like asthma. We frequently look for explanations of this type in areas where we employ the tools of the natural sciences—physics, chemistry, biology—and technology.

A second kind of explanation—**psychological explanation**—appeals to mental causes such as purposes, desires, beliefs, intentions, reasons, or motives to explain why we do something.

- In order to attract the attention of the referee who didn't see she was hit in the face by the soccer ball, she fell to the ground.
- Like President Truman, the President campaigned from the back of a train because he wanted to identify with the common people.
- Lacking the motivation to read the material and study, he failed the test.

Psychological explanations address the question of what causes us to behave in a specific way. We frequently ask for this type of explanation when we want to understand why someone did something. For example, the City Council voted to install new sewers because it believed that leaks in the old system were polluting the lake. Its belief about the old system caused the Council to vote as it did.

As you might expect, physical explanations are more amenable to scientific exploration than psychological explanations. Although they are not always successful, scientists attempt to formulate laws that govern natural events. Often the goal is to quantify the causal relationship by expressing it in a complex mathematical formula. Even if we cannot formulate any physical law to cover the relation between cause and effect, in our daily life we rely on the physical regularity between the cause and effect to act. You might not be able to formulate mathematical laws governing the flow of water and water pressure, but you rely on the causal relationships that hold between opening the spigot and filling your sink with water.

Psychological and sociological explanations are more difficult to formulate in precise laws because human behavior so greatly varies. Hence, social scientists who deal with psychological explanations resort to more general statements of the relation of psychological causes and behavioral effects, using statistical analyses to present laws covering these relationships. Although often these relations cannot be quantified as precisely or easily as physical relations, social science analyses are no less important than physical science analyses for understanding our world. Indeed, since we spend so much of our time, energy, and attention interacting with people, psychological and sociological explanations are critical to our own personal development and our involvement in society.

Exercise 2

In the following statements, first identify what is being explained (the given, which is the effect) and the proposed explanation (the cause). Then note whether the explanation is physical or psychological.

1. The Federal Reserve Board has not reduced interest rates because it does not want to fuel inflation in the economy.

2. Why are there no fish in Lake Wabasso? It is a shallow lake that completely freezes in winter.

3. The Russian teacher explained to the Academic Dean that the reason the number of students taking Introductory Russian declined was that the class was scheduled at the same time as a very popular soap opera.

4. Dustin uses a weight belt when he lifts weights so that he does not get a hernia.

5. After a long investigation into the operations of the Burton Frozen Food Company, it was determined that the two deaths were caused by tainted

containers of ice cream. Investigators also determined that the ice cream was tainted when the milk used to produce it was delivered by trucks that had been used to transport eggs and that had not been properly sanitized.

6. [The Dead Sea Scrolls contain a] provocative rewrite of the story of Abraham's near sacrifice of his son Isaac. In the traditional Bible, God commands Abraham to sacrifice Isaac. At the last second, an angel stays Abraham's knife and points to a ram trapped in a thicket as a substitute sacrifice. The biblical tale . . . has always posed a difficult theological question: How could God tempt Abraham to slay his son? The Qumran text . . . attempts to "soften the blow of God's action" by introducing a Satan figure, called Mastemah or "prince of malevolence," who goads God into the test. God thus does not originate the evil but merely countenances it and permits Abraham to prove his faithfulness. . . . (Jeffery L. Scheler, "The Reason God Tested Abraham," *U.S. News & World Report,* July 7, 1997, p. 71. Copyright, 1997, U.S. News & World Report. Visit us at our website www.usnews.com for additional information)

7. Recently small explosions hurled hot "rock bombs" a kilometer or more into a nearby settlement. This energetic behavior is consistent with the scientists' conclusion that the rising magma [in the volcano] is now moving upward more rapidly. . . . (David Schneider, "Awaiting the Big Bang?" *Scientific American,* January 1997, p. 31)

8. It's a scientific fact. A child naturally learns a language far more easily than an adult does. In Europe, kids commonly learn a second language at the same time as their first—in early childhood. Why? Because it will never be as easy again. (Advertisement)

9. Wizard of Id

Source: By permission of Johnny Hart and Creators Syndicate, Inc.

10. Shoe

Source: SHOE © Tribune Media Services, Inc. All rights reserved. Reprinted with permission.

11. Marmaduke

Source: MARMADUKE. Reprinted by Permission of United Features Syndicate, Inc.

12. After examining 81 fossils of trilobites that had obviously been bitten, Loren Abcock and Richard Robison of the University of Kansas found that 73 percent of the animals had been attacked on their right flank. . . . Some suggest that the trilobites caused the bias by habitually curling up in a way that exposed their right flanks. Others argue that the finding simply means that trilobites had fewer vulnerable organs on the right and, so, were more likely to survive an attack from that side. (28th International Geological Congress, "Right Bite on Trilobites," *Science Digest,* April/May 1990, p. 51)

13. I take it that you are in love, or have been, or think you might be in time. . . . And since you go to the trouble to seek an expert opinion, you must value the investment of emotion and the creative effort you have put into your relationship. Intimacy matters to you. (Peter Kramer, "Should You Leave?" *Psychology Today,* September/October 1997, p. 40)

14. NGC 891 [a spiral galaxy in Andromeda] has astronomers scratching their heads. . . . [A photo] shows so many [dust] streamers above and below the [galaxy] plane that researchers were surprised at their find. They conclude it is unlikely that supernovae alone could have propelled the galaxy's tremendous network of murky clouds into place. . . . They hypothesize that perhaps some gentler processes, such as the pressure of starlight, have "polluted" NGC 891's inner halo with dust. . . . ("A Dust-Choked Spiral," *Sky and Telescope*, November 1997, p. 57)

15. All 70 of the gender disturbed boys were found to be normal physically and the more completely evaluated boys were found to be normal physically, with the single exception of one boy with one undescended testicle. No evidence was found for maternal hormone treatment during pregnancy nor were there any histories of hormonal imbalance in the mothers. In these cases, therefore, the social environment of child-rearing is primarily implicated in the psychosexual disturbance. (George Rekers, "Gender Identity Disorder," *The Journal of Human Sexuality*, 1996)

PERSUASIVE DISCOURSE: ARGUMENTS

A second purpose of communication is to persuade. Authors want to persuade their readers about the truth of particular ideas. Advertisers attempt to persuade consumers to purchase their products. Prosecutors argue to persuade the jury that the accused is guilty, while on the other side the defense attorneys counter to convince the same jury that the accused is innocent. Politicians desire to persuade the electorate to vote for them while perspective employees strive to persuade employers to hire them. The kind of discourse more frequently used to persuade is the argument.

Often we use the word *argument* with negative connotations. For example, "Scott had an argument with his girl friend." Here *argument* refers to a kind of verbal battle between two persons. Used in this sense, *argument* has negative connotations. These kinds of arguments often are to be avoided because they fail to provide effective communication; rarely are they persuasive enough to resolve the problems among people.

We use *argument* in another, more neutral, way. An **argument** is a form of reasoning in which one draws a conclusion based upon particular pieces of evidence. Arguments involve making an *inference* from one set of claims (the premises) to another (the conclusion). The premises are believed to provide evidence for or some reason to believe the concluding claim. For example:

> Vitamin E can lower heart-disease and cancer rates—and works even better, new findings suggest, when taken with vitamin C. A nine-year study . . . polled more than 11,000 people age 67 and over about vitamin use. Those who took vitamin E supplements—separately, not in a multivitamin—had 34 percent fewer deaths from any cause than those who took none. Vitamin C alone had no effect on mortality. But subjects who took both vitamins had 42 percent fewer deaths. Researchers didn't track doses, but vitamin E capsules typically contain at least 100 IUs, and daily doses of up to 800 IUs are not toxic. (Excerpted from "Newswatch: C Plus E Equals Longer Life," *U.S. News & World Report*, August 19, 1996, p. 62. Copyright, 1996, U.S. News & World Report. Visit us at our web site at www.usnews.com for additional information.)

In this example, the author claims that when taken with vitamin C, vitamin E can lower risk of heart-disease and cancer. The evidence for the truth of this claim is found in the study the author reports.

Arguments consist of statements. We noted in Chapter 4 that statements are assertions that are either true or false; they are expressed by complete sentences or sentence fragments. Arguments serve to *rationally support* or provide evidence for some opinion or belief. *To support a claim is to give reasons for thinking that a claim is true.* People may argue for their own benefit, either to confirm what they already believe or to find out the truth about something. People may also argue to rationally persuade another to their opinion.

The evidence that we use to support the thesis is called the **premise.** The premise is what the author of the argument already accepts as true or less in dispute. Someone else might not agree with this evidence, but at this stage of our analysis whether or not someone else agrees is beside the point. We are not evaluating the argument, only trying to recognize and analyze it.

The statement that is drawn or inferred from the evidence is called the **conclusion.** The author of the argument believes that the conclusion is more in doubt than the premises and hence uses the premises to support or provide evidence for the conclusion. Put another way, the author believes that the conclusion follows from the premises.

Here are two examples of simple arguments.

> If there are cookie crumbs all over the floor, Molly must have eaten a cookie while I was out. There are cookie crumbs all over the floor. So Molly must have eaten a cookie while I was out.

The truth of the claim that Molly must have eaten a cookie is supported by the evidence of the cookie crumbs on the floor.

> All Scandinavians are blonde. Ingmar is a Scandinavian, so he must be blonde.

Here the truth of the claim that Ingmar is a blonde is inferred from the claims that he is Scandinavian and that all Scandinavians are blonde. Again, our concern is not about the truth of the universal statement that all Scandinavians are blonde, which is not true, but about the connection between this universal statement and what is believed to follow from it *if it were true.*

There are several important things to note in constructing a good argument.

- In a good argument, the premises must be different from the conclusion.

Probably you have been in an argument where someone tried to support or defend his or her conclusion by sneaking the conclusion into the premises. A person may do this blatantly by simply repeating the conclusion or else by saying the conclusion in different words so that it is not so obvious what the arguer is doing. In Chapter 11 we will see that this is an example of a bad argument (a fallacy called *Begging the Question*).

You might note how the following advertisement for a passion fruit juice aptly illustrates the failure to differentiate the conclusion from the premise. The advertisement shows two women sitting after sunset at a table drinking margaritas while in the background a man in an office works at his computer. "Cathy and Rita could have stayed late at work and looked really dedicated, but that would have entailed staying late at work and looking really dedicated."

- The arguer must consider the premises to be more obvious than the conclusion. We reason from the more to the less obvious, from the more known to the less known.
- The premises must be relevant to the conclusion and provide enough evidence for us to infer the conclusion from them.

Consider this example of an advertisement that uses both relevant and irrelevant reasons for purchasing an automobile.

> The Rabbits of Lahaska, Pennsylvania. It's true. Meet Peter Rabbit. His wife, Bunny Rabbit. Their son, Jay Rabbit. And their brand-new Volkswagen Rabbit. Now when we read about them in the newspaper, we couldn't wait to ask the big question: "What was it that got you to add another Rabbit to the family? The 38 miles to the gallon? The incredible acceleration? The handling ease? The head and leg room inside of some mid-size cars? "It was all those things" answered Peter Rabbit. "Plus something I've been fond of for 14 years," added Bunny. "What's that?" we asked. "My last name," she smiled.

In this example Peter's response—"all these things"—is appropriate, for many miles per gallon, acceleration, and handling ease are relevant considerations in purchasing a car. But Bunny's (humorous) response would indicate a bad argument, for the name of the car would normally not be a relevant reason for purchasing a car.

Or consider a shoe ad, in which a woman dressed in a white sun suit sits on a dock and holds a shoe to her ear. The ad simply says:

> If you listen very carefully, you can hear the ocean. Bass shoes.

If one considers this an argument for purchasing a specific brand of shoes, it appears to be a very poor argument, for the reason given (you can hear the ocean if you hold the shoe to your ear) is quite irrelevant to the purchase of a particular brand of shoe (or perhaps to the purchase of any shoe). Arguments where the premises are irrelevant to the conclusion are bad arguments; they commit what is called the *Fallacy of Irrelevance*.

We will look at other features of good arguments in Chapters 10 through 12, features that are necessary to avoid bad reasoning. But for starters, remember that the premise must be different from, yet relevant to and more obvious or more known than the conclusion, when you construct arguments in favor of a position.

Locating Arguments

To evaluate an argument, you must first find it. The best way to find the argument is first *to identify the conclusion* and then search out the reasons or evidence given for it. People sometimes have difficulty distinguishing the premises from the conclusion. They tend to confuse the two, treating the conclusion as the premise and the premise as the conclusion. Unless you can distinguish the conclusion from the premise, you will miss the point of what is written or said, for the *conclusion of the argument is often the thesis of the paragraph or article.*

Since the thesis is what the author wants to say, it is the most important feature and hence worthy of support or defense.

How do you find the conclusion? Here are several suggestions.

- Location

As we have noted, the thesis of the paragraph, section, or article often is the conclusion. In a well-written paragraph, the thesis generally is either at the beginning or at the end or both. For example:

> When the city reconstructs our street next fall, it should not widen it. I live on a hill and my current driveway is very steep where it connects with the street. If the city widens the street, my driveway will be so steep that I will scrape my tailpipe and bumper on the asphalt, ruining my car and gouging the new street. Keep the street that same width!

The thesis in this paragraph is "The city should not widen the street when it rebuilds it." This is expressed in both the first sentence (the *topic sentence*) and in the final sentence. You might wonder about the final sentence, since it expresses a command. As we noted in Chapter 4, a command often can be translated into a statement; here: "You should keep the street the same width." Though what is lost is the emotional content (note the exclamation point), the assertion underlying the command is retained.

- Logical indicator words.

While many of our words have meaning, other words have a function. Some words have functions that help us identify premises and conclusions; we call them **logical indicators.** They are like road signs through the material you are reading or writing. Imagine that you have to get from your town to a town in another state to which you have never traveled. Suppose there are no road signs between your town and that town—no route signs, no direction signs, just roads. You can imagine how difficult it would be to get to that town; you would have to be stopping continually to ask directions.

Signs are important in communication as well. They help the reader through what you write and the listener through what you say. They indicate what you treat as premises and as conclusions in your reasoning. The more you use these road signs, the clearer your communication is. At the same time, however, overuse of logical indicators makes for very boring writing. So you have to find a middle ground in using them: enough to give clarity to what you write; few enough to avoid repetition and make what you say interesting.

Some words are called **premise indicators;** the statement that *comes after* these words is a reason for a conclusion. For example, "You should vote for the current office holder because he has been in Congress for many years and holds a high office on the Appropriations Committee." The premise indicator here is the word *because.* What comes after the word *because* is the premise, which is why *because* is called a premise indicator.

No standard order exists to determine the relation between premise and conclusion. In our example the conclusion precedes the premise; *because* in this sentence is like glue holding the conclusion together with the premise. But other orders are equally possible. Consider this example: "Because the current office holder has been in Congress for many years and holds a high office on the Appropriations Committee, you should vote for him." *Because* still functions as a premise indicator because the premise for the conclusion still follows it. Here, however, the conclusion follows the premise. To repeat, there is no set order for relating the premise and conclusion; in one context the premise comes before the conclusion; in another context it comes after the conclusion. But in either case, what comes immediately after the premise indicator (with no punctuation in between) is the premise.

Here are some other examples of premise indicators.

"Since Freon damages the ozone layer, it should be banned."

"Freon should be banned, for it damages the ozone layer."

Since and *for* function as premise indicators because the premise that provides evidence for the conclusion follows each of them. The following list of premise indicators is not meant to be complete. You should add to it as you find other examples in your reading.

PREMISE INDICATORS

because	for	since
as	given that	assuming that
for the reason that		

Other words function as **conclusion indicators.** What directly (with no punctuation in between) *comes after* conclusion indicators is the conclusion. For example, "The current office holder has been in Congress for many years and holds a high office on the Appropriations Committee; therefore you should vote for her." What comes after the word *therefore* is the conclusion. Here is an incomplete list of conclusion indicators to which you can add.

CONCLUSION INDICATORS

therefore	so	hence
thus	entails that	implies that
follows that	consequently	whence
it must be that	for this reason	that is why
why _____ ? (in a question form)		

You already use premise and conclusion indicators without thinking about them. For example, perhaps your mother asked you why you were out so late, and you said "Because." You didn't want to give the reason, so all you gave was the indicator. Of course, if your mother was wise, she said that *because* is not a reason and pressed you for a reason. But although people use indicator words without much thought about their function, critical thinkers are very much aware of them and use them to organize their presentations for the sake of clarity.

Indicator words are so useful that sometimes without even knowing the content of the statements we can discern the pattern of the argument just by looking at the indicator words. For example,

♦ "Because x, y; therefore z." Here x is a reason for y, and y is a reason for z.

Or again,

♦ "Since w and x, y. So z." Here w and x are reasons for y, which in turn supports (provides evidence for) z.

Sometimes, however, the structure is vague, and we definitely need content. For example,

♦ "Because of w and x, y since z." What is unclear is whether w and x support (provide evidence for) z, which in turn supports y, or whether w, x, and z all are used to support (provide evidence for) y.

Since our language contains an indefinite number of structures, it is impossible to list them all. The important thing is to look for these indicator words and to note how they function. They will guide you through even the most difficult arguments.

You should not be misled by the mere presence of words like *for, because,* and *since.* They do *not* always function as logical indicators. Two caveats must be noted. *First,* people can misuse indicator words. For example, an acquaintance of mine has the habit of describing some event over the phone, like running into a deer with his car, and then saying, "So, that's the story from here. " The word *so* here does not indicate a conclusion but simply links ideas or puts an end to the story. In sum, though the presence of an indicator word provides good reason to think that the person is presenting an argument, it is not conclusive evidence.

Second, because our language is complex and varied, the same words may have different meanings or functions in different contexts. In the case of logical indicators, you need to carefully distinguish among their respective functions.

Consider the word *since. Since* is a premise indicator when what follows *since* supports or gives evidence for a thesis. "Since he is seven feet tall, we have to heighten the doorways in his house." But *since* also can be a time word. "I have been here since 5 o'clock this morning." Five o'clock this morning is not the reason I am here; the statement merely notes the time I arrived.

Similarly, *for* can be a premise indicator: "Lions should not be made into household pets, for when they become adults they are temperamental and dangerous animals." But *for* can also function as a preposition: "She has been here for three hours." Or again, "He bought the tool chest for thirty dollars." Neither "three hours" nor "thirty dollars" provides a reason for anything else in these examples.

The word *because* is also tricky. At times it can function to indicate a reason; "You should go to the store because we are out of milk." At other times— as we already noted in this chapter—it functions in an explanation to indicate the cause of an event. "Our basement was flooded because the copper pipe had a hole in it." In this example the speaker is not arguing the truth of the claim that the basement was flooded and giving the hole as evidence for it, but rather is attempting to explain the cause of the disaster.

In short, just as the same symbol can have different meanings—*lead* can mean a metal, to conduct, what you put in a mechanical pencil—so the same symbol can have different functions. Critical thinkers pay attention to the context to determine whether the word is functioning as a logical indicator or is serving a different function.

Here is a third way of locating the conclusion

- Analyze the *content* of the paragraphs

Throughout this book we have stressed how to find the content: find the topic, the issue, and then the thesis. The thesis should be the main conclusion, while the main points provide the evidence for the conclusion. The main points themselves are often conclusions of the paragraphs in which they are found. Careful reading helps you find these components of the argument.

You might have noted in this suggestion a bit of circularity. How do we find the thesis? It is the conclusion of the argument. How do we find the conclusion? Look for the thesis. The circularity is there because the thesis and the conclusion are often the same statement. Knowing this fact helps you identify the conclusion, thesis, or main point of the paragraph or section. *Once you discover this relationship, you can work backward to find the evidence given in support of the thesis or conclusion.*

Testing for Premises and Conclusions

Since not all passages contain logical indicators, once you find what you think are the conclusion and the premise(s), you can temporarily put a logical connector between them *to see whether the connection makes sense.* Although this procedure provides no guarantee that you have correctly identified the premise and conclusion, it helps you not to reverse or confuse the two. Your common sense often tells you which statement is most obvious (the premise) and which statement needs argumentative support (the conclusion). For example,

- The prison guards lined up the prisoners, handcuffed and beat them; the guards responsible should not only be relieved of their duty but prosecuted for their crime.

Since this sentence lacks logical indicators, we can supply them to see what makes better sense.

- The guards responsible should not only be relieved of their duty but prosecuted for their crime [*because*] the prison guards lined up the prisoners, handcuffed and beat them.
- The prison guards lined up the prisoners, handcuffed and beat them [*because*] the guards responsible should not only be relieved of their duty but prosecuted for their crime.

The first sentence makes sense; the second one does not. Once we supply the indicator it often becomes obvious which statement is the premise and which is the conclusion.

Exercise 3

For each argument, (1) circle any logical indicators and tell whether they are premise or conclusion indicators. (2) Underline the conclusion; double underline each premise. (3) Where there are no logical indicators, supply them to test your belief about which statements are premises and which are conclusions. Note that not every statement functions as a premise or conclusion. You need to separate out descriptive material from argumentative material. Some paragraphs may not express an argument.

1. The university should be able to beat its rivals because it offers more football scholarships than they offer to attract better players.

2. Seventeen people have showed up for our Green River raft trip, so we have to find a third raft.

3. I hope I'm not doing the wrong thing in throwing out all these old school papers. The kids just might need them next year to review.

4. The fact that people have depended on their future Social Security benefits to carry them through retirement is a good reason for Congress not to alter the current Social Security system in a way that would reduce benefits.

5. Either the campus police do not detect parking violations, in which case they are incompetent, or they do but don't ticket them, in which case they are corrupt. Not much of a choice.

6. Reduced to unemotional basics, when a person decides to purposefully murder another, that is a choice he or she has made. So, understanding that a death penalty exists for such an act, those who commit it consciously choose death for themselves. This is not a profound or complicated idea. But it makes it clear that we each have to take responsibility for our own actions. (Darrell Hare, letter, *U.S. News & World Report,* July 7, 1997, p. 4. Reprinted by permission.)

7. Instead of piling overkill upon overkill, why not start now with a [nuclear] freeze? . . . A nuclear freeze can give the two great powers breathing room before they rush into a nuclear future that may threaten the future itself. It can halt new technologies that will be dangerous and destabilizing. (Edward Kennedy, *Congressional Record,* 98th Congress)

8. Since no man has any natural authority over his fellow men, and since force is not the source of right, conventions remain as the basis of all lawful authority among men. (Jean-Jacques Rousseau, *The Social Contract*)

9. Some species of trees have been 'read out of the party' by economics-minded foresters because they grow too slowly, or have too low a sale value to pay as timber crops: white cedar, tamarack, cypress, beech, and hemlock are examples. In Europe, where forestry is ecologically more advanced, the non-commercial tree species are recognized as members of the native forest community, to be preserved as such, within reason. (Aldo Leopold, "The Land Ethic," *A Sand County Almanac*)

10. "This earthquake is not a new thing," replied Pangloss. "The town of Lima suffered the same shocks in America last year; same causes, same effects; there is certainly a vein of sulfur underground from Lima to Lisbon." (Voltaire, *Candide*)

11. We consider that the whole universe is animated, and that all the globes, all the stars, and also the noble earth have been governed since the beginning by their own appointed souls. (William Gilbert, *On the Magnet*)

12. Do not the wicked do some harm to those who are ever closest to them, whereas good people benefit them? And does the man exist who would rather be harmed than benefited by his associates? Then do you accuse me here of corrupting the young and making them worse deliberately? (Plato, *Apology*)

13. Rationality is a fine and useful tool, but it is just that—a tool, one way of analyzing matters. Equally valid, perhaps more so, is intuitive, instinctive awareness. We can become more cognizant of ultimate truths by sitting quietly in the wild than by studying in a library. Reading books, engaging in logical discourse, and compiling facts and figures are necessary in the modern context, but they are not the only ways to comprehend the world and our lives. Often our gut instincts enable us to act more effectively in a crisis than does careful rational analysis. (Dave Foreman, *Confessions of an Eco-Warrior*)

14. I do not think that, practically or morally, we can defend a policy of saving every distinct local population of organisms. I can cite a good rationale for the preservation of species—for each species is a unique and separate natural object that, once lost, can never be reconstituted. But subspecies are distinct local populations of species with broader geographical ranges. (Stephen Jay Gould, "The Golden Rule—A Proper Scale for Our Environmental Crisis," *Natural History*, September 1990, p. 26)

15. Depending on one's point of view, [Peter] Larson is either the worst culprit or the most egregious victim in these bone wars. "Public lands belong to us all, and fossils tell our prehistoric past," argues Richard Stucky, chief curator at the Denver Museum of Natural History. "We have a responsibility to be good stewards of this national heritage, and the primary concern should be science and education, not dollar values." . . .

   Michael Triebold, a respected dealer who sells specimens to museums and private collectors, says more fossils are destroyed by erosion than are ever recovered. He insists most for-profit dealers have strong science backgrounds, do good fieldwork, and provide a valuable service. "Fossils are not going to wait for the politically correct person to find them," he says. . . . (Excerpted from Michael Satchell, "Dinosaur Bone Wars: Should Dealers Be Allowed to Sell Fossils They Have Found on Public Lands?" *U.S. News & World Report*, August 26, 1996, pp. 43–4. Copyright 1996, U.S. News & World Report. Visit us at our web site at www.usnews.com for additional information.)

DIAGRAMMING ARGUMENTS

We now come to the hardest part of recognizing arguments, namely, identifying the structure of the argument in the context of ordinary discourse. Critical thinkers need to understand how arguments are constructed so they can better evaluate them.

One way of identifying an argument's structure is to construct a flow chart of the argument. This is a fancy way of saying that we can discern the argument structure by diagramming the argument. Diagramming provides a way to see how the argument is assembled. To accomplish this, we use the basic format where

> P stands for the premise,
> C stands for the conclusion, and
> the → shows the direction of the reasoning from
>   premise to conclusion.

So, for example, in the argument "We should not throw rocks over the cliff because hikers may be below us," "hikers may be below us" is the premise (P), and "We should not throw rocks over the cliff" (C) is the conclusion. We diagram the argument:

$$P \rightarrow C$$

Since what is written may contain many statements, first number the statements presented. Then use these numbers to construct the diagram. In our example, we label "We should not throw rocks" as 1 and "hikers may be below us" as 2. Thus, we visually represent the reasoning as follows:

$$2 \rightarrow 1$$

To make it easier, let us begin with the *steps* to successful diagramming.

1. Number the statements (not the sentences).
2. Circle the logical indicators. These guide you through what you are analyzing.
3. Find the main conclusion. If the piece is well written, the main conclusion is at or near the beginning and/or at the end. It may also be preceded by a conclusion indicator.
4. Using the logical indicators you have identified, work backwards from the conclusion to the first premise. Where no indicators are given, supply your own to make sure that the connections you suggested make sense.

We can note four important things about diagramming paragraphs.

- Number the statements, not the sentences.

We noted earlier in this book that the sentence is the vehicle that communicates statements. One sentence can contain several statements, and it is statements that play the crucial role in arguments. Hence, since arguments are composed of statements, each statement should have its own number.

- Number the statements consecutively from the beginning of the piece to the end.

This does not mean that your diagram will be numbered sequentially, with the lower numbers always leading to the higher numbers. It would be nice if the numbers proceeded sequentially from low to high because this would make the argument easier to follow. But since not everyone argues in an orderly fashion, you cannot predict whether the diagrammed argument will follow a pattern of consecutive reasoning.

- You might not use every number in your diagram.

If you numbered every statement, your numbering probably includes statements that are informative and hence not part of the argument. Also watch for initial statements in paragraphs that introduce a topic, issue, or thesis but then are followed with contrast words like *but,* indicating that the author takes a different direction than initially employed in the paragraph. (We spoke about such structures in Chapter 3.) Since these statements are not part of the author's own argument but are those of another or express common opinion, they can be ignored.

- Sometimes the same statement appears more than once.

For example, the same statement (though put in different words) may appear both in the topic sentence and in the concluding sentence of a paragraph. You may either assign the two statements different numbers (and note in the diagram that they are the same) or assign the statements the same number.

Four Types of Argument Structures

There are many variations of argument structures, but let me note four basic types. Learning the names might help you recognize these fundamental argument structures.

The first type is a **conjoint argument.** In this type of argument, the author gives one or more premises to support or provide evidence for the conclusion. Where more than one premise is presented, these premises work in conjunction with each other to yield the conclusion.

For example, "Since (1) today is Tuesday, (2) it is almost noon, and (3) on Tuesdays I play racquetball at noon, (4) I should be heading toward the gym." In this argument, all three premises work conjointly to support the conclusion. One can see that they work conjointly because *if one of the premises is false, the argument fails.* We diagram conjoint arguments as

$$1 + 2 + 3$$

$$\downarrow$$

$$4$$

This is a good time to point out the function of connector words like *and, moreover,* and *also.* These words are *not* logical indicators, but they usually indicate that the statements they connect function on the same level. If one statement is a premise, the statement connected to it by words like *and* is probably also a premise. If one statement is a conclusion, often so is the other. The word *but* can also function in this way, although more often it is a contrasting word, separating what follows from what comes before.

Here is a second example of a conjoint argument. "(1) You should not vote for Martha because (2) she is over 60." Here 2 → 1. This is a conjoint argument because the argument contains an assumed premise: (3) you should not vote for people over 60. If we add this assumed premise to our diagram, putting it in parentheses since it is assumed, we get

2 + (3)

↓

1

A second kind of argument structure is the **converging argument.** In arguments of this type, two or more premises are given as evidence for the truth of the conclusion, but the premises *function independently* of each other. If one premise is false, the other can continue to provide evidence for the truth of the conclusion. In effect, the author provides two separate arguments for the same conclusion. You can observe this effect by noting that the two premises address different topics.

For example,

> (1) Capital punishment is appropriate in cases of first degree murder, for (2) the killer has deprived an innocent victim of his or her life. (3) It also serves as a deterrent to society, warning others what will happen if they commit similar acts. Finally, (4) capital punishment gives relatives of the victim a real sense of justice in that the murderer has paid with his or her own life for the life taken.

In this argument premises 2, 3 and 4 support 1, but each premise addresses a different topic. Premise 2 deals with retribution for murder; premise 3 indicates that punishment serves as a deterrent, and premise 4 identifies the concern about justice for the victim. If 2 were false, 3 and 4 would be unaffected and could still provide separate arguments for the conclusion. Likewise if 3 were false, 2 and 4 could be used to construct an argument for 1. We diagram converging arguments as follows:

2   3   4

↓ ↓ ↓

1

This kind of argument differs from the conjoint argument in that there are three separate arguments for the same conclusion. *Each arrow symbolizes a separate argument.*

A third kind of argument structure is the **diverging argument.** In this argument one premise leads to two conclusions. You might wonder how this could be, and the visualized structure is a bit misleading. But what happens is that the given premise works with two different, assumed premises to yield the two conclusions. For example,

> (1) The first sergeant has been found guilty of stealing from the unit's payroll. (2) He should be required to repay what he has stolen and (3) given a dishonorable discharge.

Our diagram for this argument looks like this:

1
↓   ↓
2   3

The assumed premise that leads from 1 to 2 is that (4) people found guilty of stealing from their unit's payroll should be required to repay what they have stolen. The assumed premise leading from 1 to 3 is that (5) people found guilty of stealing from their unit's payroll should be given a dishonorable discharge. Two different arguments are given for two different conclusions; it is just that they share one premise. Thus, a fuller diagram, using the assumed premises 4 and 5, would look like this:

1 + (4)   1 + (5)
  ↓   ↓
  2   3

You can see that since 4 and 5 are different premises, although they share premise 1, they produce different conclusions.

A fourth argument structure is the **serial argument.** In this argument the conclusion of one argument becomes the premise for a subsequent argument. Thus, a chain of arguments unfolds. For example:

> (1) Jeff lost his job last week, so (2) he should not be required to make the payments on his new truck. Consequently, (3) you can repossess his truck if you don't penalize him.

The ultimate conclusion is that (3) you can repossess his truck if you don't penalize him. The premise supporting it is (2) he should not be required to make payments on his new truck, and the reason for this is that (1) he lost his job last week. We can diagram the argument as follows:

1
↓
2
↓
3

This serial argument contains two separate arguments: 1 → 2, and 2 → 3. But they share statement (2). In the first argument, 2 functions as a conclusion. In the second argument, 2 functions as a premise. This shows that the same statement can function in different ways in different arguments. The conclusion of one argument can in turn be used as a premise in another argument.

Combining Argument Structures

These four basic argument structures can now be combined to represent more complex arguments. Think of the Legos pieces that come in four basic shapes: squares, double-rowed rectangles, single-rowed rectangles, and round pieces. By combining these four basic designs, you can create greatly varying objects.

Here are two examples of more difficult arguments.

> (1) Consider the case of a sealed-bid auction, in which no one knows how much to pay for a prize. (2) The collected bids do not reveal much about the true value of the prize, because (3) the bidders may be looking for bargains. (4) The odds are that the winner will end up paying too much (because (5) she valued the prize significantly more than her competitors) or (6) too little (because (7) everyone bid low). (8) Either result harms economic efficiency because (9) the price paid does not reflect real worth. . . . (William Vickrey and James A. Mirrlees, "Making Honesty Pay," *Scientific American,* January, 1997, p. 18. Statement numbers added.)

We may diagram this argument as

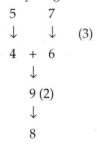

This paragraph has numerous indicators to help us through it. The first *because* indicates that 3 is a reason for 2. *Because* similarly connects 5 with 4, 7 with 6, and 9 with 8. The author connects the argument 9 → 8 with 4 and 6 (which is a compound statement because 4 and 6 are connected by *or*) by use of the word *either.* The more difficult part is to see how the argument 3 → 2 fits in. Statement 2 makes approximately the same statement as 9 (which we indicate by the use of the parenthesis around 2), whereas 3 might be interpreted as a general statement that is unpacked by the arguments 5 → 4 and 7 → 6. Statement 1 is description and hence does not play a role in the argument itself.

Here's a second example.

> (1) A mandatory notification program seems the ideal way to protect the welfare of a sex or drug partner of someone who tests HIV positive. One might reason that (2) violating the confidentiality of the HIV-positive person is warranted by his or her partners' need to know. (3) Although this may be so, (4) an additional consequence of such a policy is that it discourages those who are at highest risk for AIDS from seeking testing. (5) Few people would be willing to risk such serious consequences as losing their jobs, not being able to find a place to live, or not being able to get insurance if information about their being HIV positive was deliberately or even accidentally made public. (Ronald Munson, *Intervention and Reflection*)

This example illustrates a point we made earlier in the book, namely, that authors sometimes begin their discussion with a point contrary to the point they are making. Note the function of statement 3 and its *although.* Thus, in this paragraph, statements 1, 2, and 3 do not contribute to the author's argument. Further, the conclusion, which is not stated, is the opposite of the initial thesis (1). We might diagram the argument as follows.

    5

    ↓

    4

    ↓

[There should not be mandatory testing for HIV.]

Statement 5 might also be another way of saying 4, in which case the argument would be

    4 (5)

    ↓

[There should not be mandatory testing for HIV.]

Diagramming arguments serves several important functions.

1. Diagramming visually reveals the structure of the paragraph(s), allowing you to see more easily how the extended argument is put together.
2. You can determine how many topics are included in the paragraph. Has the author addressed one topic or mixed topics?
3. It helps you determine how well something is written. Determining this is particularly important in assessing one's own writing. If the numbered statements have a sequential order, going from low to high, that order provides a clue that the paragraph is reasonably well organized. Conversely, if the numbers have little or no sequence, the author probably has jumped around in the paragraph, making it difficult to understand. The more sequential the numbers, the easier it is to understand the paragraph.

Exercise 4

For each of the following paragraphs, (1) number the statements, (2) state the topic, (3) identify the thesis or conclusion, (4) circle the logical indicators and label them P(remise) or C(onclusion) indicators, (5) diagram the paragraphs, using the numbers you assigned to the statements.

1. Augustine advises the Christian who goes to war to repent in advance, because the ambiguities of the situation confuse moral issues and because passions confuse the moral intention. (Robert Clouse, ed., *War*)

2. Truckers who use double and triple trailers have the best safety record. That's because it is a highly controlled operation, using the best drivers, operating under permit only. It is a privilege to operate a triple. (Bernard Gavzer, "Should the Big Trucks Get Bigger?" *Parade,* July 20, 1997)

3. Many people expect me to support the prison smoking ban. These are prisoners. They shouldn't have any rights. ("Cruel and Unusual: Prison Smoking Ban," *St. Paul Pioneer Press,* July 30, 1997)

4. Reptiles make unusual pets, but tending for them is no easy matter. Green iguanas need a special diet of one third chopped leafy greens, one third chopped other vegetables, and one third fruit. They also grow fast, reaching four to six feet. So think twice before taking on a scaly pet.

5. If Bryan Cox of the Chicago Bears was a decent football player, we fans might offer him a little more slack, but all we see is a mediocre player making a scene—and a fool of himself—and then missing the tackle. Cox should stop telling us how misunderstood he is and how great a competitor he is and start performing. (Brian Axtman, letter, *Sports Illustrated*, October 20, 1997)

6. It's great to see such enthusiasm, and I wish more players were like Cox. Gone is the day of Dick Butkus and Jack Lambert, so let's enjoy this wild man while we can. (John Manley, letter, *Sports Illustrated*, October 20, 1997)

7. Marilyn Monroe believed her fame would be brief, but she was wrong. We are still on a first-name basis with the sex symbol. . . . She was on the cover of *Playboy* in January [1997] and appeared in the *Sports Illustrated* winter swimsuit issue. Every week at least one new Marilyn Monroe product is licensed, from Christmas ornaments to debit cards. A Marilyn Monroe *Gentlemen Prefer Blondes* Barbie doll costs about $70. . . . (Excerpted from Lee Neville, "Database: Icon," *U.S. News & World Report*, July 28, 1997, p. 15. Copyright, 1997, U.S. News & World Report. Visit us at our web site www.usnews.com for additional information.

8. She ate Maple Leaf Farms' chicken cordon bleu and contracted salmonella poisoning when she was seven weeks pregnant. . . . Her suit blamed the company for carelessly causing the miscarriage of her fetus. . . . Maple Leaf's lawyers requested a dismissal for two reasons: First, a nonviable fetus is not "an unborn child." Second, to allow a suit for the wrongful death of a seven-week-old fetus would conflict with a state law allowing an abortion up to the 24th week of pregnancy. (Aaron Epstein, "Recent Fetal Protection Efforts Cloud Abortion Issue," *St. Paul Pioneer Press*, August 5, 1996. Reprinted by permission.)

9. Rape is a unique crime in our society because of the stigma attached to it and the extreme psychological and physical harm caused by it. Good public policy recognizes this and gives the victim, not the media, the choice of revealing her identity. To establish such a public policy and ensure that it will withstand a constitutional challenge, one must also review the legal issues involved and determine the proper balance a policy must maintain to protect the victim's right of privacy without unduly interfering with the media's first amendment rights. (Paul Marcus and Tara L. McMahon, "Limiting Disclosure of Rape Victim's Identities," *Southern California Law Review*, 1991)

10. The orderly process of sedimentation may be modified by currents and bottom conditions that control wave action or interfere with the movement of the water shifting the sediment. Hence the different types of sediment are rarely pure, for the gravels generally contain sand, the sands generally contain mud or clay, the muds contain fine sand or some calcareous matter, and the calcareous rocks may contain both clay and sand. (William Emmons et al., *Geology*)

11. The first hominids were faced with a new, complex, and highly unpredictable world. Yet they had the brains, the freedom from dependence on only one type of food, and the freedom that bipedalism gave them to use their hands in ways that would promote their survival. Thus their emergence during the course of evolution was a modification of patterns observed among other primates; it was based on the primate heritage. (Cecie Starr and Ralph Taggart, *Biology*)

12. Because the Christian church viewed care of the soul as far more important than care of the body, medical treatment and even physical cleanliness were little valued, and mortification of the flesh was seen as a sign of saintliness. In time, nearly all Europeans came to look upon illness as a condition caused by supernatural forces, which might take the form of diabolical possession. Hence, cures could only be effected by religious means. (David W. Tschanz, "The Arab Roots of European Medicine," *Aramco World,* May/June, 1997, p. 23).

13. Like us, animals have certain basic moral rights, including in particular the fundamental right to be treated with the respect they are due as a matter of justice. Like us, therefore, they must never be treated as mere receptacles of intrinsic values, and any harm that is done to them must be consistent with the recognition of their equal inherent value and their equal prima facie right not to be harmed. (Tom Regan, *The Case for Animal Rights*)

14. What about those experiments which carry no appreciable risk—the "wrongful touchings" sort? In an adult, it would seem, the right to autonomy is sufficient basis for the action of wrongful touching. But the child does not have a right to autonomy, except insofar as some measure of autonomy is necessary to promote the child's development and well-being. Harmless experiments on children, therefore, which satisfy the other canons of medical ethics—could be performed. Parents would not be derelict in their duty should they consent, on behalf of their child, to experiments of this sort. (Benjamin Freedman, "A Moral Theory of Consent," in Ronald Munson, *Intervention and Reflection*)

15. The refusal of James Grant George's biological mother to provide information that would enable him to obtain a lifesaving bone-marrow transplant is shockingly inhumane. Only in the worst soap opera would one expect to find a woman who valued her reputation more than the life of her child. No person's privacy outweighs the value of a life. (Catlin Smith, letter, *Newsweek,* August 31, 1981, p. 8)

16. Global warming is a serious issue. By switching to clean, renewable energy and making our cars and trucks go farther on a gallon of gas, we can curb global warming and create jobs. We don't need to burn coal and guzzle gasoline in order for our economy to grow. A change that moves America toward a cleaner, more-sustainable future is a change for the better. The President should take strong steps now to curb greenhouse-gas emissions. (Bret Coleman, letter, *Seattle Times,* October 24, 1997)

17. Forty-seven years after becoming a UN member, Israel is still not eligible to sit on the Security Council and other key UN bodies. Sponsors of

terrorism—including Iran, Cuba, Libya, North Korea, Sudan and Syria—are among the 184 member countries that are eligible. Ted Turner ought to reconsider his billion dollar gift to a body operating in an openly anti-Semitic fashion. (Erna Martino, letter, *Atlanta Constitution*, October 14, 1997)

18. During the past 2,000 years, Jewish people have been oppressed, tortured and killed for the glory of a Christian God. The soil of Europe is drenched with Jewish blood. The majority of Europeans still hate Jews senselessly. Is it proper, therefore, in describing Jews, to use a word denoting delusions of persecution? The sad fact is that Germany today is still sick with blind anti-Semitism, and many of its people want only to forget what it did to the Jews. [Forgiving the Germans] cannot be allowed to happen. (Saul Schoenfeld, letter, *Newsweek*, June 8, 1981, p. 13)

19. Visiting small groups after you've set them a task can seem like a form of assessment—a way of checking up to see whether they're doing what you told them to do. This can be insulting to students since it implies that you don't trust them enough to do what you've asked. Students might change their behavior during your visit to their group as a way of impressing you with the kinds of behaviors they think you want to see. Their overwhelming concern is showing you what good, efficient, task-oriented learners they are rather than thoughtfully analyzing and critiquing the task at hand. (Stephen D. Brookfield, *Becoming a Critically Reflective Teacher* (Jossey-Bass, 1995))

20. The commission concluded that at this time it is morally unacceptable for anyone in the public or private sector to attempt to create a child using somatic cell nuclear transfer cloning. We reached a consensus on this point because current scientific information indicates that this technique is not safe to use in humans at this time. Indeed, we believe that it would violate important ethical obligations were clinicians or researchers to attempt to create a child using these particular technologies. . . . Moreover, in addition to safety concerns, many other serious ethical concerns have been identified that require much more widespread and careful public deliberation before this technology may be used. The commission therefore recommended . . . [a] continuation of the current moratorium on the use of federal funding to support any attempt to create a child by somatic cell nuclear transfer. . . . (Excerpted with permission from Harold T. Shapiro, "Ethical and Policy Issues of Human Cloning," *Science,* July 11, 1997, pp. 195–6. Copyright, 1997, American Association for the Advancement of Science.)

Cooperative Learning Exercise

Take a paper you have written and diagram three paragraphs to see how well the paper is written. Bring this paper to class and have your partner diagram the same three paragraphs. Compare your diagram with your partner's and resolve where you disagree, giving reasons for preferring one diagram over the other.

This chapter presented various types of discourse, with an emphasis on arguments. It developed the structure of arguments and helped you understand them by means of diagrams. There is much more to learn about arguments; in particular, you need to distinguish among different kinds of arguments. To this task we turn in the next chapter.

ANSWERS TO THE EXERCISES

Answers to Exercise 2

1. Effect: The Federal Reserve Board has not reduced interest rates.
   Cause: They do not want to fuel inflation in the economy.
   Psychological explanation
3. Effect: The number of students in Introductory Russian declined.
   Cause: It was scheduled at the same time as the most popular soap opera.
   Psychological explanation
5. Effect: Two people died.
   Cause: The containers of ice cream were tainted.
   Effect: The containers of ice cream were tainted.
   Cause: The milk delivery truck has been used to transport eggs and had not been properly cleaned.
   Physical explanation
7. Effect: Small explosions hurled hot "rock bombs" a kilometer or more into a nearby settlement.
   Cause: The rising magma in the volcano is now moving upward more slowly.
   Physical explanation
9. Effect: The thief let him go
   Cause: The thief saw that the IRS agent was also a thief.
   Psychological explanation
11. Effect: Marmaduke fawns over Linda.
    Cause: Linda's husband is a butcher.
    Psychological explanation
13. Effect: A person went to the trouble to seek expert opinion about a marriage.
    Cause: The person values the investment of emotions and creative effort the person put into the relationship.
    Psychological explanation
15. Effect: Boys with gender disturbance
    Cause: The social environment of child-rearing
    Psychological explanation

Answers to Exercise 3. Added indicators are in brackets.

1. (C) The University should be able to beat its rivals *because* (P) it offers more football scholarships than they offer to attract better players.
3. (C) I hope that I'm not doing the wrong thing in throwing out all these old school papers [*because*] (P) The kids just might need them next year to review.
5. (P) Either the campus police do not detect parking violations, in which case they are incompetent, or they do but don't ticket them, in which case they are corrupt. [*Therefore*] (C) Not much of a choice.
7. *why* not (C) start now with a [nuclear] freeze? . . . (P) A nuclear freeze can give the two great powers breathing room before they rush into a nuclear future that

may threaten the future itself. (P) It can halt new technologies that will be danger-ous and destabilizing.

9. (C) Some species of trees have been 'read out of the party' by economics-minded foresters *because* (P) they grow too slowly, or have too low a sale value to pay as timber crops.

11. No argument. *Since* is a time indicator.

13. (C) Equally valid, perhaps more so, is intuitive, instinctive awareness. (P) We can become more cognizant of ultimate truths by sitting quietly in the wild than by studying in a library. (P) Often our gut instincts enable us to act more effectively in a crisis than does careful rational analysis.

15. (P) "Public lands belong to us all, and fossils tell our prehistoric past." [*Therefore*] "We have a responsibility to be good stewards of this national heritage, and the primary concern should be science and education, not dollar values. . . .

    (P) more fossils are destroyed by erosion than are ever recovered. (P) Most for-profit dealers have strong science backgrounds, do good field work , and provide a valuable service. (P) "Fossils are not going to wait for the politically correct person to find them." [*Therefore,* (C) dealers should be allowed to sell fossils they have found on public lands].

Answers to Exercise 4

1. Augustine advises (1) the Christian who goes to war to repent in advance, because (2) the ambiguities of the situation confuse moral issues and because (3) passions confuse the moral intention.
   2. Topic: Christian fighters
   3. The Christian who goes to war should repent in advance.
   4. Because: premise indicator
   5. 2   3
        ↘   ↙
            1
   6. Both arguments are deductive.

3. Many people expect me to (1) support the prison smoking ban. (2) These are pris-oners. (3) They shouldn't have any rights.
   2. Topic: smoking for prisoners
   3. Thesis: Prisons should ban smoking for prisoners.
   5. 2 + 3   2
        ↓   ↓
        1   or   3
              I don't support . . .   ↓
                                      1
   6. Deductive

5. (1) If Bryan Cox of the Chicago Bears was a decent football player, we fans might offer him a little more slack, but (2) all we see is a mediocre player making a scene—and a fool of himself—and then (3) missing the tackle. (4) Cox should stop telling us how misunderstood he is and how great a competitor he is and (5) start performing.
   2. Topic: Bryan Cox
   3. Thesis: Cox should stop telling us how misunderstood he is and how great a competitor he is and start performing.
   5.   2 + 3
         ↙   ↘

         4   5
   6. Deductive argument

7. (1) Marilyn Monroe believed her fame would be brief, but (2) she was wrong. (3) We are still on a first-name basis with the sex symbol. (4) She was on the cover of *Playboy* in January and (5) appeared in the *Sports Illustrated* winter swimsuit issue. (6) Every week at least one new Marilyn Monroe product is licensed, from Christmas ornaments to debit cards. (7) A Marilyn Monroe *Gentlemen Prefer Blondes* Barbie doll costs about $70.

   2. Topic: Marilyn Monroe's fame
   3. Thesis: Marilyn Monroe was wrong that her fame would not last.
   5. 4 5 6 7
      ↓ ↓ ↓ ↓
         3
         ↓
         2
   6. All are probably deductive

9. (1) Rape is a unique crime in our society because of the stigma attached to it and the extreme psychological and physical harm caused by it. (2) Good public policy recognizes this and gives the victim, not the media, the choice of revealing her identity. (3) To establish such a public policy and ensure that it will withstand a constitutional challenge, one must also review the legal issues involved and determine the proper balance a policy must maintain to protect the victim's right of privacy without unduly interfering with the media's first amendment rights.

   2. Topic: naming rape victims
   3. Thesis: To establish such a public policy and ensure that it will withstand a constitutional challenge, one must also review the legal issues involved and determine the proper balance a policy must maintain to protect the victim's right of privacy without unduly interfering with the media's first amendment rights.
   4. Because: explanation indicator
   5. 1
      ↓
      2
      ↓
      3
   6. Both arguments are deductive.

11. (1) The first hominids were faced with a new, complex, and highly unpredictable world. Yet (2) they had the brains, the freedom from dependence on only one type of food, and the freedom that bipedalism gave them to use their hands in ways that would promote their survival. Thus (3) their emergence during the course of evolution was a modification of patterns observed among other primates; (4) it was based on the primate heritage.

   2. Topic: first hominids
   3. Thesis: Their emergence during the course of evolution was a modification of patterns observed among other primates.
   4. Thus: conclusion indicator
   5. 2
      ↓
      4
      ↓
      3
   6. Inductive (causal hypothesis); Deductive

13. (1) Like us, animals have certain basic moral rights, including in particular the fundamental right to be treated with the respect they are due as a matter of justice.

(2) Like us, therefore, they must never be treated as mere receptacles of intrinsic values, and (3) any harm that is done to them must be consistent with the recognition of their equal inherent value and their equal prima facie right not to be harmed.

2. Topic: Treatment of animals
3. Thesis: They must never be treated as mere receptacles of intrinsic values and any harm that is done to them must be consistent with the recognition of their equal inherent value and their equal prima facie right not to be harmed.
4. Therefore: conclusion indicator
5.   1

   ↙ ↘

  2   3
6. Both are deductive.

15. (1) The refusal of James Grant George's biological mother to provide information that would enable him to obtain a lifesaving bone-marrow transplant is shockingly inhumane. (2) Only in the worst soap opera would one expect to find a woman who valued her reputation more than the life of her child. (3) No person's privacy outweighs the value of a life.

2. Topic: a lifesaving transplant
3. Thesis: The refusal of James Grant George's biological mother to provide information that would enable him to obtain a lifesaving bone-marrow transplant is shockingly inhumane.
4. None
5. 3   2

   ↓   ↙

     1
6. 3 → 1: Deductive; 2 → 1: inductive (persuasive comparison)

17. (1) Forty-seven years after becoming a UN member, Israel is still not eligible to sit on the Security Council and other key UN bodies. (2) Sponsors of terrorism—including Iran, Cuba, Libya, North Korea, Sudan and Syria—are among the 184 member countries that are eligible. (3) Ted Turner ought to reconsider his billion dollar gift to a body operating in an openly anti-Semitic fashion.

2. Topic: Ted Turner
3. Thesis: Ted Turner ought to reconsider his billion dollar gift to a body operating in an openly anti-Semitic fashion.
5. 1 + 2

  ↓

  3
6. Deductive argument

19. (1) Visiting small groups after you've set them a task can seem like a form of assessment—a way of checking up to see whether they're doing what you told them to do. (2) This can be insulting to students since (3) it implies that you don't trust them enough to do what you've asked. (4) Students might change their behavior during your visit to their group as a way of impressing you with the kinds of behaviors they think you want to see. (5) Their overwhelming concern is showing you what good, efficient, task-oriented learners they are rather than thoughtfully analyzing and critiquing the task at hand.

2. Topic: visiting small groups in class
3. Thesis: Teachers should not visit small groups in their classes.
4. Since: Premise indicator

5. 1 + 3
      ↓
    2   4 + 5
      ↘   ↙

[Teachers should not visit small groups in their classes.]
6. Deductive

CHAPTER 7

Analysis

Discovering How Arguments Work

The darker it got the worse my nerves became. I screamed at the slightest noise, left my kerosene lamp lit all night, stayed awake with my head under the covers—and nothing happened. So much for ghosts . . . When the sun appeared and bathed the barn in light, I returned to my spinning loft. I sat down at my loom and picked up my shuttle only to drop it again. Two uneven rows straggled across the face of my rug below the knots I had tied the night before. Unlike the tabby pattern I had used, the yarn dipped under two warp strings and over two warp strings instead of one. I sat there for a long time trying to explain away what I was seeing with my own eyes. There was no explanation. In the space of a second I became a believer. Someone had come back, through those swinging doors and said hello. (Cora Holmes, "Another Ghost at Chemofski," *Alaska*, October 1997)

What is the topic of this paragraph? _____

Its issue? _____

Its thesis? _____

Its main point? _____

By providing evidence from her experience, Cora Holmes creates an argument for her thesis that a ghost haunted her Aleutian ranch. Do you agree that she has good reason to believe in ghosts? To answer this question, you have to look at her argument and the evidence she advances. But how do you evaluate her argument? To accomplish this accurately, you must first understand the kind of argument she presents. Since not all arguments have the same structure, individual arguments may require different methods of evaluation. Application of the wrong methods of evaluation leads to an inaccurate assessment of an argument's strength. To prepare you for the later steps of evaluation, this chapter details different argument structures.

Arguments generally are divided into two types, deductive and inductive. In **deductive arguments** the premises claim to support or provide evidence for the conclusion in such a way that, if the premises are true and the argument breaks no rules (is valid), the conclusion *must* be true. The truth of the conclusion follows *necessarily* from the premises in that you cannot deny the conclusion without denying the truth of one of the premises. Note that we are *not* claiming that the premises of deductive arguments are true. Rather, we are looking at the relation between the premises and the conclusion. We are saying that *if* the premises are true, the conclusion must be true. We term a deductive argument that breaks no rules and has true premises **sound.** We will say more about these rules in Chapter 12.

Here are some deductive arguments.

1. All the rooms in this house reek of onions. If all the rooms reek of onions, my wife must have been cooking soup. Therefore, my wife was cooking soup.

If it is true that all the rooms reek of onions and that if so, my wife was cooking soup, then there is no escaping the fact that she was cooking soup.

2. The entire soccer team must purchase red jerseys before the first game. Rachel is on the soccer team, so she must purchase a red jersey before the first game.

Again, if the premises are true, the conclusion that Rachel must purchase a red jersey before the first game must also be true.

3. The Sears Tower is taller than the Empire State Building, and the Empire State Building is taller than our nation's Capitol Building. So it follows that the Sears Tower is taller than our nation's Capitol Building.

As before, the truth of the premises and the structure of the argument establish the conclusion about the Sears Tower as true. You can recognize that this is a deductive argument by noting that if you deny the conclusion, you must also believe that one of the premises is false.

In **inductive arguments,** even though the premises are true and the argument is strong, the conclusion is at best *probable.* That is to say, you can deny the conclusion without denying the truth of any of the premises. An inductive argument is *strong* when the premises provide good reason for thinking that the conclusion is true. The stronger the argument, the more *likely* it is that the conclusion is true. But the conclusion never follows with certainty from the premises. It is appropriate to say that inductive arguments are strong or weak. An inductive argument is **cogent** when the premises are true and the argument is strong. The term *cogent* applies to inductive arguments parallel to the way *sound* applies to deductive arguments.

Here, then, is an important difference between deductive and inductive reasoning. Assuming that the premises are true in both cases, deductive reasoning yields conclusions that are surer or more certain than inductive arguments. Put another way, inductive arguments are weaker than deductive arguments.

This is not necessarily bad, for often the best argument we can raise is an inductive one. But critical thinkers are aware of what the argument can and cannot establish and of how much confidence they can place in the conclusion given the truth of the premises. In this way they are not misled by claims that are stronger than warranted.

Here are examples of four types of inductive arguments. We introduce these inductive arguments types here and explore the first three in greater detail in the following sections.

> 1. Bobbie, Jean, and Randy are siblings and have blue eyes. So it is likely that all their brothers and sisters have blue eyes.

In this *generalization,* an arguer concludes something about all or most of a group based on the evidence provided by a sample of three cases. The conclusion is at best probable, since if one of the parents has brown eyes, it is possible that at least one of the children has brown eyes.

> 2. The government is like a ship. When the captain becomes incompetent for some reason, it is necessary to replace that person with someone who is qualified to safely pilot the ship.

This argument from *analogy* compares two things and draws a conclusion from that comparison. The arguer infers that since two things—ships and governments—are relevantly similar, other aspects about them are relevantly similar.

ships	replace the captain when incompetent
--------- :	--------------------------------------
governments	therefore, replace the captain when incompetent

You can readily see that the conclusion is at best likely, depending on how closely governments are like ships.

> 3. Jack has won more than twenty games each of the last three seasons, yet he is thirty pounds overweight. It must be what the Tigers feed him that makes him a winning pitcher.

Causal arguments infer a cause or causal hypothesis from an analysis of specific effects. In this argument, the arguer suggests a causal explanation or hypothesis for the fact that Jack has such a good winning record. The argument is inductive, for other causes might be presented to explain Jack's record (Jack has unusual control; he has a good split-finger fastball; the team has quite an array of 300 + hitters).

> 4. An a*ppeal to authority* draws a conclusion based upon the recommendation of some alleged authority or person with prestige or popular appeal.

In our example on the next page the advertiser concludes that you should drink milk because Michael Johnson, who is a track superstar, recommends it. We will examine the role of authorities more closely in Chapter 10. Here we merely note that any conclusion that follows from the testimony of an authority is at best probable.

The examples we used are simple arguments, easy to recognize. Arguments in real life are often much harder to differentiate in terms of being

In the time it takes to read this, I became the world's fastest man. Was it my unique posture and upper body strength? Or did the skim milk in my healthy diet help? After all, that's what many pro trainers recommend. One thing's for sure. It wasn't just the gold shoes.

MILK
Where's your mustache?

Appeal to authority

deductive or inductive. One way to distinguish the two is to ask how much confidence you would have in the conclusion if the premise(s) were true. If you cannot see any way of denying the conclusion in such a case, the argument is deductive.

A second way is to look for **argument-type indicators** like *must* or *likely*. *Must* and its synonyms (*certainly* or *necessarily*) usually indicate a deductive argument, while *likely* and its synonyms (*probable, good reason to believe that*) indicate an inductive argument. These signposts are at best indicators and not sure guarantees of argument types, for we sometimes misuse these words. In particular, it is not unusual for someone to use the word *must* in reference to the conclusion of an inductive argument. Note Example 3 about the Tiger baseball player Jack. The arguer misused *must* in what is an inductive argument. Here is another example:

The back door is locked. No windows are broken. So the burglar must have left through a window.

The arguer would better have said, "Probably the burglar left through a window." Other options might explain the locked door. For example, the burglar might have found a house key inside the home and locked the door on the way out to fool the police. Given the truth of the premises, the conclusion is probable, not certain. These examples show that you should look for argument-type indicators to help you identify the type of argument given, but at the same time you must test any indicators that are given to see whether they truly fit the kind of argument the author has suggested.

One note of caution. *Don't confuse argument-type indicators with logical indicators.* The first indicate the type of argument being given, whether deductive or inductive; the second indicate premise and conclusion. However, some words, like *must,* can serve both functions. For example,

> He must have had an accident; his right front fender is crumpled and the headlight is dangling.

Must indicates both the conclusion and that probably we have a deductive argument. The missing premise to the deductive argument is "If his right front fender is crumpled and headlight is dangling, he must have had an accident."

You might protest that there is another way to interpret this argument about the crumpled fender. You might claim, correctly, that his crumpled fender is only a sign that he might have had an accident. The crumpled fender could have been caused by other events (his girlfriend got mad and hit his car with a sledge hammer). The conclusion that he had an accident is only probable. This argument, then, also might be interpreted as an inductive argument and hence provides another illustration of a misuse of *must.* Which way the argument goes often depends on the context or on what is assumed in the argument. We will say more about assumptions later.

Try your hand at the following exercises. If you have difficulty distinguishing deductive from inductive arguments, ask yourself two questions. (1) How certain would the conclusion be if the given premise(s) were true? (2) If the argument were an inductive argument, which of the preceding four types of inductive arguments would it exemplify?

Exercise 1

In the following arguments, (1) bracket and number the statements; (2) circle the logical indicators and underline the argument-type indicators; (3) diagram the argument; (4) decide whether the argument is deductive or inductive.

1. Since taking some vitamin C daily is good for your health, I take several thousand milligrams daily to really protect my health.

2. The nutritionist said that taking vitamin C daily is good for your health. So I never miss a day without taking my vitamin C.

3. Although my street is normally quiet, today cars from all around the neighborhood are driving past my house. The city must have one of the nearby roads blocked.

4. Because the number of personal bankruptcies in our county has doubled in the past year, we must vote to close down the riverboat casino.

5. *U.S. News* tallied 76 deaths [in day-care facilities] in 1996. The causes included drowning, falls, being struck by autos, and sudden infant death syndrome—but the data are sketchy, since many states do not report the causes of these deaths. (Victoria Pope, "Day Care Dangers," *U.S. News & World Report,* August 4, 1997, p. 34)

6. This is doubtless not the full total, since seven states as well as the District [of Columbia] did not respond to repeated requests for information—and 16 others, including California and Ohio, said they do not track deaths in day care. (Victoria Pope, "Day Care Dangers," *U.S. News & World Report,* August 4, 1997, p. 34)

7. Zebra mussels have been found above the dam separating the lower from the upper St. Croix River. Boaters have not been careful to scrape off all the mussels attached to their boat when they transported them around the dam.

8. Troopers staffing special overtime enforcement patrols . . . issued 50 percent more tickets than normal through June 30; they have tagged 42 percent more speeders than [last year]. Based on results to date, speeding tickets issued by the patrol will likely exceed 17,000 this month, compared with the 12,000-plus issued last July. (Gary Dawson, "New Speed Limits Being Enforced," *St. Paul Pioneer Press,* July 30, 1997)

9. Yes, it was settled; his career was determined. He would run away from home and enter upon it. He would start the very next morning. Therefore, he must now begin to get ready. (Mark Twain, *Tom Sawyer*)

10. In the time of peace in December, 1932, at one time 265 condemned prisoners were awaiting execution in Leningrad's Kresty Prison alone. And during the whole year, it would certainly seem that more than a thousand were shot in Kresty alone. (Aleksandr Solzhenitsyn, *The Gulag Archipelago*)

11. As the fire which is kindled makes its fuel into ashes, so the fire of knowledge makes all actions into ashes. (*Bhagavad Gita,* IV)

12. Since I transcend the perishable and am higher even than the imperishable, I am renowned in the world and in the Vedas as the highest Spirit. (*Bhagavad Gita,* XV)

13. I say we shall always have native crime to fear until the native people of this country have worthy purposes to inspire them and worthy goals to work for. For it is only because they see neither purpose nor goal that they turn to drink and crime and prostitution. (Alan Paton, *Cry, the Beloved Country*)

14. Even so, these children seldom abandoned fairness entirely. They may have switched from one idea of justice to another—say, from merit to equality—but they did not resort to egoistic justifications. . . . Older children were more likely to believe in fairness and to act accordingly, even when such actions favored others. This finding was evidence for the reassuring proposition that ideals can have an increasing influence on conduct as a child matures. (William Damon, "The Moral Development of Children," *Scientific American,* August 1999, p. 75)

15. You must strive to guide policy indirectly, so that you make the best of things, and what you cannot turn to good, you can at least make less bad. For it is impossible to do all things well unless all men are good, and this I do not expect to see for a long time. (Thomas More, *Utopia*)

INDUCTIVE ARGUMENTS

We have observed that there are various kinds of inductive arguments. Let us look in more detail at three common ones in order to understand their structure. The ability to recognize the structure of these arguments enables you to better identify inductive arguments.

Generalizations

One kind of inductive argument is a **generalization.** *Generalizations argue from a limited sample to a statement about all, most, or a certain percentage of the whole.* Suppose I buy a crate of oranges at the supermarket. When I get it home and examine it, I find that all the oranges on the top layer are rotten. Rather than sorting through the entire crate, I take it back, telling the manager that from looking at this top layer I concluded that all (or most) of the oranges are rotten, and I want my money back. Here the *sample* is the oranges on the top layer, and what I generalize about are all, most, or a certain percentage of the oranges in the crate.

What I generalize about must be of the same type or category as the items in the sample. In the example, I generalize about the crate of oranges. The *relevant category* is oranges. If I also bought a crate of apples from the supermarket, whether or not I can argue to return the apples as well depends on what I take as the relevant category about which to generalize. If the category is oranges, I cannot argue from the sample of rotten oranges that I should be able to return the apples as well, since the new relevant category covering both oranges and apples (fruit) is of a different type than the sample (oranges). If, however, I broaden the sample category to fruit, I can make the generalization from the rotten fruit to cover both crates—the oranges and the apples. The point here is that generalizations are strictly controlled in the sense that *what you generalize about must be of the same type as the sample from which you generalize.*

You can readily see that generalizations are forms of inductive, not deductive, reasoning. If I do not examine all the oranges, then although the premise (the oranges in the top layer are rotten) is true, the conclusion (all the oranges in the crate are rotten) may still be false, for there may be one or many good ones in the layer below which I looked. Only if I had examined every orange would I be entitled to say with certainty that all the oranges in the crate are rotten. But then I am no longer giving an inductive argument. In fact, I would be making not an inference but an assertion based on the observation that all the oranges are rotten.

Generalizations may lead to conclusions of varying strengths. Based on the sample, I may make a universal claim that *all* the oranges are rotten. This is a very strong claim. A weaker claim would be that most or a certain percentage—say 75 percent, based on the fact that three-fourths of those I sampled are rotten—of the oranges are rotten.

Generalizations play an important role in our lives. We have neither the time nor the resources to investigate every event, yet we want to make claims that go beyond our limited experience. Generalizations do this for us. One important use is in polling. In the lead-up to the 1996 presidential election, poll takers were at work every week.

> A new Newsweek poll shows Clinton's lead plunging to two points, 44–42. With a margin of error of plus or minus 4 percentage points, the race is a statistical dead heat, according to the poll of 933 registered voters taken on Thursday and Friday. (Stephen Thomma, "Clinton, Dole in Dead Heat, Spar on Taxes," *St. Paul Pioneer Press*, August 18, 1996)

The pollsters generalize from a sample of 933 persons to the entire electorate. *Newsweek* could not sample the entire electorate, but a good sample should get close to the results *relevant at the time the poll was taken.* Note that in this example the pollsters were aware that generalizations are forms of inductive reasoning, for they included a *margin of error* in their results; note the words *plus or minus 4 percentage points.* In this case the margin of error means that on the day the poll was conducted Clinton could have gotten anywhere between 40 and 48 percent of the votes, while Dole could have received between 38 and 46 percent—each having a range of eight percentage points.

The margin of error in polling depends on a number of things, including the sample size. The chart shows the margin of error that correlates with a random sample of persons.

Persons	Margin of Error	Range
100	+/– 11 percentage points	22 points
200	+/– 8 points	16 points
600	+/– 5 points	10 points
800	+/– 4 points	8 points
1,500	+/– 3 points	6 points
4,000	+/– 2 points	4 points

As you can see, the margin of error diminishes as you get a larger and larger sample, so that at some point it becomes economically unfeasible and statistically insignificant to extend the size of the sample.

The critical thinker, while accepting the importance of generalizations, is aware of the shortcomings of polling. In Chapter 10 we pay attention to these shortcomings and note how they might be rectified when we consider how to evaluate generalizations; for now the goal is to help you recognize generalizations.

Analogies

A second type of inductive argument involves arguing from **analogy.** *An analogy says that two things are like each other in some respect.* Love is like a rose, defensive football lines are like bulldogs, the tired rock climber's legs are like jelly, and so on. One of my favorite lines about my father was that his teeth were like stars: they came out at night.

Analogies play an important role in our understanding. When we cannot clearly grasp what something is like, it helps to compare what is unclear to something that is clearer or better understood. Thus, one use of analogy is as an *example or illustration,* whose purpose is clarification. For example, one author uses analogy to help his readers understand one stage of mitosis (cell division).

> Around the same time, the cell begins to erect a spectacular system of protein wires around the chromosomes that will alternatively serve to guide and propel them along a genetically plotted pathway to two separate destinations. Called the spindle apparatus, this system of slender cables is spun by two sets of freshly duplicated organelles called *centrioles.* . . . Together, the two sets of centrioles spin a silken bridge of spindle fibers between the two poles of the cell, eventually surrounding the troupe of chromosomes in a cocoon of microscopic parallel fibers. (David Suzuki and Peter Knudtson, *Genethics*)

Suzuki employs several analogies: wires formed into cables that guide an object from one location to another; a bridge of fibers; a cocoon that surrounds the chromosomes. Perhaps there are too many different illustrative analogies in this passage so that it confuses as much as it helps the reader understand the process. Nevertheless, the author intends the analogies to assist the reader's understanding of reproduction.

But some people go beyond using analogy as an illustration to actually construct arguments based on an analogy. The **argument from analogy** has three parts.

1. The analogy assumes that two things (called analogues) are basically like each other. To make the analogy stronger, the arguer might list the ways these things are alike.
2. The analogy notes that one of the things or analogues has a certain property.
3. The analogy concludes that the other thing or analogue has that property as well.

On the next page is an advertisement that argues from analogy.
The advertiser compares vaccinating an animal to house painting. The property the arguer focuses on is that you would not vaccinate your own dog. So, the argument concludes, you would not paint your own house.

vaccinating an animal	you don't do it yourself
- - - - - - - - - - - - - - - - - :	- -
painting	therefore, don't do it yourself

As you can readily see, arguments from analogy are inductive arguments. Even if the premises are true, the conclusion does not follow with certainty. Even though two things are similar, their similarities might not extend to the property in question. We will learn how to evaluate analogies in Chapter 10.

Exercise 2

For each of the following, (1) bracket and number the statements, identify the conclusion, and diagram the argument. Then (2) determine whether it is a generalization or an analogy. (3) If it is a generalization, what is the sample from which the arguer generalizes? If it is an analogy, note what two things are being compared.

1. Introducing thick, fuzzy wool mittens for your immune system. Shield yourself . . . during the cold season and throughout the year. (Advertisement for throat lozenges)

Source: Minnesota Painting & Decorating Public Relations and Apprenticeship Bureau

2. What other name conjures up so many memories? So many smiles? Remarkable how frequently life's special moments happen in Bass shoes. Call it coincidence, but that Bass coincidence just keeps happening over and over again. For many women, a closet filled with Bass shoes is like a diary. (Advertisement)

3. Although there are signs that the wall of ageism is beginning to crumble— welcome back the craggy, world-weary faces of Mick Jagger (51), Keith Richards (51), Eric Clapton (50), Robert Plant (46), Don Henley (47), and, yes, Tom Jones (54)—with the exception of Tina Turner, . . . it seems only males are granted special dispensation to pass through [to musical stardom at an older age]. (Charles Gandee, "Triumph of the will," *Vogue,* April, 1995, p. 191)

4. The Hispanic population's share is much larger in many of the smaller Texas metropolitan areas and cities, especially those along the Mexican border. The 1990 census showed Hispanics made up 48 percent of the residents

of San Antonio, 70 percent of El Paso, and more than 80 percent in the border cities of Brownsville, Laredo, and McAllen. (Jorge del Pinal and Audrey Singer, "Generations of Diversity: Latinos in the United States," *Population Bulletin,* October, 1997, p. 12)

5. In the fullest definition, harmony is an experience that engages any or all of the five senses in addition to delighting the mind. Harmony can stir the spirit as well as soothe the soul. Consider the harmonious interplay of petals with the rose. Or the full chorus soaring to the last movement of Beethoven's Ninth Symphony. Can there be beauty without harmony? Not if one agrees that beauty arises from the perceived harmony of an object. An object, often made up of divergent parts that come together in an aesthetic whole. Thus, the highest praise one can bestow on an intricate timepiece is "created in harmony." (Advertisement for Concord watches showing a rose and a watch)

6. In 1957 . . . geologist [William] Stokes discovered a trackway in a 145-million-year-old sandstone bed in Arizona. The tracks showed that the animal had a wide reach, and when it walked its front feet landed behind its rear ones. . . . Stokes declared them to be pterosaur tracks. [More recently, Kevin Padian argued that the] tracks belonged to a crocodile. To prove it, he and his colleague Paul Olsen took a small crocodile called a caiman, ran it across a patch of mud, and came up with tracks similar in many ways to the ones Stokes had found. The experiment convinced most paleontologists that Stokes's tracks should be reclassified as crocodilian, or at least as "origin unknown." (Mary K. Miller, "Tracking Pterosaurs," *Earth,* October 1997, p. 20)

7. I switched from European cars to American cars in 1991, buying one by Chrysler and one by Ford, and I wound up with two limes—not quite lemons, but nothing to write home about either. Next time, I'll give a Japanese car a try. (Alan Meisel, letter, *Business Week,* December 22, 1997, p. 16. Reprinted by permission.)

8. The real story is that nothing has changed in Detroit: The old arrogance is alive, well—and in complete control. My Mercury Sable was delivered with defective motor mounts; it is now on its fourth set at more than $250 per set. Further, after two tries and $200, I have given up on having my local dealer replace a $12 interior trim piece. (David W. Harlowe, letter, *Business Week,* December 22, 1997, p. 16. Reprinted by permission.)

9. At the time of the birth of Christ, Rome was a prosperous, thriving empire with a standard of living significantly higher than that of any other city in the Western world, if not on the entire planet. . . . [Rome] thrived as a government center living largely off the tribute (taxes) of the provinces and conquered lands. . . . The parasitic nature of Rome's opulent existence contributed to its eventual downfall. Is a similar redistribution of income and wealth taking place in America? Resources are being extracted from the general tax-paying public to feed the bureaucrats and government officials who tend . . . to concentrate themselves in state or national capitals . . . America's government centers have become parasite economies . . . The affluence of government centers is making the

rest of America poorer. "Capital crimes" gradually are sapping the nation of needed economic vitality. (Richard Vedder, "Capital Crimes: Political Centers as Parasite Economies," *USA Today,* September 1997, pp. 20, 22)

10. [Spanish] scientists dubbed the 780,000-year-old fossil *Homo antecessor.* The partial skull has the cheekbones and nose of modern humans but the sloped brow of our extinct cousins, the Neandertals. The Spanish team argues that the species established this branch of our family tree, giving rise to one twig that flourished—us—and another that led to the Neandertals and has since gone extinct. ("Neandertal Origins," *Earth,* October 1997, p. 11)

Causal Arguments

A third kind of inductive argument involves causal reasoning. We might distinguish two types. One argues from known causes or something related to a common cause to projected effects (a prediction); the other infers a cause from given effects (causal explanation).

Arguing from causes to projected effects involves making a **causal prediction.** In predictions we say that a statement about the future is true based on what we know about the past and present (The boat will sink because it has a hole in the bottom) or about other truths causally related to what is predicted (It will rain tomorrow because there is a ring around the moon). Put another way, in a prediction we infer from what we think is a cause to a possible effect of that cause. The cause (which is given) is known; the possible effect we infer to is less known or unknown. Since many things can affect the future, the conclusion of a prediction is at best probable. The stronger the causal link between what we know and what we predict, the better grounded is the prediction.

The strength of our confidence in the causal link is often determined by our past experience of how similar causes have been related to what is projected as the effect. For example:

> Frankie will probably pass the test tomorrow because she studied regularly since the last test and really seems to understand the material.

We might say that prediction about Frankie here is strong because we have often noted for other students that studying regularly and understanding the material seem causally related to their doing well on tests.

Here is a second example where the causal connection is more indirect.

> It will probably rain tomorrow since the wind has shifted to the south.

A change in today's weather is the basis for making a prediction about tomorrow's weather. Though the shift in the wind might not be a cause of tomorrow's rain, both are causally related to something broader, namely, a change in the weather pattern that probably will cause it to rain.

> The White Sox have won the first three games of the series; they will probably finish off the Brewers in the final game tomorrow.

Past experience about the success of the White Sox provides grounds for making a prediction about the future. The relation between the White Sox winning the first three games and the fourth is not directly causal; that is, winning the first three games does not cause the team to win the fourth. As in the previous example, however, both stem from an alleged similar cause: the superiority of the White Sox, which enabled the team to win the first three games.

We can use this last example to show that predictive reasoning can be interpreted not only in terms of causal reasoning, but also as analogies or generalizations.

The argument about the White Sox can be analyzed as an analogy.

The first three games		the White Sox won
-----------------	:	---------------------------
The fourth series game		therefore, the White Sox will win

The fourth game resembles the first three games. The first three games had the property of the White Sox winning, so the fourth game will have that same property. What this analysis loses, however, is the notion that there is a *causal* connection, either direct or indirect via unstated or common causes (for example, the White Sox's superior ability), between the White Sox winning the first three games and winning the fourth.

A second way of understanding predictions appeals to a generalization. Here the extended argument would look like this.

1. The White Sox won games 1, 2, and 3.
2. Therefore the team will win every game with the Brewers. (The argument from 1 to 2 is a generalization.)
3. Tomorrow the White Sox play the Brewers.
4. Therefore, the White Sox will win tomorrow. (The argument from 2 and 3 to 4 is deductive.)

This formulation is more dubious, since it makes a very broad generalization (from premise 1 to 2) based on what appears to be insufficient evidence. In Chapter 10 we note that this formulation is guilty of the *Fallacy of Hasty Generalization:* generalizing from a too small or an unrepresentative example. Furthermore, again the causal connection is suppressed. However, it is a possible way of understanding predictions. The point here is that *predictions can be argued for in diverse ways, involving causal reasoning, analogy, and generalization.*

A second kind of causal reasoning proceeds from effects to infer something about their cause. This kind of inductive argument is called a **causal inference.** In a causal inference, from the effects we infer something about their cause. What we know (the given) are the effects; the inferred is the cause, which is uncertain.

This kind of reasoning occurs in detective stories and is the backbone of science. For example,

> The door of my canary's cage is open; the carpet has a red stain; my cat on the couch is smiling; my canary is missing. The cat probably ate my canary.

The word *probably* indicates that this argument makes an inductive inference. Since the red stain might be from my son's spilling catsup on my carpet as he traipsed through the living room to feed my cat, and since the living room window is open, it is possible that my canary flew out the window when I forgot to shut the cage door properly.

Consider another example.

Whereas malaria can strike any individual in the region, those with a particularly strangely shaped red blood cell appear resistant to it. Hence, having sickle-shaped red blood cells helps provide an immunity to malaria.

Here a **hypothesis,** which is a supposition that is tentatively accepted to explain certain facts or to provide the basis for further investigation, is presented. The hypothesis (having sickle-shaped red blood cells helps provide an immunity to malaria) accounts for the effect (people with a particularly strangely shaped red blood cell appear resistant to malaria) and can be used to generate other facts that can be investigated and tested. The reasoning is from effect to cause and is at best probable.

To distinguish causal prediction from causal inference, you should look for two things.

1. Causal prediction goes from causes, what signifies causes, or is related to causes, to an effect that has not occurred or, if it has, is unknown to us. Causal inference goes from effect to cause.
2. The causal prediction does not explain the data from which one predicted, whereas the causal hypothesis can be used to explain the effect or data from which the inference was made. For example, the hypothesis that my cat ate the canary explains the data that the canary is missing, that there is a red stain on the carpet, and that the cat seems pleased. But the prediction that the White Sox will win the fourth game of the series does not explain why the team won the first three.

As critical thinkers, we need to pay attention to what we are given, determining whether it is the cause or the effect. If it is the former, we might then look for what predictive conclusion is derived from that cause. If it is the latter, we might look for a cause or hypothesis that best explains the effect we are given initially. In each case, the direction of the causal inference brings the structure of the argument into focus.

Exercise 3

For each of the following, (1) bracket and number the statements; (2) circle the logical indicators; (3) diagram the arguments; and (4) indicate whether the conclusion inferred from the evidence is a causal prediction or a causal inference.

1. There have been a number of earthquakes in and around Los Angeles in recent years. They appear to be increasing in intensity. In the next few years we will see a really big one hit this area.

2. I checked out the air pressure in the tires and even had the tires balanced and aligned. Yet the front end shimmy remains. One of my tires must be out of round.

3. They must have forgotten my birthday this year. I looked in the closet, under the bed, even downstairs under the Ping-Pong table, and haven't found anything even resembling a wrapped present.

4. The polls put the challenger far ahead of the incumbent. In this district the incumbent has never won when he or she was behind in the polls. So it is easy to see that the challenger will win the congressional race this year.

5. The victim's blood was on the front seat of the car, and there were bloody tracks leading to the front door of the house. The victim's blood was also on the accused's socks. He also could not explain where he was during that crucial half hour before he was taken to the airport. There is little doubt that he is guilty of the murder.

6. On Monday I had a pizza and a tequila and woke up with a terrific headache; on Tuesday pizza and rum and woke up with a terrific headache; on Wednesday pizza and bourbon and woke up with a terrific headache; on Thursday I ate a pizza with two beers and got a headache. I think I should give up eating pizza.

7. When the shortstop played the ball, it took a wicked hop. It must have hit a small stone on the edge of the infield grass.

8. People who fished the lakes in New England began to notice a common feature in the lakes—namely, that the fish were much fewer and smaller. When they analyzed the water, they noticed a high acidic content. The sulfur from the coal burning plants in the Midwest must be precipitating into the lakes and killing the fish.

9. Before mid-century, there were no significant holes in the ozone layer over Antarctica, but the size of the holes has increased dramatically since then. During that same period we have also seen a dramatic rise in the number of air conditioners and refrigerators. Perhaps the CFC emissions from these appliances affect the ozone layer.

10. The team compared the Neandertal sequence with 986 distinct sequences from living humans. They found, on average, three times more differences between the Neandertal and modern human sequences than between pairs of modern humans. Specifically, pairs of modern human sequences differed at an average of only eight positions, while human-Neandertal pairs differed at an average of 25.6 positions. . . . These data . . . make it "highly unlikely that Neandertals contributed to the human mtDNA pool." (Patrick Kahn and Ann Gibbons, "DNA from an Extinct Human," *Science,* July 11, 1997, p. 177.)

Exercise 4

For each of the following, circle any logical indicators and indicate whether they are premise or conclusion indicators. Then determine whether the argument is a generalization, analogy, or causal argument. Some paragraphs might present more than one argument.

1. The Boundary Waters has been referred to as the "crown jewel" of the wilderness system. Picture a man five generations ago. He looks and looks and finally finds the most beautiful diamond to give his wife. She loves, cherishes and cares for this precious jewel until she grows old. The dia-

mond is passed along to her daughter. As her grandchildren grow, they admire the stone. . . . This diamond is passed down from generation to generation, until today, in 1996, when it is in the hands of the fifth generation. This great-great granddaughter loves, cherishes and cares for this precious jewel. The Boundary Waters is that "precious jewel" to many who live nearby. Anyone who thinks we locals are going to hurt our beloved inheritance is dead wrong. Please, let us have the three motorized portages back. (Dea Whitten, letter, *St. Paul Pioneer Press*, August 22, 1996)

2. How typical of Americans! They cannot appreciate any exquisite foreign food without vulgarizing and prostituting it. Just look what has happened to pizza, to crêpes and to Chinese and Japanese food—and now it is the turn of that French delight, *le croissant*. How sad that instead of elevating their taste to the food, Americans always insist on debasing the food to their taste. (Alain Dubois, letter, *Newsweek*, May 25, 1981)

3. As far as we can tell, [the Greenlanders] starved to death. . . . Excavations have turned up many expensive portable items, like crucifixes, that would probably have been removed by the settlers in an evacuation. And had the colony's population gradually diminished, . . . the wood in many of the farms—a valuable commodity in a place with few trees—would have been scavenged by the remaining settlers. Such was not the case. . . . Cut marks on [dog] bones suggest the dogs were butchered; even the cow hooves were eaten. (Kathy A. Svitil, "The Greenland Viking Mystery," *Discover,* July, 1997, p. 30)

4. Curiously, the giant white clams, long thought to have been a dominant and characteristic vent species, have not yet appeared. These must be a late-stage colonizer, indicative of an old hydrothermal field. Lutz expects the clams will have arrived by his next visit this fall. (Shanti Menon, "Deep Sea Rebirth," *Discover,* July 1997, p. 34)

5. Diadoras: They're like Ferraris for your feet. Like the famous racing car, Diadora shoes are very quick, precisely engineered, responsive and— I think—good to look at. . . . Seek out the Diadora tennis shoe. Inspect it. Try it on. If you are as serious about winning as I am, to take a lesser shoe on the court would be like driving the family sedan at LeMans. (Advertisement)

6. I read with dismay your article about the use of pesticides in Third World countries. This is another example that makes plain the need to monitor and, if necessary, regulate the activities of the business community, which has shown once again that profits have a higher priority than the well-being of the planet and its inhabitants. (Gaye Clemmer, letter, *Newsweek*, August 31, 1981, p. 8)

7. How to judge a Kentucky champion. Pedigree. Performance. Physical appearance. Sure. But there is a quality that sets champions apart from other thoroughbreds. Maybe it's heart. Something you can't define. But you know it's there. How to judge fine Kentucky whiskey. Taste. Aroma.

Smoothness. Qualities that are hard to define. But one taste of Burke & Barry [whiskey] and you know they're there. (Advertisement)

8. I was a patient in Deaconess Hospital in August. One evening while looking out the window overlooking the main entrance parking lot, I observed a young man tampering with the wheels of a car. I noted down the license number of the car he was in and turned it over to the security guard. It turned out he had let the air out of two of the tires. The car belonged to a woman employee of the hospital. She did not even say thank you or acknowledge me for relaying this information. I learned a lesson. Don't get involved. People really don't care. (Beatrice Finn, letter, *Minneapolis Tribune*)

9. [The survey] comprised 17,077 girls aged 3 to 12; 9.6 percent of them were African American, the rest white. Although textbooks say it is abnormal for girls to show signs of sexual maturation under the age of 8, the researchers found that 1 percent of whites and 3 percent of blacks already showed signs of pubic hair or breast development by age 3. By age 8, those figures had jumped to 14.7 percent and 48.3 percent, respectively. The racial differences are in line with other evidence that blacks develop more quickly than whites do. . . . [To] some people, the across-the-board earlier development suggests that hormone-like chemicals—so-called endocrine disrupters, such as certain pesticides—are at work. . . . (Excerpted with permission from "Early Puberty Getting More Common," *Science*, April 25, 1997, p. 537. Copyright, 1997, American Association for the Advancement of Science.)

10. David Hoppe notes that in the course of handling thousands of frogs between 1975 and 1995, he saw only two with visible limb defects; in 1996 alone he saw more than 200. He speculates that an environmental agent in the water where the creatures breed could be the cause. (Sasha Nemecek, "Amphibians On-line," *Scientific American*, March, 1997, p. 18)

11. Case for Abortion. A counselor, following the philosophy of a recent U.S. Supreme Court decision, would have decided their case in short order. The father had syphilis; the mother, tuberculosis. They had had four children already. One was blind; another had been born dead; the third was a deaf-mute; the fourth, tubercular. Now the mother was pregnant again. The U.S. Supreme Court would have counseled an abortion. But the mother had her baby. And that baby turned out to be Ludwig van Beethoven. (Source unknown)

12. What a poor example our government is showing us with its attacks on Iraq—especially to our youth. Its actions say that it is perfectly fine to retaliate against violence with more violence, not so much for attaining concrete goals such as saving lives or self-defense, but for something as obscure as maintaining "credibility." Insightfully, the same concern for credibility is at the heart of our urban gang wars. In light of these considerations, we should rightfully fear for the future of our country under the leadership of people with no more restraint than a 5-year-old. (Dan Pinotti, letter, *St. Paul Pioneer Press*, September 8, 1996)

13. Despite their surprising similarity to terrestrial rocks in silicate content, Barnacle Bill, Yogi, and the soil exhibit other chemical signatures . . . that losely match the 12 Martian meteorites. This indicates that these meteorites . . . did in fact come from Mars. (Robert Naeye, "Mars Pathfinder Update," *Astronomy*, November, 1997, p. 30)

14. Your article describing juvenile delinquency among orphaned elephants in South Africa carried important information about all social mammals, humans included. You quoted a zoologist as saying that normally "a dominant older male elephant is around to keep young bulls in line." Without this control, young males become killers. We see the same phenomenon in the United States in the human species when government replaces the father. Statist contempt for the family flys in the face of biology. (Robert Koch, letter, *Time*, November 3, 1997, p. 31. Reprinted by permission.)

15. To refute some of the criticisms made of our food service (such as: "dinner rolls could be used as basketballs," "biscuits remain very resilient and of remarkable density") I will present some of my own evaluations from my experiences. In evaluation, I looked for tastiness, appearance, and cost of the food, cleanliness, and the politeness and friendliness of the kitchen staff. I found that the food tasted very good and appeared very attractive. The cooks are so concerned about the attractiveness of their food that they wipe off any soup that drips down the side of each cup before presenting it to someone. As far as cleanliness is concerned, I have not once found a dirty fork, plate, or glass nor has any food been less than wholesome. Another outstanding facet is the politeness and friendliness of each person on the staff. All in all, the college has a quality food service that is deserving of praise from our newspaper rather than scorn. [Neil Pauluk, letter, *Echo*, February 22, 1974]

Exercise 5

In the following article, (1) identify the data the researchers gathered. (2) What hypothesis does the author give to explain this data? (3) Note and develop any analogies or generalizations that you might find.

Anti Gravity
Space Invaders

Discretion, rumor has it, is the better part of valor. When it comes to driving, however, discretion often goes out the window, usually the driver's. Normally mild-mannered, deferential individuals metamorphose into zealous defenders of territorial rights when behind the wheel. Two centuries ago one sure way to get a rise out of a guy was to backhand your glove across his face. One can achieve the same result today by cutting off another driver on the highway. A recent study shows, however, that even in stationary cars drivers cannot resist the urge to mark their territory.

The research took place at the epicenter of late 20th-century social interaction— the shopping mall. As any Saturday

continued

Anti Gravity
Space Invaders continued

shopper can attest, nowhere are cars more stationary than at a mall parking lot. The inevitable game of musical chairs that occurs over parking spaces leads to what exosociologists might call close encounters of the third kind. "Primary territories are those that are central to our lives—our home or office," explains Pennsylvania State University researcher R. Barry Ruback, whose study appeared in the *Journal of Applied Social Psychology.* "Secondary territories are those that we occupy on a regular basis; Norm's bar stool at *Cheers* would be one. It's sort of generally acknowledged that when you're there, it's your place. The third are public territories, the things that we own temporarily." Such as mall parking spaces.

Ruback decided to examine the speed with which the possessors of parking spaces accomplished spot removals, thereby relinquishing their temporary ownership. The question is intriguing because once the bargain hunting is done, a mall parking space is perhaps the area least worth defending on the face of the earth. Defense is actually counterproductive because the intention once a driver has returned to the car is to leave the scene of the carnage and bring home the kill. Nature, however, has been described as "red in tooth and claw," and vestiges of ancient behaviors survive the millions of years between maul and mall. The average driver spent 32 seconds leaving his or her spot when no one else was jockeying for it, but an additional seven seconds maintaining possession when another car appeared eager to enter.

Part of that difference may result from performance anxiety, a common problem in tasks involving the insertion or removal of objects into and out of tight spaces. Ruback believes, however, that an additional response accounts for at least some of the extra time. A second part of the study bears him out. He and his students fixed the game by confronting those about to pull out with a shill vehicle that either waited patiently or—and here's where things really get ugly—honked. The result: blow your horn, pal, and you can sit there for another 12 seconds. "Somebody infringes on your freedom," Ruback says, "and the first thing you do is react against it." Or, as high-strung taxi driver Travis Bickle might put it after returning to his cab after a hard afternoon accessorizing at Weapons 'R' Us, "You honkin' at *me?*"

For better, or more likely for worse, we all have at least a bit of Bickle in us and are quite willing to squander time and energy in senseless posturing when strangers attempt to horn in on our spaces. What we think of as civilization, then, may be less a wholesale move away from primitive reactions than a substitution for them—a trade of head busting for 12 seconds of chop busting. And if that is true, the old notion of counting to 10 to diffuse an emotionally charged situation is probably a good idea, although counting to 12 is most likely even better.

[Reprinted by permission of the author from Steve Mirsky, "Space Invaders," *Scientific American,* August, 1997, p. 24. Steve Mirsky is a contributing editor at *Scientific American* magazine.

EXPLANATION AND ARGUMENT

Often it is difficult to distinguish causal reasoning (which is inferential) from causal explanation (which is merely informative). The reason is that causal explanations often look like arguments. Indeed, both explanations and arguments can use the same indicator words, such as *because.*

The main difference between causal explanations and causal arguments is that explanations do *not* involve inferences, whereas arguments do. That is, causal explanations do *not* intend to establish the truth of a claim but rather suggest or indicate a cause for the known effect. But establishing the truth of a claim or giving reasons for a conclusion is the function of an argument.

We might put this distinction another way. *Arguments give us a reason for thinking that some claim is true; explanations tell us what brought something about.* For example,

> You should vote Republican because Republicans offer the best chance of balancing the budget and addressing the deficit.

Here we have an argument providing a reason for voting Republican. But consider this:

> She will vote Democratic because that is how her parents voted.

Here we probably have an explanation, telling us that the cause of how she votes is her heritage.

We say *probably* because this example might also function as an argument for the truth of the claim that she will vote Democratic. That is, we might interpret this sentence to say that it presents a reasoned prediction, based on the evidence about how her parents voted. This example shows that sometimes it is difficult to tell the difference between an explanation and an argument. At times they look alike, and we need more of the context to tell what the author had in mind.

Consider this example:

> Women are less susceptible to heart attacks because of the estrogen in their body.

On one hand, this could be an explanation. The given or the effect is that women are less susceptible to heart attacks; the cause is the presence of estrogen. On the other hand, it could be seen as an argument. We know the truth of the premise that women have estrogen in their bodies. This fact provides a basis for the truth of the claim that they are less susceptible to heart attacks. If it is an argument, it assumes the missing premise that "All people who have estrogen in their bodies are less susceptible to heart attacks."

Or consider a modification of the example we gave earlier in the chapter about skim milk.

> Skim milk has less fat than whole milk because the fat has been processed out of it.

This might be an explanation. But suppose we replace *has* with *must have.* Now we have an argument trying to establish the truth of the claim that skim milk has less fat. If we know that the fat has been processed out of the milk, we can conclude that skim milk has less fat than whole milk. The tipoff that we have an argument in the revised statement is the word *must,* which often functions as a conclusion indicator.

Consider this cartoon.

Source: ONE BIG HAPPY by Rick Detorie. By permission of Rick Detorie and Creators Syndicate.

Does this cartoon contain an argument, trying to establish that the bad things the boy has done are not his fault, or is he presenting an explanation for his conduct? It is not very clear; we could make a case for either of these possibilities.

There are several reasons that arguments and causal explanations are not easily distinguished. One is that the same words, including words like *why*, *because*, and *the reason that* are used in both. This means that we cannot rely simply on language to differentiate arguments and explanations. Second, whether the statements constitute an argument or an explanation often depends upon the context, and in particular, on the intent of the author. But it is often difficult to determine whether the author intends a description or a causal inference. Indeed, the author may not be clear about whether he or she is offering an argument or an explanation. Consequently, not only it is often difficult to distinguish between arguments and explanations, but sometimes it is not very profitable to attempt to do so.

Is there a way to tell causal explanations and causal arguments apart? One stategy is to *ask what is in doubt.*

- If neither the cause nor the effect is in doubt, or if both are on the *same level of surety,* then it is a causal explanation, not an argument.

The reason is that if the author has the same confidence in both, then the author is not making any inferences from one to the other but is merely describing a causal relationship. Arguments involve inferences that move from the more known to the less known. For example, "The toaster is not getting hot because I unplugged it to move the table." This is a causal description if I know both that the toaster is not getting hot and that I unplugged it. I am merely reporting a causal connection and not making any inferences.

- If we know the effect but are in doubt about the cause, then the affirmation that something is the cause is the result of an inference. An inductive causal argument is presented that infers a cause or hypothesis that explains what is given (the effect).

For example, "The furnace won't start again; Kathy must have blown a fuse." In this case I know the effect: that the furnace won't start. From this effect I infer that Kathy must have blown a fuse. And Kathy's blowing the fuse explains why the furnace won't start.

We might summarize as follows:

- *Causal Explanation:* The cause and effect have the same surety; the causal relation is described.
- *Causal Argument:*

  Effect (treated as a fact or given that is more known)

  ↓

  Cause or hypothesis (treated as somewhat in doubt)

Looking for what, if anything, is in doubt should help you be more successful at distinguishing explanations from arguments, causal or not. To resolve the puzzle about the cartoon where the boy says his prayers, we have to ask first whether the boy thinks that anything is in doubt. On one hand, if nothing is in doubt, we have a causal explanation functioning as a description; the boy merely presents a cause for his behavior. On the other hand, if what is in doubt is whether the boy is to be blamed for his bad behavior, we have a causal argument in which the boy argues that his environment caused his bad behavior. As already mentioned, sometimes it is not clear which is intended; you can only do your best to penetrate the author's intent.

Exercise 6

(1) Determine which of the following are explanations, which are arguments, and which have other functions. (2) Where there is an explanation, identify the effect and the cause (explanation). (3) For each explanation, tell whether it invokes a physical or a psychological explanation.

1. The price of crude oil must have declined last week because the government decided to again restock its reserves with large purchases.

2. The price of crude oil declined last week because the border dispute between two oil producing countries was settled.

3. He quickly ran from the house because he could smell smoke in the hallway.

4. He wrecked his car coming home from work today. I saw his broken headlight and damaged bumper.

5. He wrecked his car coming home from work today because an inconsiderate driver cut him off on the freeway and he hit an embankment.

6. If your stove is not working, make sure the fuse is off before you open the rear cover over the electrical terminals.

7. Men are less likely to develop osteoporosis until later in life than women and seldom suffer as severely because they have 30 percent more bone mass on the average and don't undergo the sudden drop in estrogen that occurs with menopause. . . . (Matt Clark, "The Calcium Craze," *Newsweek,* January 27, 1986, p. 50)

8. A prisoner stood at a checkpoint, a bruise on his head and neck. He must have been beaten.

9. A prisoner stood at a checkpoint, a bruise on his head and neck. His arms were pinioned behind his back, and he was guarded by another soldier armed with an AK-47.

10. A prisoner stood at a checkpoint. Next to him were three other unarmed and bound prisoners. The Russian assault on the command post probably failed.

11. Armed with assault rifles and armor-piercing, rocket-propelled grenades, the fighters have been careful about conserving their arms and ammunition, rarely wasting it on targets where they are not likely to do immediate damage.

12. If you throw a ball at a stationary wall, the ball will rebound with about the same speed as it had before hitting the wall. Now imagine what happens if the wall is moving toward you. The ball rebounds with additional speed. The wall has transferred some of its momentum to the ball, causing it to speed up. And likewise, the ball has slowed the wall a negligible amount. The opposite occurs if the wall is moving away from you. A tossed ball rebounds with less speed. That's because the receding wall absorbs energy from the tossed ball, causing it to slow down. And likewise, energy from the ball causes the wall to speed up a tiny amount. (James Oberg, "The Spacecraft's Got Swing," *Astronomy*, August, 1999, pp. 50, 53)

13. Your article states that the sale of deadly pesticides is tightly regulated in America. As a small farmer in the state of Washington, I find that for large corporate farms there is easy access to deadly chemicals—both pesticides and herbicides—and that enforcement of regulations is lax or nonexistent. Mass pesticide pollution of our air, water and soil in America needs more than "tight regulations" that are not enforced because of the power vested interests have over our enforcement agencies. (Quentin Mehlenbacher, letter, *Newsweek*, August, 31, 1981. p. 8. Reprinted by permission.)

14. Garfield

Garfield ® by Jim Davis

15. The amount of money wagered through legal gambling in America has become so immense so quickly that it would be irresponsible to not thoroughly study its social, economic and political impact on the nation. That is why Congress passed legislation to create the National Gambling Impact and Policy Commission.

16. . . . Scientists now know why wintergreen mints give off flashes of light when you crunch them. Linda Sweeting of Towson State University and colleagues . . . found that among pure crystals, only those lacking rotational symmetry—be it natural or because of impurities—lit up. The finding confirms an earlier theory: flashes appear when opposite charges on different faces of the fragmented crystal recombine and excite gas molecules. Such charges occur when voltage arises in a crystal under stress—a "piezoelectric" effect seen only in asymmetrical materials. ("Flashy Mints," in "In Brief," *Scientific American,* August 1997, p. 20)

17. Tobacco use among children is at a 16-year high. And I just don't see the enthusiasm for anti-smoking campaigns directed at kids that I saw as recently as the late 1980s. Perhaps it's because today's generation of young people is growing up more disconnected from adults and adult guidance than any other generation in our nation's history. Many children have been left to raise themselves. Maybe it has to do with our modern preoccupation with "rights." Don't people have the "right" to do whatever they please—even kids? Or maybe it has to do with the image of smoking itself. Nicotine addiction is a stealth pediatric disease. Kids smoke, but they don't die until they're older, and we don't see the awful consequences when they're young. . . . (C. Everett Koop, "Let's Get Serious about Deterring Youth from Starting to Smoke," *Lexington Herald-Leader,* September 8, 1996)

18. Artifacts unearthed at Great Zimbabwe have not clarified the social and cultural organization of the settlement, but they have distinguished it from other Iron Age sites. In particular, a group of soapstone birds, many of them 14 inches high and sitting atop three-foot-tall columns, is unlike any sculpture found elsewhere. Each bird has a different pattern or marking; none is identifiable as a local creature. Because of the regard contemporary Shona people hold for their dead and because some Shona tribes use iron rods to mark tallies of their dead, some archaeologists have speculated that the avian icons indicate aggregates of ancestors used in rituals. (Webber Ndoro, "Great Zimbabwe," *Scientific American,* November, 1997, pp. 97–8)

FINDING UNSTATED ASSUMPTIONS

Diagramming arguments and identifying the kind of argument employed enable us more easily to find unstated or implicit assumptions in arguments. When we see what arguers actually have said, we are then in a position to inquire *what else they need or presuppose* to make their argument succeed. This "what else" amounts to the implicit assumptions of their argument.

Assumptions are statements that the arguer takes to be true without providing evidence for them. There are two kinds of assumptions. **Implicit** or **unstated assumptions** are statements that the arguer assumes to be true without actually stating them. For example, if I argue that since the dinosaur fossil found in Africa had long, curved teeth and claws, it must have been a fish eater, I am implicitly assuming that all dinosaurs with long, curved teeth and claws were fish eaters. This argument also has an explicit assumption, namely, that the dinosaur fossil had long, curved teeth and claws. An **explicit assumption** is a premise the arguer states but leaves unsupported. In an argument where 1 is a reason for 2, and 2 is a reason for 3 (1 → 2 → 3), 1 is an explicit assumption (stated but unsupported) while 3 is the conclusion. Since 2 is supported by 1, it is not assumed in the argument.

As we noted earlier in this book, making implicit assumptions is not necessarily bad. Were we to include everything in our arguments, the arguments would be tedious and unnecessarily long. Thus, often we shorten the argument simply by assuming certain premises that seem to be obvious truths or that our audience would accept. Making implicit assumptions helps us and our readers or listeners focus on what is critically relevant to the argument.

Although assumptions are necessary, as critical thinkers we especially need to discover and pay attention to the implicit assumptions that people make. Although often the implicit assumptions are so obviously true that they are not worth stating, sometimes people make implicit assumptions that are downright dubious. Sometimes they do this subconsciously, unaware of what they are assuming. At other times, people consciously omit the assumptions to hide the weaknesses in their argument. Therefore, it is important for critical thinkers to find the unstated assumptions in arguments so that they can decide for themselves whether those assumptions are obviously true and hence innocuous or whether they are dubious and need defense.

Finding implicit or unstated assumptions is no easy task, but here are some suggestions.

1. In *deductive arguments*, the conclusion finds new relationships among the data presented in the premises. The conclusion should not add new information to the premises. Consequently, the conclusion should not contain anything that is not found in the premises. Since a deductive argument requires at least two premises, to find the missing premise look at the stated premises and then look at the conclusion to see what is in the conclusion but missing from the premises. What is missing provides the core content for the assumed premise.

   For example,

   Patients do not generally want to know the truth about their diagnosis of serious illnesses like cancer. Hence, as a rule most doctors do not inform patients that they have a serious illness like cancer.

   The conclusion of this argument speaks about doctors; yet this term is absent from the given premise, which is about patients. Hence, the argument makes an assumption about doctors. In this case, the assumption is that doctors generally do not tell patients what they do not want to know.

Or again,

Because there is no evidence of a drainage system in the ruined building, archaeologists presume that the building had a roof.

The conclusion speaks about a building with a roof. This is not mentioned in the given premise, which talks about a drainage system in the ruined building. Hence, the assumed premise must concern a building with a roof. We might write the assumption as: "If there is no evidence of a drainage system in the ruined building, the building must have had a roof."

2. In *inductive arguments,* since the conclusion can contain material not in the premises, we have to ask what else is needed to make the inductive argument strong. We ask what else is needed because we assume that the arguer thinks that the argument is strong; otherwise he or she would not be using the argument to persuade you about the truth of some thesis. What makes the argument strong depends upon the type of inductive argument it is.

- If the argument is a *generalization,* the unstated assumptions have to do with the quality of the sample: the sample was large enough to generalize from, it was a random sample, and the sampling activity was unbiased. For example, since the day my daughter found a beetle in her blueberry yogurt, she will not eat yogurt. She has generalized about this food from one case, assuming that the yogurt with the beetle in it was a normal sample.

- If the argument is an *analogy,* the unstated assumptions relate to the similarity of the things being compared. The author of the analogy assumes that the things being compared are relevantly similar enough to enable us to draw a good conclusion. For example, one advertisement suggests that we should eat a particular brand of jam because it is made like grandma's soap. The advertiser implicitly assumes that there are relevant analogies between making jam and making soap so that one can argue from the one process to the other.

- If the argument is a *causal hypothesis,* the unstated assumptions have to do with the author's belief that the hypothesis to which he or she has concluded provides a better explanation than the alternative hypotheses. For example, if I argue that the stain on my basement ceiling probably is caused by a leaky pipe in the bathroom above, I am implicitly assuming that other hypotheses—such as rainwater seeping in from the outside—are less plausible.

- If the argument is a *causal prediction,* the author assumes that there is adequate past experience from the data gathered to warrant the prediction and that the case in hand is relevantly like those past cases. That is, the author assumes that "all things are equal" about the past cases and the predicted future case. For example, it is predicted that the winter that follows the year dominated by the weather pattern called El Niño will be wetter and colder than normal because this is what happened in the early 1980s. The meteorologists implicitly assume that other factors affecting the weather systems this coming year will be basically the same as those that affected the systems in the early 1980s.

In short, critical thinkers want not only to identify the type of argument used, but also to discover the assumptions made so that they in turn can be evaluated. Recognizing the type of argument assists us in the process of discovering those assumptions. We will say more about assessing these assumptions when we turn to evaluating inductive arguments in Chapter 10.

Exercise 7

Go back to Exercise 1 and identify the implicit assumptions made in each of the arguments.

Exercise 8

In the following articles,

1. Identify the topic, issue, and thesis.

2. Identify the main points (the conclusions that support the thesis).

3. Circle and identify any logical indicators.

4. Diagram the arguments.

5. Determine whether the arguments you identified in #4 are inductive or deductive.

A. There is hardly a stadium built more than 10 years ago that isn't on the endangered species list. Fans don't love plastic-grass, multiuse ballyards like Veterans Stadium in Philadelphia anymore. We don't want Eighth Wonders of the World like Houston's Astrodome. We don't even see the need to preserve old ballparks like Detroit's venerable Tiger Stadium, which will be replaced in 2000, and Boston's 85-year-old Fenway, which—if the Red Sox have their way—could be razed soon after the millennium.

Instead we want new ballparks that just *look* like Fenway, faux-old ballyards like Baltimore's Oriole Park at Camden Yards, urban confections designed to soothe the eye and fatten a franchise's wallet. Fenway, by contrast, is a classic, replete with nooks and angles and the Green Monster and a sense of proximity to the players that no other stadium offers. Despite players' complaints about the park's old, dingy locker rooms and weight-training area, . . . the game will be forever diminished if the old girl disappears. (Michael Farber and Richard Deutsch, "Endangered Species: Ball Game's Over," *Sports Illustrated,* September 29, 1997, p. 96)

B. The context for the following piece was the debate about the effectiveness of the Joe Camel ads in getting young people to smoke.

Thanks to the cartoon character Old Joe, Camel cigarettes are now a drug of choice among American smokers under 18. Since 1987, when R. J. Reynolds introduced the suave and debonair symbol to these shores, Camel's share of the illegal youth market has soared from a barely perceptible 0.5 percent to a stunning 33 percent, according to figures from the antismoking side of the debate.

Reynolds says these kids would have smoked anyhow. And of course it doesn't want kids to smoke.

"If we believed for a minute that the camel ad induces children to smoke," a spokeswoman said, "we wouldn't wait for the FTC or anyone else to act. We would immediately change the campaign."

Sure.

. . . Cigarette promotions are aimed primarily at kids. Old Joe symbolizes "cool." Brands pitched at the female market are keyed to slimness, sex appeal and sports. Marlboro seeks to identify with athleticism and the outdoors.

The messages are not merely subliminal, they are overt: Smoking will make you all the things you want to be. But the companies say this is only to promote brand loyalty among people who already smoke.

Right.

. . . Canada has banned cigarette advertising. The ban is being appealed to the Canadian Supreme Court. The United States, despite evidence that 9 of 10 smokers begin before they turn 21, is unlikely to follow Canada's lead. Here the tobacco industry has far deeper historic, cultural and economic roots. Here more politicians are for sale. Here, too, we have a First Amendment that probably—but not certainly—would be held to prohibit a total ban on the promotion of an otherwise legal product.

Whether to ban Joe Camel, however, has become a ripe question. More than a year after antismoking groups formally petitioned for this, the staff of the Federal Trade Commission (FTC) apparently has recommended that the agency find the symbol unfairly attractive to children and banish him from public sight.

The government would have stronger constitutional grounds for banning all cigarette ads than for proceeding against just this one.

While the courts have many times upheld the government's power to censor commercial speech that is untrue or deceptive, there is no showing that Joe Camel ads are any more untruthful or deceptive than the ads that are calculated to make teenage girls think smoking will make them attractive or help them stay slim.

What, then, is Joe Camel's peculiar sin? That he is simply more effective? You can say what you like in an ad, but only so long as you don't say it too well? That is a terribly dangerous line for any government agency to cross. . . .

But if Joe Camel is banned, the Marlboro Man and the Virginia Slims ladies will still be around, and I suspect it wouldn't take long for Reynolds to find an able successor for Joe.

Then we would have the FTC and the courts in the endless, ponderous business of deciding which of these wicked ads are impermissibly more wicked than the others. And while that went on, Congress and the legislatures would have yet another excuse for postponing the higher taxes that, as smokers themselves will tell you, would best hasten the decline of the tobacco industry.

Children in particular are price-sensitive shoppers, and even the tobacco lobby has yet to claim that higher taxes would be unconstitutional.

Journalists, some say, are suspect on this issue. Is it that we love the First Amendment so much, or the profits from tobacco advertising? If there is a moral obligation to the principle of unfettered commercial speech, there is also an equivalent burden to recognize the great harm tobacco causes.

But we must take care to get rid of Joe Camel in ways that don't do harm to the Constitution. Let's let taxes break that camel's back. (Martin Dyckman, "Breaking the Camel's Back," *St. Petersburg Times*, August 15, 1993)

C. Imagine if it were happening here. Imagine if our government were sponsoring research in the poorest pockets of our own country where masses of pregnant women are infected with HIV. The researchers know that AZT could save many of their babies from being born infected. Without AZT one baby in four is infected by the mother, with it only one in ten. But AZT is expensive, $1,000 a mother as it is prescribed now, and the need for a cheaper regimen is critical. So with the best of motives, they set up a study to see if lower, less costly doses are as good as higher doses. Some mothers are given the current AZT protocol, some are given smaller doses. But half—this is the crucial fact—are given placebos, those doses of nothing pills. After all, they reason, how else can they find out if something is better than nothing?

Imagine now what happens when the placebo children are born, when it is discovered that in the name of science the researchers withheld a known treatment. When it becomes known how the government justified this research by saying that these few babies were sacrificed today for the good of more babies tomorrow. And that their mothers would never have had any medical care anyway. It is, of course, unimaginable. Yet it is happening in Uganda, Malawi, Zimbabwe, Ethiopia and other countries where AIDS has spread like, well, AIDS. And happening with the best of American intentions and funding.

In some African countries up to 40 percent of pregnant women are infected. On average the annual health care budget in Africa hovers around $11 a person. The likelihood that these women will get AZT as it is given in our country is virtually nil.

So the urgency of the problem and the poverty of the people are used to explain research that would simply never pass ethical muster here. In the heated controversy that has arisen over their use of placebos, the question has come up: Does a double medical standard justify a double ethical standard? Here, giving a placebo when a known effective treatment exists violates all the canons for research on human subjects. But in the seven AZT studies funded by our government abroad, the women being given dummy pills will give birth to more than a thousand infected babies. . . .

But many respected AIDS researchers hotly disagree, arguing that in the real world of African AIDS, where women have little prenatal care and nothing is the norm, these placebo studies offer the best, fastest hope. They argue that African leaders know best the ethical balance for their own countries. As two supporters of the research added in a New York Times op-ed piece, "Americans should not impose their standards of care on developing countries."

The argument about universal human rights in a diverse world underlies a host of issues from child labor to women's equality to free speech. It is often said that poor countries cannot afford universal human rights. But if AZT is too expensive for Africa, do we deal with a low economic standard by lowering an ethical standard? If so, developing countries could become convenient offshore research factories for ethically cheap science. . . .

Just a few months ago, our government publicly apologized for Tuskeegee. Now I wonder: Did we shut down Tuskeegee? Or did we export it? (Ellen Goodman, "An AIDS Ethical Dilemma," *Boston Globe,* September 24, 1997. © 1997, The Boston Globe Newspaper Co./Washington Post Writers Group Reprinted with permission.)

LOOKING AHEAD

We have clarified the difference between deductive and inductive arguments and have concentrated on helping you recognize arguments, particularly those that are inductive. In doing so we distinguished between several kinds of inductive arguments: generalizations, analogies, causal inferences, and appeal to authorities. In the next two chapters we attend to writing and problem solving. In doing the exercises in these chapters, you will be asked to construct arguments, and more than likely you will use both types of arguments that we have described. In the final three chapters of the book we return to these argument types and study appropriate ways to evaluate them.

ANSWERS TO THE EXERCISES

Answers to Exercise 1

1. (1) Since taking some vitamin C daily is good for your health, (2) I take several thousand milligrams daily to really protect my health. *Since* is a premise indicator. Inductive generalization. 1 → 2
3. (1) Although my street is normally quiet, (2) today cars from all around the neighborhood are driving past my house. The city must have one of the nearby roads blocked. Inductive causal hypothesis (inappropriate use of a deductive-type indicator *must*). It could also be a deductive argument, with the assumed premise that if cars from all around the neighborhood are driving past my house, the city must have one of the nearby roads blocked. (1 + 2) → 3
5. *U.S. News* tallied 76 deaths in day-care facilities in 1996. The causes included drowning, falls, being struck by autos, and sudden infant death syndrome—but (1) the data are sketchy, since (2) many states do not report the causes of these deaths. *Since* is a premise indicator. Deductive. 2 → 1
7. (1) Zebra mussels have been found above the dam separating the lower from the upper St. Croix River. (2) Boaters have not been careful to scrape off all the mussels

attached to their boat when they transported them around the dam. Inductive causal hypothesis. It could also be a deductive argument, with the assumed premise that if zebra mussels have been found above the dam separating the lower from the upper St. Croix River, boaters have not been careful enough to scrape off all the mussels from their boats when they transported them around the dam. 1 → 2

9. (1) Yes, it was settled; his career was determined. (2) He would run away from home and enter upon it. (3) He would start the very next morning. Therefore, (4) he must now begin to get ready. *Therefore* is a conclusion indicator. Deductive. (1 + 2 + 3) → 4

11. (1) As the fire which is kindled makes its fuel into ashes, so (2) the fire of knowledge makes all actions into ashes. *So* is a conclusion indicator. Inductive analogy. 1 → 2

13. I say (1) we shall always have native crime to fear until the native people of this country have worthy purposes to inspire them and worthy goals to work for. For (2) it is only because they see neither purpose nor goal that (3) they turn to drink and crime and prostitution. *For* and *because* are premise indicators. Deductive. 2 → 3 → 1

15. (1) You must strive to guide policy indirectly, so that you make the best of things, and what you cannot turn to good, you can at least make less bad. For (2) it is impossible to do all things well unless all men are good, and (3) this I do not expect to see for a long time. *For* is a premise indicator. Deductive. (2 + 3) → 1

Answers to Exercise 2

1. (1) Introducing thick, fuzzy wool mittens for your immune system. (2) Shield yourself . . . during the cold season and throughout the year. 1 → 2 Analogy comparing lozenges to mittens.

3. (1) Although there are signs that the wall of ageism is beginning to crumble—(2) welcome back the craggy, world-weary faces of Mick Jagger (age 51), Keith Richards (age 51), Eric Clapton (age 50), Robert Plant (age 46), Don Henley (age 47), and yes, Tom Jones (age 54)—(3) with the exception of Tina Turner, . . . it seems only males are granted special dispensation to pass through (to musical stardom at an older age). 2 → 3 Generalization from six male singers.

5. In the fullest definition, (1) harmony is an experience that engages any or all of the five senses in addition to delighting the mind. (2) Harmony can stir the spirit as well as soothe the soul. (3) Consider the harmonious interplay of petals with the rose. (4) Or the full chorus soaring to the last movement of Beethoven's Ninth Symphony. (5) [There cannot] be beauty without harmony. Not if one agrees that beauty arises from the perceived harmony of an object. An object, often made up of divergent parts that come together in an aesthetic whole. Thus, (6) the highest praise one can bestow on an intricate timepiece is "created in harmony." Analogy comparing a watch with a rose and with Beethoven's Ninth Symphony.

    3   4   (+5)
    ↓   ↓
        6

7. (1) I switched from European cars to American cars in 1991, buying one by Chrysler and one by Ford, and wound up with two limes—not quite lemons, but nothing to write home about either. [(2) American cars are nothing to write home about.] (3) Next time, I'll give a Japanese car a try. 1 → [2] → 3 Generalization from buying a Chrysler and a Ford.

9. (1) At the time of the birth of Christ, Rome was a prosperous, thriving empire with a standard of living significantly higher than that of any other city in the Western world, if not on the entire planet. (2) Rome thrived as a government center living largely off the tribute (taxes) of the provinces and conquered lands. . . . (3) The

parasitic nature of Rome's opulent existence contributed to its eventual downfall. (4) Is a similar redistribution of income and wealth taking place in America? (5) Resources are being extracted from the general tax paying public to feed the bureaucrats and government officials who tend to concentrate themselves in state or national capitals . . . (6) America's government centers have become parasite economies. . . . (7) The affluence of government centers is making the rest of America poorer. (8) "Capital crimes" gradually are sapping the nation of needed economic vitality. (1–3, 5–8) → 4 Analogy comparing U.S. centers of government (Washington, D.C.) with Rome.

Answers to Exercise 3

1. (1) There have been a number of earthquakes in and around Los Angeles in recent years. (2) They appear to be increasing in intensity. (3) In the next few years we will see a really big one hit this area. (1 + 2) → 3 Prediction.

3. (1) They must have forgotten my birthday this year. (2) I looked in the closet, under the bed, even downstairs under the Ping-Pong table, and haven't found anything even resembling a wrapped present. 2 → 1 Causal inference.

5. (1) The victim's blood was on the front seat of the car, and (2) there were bloody tracks leading to the front door of the house. (3) The victim's blood was also on the accused's socks. (4) He also could not explain where he was during that crucial half hour before he was taken to the airport. (5) There is little doubt that he is guilty of the murder. (1 + 2 + 3 + 4) → 5 Causal inference.

7. (1) When the shortstop played the ball, it took a wicked hop. (2) It must have hit a small stone on the edge of the infield grass. 1 → 2 Causal inference.

9. (1) Before mid-century, there were no significant holes in the ozone layer over Antarctica, but the size of the holes has increased dramatically since then. (2) During that same period we have also seen a dramatic rise in the number of air conditioners and refrigerators. Perhaps (3) the CFC emissions from these appliances affect the ozone layer. (1 + 2) → 3 Causal inference.

Answers to Exercise 4

1. Conclusion: Please, let us have the three motorized portages back.
   Premises: It is a precious treasure and we will protect it and pass it on.
   Analogy: Boundary Waters is compared to a diamond. As one protects and passes on a diamond, so one would do so to the Boundary Waters.

3. Conclusion: The Greenlanders starved to death.
   Premises: Excavations have turned up many expensive portable items, like crucifixes, that would probably have been removed by the settlers in an evacuation. And had the colony's population gradually diminished, the wood in many of the farms—a valuable commodity in a place with few trees—would have been scavenged by the remaining settlers. Such was not the case. Cut marks on the dog bones suggest the dogs were butchered; even the cow hooves were eaten.
   Causal argument

5. Conclusion: Use the Diadora tennis shoe on the court.
   Premises: Diadoras are like Ferraris for your feet. Like the famous racing car, Diadora shoes are very quick, precisely engineered, responsive and—I think—good to look at. . . . To take a lesser shoe on the court would be like driving the family sedan at LeMans.
   Analogy

7. Conclusion: Burke & Barry [whiskey] has an indefinable quality that sets it apart.
   Premises: There is a quality that sets champions apart from other thoroughbreds. Maybe it's heart. Something you can't define. But you know it's there. How to

judge fine Kentucky whiskey. Taste. Aroma. Smoothness. Qualities that are hard to define. But one taste of Burke & Barry [whiskey] and you know they're there.
Analogy

9. Conclusion: Endocrine disrupters are at work.
Premises: Girls are undergoing earlier puberty.
Causal argument

11. Conclusion: Don't abort.
Premise: Though his prospects were dim, the baby born was Ludwig van Beethoven. [That is, this case turned out to be a genius.]
Intermediate conclusion: Any child could turn out to be a genius.
Generalization

13. Conclusion indicator: This indicates
Conclusion: These meteorites did in fact come from Mars.
Premise: Barnacle Bill, Yogi, and the soil exhibit other chemical signatures that closely match the 12 Martian meteorites.
Analogy

15. Conclusion: The college has a quality food service that is deserving of praise from our newspaper rather than scorn.
Premises: I found that the food tasted very good and appeared very attractive. The cooks are concerned about appearance. I have not found a dirty fork, plate or glass. The people are polite and friendly.
Generalization

Answers to Exercise 5

1. Data: The average driver spent 32 seconds leaving his or her spot when no one else was jockeying for it, but an additional seven seconds when another car appeared eager to enter.
When cars honked, drivers took an additional 12 seconds.

3. Analogies or generalizations.
Analogy between backhanding another's face with a glove two centuries ago (dueling) and hanging onto a parking space today. Also an analogy of hanging on to one's parking space with Norm keeping his bar stool in *Cheers*. Generalization: "We all have at least a bit of Bickle in us and are quite willing to squander time and energy in senseless posturing when strangers attempt to horn in on our spaces."

Answers to Exercise 6

1. Argument. The argument is an inference from the effect (the government restocked its reserves) to the cause (oil prices declined).

3. Causal explanation. The effect—he quickly ran from the house—is explained by the cause—he could smell smoke in the hallway. Psychological explanation.

5. Causal explanation. The effect—he wrecked his car coming home from work today—is explained by the cause—an inconsiderate driver cut him off on the freeway and he hit an embankment.
Psychological and physical explanation.

7. Causal explanation. The effect—men are less likely to develop osteoporosis until later in life than women and seldom suffer as severely—is explained by the fact that they have 30 percent more bone mass on the average and don't undergo the sudden drop in estrogen that occurs with menopause.
Physical explanation.

9. Description

11. Description
13. Causal explanation. The effect—the lax enforcement of anti-pollution regulations—is explained by the cause—the power vested interests have over our enforcement agencies. Psychological explanation. The paragraph also contains a noncausal argument: because of the power vested interests have over our enforcement agencies, America needs more tight regulations.
15. Argument. The conclusion—we ought to thoroughly study its social, economic and political impact on the nation—is argued for on the grounds that the amount of money wagered through legal gambling in America has become so immense so quickly. The paragraph also contains an explanation. That the amount of money wagered through legal gambling in America has become so immense so quickly is given as a reason why Congress passed legislation to create the National Gambling Impact and Policy Commission.
    A psychological explanation.
17. Probably a causal argument, since the causes are unsure. For the effect—There is no enthusiasm for anti-smoking campaigns directed at kids that I saw as recently as the late 1980s—the author suggests three possible causal hypotheses: (1) Perhaps it's because today's generation of young people is growing up more disconnected from adults and adult guidance than any other generation in our nation's history. (2) Maybe it has to do with our modern preoccupation with "rights." (3) Or maybe it has to do with the image of smoking itself. If it contains explanations, they are psychological.

Answers to Exercise 7

1. Assumes that each dose of vitamin C taken will contribute to good health.
3. Assumes that other, unstated hypotheses—for example, that a delivery truck is blocking the road—will not explain the presence of the cars on the street as well as the given hypothesis.
5. When many states do not report the causes of these deaths, the data is sketchy.
7. Assumes that other, unstated hypotheses will not explain the presence of the mussels as well as the hypothesis about failure to clean off contaminated boats.
9. If he is going to run away tomorrow, he must get ready now.
11. Assumes that the analogs—fire and knowledge—are relevantly similar in other respects.
13. The natives of the country see neither purpose nor goal.
15. If you cannot do all things well, you can at least make them less bad.

Answers to Exercise 8

A. Topic: baseball parks; Fenway Park
   Issue: Whether Fenway should be replaced
   Thesis: (3) Fenway should not be replaced.
   Main points: (1) Fenway is a classic, replete with nooks and angles and the Green Monster and a sense of proximity to the players that no other stadium offers. (2) The game will be forever diminished if the old girl disappears. 1 → 2 → 3 Deductive arguments.
C. Topic: AIDS research
   Issue: Whether AIDS research should be done in Africa by using samples that are not given any AZT
   Thesis: (1) We should not do AIDS research in Africa by using samples that are not given any AZT.
   Main points: (2) We would not allow such research to happen here. (3) Giving a placebo when a known effective treatment exists violates all the canons for research

on human subjects. (4) The researchers know that AZT could save many of their babies from being born infected. (5) Without AZT one baby in four is infected by the mother, with it only one in ten. (6) We don't deal with a low economic standard by lowering an ethical standard. (7) If we did, developing countries could become convenient offshore research factories for ethically cheap science.

Deductive arguments

CHAPTER 8

Synthesis

Writing with Critical Thinking

At various points along our journey into critical thinking you have been encouraged to put your ideas into writing. Writing assists you in making ideas your own, in clarifying your opinions or beliefs, and in sorting out the evidence you have for thinking your beliefs are true.

Putting your ideas down on paper in a manner suitable for critical reflection is a difficult task; it involves more than merely journaling or chronicling your ideas. You need to

- set out a problem or issue that is worthy of reflection
- take a position on it by stating a thesis
- find evidence or main points to justify your confidence in answering the problem in the way you did.

This chapter provides assistance in developing your ideas into a written piece of persuasive reasoning. You will not find an easy formula for writing a good paper here because no such formulas exist. Writing is not a linear process by which you start at point A and arrive at point G—a Good Paper. Even the structure we suggest provides only an initial model that, as you progress, you will modify to suit your own communication style. But although future modification will occur, to promote your ideas in writing it is best to begin with a strong foundation.

The writing process is filled with uncertainty. You might begin to work on some topic and then have to change and start on another when the first leads to a dead end. You might have to revise your issue and thesis as you proceed. You probably will encounter interesting information in your research that you will never use. You might also have to go back and find additional information to carry out your project, either in the same sources where you already looked or in new sources. You might discover counter-arguments to what you presented that are so strong and convincing that you have to alter what you initially wrote. You might even uncover a subsidiary problem that is much more interesting, important, and controversial than the original problem, leading you to change the direction of your paper.

But despite these uncertainties in the writing process, you can begin with several certainties.

- Good writing is hard work.

For most of us, writing takes great mental and physical energy. Perhaps this is one reason that writing is so rewarding, for when the project is done, you will have produced something tangible through your travail. In any case, you must set your mind and energies to the task, realizing that significant effort is required to produce a quality product.

- Good writing depends upon reading.

Every system needs the introduction of new energy to keep functioning. Your mind also needs new energy to produce new ideas. This energy comes from your experiences and your reading about what others have experienced or thought. To change the metaphor, experience and reading are the fertile soil that generates new ideas. While personal experience provides basic but essential access to the world, your limits restrict what you can encounter. To get beyond those limits, to incorporate others' experiences and reflections, you need to read what others have written—in books, articles, newspapers, and reference sources. This reading may be of two types. *General reading* unconnected with a specific research project stimulates you with new topics, new vocabulary, and new ideas that may capture your interest and intrigue you to pursue them further. *Specialized reading* on the topic of your research paper connects you with those who have also thought, researched, and written about your topic and issue. Those who read little almost always have difficulty writing.

- Writing gives birth to more writing.

Once you have produced a written piece, you need to sit back and let the words and ideas mellow. Setting it aside for a while gives you distance from what you have written so that when you reread it, the ideas and their phrasing are somewhat fresh. That temporal difference allows you to rethink and rewrite more clearly. Obviously this is an argument against writing a paper at the last minute before it is due.

After a time, reread what you have written, noting what needs changing, developing, and supporting. Possibly you will change some of your ideas; doing this will require that you go back and rewrite sections of your paper. You will discover ambiguities, vagueness, lack of clarity, bad reasoning, unwarranted use of emotive language, lack of sufficient detail, and lots of other reasons to rewrite. In short, writing necessitates rewriting.

- Writing is fun and rewarding.

Don't forget this last point, which is of great importance. You can achieve great satisfaction when you see the results of your mental labor. Producing a paper that contains your own ideas, carefully thought out and researched, well written and clearly explained, is a significant accomplishment; the results are worth sharing with others. Writing lets your ideas loose.

GENERATING A TOPIC

Suppose one of your teachers asks you to write a paper for the class, or you decide on your own to write something. You now face one of the most daunting tasks in argumentative writing: generating a topic. "Where do I begin?" you ask yourself. Without a good topic, your writing project cannot begin.

As you recall from Chapter 3, the topic is the subject of your paper, expressed in a few words or a phrase. Let us begin with a few suggestions for choosing a topic on which to write.

- Choose a topic in which you are interested.

Writing several paragraphs, let alone a paper, about a topic in which you have no interest is difficult. You will find that you cannot convey the ideas with the enthusiasm necessary to intrigue and persuade others. But if you write about something that interests you, even the research will go more smoothly. You will want to read and learn more about the topic, see its connections with other things you know, and discover what others have thought and said about it. To begin a paper on an open topic, write a paragraph or two about some things, people, ideas, or events that interest or concern you and tell why you are interested in them. After writing these paragraphs, identify a topic that applies to each of these areas.

- Choose a topic that will interest your audience.

When you write, you need to consider who your audience is. To capture the attention of your prospective readers, think about their interests and background so that they will want to read what you write. Ask what your readers already know and do not know so that you can add to their knowledge and understanding or persuade them to a different opinion. You want to consider what they accept or believe, what presuppositions you share in common with them and what they would require arguments for so that you can write about things that are significant while not assuming too much.

- Choose a topic either that you know something about or about which someone else can assist you to find information.

Select a topic that is addressed by adequate quality resources. Your instructor or a librarian can assist you in searching for materials on your topic. When you are given an open agenda, it is wise to explore several topics so that if one leads to a dead end, another may prove fruitful.

- Choose a topic that is neither too broad nor too narrow.

You must avoid both generalities that make a topic too broad and a parochialism that narrows a topic too severely. Topics like U.S. presidents, baseball, euthanasia, movie stars, and the Second World War are so broad that they make it difficult to narrow your focus. Topics like the ninth inning of yesterday's ball game, abortion in Manhattan, or last week's episode of *Home Improvement* might prove too narrow to generate enough research materials. The rule of thumb is this: if you are overwhelmed by materials, probably your topic is too broad; if you are underwhelmed by materials, probably your topic is too narrow.

If your choice is between too broad and too narrow of a topic, it is better to avoid an overly narrow topic. If your topic is overly narrow, the slightest shift in topic as you write your paper might move you to a different topic. If your topic is broader, you can develop different aspects of that topic without getting off course. As you work with your topic, feel free to narrow or broaden its scope while avoiding the extremes.

- If you are working in an unfamiliar area, find resource materials that might suggest topics to you.

Look at the chapter headings of a standard textbook in the field. If the text has study questions, read them to find ideas you might want to address. Find an index for academic journals in the field you are asked to investigate and look at the subject headings. The advantage of these methods is that the textbook probably has a bibliography, while the journal indexes list recently published articles or books relevant to the topic. This will get you started with resource materials.

- Look at the editorial pages of your local or a national newspaper to find what is currently being debated.

Here you will find topics about which there is serious discussion and disagreement. The editorials will also introduce you to current thinking on the topic.

Remember that the topic guides your writing. Since it is the subject you will address, select the topic with care and enthusiasm.

Exercise 1

By the time you have completed this chapter, you will have written and rewritten an argumentative paper.

1. Write a paragraph about three things, people, ideas, or events that interest you, and tell why you are interested in these.

2. For each of these three interests, identify a topic about which you would like to write. Make sure it is neither too broad nor too narrow.

3. Select one of these topics for your argumentative paper.

GENERATING AN ISSUE

After you have identified your topic, the next step is to generate a problem or issue that you want to address. As Chapter 3 noted, you state the issue in the form of either a direct or indirect question. This question identifies what you intend to address or answer in the paper. Since this issue guides the rest of what you write, choose it carefully. At the same time, you should feel free to modify the issue as you go along. The issue you choose is not written in stone. But remember that if you alter the issue, you have to go back and review what you have researched and written to see whether these materials are now relevant to your new formulation of the issue.

You generate the issue by asking a question about your topic. In fact, to get started you might *list half a dozen or more questions that relate to your topic.* You may even mention your topic to your friends and have them suggest some questions about this topic. The more questions you ask about the topic, the more issues you have from which to choose. This diversity of questions provides some flexibility so that you do not feel trapped by thinking that there is only one problem on your topic. Remember that the issue posed contains your topic.

Suppose you chose the topic of automobile air bags. What issues can you raise regarding this topic? Here are some questions:

1. Should consumers have to pay for air bags in their automobiles even if they do not want them?
2. Should people be allowed to disconnect their air bags if they think they are unsafe?
3. Should automobile manufacturers be held legally accountable for deaths caused by air bags?
4. Do the few children's lives saved by disconnecting automobile air bags outweigh the greater number of adult lives that will be lost because of disconnected air bags?
5. Would weaker air bags result in fewer or more deaths?
6. Should the government require auto manufacturers to design air bags for all passenger sizes and weights?

Once you have listed these questions about your topic, you need to choose one of them on which to proceed. Not all of these questions will lead to a good paper; some questions are better than others in generating arguments. You need to sort through the questions to find the particular issue you feel is significant and want to address.

Many of the same suggestions noted about how to go about choosing a topic apply to selecting an issue as well.

- Choose an issue of interest to you and others.
- Choose an issue that either you know something about or on which someone else (your professor, librarian, parent, peers) can help you find information.
- Your issue should be neither too broad nor too narrow.
- Choose an issue about which there is some significant disagreement.

Your paper should address a topic that is significant both to you and to others. Writing a paper about today's weather will not get you very far. Neither will writing a paper that takes a position that most people accept. You, your teacher, and your readers will wonder why you are spending your time writing about something on which you all agree. The *disputability* of your topic keeps you and the reader interested, wanting to know the reasons why you believe as you do, and why others take differing stands.

If you cannot find people who have written on both sides of your issue, you should begin to question whether your issue is significant or disputable enough to warrant your time and energy researching and writing about it. Generally, the more you find people responding on both sides of your question, the more interesting, important, and disputable the issue is. One test of disputability is to give your issue to some friends. If they do not give different answers to your issue, probably it is not very disputable.

Exercise 2

1. List half a dozen questions you might ask about the topic you chose in Exercise 1. The questions should be of the sort that people could reasonably answer in different ways.

2. Choose from these questions the question you intend to address as your issue in your paper.

3. Evaluate the issue you have chosen using the four items listed in this section.

GENERATING A THESIS

Once you have chosen the issue you want to address, it is time to stake out a position on the question posed. In your paper do not provide a survey of different views; that would be a mere report. Rather, in an argumentative paper you attempt to persuade your readers about the truth of a certain point. This point constitutes your main thesis; it asserts your opinion on the issue you chose to address. The thesis that initially directs your research derives from your experience, reading, and reflection.

When you write your paper, no matter how long it is, the first paragraph or two and the concluding paragraph should state your thesis. It should appear in the beginning of your paper to let your reader know what you intend to show or defend. It should appear at the end of your paper to confirm to your reader that you have indeed defended that thesis.

The paragraph stating your thesis is both the first and the last paragraph you write. It is the first thing you write because the thesis provides the unifying factor for the rest of the paper. Everything in the paper relates back to the thesis, developing and defending it. The thesis paragraph is also the last thing you write as you review what you have written and reflect on how successful your reasoning has been.

As you develop your paper, you may actually change your mind about your thesis. Your initial thesis reflects your opinion or belief prior to your research into the reasons for and against holding it. Somewhere along the way you may decide that the evidence points not in favor of but against your thesis. In this case, you may have to qualify or modify your thesis to reflect your revised thinking. When this happens, you have to rewrite your thesis (and probably part of your paper) to encompass the changes. In short, while the thesis controls your paper, and while you need to continually check that you are addressing it, you should feel free to alter that thesis so that it better reflects the results of your research, careful thinking, and developed arguments.

To say that your thesis is tentative and may change sounds frightening—and it is. But it is also exciting, for research and writing can be a time of discovery, opening you to positions and views that previously you had not seriously considered. Writing provides the opportunity for you to explore new horizons, to think in new ways, to entertain unlikely or unusual ideas, and not merely cement your old views.

One difficulty, discussed in Chapter 3, that plagues many papers is that the writer gets off the topic or thesis. The author intends to go in one direction but through following a train of thought moves in another. So that this does not happen to you, frequently stop writing and read what you have written. Then go back and reread your thesis statement to see whether you are still addressing the topic and issue and asserting the thesis you said you would. If you find you are addressing some other topic or issue or are asserting a different thesis, you will have to find where you departed from the trail and begin again at that point. A clearly written thesis statement helps prevent moving off on tangents.

Exercise 3

State the thesis of the essay that you started in Exercises 1 and 2. It should be your answer to the question posed in the issue selected in Exercise 2.

GENERATING THE MAIN POINTS

It is now time to construct your paper, to develop and defend your ideas. Since this book is directed toward critical thinking, your development of the ideas must do more than summarize the data you find or the various positions others have taken on the issue. As we stated in the previous section, the paper is *not* to be *a survey* of various views. You do need to understand the data and others' views, for if you misunderstand them you will in turn misrepresent their ideas in your paper. But to present only the data or others' views leaves you and the reader at the earlier stages of critical thinking—knowledge and comprehension. Rather, your goal is to *use* the data from your research and the arguments of others to *shape arguments* that defend your position and/or refute contrary positions. Your ultimate goal is to rationally persuade your reader (and perhaps yourself) that your thesis is true.

The arguments you present to defend your view constitute the main points of your paper. Each main point is itself a subthesis, which both relates back to the main thesis and in turn needs to be developed and defended by arguments and evidence. In a sense, the development of each main point becomes a mini-paper within the larger paper. Thus, an outline develops in which the thesis is supported by main points, which themselves are supported by subpoints or arguments, and so on. The structure may look something like this.

> Thesis
> > Main Point 1 (subthesis)
> > > Support for main point 1 given by submain points
> > Main Point 2 (subthesis)
> > > Support for main point 2 given by submain points
> > Main Point 3 (subthesis)
> > > Support for main point 3 given by submain points
> > Other Main Points as needed

This skeleton provides a structure around which you can build your paper. Your research and thinking flesh out these main points, developing and strengthening your arguments for your positions and against competing views. By carefully laying out your arguments to develop the main points, you shape a carefully reasoned paper.

Continuing our air bag example, if you decided to write your paper on the thesis "People should be allowed to disable air bags if they desire," you might develop the following main points.

1. Forcing people to act contrary to their own desires or their own perceived best interest is paternalism, and paternalism is not justified for adults.
2. Older people and children have been killed or seriously injured by air bags and this is unjustified.
3. The accidental deployment of air bags is both dangerous and costly.

Main points can have two different kinds of structure. Some main points are positive in character, presenting arguments *for* your thesis. Initially, you list reasons for believing that your thesis is true. As you research, you modify this list by adding to it, discarding some of the earlier reasons as being inadequate to support your thesis, and in general developing and improving the list. One of the major functions of your research is to strengthen your initial, positive reasons for your thesis by developing what you think is true and adding new information and arguments. As mentioned previously, research might also have the opposite effect, convincing you that your original position needs to be abandoned or significantly modified.

The arguments you give in favor of your position should

- be supported by careful, documented research
- be supported by careful reasoning
- use principles or truths that are widely accepted.

Where exceptions to such principles or truths are made, you need to defend them convincingly.

Save your strongest argument for the end because this argument will stick with the reader the longest. As you lay out your main points, you might start with your weakest argument and gradually proceed to your strongest argument. However, since giving your weakest argument as your initial argument might turn the reader off from the outset, you might think about starting your reasoning with your second strongest argument.

Some of your main points may also be negative in character. That is, they present arguments *against* positions that differ from your thesis. To respond to or refute opposing views, you need to look at what other people have written and thought about your thesis. You need to understand their arguments and then interact with them, showing the reader where those who disagree with you went wrong or why their arguments are inadequate to refute your position. Here you carefully consider the other side of your thesis. When you do this, it is essential that you treat the other side with intellectual fairness.

Some writers are tempted merely to dismiss contrary positions without taking them seriously. They make those positions as weak as possible and then easily refute them. This kind of reasoning is called the *Straw Person Fallacy*. You might think of the story of the Three Little Pigs; in it the wolf easily blew down the pig's house constructed from straw. This tale illustrates the approach some take to others' positions. If by weakening their arguments you misrepresent those who disagree with you, you have created a straw person argument that may be easy to refute. Your refutation may seem persuasive at first to your readers, but it both violates the integrity for which critical thinkers strive and destroys the ultimate goal of critical thinking: to arrive at the truth. So, when you consider the views of others, treat them with integrity; present their views in their strongest form possible and then proceed with your critique of them.

Your resulting paper probably will have something like the following structure.

INTRODUCTION. Here you set the stage for your paper. You may tell

- why you are writing this paper (in the sense of providing a context for the paper). You may show how the issue arises or why it should be addressed.
- what your approach to the issue is
- what your thesis is.

BODY. This is the "meat" of your paper. Here you

- lay out your main points to develop and defend your thesis

- respond to actual or possible criticisms of your thesis and main points
- lay out your opponent's view and critique or refute it.

CONCLUSION. Here you summarize what you have said or argued. It

- should contain a restatement of your thesis
- may review or mention the main points supporting your thesis
- should *not* introduce new topics or material.

Making an outline also serves to keep your paper on track. In your own writing it is important to make sure that the main points address the same topic and thesis with which you began. If they do not, there is a good chance that you have wandered off the main topic or issue. A good outline helps assure that you still are addressing the topic or issue on which you chose to write. With an outline you can see the main points more easily and can determine whether or not they are relevant.

One important word. This structure for writing papers presents an *ideal*, as much broken as kept in good writing. Writers may depart from this ideal by beginning their piece with a story or puzzle to capture the reader's interest. They may also begin with a commonly accepted view on the issue posed and then proceed to refute that view so that their thesis comes rather late. Eventually you too will work creatively in your presentations. But as with any rule or ideal, to break the ideal you must first master it. Only then can you go on to rework the structure you have mastered to better convey your thoughts. If you depart from this ideal, you must be careful not to create a muddled presentation, for readers expect to find clarity in what they read.

Exercise 4

Here is an editorial on air bags.

1. State the issue and thesis.

2. Make an outline of main points the author presents to support his thesis.

The new prohibitionists

It gets sillier and sillier. After air bags exploding in cars traveling at low speeds killed more than 30 children and 20 adults, President Clinton announced that car owners will be allowed to deactivate their air bags with the help of a mechanic. However, there are no plans to cancel the 1991 congressional mandate that dual air bags must be installed in every car by the 1998 model year.

So a lot of car buyers will pay $400 for air bags they don't want and don't have to use.

This is what happens when the government steps in to protect us from ourselves. The usual form of government regulation, like air pollution or air safety controls, is designed to prevent people from being harmed by others. Air bags, however, belong to a whole different species of regulation. They require people to protect themselves from their own actions. The results can be ridiculous.

For adults as a whole, the most recent analysis by the National Highway Traffic Safety Administration concludes that air bags are an overall safety benefit, reducing the fatality rate by 11%. However, the same analysis shows that for a child under 10 in the passenger seat, the presence of an air bag more than doubles the statistical probability of that child's dying in an accident.

Air bags have widely varying benefits, depending on individual circumstances, and can be outright harmful to certain categories of car occupants. According to NHTSA, including accidents where adults were often killed or badly injured, accompanying children experience a large "fatality increase with passenger air bags [that] persists up through age 10."

Air bags also don't do much good for people who are already wearing seat belts. Compared with no protection, wearing a seat belt reduces the fatality rate by 45%. Adding an air bag increases this to only 50%.

Air bags also work well only in direct frontal crashes. For other types of accidents, having an air bag can actually increase the statistical fatality rate for certain categories of adults. For adults over 70, this effect largely counteracts other safety benefits. Some data also suggest that people in small cars may benefit less.

Why wasn't all this taken into account before the Naderites and others forced air bags on all of us? Because that isn't the way the government works. Congress sees a problem, it passes a law. The consequences are somebody else's affair.

The potential toll of innocent victims of air bags may actually be much larger than the official statistics show. The evidence is mounting that some drivers compensate for increased safety protections by taking significantly more risks on the road. In a 1993 article in the *Journal of Policy Analysis and Management,* two University of Chicago researchers concluded that, allowing for such "offsetting" behavior, air bags and other protective devices would have only "a modest net effect" overall.

A subsequent study of insurance data collected between 1989 and 1993, published in the *Journal of Law and Economics,* found that "air bag-equipped cars tend to be driven more aggressively," and have more accidents.

I wish the do-gooders would read a bit of history. They could turn to the chapters on Prohibition. In trying to protect people from the evils of drink Congress banned the stuff, touching off a major crime wave and a general disrespect for law. It also killed a lot of people with poisoned booze. Right now there are lots of people out there who would like to see a similar prohibition on cigarettes.

Are air bags just an expensive nuisance? No, it's worse than that. When

continued

government gets into this kind of activity, it promotes the dangerous idea that people are children who need to be looked after by their betters. Paradoxically, those who are most determined to mandate devices like air bags are often those who claim to have great confidence in the judgment of their fellow citizens. Yet they do not seem to think these same people are capable of assuming responsibility for their own safety and well-being.

Congress should start by repealing the requirement that every car must have air bags and instead require car companies to provide information that will let consumers make their own choices.

[Robert H. Nelson, "The New Prohibitionists," *Forbes*, February 10, 1997, p. 72. Reprinted by permission of FORBES Magazine, © Forbes Inc., 1997.]

Exercise 5

Present an outline containing at least three main points to support the thesis you stated in Exercise 3. The main points are to be expressed in complete sentences. At least one of your main points should respond to a denial or critique of your thesis.

DECIDING WHAT NEEDS DEFENSE

Arguments play an important role in our lives. Often we provide evidence or reasons to support our beliefs or to persuade someone about the truth of a thesis. But are the reasons we present as a defense themselves true? When our readers or listeners doubt these reasons as much as the conclusions they support, we have in turn to defend these very reasons. So reasons are used to defend other reasons, which ultimately defend conclusions.

At the same time, we cannot argue for the truth of every statement in our presentation; we lack the time, space, and energy for this endeavor. Indeed, if we had to defend every statement we used, we would be caught either in an infinite circle or an infinite regress of reasons. *Being caught in a circle* means giving a reason in support of another reason, and then a third reason in support of the second reason, so that eventually you use one of your ultimate conclusions to support a prior premise. *Being caught in an infinite regress* of reasons means that every reason is supported by another reason and so on to infinity. This regress would be like dialoging with children who respond with the question "Why?" to everything you say. Although they request a reason for every response you give, after a while you must draw the conversation to a close and proclaim that what you have said is just the way things are. Since a reasoning chain has limits, you have to make an initial determination about which statements need more careful consideration and support and which you can let pass. Those actual statements you let pass constitute your explicit assumptions. Those that need some support often function as conclusions of other arguments. Let us further explore this distinction between reasons that do and reasons that do not need defense.

Statements Not Needing Defense

Let us first consider actual statements we let pass without a defense: our explicit assumptions. As we noted in Chapter 7, explicit assumptions differ from implicit assumptions, which are statements assumed but never actually stated. Explicit assumptions are an essential and important aspect of our communication. Included in this category are the following:

• Statements grounded in our own individual, personal experience

Generally we need not defend assertions about what we have seen, heard, smelled, or touched. For example, "I saw two loons on the lake yesterday"; "Mary brought her twin girls by my office"; "I heard the crowd roar when Taylor kicked the winning goal in overtime."

• Statements about common experience

Since most of us sense colors, shapes, smells, and sounds in the same way, general statements (in contrast to personal experience statements) about how things look, smell, or sound generally need no defense. Likewise, since humans experience similar feelings, emotions, pains, and desires, we often do not need to defend statements like "Southern Californians got angry when they discovered that the gas pumps did not give them the amount of gasoline they paid for"; or "Butterflies churn even in stomachs strong enough for the Big One, a 235-foot-high roller coast at the Pleasure Beach."

• Statements about matters of common knowledge

The truth of such statements is generally acknowledged and hence not disputed. It is common knowledge that the earth is spherical or that seals try to escape from stalking polar bears by plunging down their hole into the sea, although few of us have actually experienced this fact. These statements sound reasonable enough to our limited experience to be accepted as true without needing defense.

• Statements accepted by both author and audience within the context of a presentation

For the sake of argument or to get the discussion underway, people may agree to accept certain claims as true, although these claims may be disputed by others who are not part of the audience. In this context, this common viewpoint can be assumed and need not be defended. For example, in the context of a theological debate, the presenter and listeners may carry on a conversation that presupposes the existence of God. Since they both agree on this premise, they can pass on to more disputable claims. But if the dialogue were between a believer in God and a nonbeliever, the claim that God exists would not be held in common and the matter would be disputable. Or again, two Republicans may assume that we need a tax cut and proceed to discuss the best way to achieve it, whereas in the context where a Republican debates a Democrat, there may be no shared common view and the matter of a tax cut is highly disputable.

• Claims that seem intuitively obvious to us

This is perhaps the category with which you ought to be most careful, since it is easy to claim that something is intuitively obvious to you when that same claim may be disputed by those with whom you are communicating. If you argue against capital punishment, you may take it as intuitively obvious that people who are executed for serious crimes committed suffer in their last moments, but others may doubt whether this is so. The claim, rather than intuitively obvious, may be disputable.

In summary, since we cannot defend every statement we make, we present many statements for which we do not give reasons. These explicit assumptions are taken as givens. We assume them to be true (on the grounds noted) and ask our readers or listeners to do likewise.

Statements Needing Defense

Not every statement we make, however, can be assumed to be true. When we turn to those statements we need to defend, we encounter statements or claims that are disputed or disputable. They are not matters of our own or common experience or knowledge, accepted within the context of our discourse, or intuitively obvious. Generally, statements that are disputable and require defense include the following:

- Statements about experiences only a few persons have had or of a very unusual sort

These may include things like sightings of UFOs, near-death experiences, miraculous healings, or new experimental research or laboratory results. It is important to note that although statements about such experiences generally require a defense, this should not be taken to imply that such statements are false. Rather, in such cases to question why these statements are true, to ask for further evidence in their behalf, is simply appropriate.

- Statements that make universal or near universal claims

For example, "All the theater-goers enjoyed the movie," "Most physicians recommend this product to their patients," "Everyone is wearing jeans to the concert," "The bakery down the street makes the best pies ever," "Sarah is the funniest girl ever" all need defense. We may accept without defense the claims that many theater-goers enjoyed the movie, some or many physicians recommend this product, the bakery makes good pies, or Sarah is funny. Because our experience is limited, it is easier to believe particular statements that affirm that something is the case some of the time. But rarely do we have access to information that allows us to make universal or near universal claims about all, every, most, or best. In particular, hyperbole is always suspicious. Hence, when people make universal claims, it is often appropriate to query what basis they have for making such statements.

Other statements needing defense are these:

- Statements that report data or make claims that many people actually do or may dispute

Someone may argue in defense of the pro-life position that many women who have abortions suffer from depression or serious medical complications. But whether or not this claim is true is as much a matter of dispute as the conclusion it is used to support, and hence it needs defense.

- Statements that reflect disputable inferences from data

Some people might conclude one thing from the data, whereas other people conclude something quite different from the same material.
Consider the following article.

Moroto Morass

The arid, scrub- and acacia-dotted hills of Uganda's Moroto region in East Africa are not where you'd expect to find an ape. But more than 20 million years ago, during the Miocene epoch; this area was the woodland home of a surprisingly modern-looking ape that may have swung through the tress while its primitive contemporaries traversed branches on all fours. According to a report in the April 18 issue of *Science,* this ape displays the earliest evidence for a modern apelike body design—nearly six million years earlier than expected—and may belong in the line of human ancestry.

The authors—Daniel L. Gebo of Northern Illinois University, Laura M. MacLatchy of the State University of New York at Stony Brook and their colleagues—first focused on fossils found in the 1960s. The facial dental and vertebral remains, originally dated to 14 million years, revealed a hominoid (the primate group comprising apes and humans) with a puzzling combination of features—its face and upper jaw resembled those of primitive apes, but the vertebral remains were more like modern apes. Consequently, paleontologists were at a loss to classify the Moroto hominoid definitively and tentatively placed it in various, previously established taxonomic groups.

Now Gebo and MacLatchy are placing this ape in its own genus and species, *Morotopithecus bishopi,* based on newly discovered pieces of shoulder and thigh bone and a high-quality radiometric date suggesting an age of at least 20.6 million years for all of the remains. The researchers infer that *Morotopithe-*

cus weighed between 40 and 50 kilograms and had an advanced "locomotor repertoire" that included climbing, hanging and swinging from branch to branch. This form of locomotion "allows you to be a big animal and still exploit an arboreal environment," says MacLatchy, who suspects that *Morotopithecus* was a typical fruit-eating ape.

Critical to their locomotor reconstruction is the recently unearthed scapular glenoid, or shoulder socket. Monkeys have glenoids that are teardrop-shaped in outline, whereas modern apes, humans and, according to the researchers, *Morotopithecus* have glenoids that are rounder, which enhances shoulder mobility for hanging and swinging. This and other features, the authors contend, make it more closely related to living apes and humans than are some, considerably younger fossil apes.

Other are not so sure about the shoulder evidence. Monte L. McCrossin, a paleoanthropologist at Southern Illinois University, points out that because nothing else is preserved to identify it conclusively, "the possibility exists that the glenoid will turn out not even to be from a primate." He is also skeptical about the proposed novelty of this shoulder morphology. Scapular glenoids have not been recovered for other early Miocene apes, so they, too, might share the rounded features. "Absence of evidence shouldn't be taken as evidence of absence," he quips.

This article illustrates both of the last two points. The paleoanthropologist McCrossin expresses doubts both about the data (whether the fossil shoulder bone is from an ape) and the interpretations built upon the shape of the bone. This demand for further evidence and careful critique of inferences made from evidence is a hallmark of the sciences.

A final type of statement needing defense is

- A **normative statement,** that is, an assertion about things that are good or bad or acts that are right or wrong.

Normative statements usually contain terms like *should, ought, good, bad, right,* and *wrong.* When we claim that things should be done, that someone ought to act in a certain way, or that certain programs deserve to be implemented, we enter into areas that generally require defense. The words *should, ought,* and their synonyms in a discourse usually trigger in the critical reader the request for a defense. For example, currently a debate rages in sporting circles about whether cities and states should use public funds to build new, expensive sport stadiums for privately held professional teams. Any claim that public funds should be so dispersed is disputable and needs defense.

Disputable statements, then, can be legitimately questioned by either the author or the audience. In our own writing, we need to identify disputable statements and defend them to the best of our ability. This need can be illustrated by the following letter.

(1) Major League Baseball in the 1990s is quite different from what it was in the 1890s. (2) Baseball these days isn't about green fields and red ropes. (3) It is about money. (4) Owners talk of moving teams just so more fans will come to the stadiums. (5) Effective, but is that how owners should show loyalty to their clubs? (6) The richer teams can now buy up all of the good players, leaving smaller teams with young players or worn-out veterans. (7) Another thing that has changed is the players themselves. (8) We call players who like to get dirty "throwback" players. (9) Modern players are too worried about hurting themselves, or doing something wrong, to give their best effort. (10) We accept a professional baseball player spitting in the face of an umpire and getting to play in the next game. (Scott Reese, letter, *Christian Science Monitor,* November 11, 1997)

In this paragraph, statements 1, 2, 3, 5 (which is a rhetorical question), 7, 9, and perhaps 10 need defense because they are all universal statements about which people may legitimately differ. On the other hand, 4 and 6 do not need defense because they are common knowledge, while 8 is a definition of a certain kind of player. Statement 1 [Major league baseball in the 1990s is quite different] is the thesis and thus needs defense; the author defends it by 2 (Baseball is not about green fields and red rope) and 3 (Baseball is about money); 3 is defended by 4–6. The author also defends 1 by 7 [Players have changed], which in turn the author defends by 8–10. Hence, in this paragraph the thesis 1 is defended by the subtheses 2 + 3 and 7, and these in turn are further defended by additional reasons.

In short, when you write or speak, you need to consider whether the statements you make need or do not need a defense. The place to start is whether *you* the writer think the statements need defense or not. But you cannot stop there. Since you are writing for or speaking to an audience you are trying to persuade, you need to press on to the more difficult part, to take the perspective of your *readers*. They also are involved in the communication process, and if you are to be persuasive, you need to consider what they would accept without argument and what they would treat as disputable. You might not think that a particular statement is disputable, but if you think your readers may dispute its truth, it is better to defend the statement.

Those who follow this advice are better and more careful writers and speakers. They pay attention to what they say and consider what needs support and what can be affirmed without further justification. They then seek to provide reasonable support for those claims that need it. As a result, their presentations are stronger and more persuasive.

Exercise 6

For each of the articles,

1. Give the topic, issue, thesis, and main points.

2. Identify the statements that can be asserted without defense and those that need a defense. (The statements are numbered to make your reference to them in your homework and class discussion easier.) Note that you might be unsure about how to classify some statements. Consider whether the audience for these articles might think these statements need defense.

3. Identify which statements the author has in fact supported or defended.

A. (1) The vast majority of Minnesota's 15,000 miles of (snowmobile) trails were built for snowmobiling. (2) The hundreds of snowmobile clubs in the state used money from snowmobile registrations and a very small percentage of the state gas tax to build bridges and clear trails. (3) More money was raised by the clubs through various fund raisers and used for the trail system. (4) The labor came from club members volunteering thousands of hours of their own time. (5) State employees do maintain some of the trail system, but (6) the vast majority is done by volunteers.

I don't believe that (7) snowmobilers are opposed to the trails being used for other recreational purposes. However, (8) snowmobilers are already paying state registration fees, volunteering time, and raising funds to maintain trails. . . . (9) Maybe bicyclists and roller bladers should start paying a trail user fee and volunteering their time for trail maintenance.

I'm sure (10) we can find a solution to the pavement wear problem. However, (11) snowmobilers should not be expected to bear the entire weight of this problem. [Rory Tate, letter, *St. Paul Pioneer Press*, November 18, 1996. Reprinted by permission.]

B. (1) As the Secretary of Housing and Urban Development sees it, the long and devastating "free fall" of American cities is over, and the difficult climb back has begun. (2) He may be right.

(3) New York City has a good chance of ending the year with 1,000 murders or less, a terrifying statistic in most venues but a reason to celebrate in the Big Apple, which suffered through a record 2,245 homicides in 1990.

(4) In Detroit, which came up with the quaint custom of burning itself down every Halloween, a genuine rehabilitation seems to be under way.

(5) There has been some modest job creation, an increase in home owner-ship, a commitment of $2 billion in private investments in the city's empowerment zone and a resurgence of the downtown area, which was in pitiful shape (especially at night) just a few years ago. (6) A symbol of the renewed action in Detroit is the serious effort by the football Lions to arrange a return to the city. (7) The Lions have been holed up for years in suburban Pontiac, Mich.

(8) Chicago, Philadelphia, Kansas City, Cleveland—all are making headway in the areas of employment, public safety, neighborhood revital-ization and civic pride. (9) Even Newark, N. J., comatose since the riots of 1967, appears to be waking up. (10) Among other things, Newark's rancid high-rise public housing complexes are being demolished and housing more suitable to the human species is being built . . .

(11) It's not that the Clinton administration has been a champion of the cities; far from it. (12) But since Bill Clinton became president, cities have at least been able to get a hearing in Washington. (13) And some members of the administration have been passionate and eloquent advo-cates for cities. . . .

(14) Without some federal support, local efforts are doomed. (15) The Secretary points to several things: to federal support for anti-crime initia-tives, including money to put additional police officers on city streets; to changes in public housing policies away from high-rises filled with the poorest of the poor to lower density, mixed-income dwellings; and to the creation of urban empowerment zones, which carry with them a whole load of federal subsidies and tax benefits.

(16) It is too early to gauge the impact of the empowerment zones, but the other efforts have been helpful. (17) And cities have unquestionably benefited from the continued push to make credit more readily available through programs like the Community Reinvestment Act and the low-income housing tax credit. . . . (Bob Herbert, "After Collapse, Cities Emerging From Rubble," *Lexington Herald-Leader,* October 7, 1996).

C. In this article, you have to consider both the report of the scientific study and the claims made by the study. Note where the author moves between these two perspectives. (1) The little kid was screaming at the top of his lungs. (2) The checkout lines at the supermarket were backed up. (3) Every human being in the greater Philadelphia area in need of 10, 15 or 20 items was standing with or next to me in the optimistically named "express" lanes.

(4) The kid, a boy around 6, was hanging onto the cart in front of me. (5) He kept trying to pull it back to the candy rack. (6) His mom, a woman in her late 20s, had an infant in the cart's safety seat. (7) She told her son to stop crying and to quit pulling on the cart. (8) He continued doing both. (9) She yelled at him. . . . (10) The 6-year old gave the cart another pull. (11) His mother stepped around the cart and slapped him on his behind.

(12) Did she do something horribly wrong? (13) A supplement in the current special issue of Pediatrics magazine gives the issue of corporal punishment a thorough review. (14) Twenty-three experts in children's health, psychology and human development review what science knows

about whether parents should hit their children. (15) The findings have a lot to say about what happens millions of times each week when adults use hitting or spanking to discipline a child. . . .

(16) In reviewing the studies that have been done, the experts found that infants—children younger than 2—do not understand and cannot be effectively taught by spanking or any form of physical discipline. (17) Studies that followed parents and children over time suggest that aggressiveness and antisocial behavior grow more likely when physical punishment is harsher and more frequent.

(18) Spanking and other forms of corporal punishment of children who are older than 4 [are] not effective and might be harmful in the long run, the experts found. (19) But they did find some evidence that the rare spanking of a preschool child might contribute to reinforcing other disciplinary techniques without any apparent harm to the child. (20) Still, noncorporal methods of discipline such as reasoning, positive reinforcement and "timeouts" are always adequate and are the most effective ways to discipline children of all ages.

(21) The conclusions from the experts' review of the scientific data are clear:

- (22) Getting out the belt or the strap makes no sense and is both a lousy way to parent and unethical.
- (23) The more you hit a child the worse you make things between you and the child in the long run.
- (24) Hitting or spanking an infant is pointless.
- (25) Spanking, slapping or hitting might get the attention of a preschooler.

(26) If you have ever broken down and spanked your child, as the mom did in the supermarket, you need not fret about long-term harm, but you should know that there are better ways to change bad behavior. (27) While the rare spanking of a child can be effective, rewards, firm instruction and timeouts do just as well. (28) Corporal punishment has no place in good parenting. (Arthur Caplan, excerpted from "Research Review Finds Spanking Does More Harm than Good," Oct. 30, 1996. Reprinted by permission of the author. "Spanking Experts Say It's Not Necessary," *Grand Forks Herald*, October 28, 1996).

D. Take two paragraphs from a paper you wrote for another course and analyze each of the statements in those paragraphs to determine whether or not they need a defense. Did you defend those statements that you decided needed defense?

DOING RESEARCH

One of the first questions you ask once you have chosen a topic (and perhaps issue and thesis) is where to find reliable information to help you write an informed paper. The amount of information available is mind-boggling, so where do you begin?

First, you should begin research by using tools that access the topic you have chosen. Search engines in libraries and on the Internet can help you find materials that relate to the topic you have chosen. For example, if you have chosen as your topic "air bags," you can begin to acquire information on that topic by typing in these words in the "Search" box of some search engines.

You will probably find that initially your topic is too broad, for it brings up too many entries under that heading. A library search may yield dozens of books or hundreds of articles; an Internet search may produce hundreds of thousands, if not millions, of hits. Consequently, you need to narrow the heading under which you search to make the available information manageable. You can do this by adding adjectives or other nouns that appear in your issue or thesis statements. For example, if your issue is whether people should be allowed to disconnect the air bags in an automobile, you may search for some combination of *air bags* and other terms, like *disabling*.

You may wonder whether anyone has written about your particular issue. Maybe or maybe not. It depends on how narrow your issue is. If people have written on, say, voluntary use of air bags, that provides a good starting point with lots of information to weigh. You can read what has been written about your issue and process it, deciding how strong or weak the arguments are.

But suppose no one has written specifically on your issue. You use the search engines and simply cannot call up anything on the junction of *air bags* and *disabling*. Are you then dead in the water, especially if the teacher wants a bibliography or footnotes? Not really. You will have to return to the broader topic—for example, *air bags*—and from there begin again to narrow the topic until it approaches your own particular issue—for example, conjoining *air bags* with *infant deaths*. If this area is not exactly pertinent to your thesis because you were not specifically dealing with infants, do not despair. By reading in this related area, you should be able to find principles, arguments, and discussions that can be extended or applied to what you are addressing about disabling air bags in general.

But you are not yet done. Your thesis needs the support your main points provide. You can develop your main points by further narrowing the research. To investigate each main point, the strategy developed above can be repeated. Each main point has a topic that can be accessed, addresses an issue, and makes a thesis. As before, the research words can be narrowed down so you can concentrate especially on what is relevant to your issue. If the information peters out at this point, return to the broader topic and creatively apply what you learn from it to your issue.

In short, in your research you constantly move between topics that are too broad and those that are so narrow that you cannot find direct information on them. By moving up and down on this continuum, and by moving sideways to related subtopics, you can find pertinent information for your paper.

DETERMINING THE RELIABILITY OF SOURCES

Since our experience is very limited in time and place, much of our information comes from other sources. Our life span is brief and our memories are inaccurate, so we rely on information presented by others to supplement our historical knowledge. Since our travel experience is limited, to acquire knowledge of other parts of this world we depend on what others tell us these places are like. Because we can only be in one place at a time, yet exciting events occur simultaneously in many places, we trust newspapers, magazines, radio, television, and the Internet to inform us about current events. We can conduct only very limited personal investigations. Hence, we rely on researchers' reports to give us additional information.

How good is all this information? Are the claims true and conclusions justified? It depends, in part, on the reliability of the sources.

This book began with two articles from very different print sources, a major-city newspaper and a weekly tabloid. Perhaps the fact that the one article was taken from a tabloid immediately made you suspicious, for the sensationalism of this type of media creates doubts about its truthfulness. There are many kinds of print media and not everything in print is equally reliable; merely because something appears in print does not mean that it is true.

For one thing, the authors and information they present are *fallible*. Usually they derive their information from other sources, which themselves may be mistaken or not fully knowledgeable. Errors can creep into the information at many points along the information chain. For another, *information changes*. The geology texts before the 1970s suggested that life began around 600 million years ago. Now geologists are looking at evidence that indicates figures six times that old. So merely because you find information in a reputable text does not mean that you cannot and should not question it. Even your texts may be mistaken and bear scrutiny. Again, *theories interpreting information change*. It was once an accepted theory, affirmed by many biology texts, that the origin of life on earth was to be found in prebiotic soups of methane and ammonia that, with the addition of some form of energy, were capable of producing amino acids, the building blocks of life. Now new theories of earth life's origin are heralded: some suggest that life arose from the repetitive crystalline structures found in certain clays, that it was brought to earth aboard asteroids, or that it originated from Martian rocks that reached our planet after being launched into space. In short, new theories stimulate research, and the resulting new knowledge stimulates new theories. This research may confirm or disconfirm the standard theories found in your texts. In any case, what is currently accepted as fact is open to critical questioning, and as critical thinkers you want to question what you read and hear, whether presented in books, textbooks, magazines, or newspapers.

Similar things may be said about other forms of media: radio, television, and the Internet. The recent development and expansion of electronic media has opened up new worlds of information. At the same time, the information we obtain through these sources requires assessment before it is accepted, for not everything said or shown over the air waves or downloaded on the computer is accurate and reliable. The mere fact that a reporter says something on the evening news or on *20–20*, even repeatedly, does not make it true. Claims made by advertisers on the electronic media must be carefully scrutinized. The Federal Trade Commission (FTC) regulation of media content is only that, regulation; the FTC provides no guarantee that what is said is true. We still need to investigate for ourselves the truth of important claims.

But what sources can we trust? When you write essays or papers, where do you go for information? Traditional sources include books, magazines, newspapers, and journals. These are accessed through various catalogs, periodical and newspaper indexes, and readers' guides. The instructors in your courses and librarians can guide you to the proper reference materials that provide access to this information. But what if you have no such direct guide? How do you determine the trustworthiness of your sources? You can ask several questions to help determine reliability.

- What kind of reputation does the journal, magazine, book publisher, or electronic publisher have for publishing accurate and informed articles?

Magazines for Libraries, edited by Bill Katz and Linda S. Katz, is a standard source for assembling a library collection of journals, magazines, and newspapers. It may be said that if a journal or magazine is not in *Magazines for Libraries,* unless it is relatively new, its reliability probably is in question. Though this source does not strictly evaluate or rank the magazines and journals, it provides clues to help you assess that media. It indicates whether the journal is **refereed** (a journal is refereed when the articles it prints have been reviewed and selected by an editorial board of scholars), the official journal of some society, authoritative, or recommended for libraries. It also discusses the level of reading ability required to access the source and gives a sense of the articles published. In a more scholarly vein, the various professional or disciplinary indexes (*Social Science Index, Psychological Abstracts, Philosophers Index, Religion Index*) provide another source for discerning the reputation of journals and magazines. The fact that a journal or magazine is indexed in a professional or disciplinary index usually indicates that the journal is viewed by members of the discipline as reputable.

- What is the level of readership in the magazine, journal, book, or on-line source? Is the publication meant for a popular or scholarly audience?

Magazines for Libraries answers these questions as well. It indicates whether the magazine or journal is popular or academic and whether it is written for an elementary, junior high, high school, general, academic, or specialist audience.

You can also get clues about the intended audience from analyzing the publication. In the case of books, is the dust jacket or cover plain or does it contain pictures, and if so, pictures of what sort? Who has made the endorsements found on the cover? In the case of magazines or periodicals, look at the title and layout. Scholarly illustrations, absence of advertisements, dense text in smaller print, nonglossy paper, use of citations and references, and the presence of abstracts and conclusions in the articles indicate that you are working with a *scholarly journal.* Lots of pictures of notable or popular people, advertisements, large print on glossy paper, short articles with no citations, and reports of interviews or hearsay indicate that you are working with a more general interest periodical or a popular magazine.

Substantive news or general interest periodicals play an important role in communication. Generally no special background or academic expertise in the subject matter is presumed. Their language level makes them accessible to the average educated reader. These periodicals are amply illustrated with color photographs or drawings related to the subject discussed. The articles are written by knowledgeable people from diverse backgrounds: editors and their staff, freelance writers, or scholars. Sometimes the writers cite sources but generally not. Published commercially, these magazines provide specialized knowledge to a broad but intelligent audience. Although generally not comparable to scholarly publications, they often are trustworthy, presenting important information in language and formats that are more accessible to the average educated reader. This category of publications includes *Discover, Smithsonian, Scientific American, Atlantic Monthly, Economist, Psychology Today, New Republic, USA Today Magazine, Christian Science Monitor,* and *New York Times.*

Popular magazines are written at levels accessible to a general audience. They are well illustrated, often with photographs of popular or notable persons. The paper is glossy; the print is large; the citations of sources are absent. The articles are short, often with little depth of research but emphasizing interviews and personal comments. Alluring or provocative article titles tip you off about the intent of the author and the magazine. Eye and interest catching, they aim to entertain the reader and sell the products of their advertisers, who figure prominently in the publication. Magazines in this category include *Ebony, Jet, Parent, People, Readers Digest, Sports Illustrated, Esquire, MS, Life, Time,* and *Newsweek.*

Exercise caution in taking material from the popular media. Instead of sharing their sources with their readers, writers in more popular magazines or journals simply lay out matters as they see, have researched, or have heard about them. Their emphasis on quotations from others can tend to make them less responsive to the requirements of careful scholarship. They also aim at a specific market, perhaps less to persuade rationally than to enhance the readership of the magazine. In short, you have to be especially careful in using popular magazines as sources of information; where they are reporting work printed elsewhere, you should check to see that the authors are presenting it correctly.

- Has this journal or publisher regularly published materials that have been confirmed by research? Has the material been referenced in other writings? Do those writings confirm or disconfirm the material? That is, are the materials read, accepted, and cited by authorities in the field?

You can answer these questions by noting how frequently the materials you are investigating are cited in other works. To discover this in the humanities, for example, you might consult the *Arts and Humanities Citation Index.* Although the fact that a book, article, or piece of data is referenced in another work does not make it authoritative, the frequency of such citations suggests that these works are accepted by some as authoritative. This can be important confirmation of reliability.

- Has the piece you want to use, along with others in the magazine, book, journal, pamphlet, or electronic media, been refereed? That is, have other scholars looked at the material before it was printed, evaluated it according to current standards of scholarship, and then decided whether it met the standards of scholarship adequately enough to be published? Or did the person, without apparent evaluation by others, publish it by him or herself, for example, over the Internet on a web page or in a vanity press (where you pay a publisher to print and distribute the book)?

Ulrich's International Periodicals Directory, a standard source in most library collections, contains a listing of refereed journals. In addition, some subject-related indexes in print or electronic format list journals that are refereed. You can look in the respective academic journals (usually in the front or back) to see how articles are submitted to the journal and judged to be acceptable. Some on-line indexes even allow you to limit your search results to articles that appear in refereed journals. Doing a keyword search using a World Wide Web search engine such as InfoSeek or AltaVista, however, will not inform you about what is or is not refereed; here you have to look at individual components of the article or information you discover to assess its merit.

- Who is the author? What are that person's credentials? What kind of education or experience has she or he had that is relevant to what he or she wrote? What else has that person written on a similar topic?

To assess the author's background, look for what the book or journal itself tells you about the author: his or her expertise, what group or organization he or she is associated with, or his or her credentials. You might look up the author's name in *Contemporary Authors, Who's Who, Faculty White Pages, MLA International Bibliography,* or the various subject or professional journal indexes. Is the author connected to reputable universities, government bodies or organizations, or businesses or industries where he or she would be in a position to know whereof he or she writes?

- If your source is a book, has it been reviewed? Check the reviews. (One should be careful here; reviews sometimes are not helpful because they reflect the reviewer's bias; that is, they can trumpet the reviewer's viewpoint or can be written by someone with a particular ax to grind.)

Subject-related journal indexes contain references to book reviews. You might also check *Book Review Digest* or *Book Review Index.*

- Does the material have the kind of documentation you can follow up so that you can check the resources that the author used? If there are no footnotes or references included in the document, why not? Is it because the work is entirely novel or is it because the work is largely unresearched opinion?
- Has the source contributed significantly to an on-going discussion on important topics? What is the tenor or feel of the articles in the journal or of the book? Does it give the impression of providing a carefully reasoned argument, or is it fixated on sensationalism or on pushing a particular point of view? What is the level of its emotional content; has the author used emotion in place of reasoning to persuade?

Exploring Resources on the Internet

Many students have turned to doing their research on the Internet because of the convenience and power of its search engines. The Internet contains many good and useful things. By typing in one or a combination of search words, you can find and access all sorts of materials from around the world. Documents, articles, informational pieces, newspapers, photographs, even books are now published or printed on-line and can be downloaded easily. The electronic media holds great riches for the careful explorer and critical thinker.

Much of what is on the Internet, however, fails to meet the kinds of criteria we developed above. It is important to note that the Internet, and more specifically the World Wide Web, is largely a medium for self-publication. What you find there often has not passed by an editor, editorial board, or publisher who has evaluated the ideas before deciding whether they merit publishing. In some cases, it may be impossible to determine the author of a web resource. Merely because it is present on a particular site does not mean that it originated there. In other cases where an author is listed, it may be difficult to discover the person's credentials or establish his or her credibility. Consequently, although users of keyword search engines can retrieve documents on almost any subject imaginable, they must scrutinize the results, for documents produced by an authority or amateur, scholar or hobbyist, careful researcher or crank can appear on the same level; the writings of the incompetent are listed alongside of those who are knowledgeable.

Hence, in being wary of what they get via the electronic media, critical thinkers will carefully assess the material obtained. Before it is used, they should ascertain something about its source—the author, where the material originates, the reliability of the web site itself—and think about what other information may independently confirm what they have gotten. The information explosion can easily become an information nightmare, where truth is indistinguishable from falsehood, partial truth, or trash. When assessing the credibility of the information published on the World Wide Web, ask the following questions:

- Who is the author of the material?

Does the author have a web page that includes biographical information that lists his or her training on or experience with the topic? This information helps you determine the extent of the author's competence in the field. Does the author list his or her other publications, including books or journal articles that deal with the topic addressed by the web document? Is the author affiliated with a governmental, educational, or research institution or nonprofit or professional organization that is known for its reliability? Does the author disclose this information in his or her biographical information, or do you have to assume the person's affiliation with an organization or institution based on the site where you found the resource?

- What type of site have you accessed? Who sponsors the site? What do you judge regarding its reliability?

.edu—a U.S. university or college. Its purpose is to provide information about the educational institution. It may also contain information written by people connected with that institution. The information may or may not be sanctioned by that institution.

.k12.(state).us—a school with grades somewhere between kindergarten and twelfth grade.

.gov—a governmental organization or agency. Its purpose is to provide information reflecting the point of view of the government, its officials and agencies.

.org—a nonprofit organization or trade association. Its purpose is often connected with the specific interests of the organization.

.mil—a military site.

.com—a commercial or business site. Its purpose is to engage in a commercial enterprise that will allow it to make money, entertain, or distribute information.

.net—a network administrative organization.

Is the web page on which the person publishes designated as the official site of some reputable organization, or is the web site one that ends in .com or .net, which suggests that the content may be more personal or commercial than scholarly? The previous list of abbreviations used in site designations may help you sort through the confusion.

- How recently has the site been updated?

Has the information been updated recently? Is it the kind of information that needs updating, or is it about events or ideas in the past whose interpretation does not change frequently?

You may find some of the following sites helpful in learning how to evaluate Internet information.

Elizabeth Kirk at the Johns Hopkins University, MD.

<http://milton.mse.jhu.edu:8001/research/education/net.html> (August 1999)

Trudi Jacobson and Laura Cohen at University of Albany, NY.

<http://www.albany.edu/library/internet/evaluate. html> (August 1999)

One final point. Referencing an Internet or web resource is no different from referencing traditional printed material. When you reference the Internet in a footnote or in the bibliography, you must provide an *address* complete enough to allow readers to find the same resource you used and decide for themselves how authoritative or reliable your sources are. Since web addresses change frequently, you also need to supply the *date* on which you accessed the material. You may even make a printout of the web resource you used in case the professor requests the original information and the site has changed. The goal of all referencing is to allow readers access to the same information to which you had access so as to allow them to make their own assessment of the data and arguments. Footnotes and bibliography function to further critical thinking.

Exercise 7

Find articles or presentations from five of the following magazines, TV productions, and web sites. Use the following worksheet to determine how reliable the article and its information are.

Africa Today	*JAMA*
Atlantic Monthly	*Instrumentalist*
Beijing Review	*Jenny Jones*
Black Scholar	*Life*
Byte	*New Republic*
Chemical Abstracts	*Nature*
Chicago Tribune	*Psychology Today*
Christian Century	*Reader's Digest*
Current Sociology	*Rolling Stone*
Discover	*Runners' World*
Ebony	*Scientific American*

Economist
Foreign Affairs
Hard Copy
Hypatia
http://www.er.doe.gov/
http://www.guardians.
http://norml.org

Sports Illustrated
Time
Your hometown newspaper
20-20
http://www.touregypt.net
net/egypt/pyramids.htm
http://iufomrc.com

Exercise 8

Use the following worksheet to determine how reliable three of the resources are that you are using for your paper.

RESOURCE EVALUATION WORKSHEET

Book, Magazine, Journal, or Web Site Title: _____

Article Title (if a journal, magazine or web site): _____

Publication data: _____

    What reputation does the publication have (note *Magazines for Libraries* or other sources)? _____

    Is the publication refereed? _____

    If it is a book, has it been reviewed and where? _____

_____

_____

Audience: For whom is the piece written?

    General audience   Educated audience   Scholarly audience

    Does the article contain an abstract or brief summary? _____

    Does the article contain bibliographical references?   None   Few   Many

    What kind of illustrations are included? _____

_____

    How fully is the topic covered in the article? _____

Author:

    Who is it? _____

    What organization or institution is the author connected with? _____

    What can you discover about the author or sponsoring organization (if a web site), using this or other sources (note suggestions in this chapter)? _____

_____

_____

Objectivity: What possible biases might the writers or publishers of this article,

---

continued

book, or web site have? Why do you think this? _____

_____

_____

> Your Evaluation:
>
> Based on the above questions, is the publication
>
>   Scholarly   Substantive/General Interest   Popular
>
> Give your reasons for your judgment?
>
>
>
> How reliable is the material in the publication? Defend your answer.

MOVING ON

This chapter has presented lots of advice. Now it is time for you to try your hand at writing a paper that defends a thesis you think is important. Amid all this advice, it is important to repeat that writing can be fun. Like any worthwhile endeavor, writing involves much hard work. Research also is work, but at the same time it can open doors to information and ideas about which you never dreamed. You will meet new people, authors with exciting ideas to stimulate your mind. Research will push you in new directions so that once you start reading you will find it difficult to stop; something more, something new, something interesting is always there to be learned.

Good writing is a skill, and as this chapter emphasized from the outset, developing skills takes practice. So don't get discouraged by your first draft— or your first paper. Your papers will get progressively better as you work to master the skill of writing as an essential component of critical thinking. Save some of your first work—your first drafts and papers—so that later, when you have advanced in the skill of writing, you can see how far you have come. Nothing better enhances your self-esteem as a writer.

Exercise 9

Turn your outline into a paper of a length determined by your instructor. Include at the top of your paper some of the words that you used in searches in card catalogs, computer based searches in the library, and on the Internet, to give your instructor some idea of how you went about researching your paper.

Collaborative Learning Exercise 1

First write out the topic, issue, thesis, and main points of your paper. Then let your partner read your paper. Have your partner identify what he or she takes to be your topic, issue, thesis, and main points. Then compare your list of these items with that of your partner to see how well you have communicated what you want to say. In particular, note any differences and write down how you will address those differences.

Exercise 10

Take a thesis that contradicts the thesis you developed in Exercise 3 and write a paper defending that thesis. [Doing this will help you begin to see the strength of the other side, which is necessary to being a critical thinker. If you have difficulty defending an opposite thesis, it might reveal that your original thesis was too trivial to merit attention.]

Collaborative Learning Exercise 2

Take one of your papers from Exercises 9 or 10 and number the statements. Make a copy of it for your partner. Each of you should then go through the paper and identify those statements that need defense. Finally, share your answers, noting where both of you differed regarding what needed defense. Note where you defended statements that your partner did not think needed defense and where you failed to defend statements that your partner thought needed defending.

Exercise 11

Write a final paper, combining what you have discovered in Exercises 8 and 9, giving and defending your final position on the issue you developed in Exercise 2. That final position might be the same as the one you began with, it can be its opposite, or it can be some mediating or qualified position. The defense of your position should include both arguments for your view and arguments rebutting others' views.

ANSWERS TO THE EXERCISES

Answers to Exercise 4

Topic: Air bags

Issue: Should auto owners be allowed to choose to purchase air bags, or alternatively, should the government require auto owners to purchase air bags?

Thesis: Auto owners should be allowed to choose to purchase air bags, or alternatively, the government should not require auto owners to purchase air bags.

Outline:

A. The President announced that car owners can deactivate air bags with a mechanic's help. Therefore, people are required to pay $400 for air bags they do not want.
B. Air bags increase the fatality risk for children under ten.
C. Air bags do not significantly help seat belt wearers or people in small cars.
D. Air bags can increase the fatality rate for adults over 70.
E. Air bags correlate with more aggressive driving.
F. The author presents an analogy with prohibition, which led to a major crime wave and disrespect for the law.
G. Air bags lead the government to treat us as children who are not responsible for our own safety. This is unwarranted paternalism.

Answers to Exercise 6
In the following, (ND) = needs no defense. (D) = needs defense.

A. Topic: Cost of trail maintenance
    Issue: Should other users of state trails help defray the cost of trail maintenance?
    Thesis: Other users of state trails should help defray the cost of trail maintenance.
    Main Points: 8

Statements 1–5 may be accepted within the context of the letter and hence don't need defense. The author takes 8 as needing defense; this is the function of 2–6. Because 6 says "a vast majority," it needs defense, though it is not crucial to the argument. Statements 7 and 10 are universal but not germane to the argument. Statements 9 and 11 are normative and need defense.

C. Topic: Spanking
    Issue: Does spanking have a place in good parenting?
    Thesis: Spanking has a place in good parenting (28).
    Main points: (16), (18), (20), (22–5).

Statements (1–2) ND—a personal experience; (3) ND, if taken as hyperbole; (4–11) ND—a personal experience; (12) a question; (13–14) ND (description of a study); (15) D (an interpretation of the data); (15–25) *that* the study reported this needs no defense, though *what* the study reported needs defense (note that they are conclusions from the study). (26–28) D.

CHAPTER 9

Synthesis

Solving Problems Creatively

We have arrived at the stage where *creative thinking* plays a major role in critical thinking. It is true that some creativity enters in at step 3 of our six-step critical thinking structure; in Application you take what you think you comprehend and apply it to a situation to determine whether or not you really understood. You may recall the example earlier in the book of installing a garage door opener. My belief that I understood the instruction booklet was verified by my successful installation of the opener. At the Application stage, however, creativity is limited because you are attempting to apply what you have read, heard, or learned to a like or similar situation in order to show that you truly comprehend the information. You are neither asked to adapt what you understood nor to integrate the information with other things you know—or, if you are asked, the adaptations are minor and carefully controlled.

Demonstrating comprehension of what you have read or heard is important, but creativity eventually goes far beyond merely showing that you have understood. At some point you may be asked to take what you have learned, understood, and carefully analyzed and to add to it your own significant contributions to solve unique difficulties. The opportunity to "let your own voice be heard," "to do your own thing" may be yours. Someone may ask you to develop your own position in a research paper, design a new floor plan for a kitchen or house, adapt a play to your local stage, draw up and propose a budget for a company or struggling business, conduct your own research in the sciences, or initiate a new venture to assist the poor in the community. Whatever the situation, such a request requires you to step out beyond the comfort zone of understanding what others have said and argued, to construct your unique solution to the problem at hand.

This chapter concentrates on the task of problem solving. First, we look at problem solving in general. The end of the chapter contains several scenarios for you to work out in the context of a particular approach to problem solving adapted from Alex Osborn's[1] Future Problem Solving. Though this chapter is best approached as a group project, you can apply the skills you learn to your own individual efforts at problem solving.

Before we begin, however, a word of caution. No foolproof, simple method for consistent, successful problem solving exists. Indeed, the more the problem concerns people, the more dimensions you have to consider. Problem solving involves acquiring relevant knowledge of the facts, comprehending the information learned, and carefully analyzing it. Beyond this, problem solving also involves open-mindedness or the ability to look at things from new angles, wide experience, hard work and perseverance, imagination, creativity, intuition, and sometimes (if not often) a dose of good luck. With the exception of the last, you bring these things to the problem. Finally, often you also need to develop and carefully follow a strategy to make sure that what is important is not overlooked and likely solutions are properly pursued. This chapter focuses on developing your strategy abilities to identify problems and to brainstorm and evaluate possible solutions.

STEPS IN PROBLEM SOLVING

Problem solving begins with a situation that presents problems or difficulties to be addressed. For example, last winter my son's snowblower ran into a hard pile of snow and came to a quick halt. In the front of the snowblower is an auger, a horizontal metal piece that rotates, picking up the snow and spitting it out the chute. In this case, the auger would no longer rotate. If my son was to continue his snow-blowing business, we would have to solve the auger problem and get the snowblower back on the road.

Although the initial problem may appear simple at first glance, looks can be deceiving. What you take as the problem may be caused by another or more serious problem. That is, the immediate difficulty may be symptomatic

of deeper problems that need to be resolved. Since problems are not always obvious or what they appear to be at first glance, the first step is to

1. *Identify all the possible problems or causes of the problem in the situation.*

Return to my broken snowblower. Why would the auger no longer turn to throw the snow? Was a belt broken? Was the auger or the drive mechanism frozen? Was there ice in the gears, preventing the chain from moving the auger? Was the chain stretched, and if so could we adjust the length of the chain? Was the sprocket so worn that it threw off the chain each time we installed it? The initial problem—the snowblower's auger would not rotate—could have been caused by any one of several factors. Before we could solve the problem of the auger not turning, we had to think of the problem's many possible causes.

A second example comes from medicine. In the first half of the twentieth century a serious ill manifested itself that desparately needed to be addressed. Although outbreaks of a mysterious disease that left people paralyzed occurred as far back as the end of the eighteenth century, the first serious epidemic of what became known as infantile paralysis (polio) occurred in 1916, when six thousand people died and over 27,000 people were left paralyzed. The epidemics began to come yearly with increasing intensity, until in 1952 there were over 58,000 cases of polio and three thousand deaths. The public questioned what could be the cause of this seemingly new disease that struck the most vulnerable, the children. People responsible for public health pondered a variety of possible causes in the effort to determine what really brought on the fever, paralysis, and even death. Did it come from intimate contact between persons, poor sanitation, feces, unwashed hands, insects like flies or fleas, social status, or a virus?

The first step of problem solving, then, is to discover and accurately identify the variety or complexity of possible problems that lie behind or cause the symptomatic problem. To accomplish this, you need to brainstorm what the problems or causes may be by considering the situation from many perspectives. At this initial stage, any and all problems or causes should be listed: this is the point of brainstorming. You want to discover what is obvious and what may lie hidden. Including "the hidden" is important because the underlying problem(s) or cause(s) may not be readily apparent. It is generally the case that only after brainstorming can you whittle down the problems or causes to attend to the most likely candidates for treatment. If you start narrowing down your problems or factors too soon, you may miss the real or underlying problem. You deal with symptoms but not the causes of the difficulty.

Criteria for evaluating how successful you are in arriving at the most important problems include

(a) Clarity in expressing the problems and showing what is problematic. Problems are difficult to solve if they are formulated unclearly.
(b) Showing the relevance or connection of other, possible problems to the original situation or problem.
(c) Using diverse perspectives to view the problems; that is, making your approach broad enough to catch all the problems.

(d) Originality in viewing the problems. Creativity plays an important role in problem solving.

Sometimes resolving a problem requires that you write something down. For example, in your education you have been asked to write papers of various length. As we noted in Chapter 8, argumentative or position papers focus on some problem or issue that you need to resolve. Where the situation to be dealt with requires writing something down, the problems or issues must be clearly developed. One way of doing this is to follow the pattern we established in this book. Not only your entire presentation but each of your paragraphs should be well developed, having a topic, issue, thesis, and main points.

Although there may be many problems in a situation, the goal is to discover the deeper or underlying problem or cause of major importance. Generally this is the problem or cause you must address if the more apparent problems are to be resolved. You may experience this when you visit the doctor. You have a fever, chills, runny nose, headache, and so on. You want the doctor not merely to stop your runny nose, but to diagnose and address the underlying problem of which these are the symptoms.

Sometimes the underlying problem or cause is simple, one that is listed in the brainstorming session in step 1. At other times it may be a broader, more general problem or cause that underlies many of the problems that were brainstormed. In any case, the task in step 2 is to

2. *Identify the underlying or fundamental problem or cause.*

How well you succeed in solving a complex problem will depend on how clearly you comprehend the underlying problem. The more clearly the doctor can determine the cause of your symptoms, the easier it will be for the doctor to write the correct prescription or send you to the right specialist.

In the case of our snowblower, the underlying problem seemed to be simple: the chain had gotten stretched and hence would not stay on the sprocket. When my son and I examined the snowblower, we found that the chain came off the auger. It seemed that all we would have to do would be to reinstall the chain. But each time we reinstalled it, the chain slipped off. The problem proved more complex than we thought. At first we thought we could simply adjust the adjacent, sprocketed wheel to take up the slack in the chain. But the adjustment wheel was already positioned to take up maximum slack and could not be further adjusted. So we decided to shorten the chain. But first we had to figure how to get the chain off the machine. That required removing not only the housing but other pieces of the drive mechanism. When we finally got the chain off, we removed one pair of links and reinstalled the chain. But now the chain was too short to fit around the drive wheel and the auger. So we had another problem beyond the problem that the chain came off the auger: our chain was either too short or too long and the adjustment wheel was useless for correcting the tension on the chain. The point of this example is that often a more serious problem underlies the symptom. What seems at the outset to be a simple problem often turns out to be complex and requires that one handle many facets to solve it.

The appearance of polio provides a similar example of looking for the underlying cause. After years of investigation, researchers eventually identified a virus as the cause of the symptoms. However, identification was not simple: the virus presented itself in at least three different strains, and part of the research had to be directed to typing the polio viruses to determine whether these three strains exhausted the possibilities, or whether other, unidentified strains lurked in the population.

Since comprehension involves language, it is important to try to express the underlying problem clearly and with focus. If your description is too vague, your solutions will not be specific enough. If your description is too narrow, it will restrict the possible ways you may go about solving the problem. This is particularly true when we deal with broad social problems, like racial prejudice, distribution of welfare, national health insurance, drug abuse, and raising the educational performance of students. On the one hand, vague descriptions of the social problem give us nothing specific to address; it is like picking up Jell-O—it keeps slipping through our fingers. We need clarity in expressing the problem. On the other hand, narrow descriptions of the problem fail to address its complexity. By focusing on only one aspect, we can oversimplify and make the problem worse rather than better, for we throw its other dimensions out of balance. We have already considered this when we spoke in Chapter 3 about discovering or creating the issue to be addressed. The clearer we formulate the issue, the easier it is to address the issue. That is, a clear issue paves the way for a clear thesis.

Criteria for evaluating your success in identifying the underlying problem or cause include

(e) The comprehensiveness of your underlying problem. It must underlie most of the problems isolated in step 1.
(f) Its relevance to the situation. The underlying problem must relate specifically to the situation at hand, so that by addressing it you are addressing the problem or problems that initiated the problem-solving project. By addressing it, you relieve the symptoms.
(g) Clear focus of the underlying problem. It should be narrowed down but not so much that it will not relate to the other identified problems.

Once the major problem is identified, it is time to embark on an attempt to solve it. Often we cannot solve a problem because we continue to look at it in one way and hence fail to entertain other ways to resolve the problem. Consider the following puzzle. Without lifting your pencil, connect all nine dots by four straight lines.

Did you solve the puzzle? If not, was it because you limited yourself by invoking rules not stated in the directions? Most people who attempt to solve the puzzle assume that the lines drawn must remain within the square or that the lines cannot cross each other. But no such limitations are given. Only if you break through certain assumptions or presuppositions and think of various alternatives can you come up with a solution (See note 2).

Thus, in step 3,

3. *Brainstorm as many good solutions to the underlying problem as you can.*

Solutions, like the statement of the problems, should be specific so that they can be carried out. Vague solutions—fix the chain in the snowblower or end polio—provide inadequate direction.

You can think of this step in terms of the main points we spoke about in Chapter 3. There we saw that the main points should relate specifically to the underlying thesis. They should help advance that thesis. Similarly, the solutions to your problems should relate specifically to the underlying problem and should help advance the solution of the problem.

Several solutions appeared with respect to repairing the snowblower: loosen the nut and move the adjusting wheel, remove some links from the chain to shorten it, purchase a new chain, purchase a bigger adjusting sprocket, take it to a repair shop, purchase a new snowblower.

In the case of polio, physicians, researchers, and the community suggested various solutions: nasal sprays that would deactivate whatever was inhaled; treatment of the nose with provic acid or alum, which disabled the sense of smell; ingestion of some form of peanut oil or large quantities of vitamin C; and quarantine. When a specific virus became identified as the underlying cause, researchers directed their attention to how the virus might be handled: should the virus be killed in patients; should there be a preventative vaccine; should the vaccine consist of an inactivated virus or a live but weakened virus? Initially the research community manifested little unanimity about the direction it was to take to stop the polio epidemics.

Mechanical or technical problems are one sort of problem to be solved; addressing and solving personal and social problems often can prove much more difficult. When you try to solve broad social problems, you should always think about introducing the critical thinker's friends: WHO will carry out WHAT action, HOW it will be done, WHERE and WHEN will this solution take place, and WHY it will solve the problem. These provide the specificity needed to construct definite proposals, rather than merely expressing general ideas about vague solutions.

Criteria for evaluating good solutions include

(h) How clearly you elaborate the solutions.
(i) How specific or definite your solutions to the problem are.
(j) The relevancy of the solutions to the underlying problem.
(k) The diversity of perspectives used in suggesting solutions.
(l) How flexible your solutions are to adapt to changes in the situation. Remember that each situation introduces new facts, which require adjustment of solutions to the new situations.

(m) How likely it is that those who carry out your solution will succeed.
(n) The cost in time, energy, and personnel in resolving the problem.

Sometimes you discover that deriving solutions is difficult because *first*, the initial problem situation lacks sufficient details. You may have to go back and research the problem to find more relevant details or you might have to make critical assumptions in order to generate possible solutions. Problem situations are not always clear. For one thing, a description of the problem contains many facts. Some of these facts are relevant to the problem itself; others are irrelevant. You have to distinguish the relevant facts from the extraneous facts. For another, it is possible that in describing the situation, important, if not crucial, facts go unnoticed. These facts may not be obvious but lie hidden by the very structure of the situation (I could not see into my snowblower, and early disease researchers knew nothing of viruses), or they may be so distant from the initial problem that they are ignored.

Second, your ability to generate solutions depends on your background knowledge. The more knowledge you have, the easier it is to come up with a diversity of workable solutions. You may recognize elements of the problem that have arisen in other contexts, or you may be able to apply information from other situations to the current problem. Jonas Salk, who created the first polio vaccine, had a background investigating influenza. Although most of you are not paid researchers, yet reading widely in newspapers, journals, books, and magazines plays an important role in providing you with important background knowledge.

The goal of problem solving is to come up with a suggestion that will best resolve the underlying problem. However, "best," is a vague term. What is it to resolve the problem in the *best* way? "Best" may be measured by different criteria in different cases. To arrive at the best solution for your underlying problem, the solutions given in step 3 must be weighed or evaluated for their adequacy. Since to weigh something you must have a scale, you need to have some *criteria* by which you will evaluate various possible solutions to the underlying problem. Hence:

4. *Identify the criteria that you will use to decide which solution is the best or most promising.*

If you go to purchase a new dress, you do not simply enter a store and buy the first one you see. You evaluate several dresses, if not many, for their fit, style, color, pattern, cost, quality, and so on. Then you weigh which dress best satisfies these criteria. Of course, the criteria themselves may not have equal weight. If you have lots of money, cost is a small factor; for other persons cost may be more significant than style. So even the criteria can be ranked in order of importance.

In fixing my snowblower, deciding on the best solution required considerations of the time required for us to repair it, the cost of taking it to a repair shop, the time that the repair shop would need to repair the machine given that it was the height of the snow season, the cost of the repair versus the high cost of buying a new machine, the cost of the repair versus shoveling the snow, and the age of the snowblower. These criteria, having primarily to do

with time, energy, and cost, had to be applied to the solutions that we identified in step 3 so that we could decide what to do. In this case too we had to
rank the criteria, since my son was earning money with the snowblower and
there were only so many snowfalls in a season. Time meant more than cost—
within limits.

With the polio epidemics, the critical issue had to do with whether the
researchers were to find a cure or a prevention, and if prevention were sought,
whether they would use live or inactivated viruses. It was believed that live
viruses stimulated antibodies more effectively since they created the most natural immune response. The danger was in making sure that the injected
viruses could not mutate and themselves cause the disease. Inactivated viruses
stimulated antibodies by their presence and appeared safer, since treating
viruses with heat, chemicals, or radiation would kill them. At the same time,
the viruses had to be completely inactivated while making sure that the vaccine was strong enough to stimulate antibodies to prevent the disease. Further,
initial production of the viruses required the use of monkeys. But should the
process initially used be the only way to produce the live viruses, there would
not have been enough monkeys to produce enough vaccine viruses to vaccinate all humans. Hence, investigators needed to develop alternative production procedures. Criteria for choosing between solutions included safety, effectiveness in preventing the disease, avoiding harmful side effects, implications
for other species like monkeys, and producibility in large enough quantities.

Here again creative brainstorming is the key to come up with the criteria
to evaluate potential solutions. When we deal with solutions to social and personal problems, additional criteria for solving problems may include

(o) Humaneness of the solution.
(p) Equity and justice of the solution.
(q) Which solution has the fewest adverse side effects.
(r) The cost of the proposed solution.
(s) Whether the benefits outweigh the costs.
(t) The amount of time needed to implement the solution.
(u) Whether governmental bodies would approve the solution.

Once you have decided on the criteria you will use to evaluate your solutions, you need to

5. *Evaluate your potential solutions according to the criteria developed in step 4.*

In the example of my snowblower, I had to apply my criteria to my proposed solutions—order a new chain and install it ourselves, try to fix the old
chain, take the machine to a repair shop, junk the machine, get a new snowblower, have a friend fix it—to see which ranked the highest overall. In the
case of polio, the research community was not of one mind on which direction
to go with the vaccine. Jonas Salk chose to go with the deactivated virus,
which in this case ultimately proved successful. For him a vaccine made from
deactivated viruses was more efficient, less costly, and certainly more effective.

You might wonder what happens when the solutions that best meet your
criteria differ from what you think deep down ought to be done to resolve the
problem. That is, your intuition about what will work or your emotions may

conflict with what results from a rational evaluation of the situation. Think about such a conflict arising when you consider dating someone who does not fit certain criteria you have preestablished. It is not always easy to resolve this disagreement between your present feelings and some preselected criteria of the perfect mate. When critical thinkers choose to go with "their heart," they will want to understand why they did not follow the criteria in this case. It is not that following your heart or intuitions is wrong or disastrous; sometimes it works out for the best. But following your heart raises questions about how carefully you selected the criteria initially and how important the criteria are, either individually or jointly, that were used to assess possible solutions.

This brings us to step 6 in problem solving: implement the solution. In an academic or corporation setting, you may be required to

6a. *Describe in written form the most promising solution to the Underlying Problem.*

In the real world, step 6 may require you to

6b. *Carry out the plan of action that you have formulated by means of steps 4 and 5.*

If you are required to explain something, unless the context is otherwise, you should not assume that your reader is as fully aware of the details of the problem as you are. So any explanation should be clear, concise, and yet thorough. It is essential that you relate your best solution back to your statement of the underlying problem (step 2) and indicate how it will solve that problem in terms of the criteria you have used for evaluation, with the fewest negative side effects. Again, one should always remember that one's best friends in writing are Who, What, Where, When, Why, and How.

The solution on which you settle may actually be a combination of the various solutions you have weighed, perhaps encompassing important elements in some or all of them. The solution may be simple—take the snowblower to the shop—or it may be complex—like creating a preventative vaccine and testing it on significant numbers of schoolchildren, or taking diverse steps to improve the educational system so that a greater number of students graduate. Hence, the evaluation in step 5 only provides the beginning, indicating what you think is important to resolve the problem.

When you go through this process of problem solving, you may discover that your solution won't work. The underlying problem may be different than you thought it was, or the solution on which you settled may be inadequate to the task. In fact, this is what happened with my snowblower. I measured the chain, but it seemed the same length as the new one. So I took the machine into the shop. The problem, it turned out, had to do with the bushings in the ends of the auger and not with the chain at all. But I never thought (nor even knew) about the bushings, for these were hidden from my view and hence were not part of my list of facts to be considered. Replacing the chain ourselves would not have been enough to get my son back on the driveways blowing snow.

Another possibility is that you may discover that the byproducts or side effects of your solution are unacceptable. These other effects might turn out to be worse than the original problem. An original vaccine, which had been successfully tested on twenty monkeys, turned out to be not only useless but could produce severe alergic reactions. A vaccine developed by another researcher caused a number of cases of polio and led to several deaths. Thus, in looking at your ultimate solution you should

7. *Think about some implications of and objections to your solution, and how any negative implications or objections may be avoided or overcome.*

Perhaps negative side effects cannot be avoided or objections cannot be overcome, but at least you should be aware of possible objections, problems, or complications. One has to be open to failure in problem solving. But having failed, one gets back into the harness and undertakes trying again to resolve the problem. Going back through these seven steps will help you to do a better job in your second attempt.

As can be expected, variations in the real world will require changes in the procedure. Yet at the same time this procedure provides a basic, helpful framework for creative problem solving.

RESOURCES

By now you are probably wondering on what resources to draw to solve your problem. It seems that we often start solving problems either with a blank mind (we have no idea where to go) or with one solution that precludes us from considering all others. An essential part of problem solving is both *generating possibilities* and *breaking out of the rut*.

Several suggestions that might assist brainstorming and problem solving in general can be suggested.

- *Get help from others.*

When I needed to repair my snowblower, I called on the aid of my neighbor, who is a much better mechanic than I. He helped remove the parts and showed me some of the problems. But I still had to come up with the solution.

In the scenarios at the end of this chapter, you should remember that this is a group project. Hence, you need to welcome all the ideas the group members put forth. Some will be good, some terrible, some wild and way out, some seemingly so sensible. All these ideas should be considered initially. The wild idea might be the one that works; the sensible one much too costly. Brainstorming means opening up to many ideas initially. As you go along, these ideas will be altered, pared down, revised, even piggy-backed on.

- *Bring in materials from your experience.*

Specific examples that worked for you or others in the past are a good place to start in solving problems. What worked in the past for you or someone else might work in resolving your new problem. Here you are rich, for you have had many experiences over the years on which to draw. The older you are, the more resources from your experiences you will have. It was the rich previous experience of working with influenza that enabled Salk to move ahead successfully with his polio vaccine.

- *Research your problem and suggested solutions.*

You both can learn from the past and need not repeat the mistakes of the past. What happened in the past with similar problems can help shed light on your problem. With complex problems, you can bring research to bear on step 1. But at least by step 4 it is time to see if you can locate some information on the underlying problem. Since the underlying problem by now is well formulated, various indexes in books, on-line services, or libraries should help you locate articles or books on the topic. Of course, merely because a particular solution is written down and published does not mean that it is *the* solution to the problem. In fact, it might not be a solution to your problem at all. Thus, critical thinkers bring together their own ideas with those found in their research to solve creatively the problems facing them. We addressed research resources in Chapter 8.

- *Separate ideas from the persons who hold them.*

This is a hard concept. We tend to think that our ideas are an extension of ourselves so that if they are rejected, amended, or altered, we must have been deficient in some way. Part of the trick of brainstorming is to divorce yourself from your ideas so that everyone is free to take the ideas and see whether they will fly. Don't be put down if your idea is rejected; congratulate yourself on the fact that you entertained an idea that people could consider.

Similarly, if your idea is accepted, don't be overproud, refusing to let your idea be altered, pared down, revised, even piggy-backed on. Where you work in groups, congratulate yourself on the fact that you entertained an idea that people could accept, but at the same time remember that it is a group project, where all can contribute.

SUMMING UP

This seven-step program is an ideal. As we noted, in real life you will modify some of the steps, do some steps simultaneously, and perhaps even backtrack. Yet this structure provides a very helpful model for solving problems, whether simple ones like which car to buy or more difficult ones like resolving a personnel conflict in an organization or company.

Following these seven steps does not guarantee that you will resolve the problem. No method can assure success. But it provides one way of helping you to understand and address the problem, to distinguish the underlying problem from the symptoms, and to come up with possible solutions. It will broaden your approach and encourage you to pay attention to additional features and to look in various places for pieces that can be used to construct your solution.

Exercise

The following three scenarios pose problems needing resolution. Choosing one of the scenarios, your group should follow the steps developed in this chapter to arrive at what it thinks provides the best solution to the underlying problem it identifies. Each individual in the group should be equally involved in the project. Since some of this project probably will have to be done outside of class, you may need to arrange a time when you can get together to complete the project.

Step 1: In critical thinking, before you can deal with a situation, you must *identify the problems or causes* to be addressed. Only when the problems have been clearly identified can solutions begin. Thoroughly read and discuss the scenario that you have chosen or been assigned. Brainstorm and list as many problems or causes in the assigned scenario as you can. Select the ten that you think are the most important. Write out your ten problems or causes clearly and thoroughly, giving a one paragraph description for each.

Consider the scenario from a variety of perspectives, which may include

1. arts and aesthetics
2. basic needs
3. business, commerce, economics
4. education
5. environment
6. ethics and religion
7. government and politics
8. law and justice
9. physical health
10. psychological health
11. recreation
12. social relationships
13. technology
14. transportation

Criteria for grading step 1:

Clarity of stating the problems

Problems, not solutions, clearly indentified

Relevance of the problems to the scenario

Diversity of perspectives used in stating the problems

Originality

Good writing

Step 2: *The Underlying Problem.* Based on the problems you listed in step 1, identify the underlying problem in the scenario. It should be the one that, if solved, may solve many of the other problems you listed in step 1. (It may be one of the ten, though probably it will be a problem that underlies several of the problems noted in step 1.) Write a paragraph clearly developing this underlying problem and showing how it relates to the ten problems listed in step 1. Step 2 is crucial, for all else that you do hangs on how well you identify this underlying problem.

Criteria for grading step 2:

Relevance of underlying problem to the situation posed

Clarity and specificity of the problem

Distinguishes the underlying problem from the symptoms

A focus narrow enough to be specific but broad enough to encompass the problems that arise in the scenario

Step 3: *Brainstorm* as many *solutions* as you can to your underlying problem. List the five most promising solutions. Each solution should address all of the aspects of the underlying problem. Write a paragraph for each solution, stating WHO will carry out WHAT action, HOW it will be done, WHERE and WHEN this solution will take place, and WHY it will solve the problem. Again, be aware of diverse categories or perspectives from which a solution to the underlying problem may be generated. Solutions should be definite proposals rather than possibilities. Specificity and thoroughness are important.

Criteria for grading step 3:

Clarity of solutions

Relevance to the situation

Diversity of perspectives the solutions represent

Flexibility of viewpoints

Elaboration

Adequacy to the story

Specificity and completeness

Likely to succeed

Originality

Good writing

Step 4: *Identify* the *criteria* by which you will decide which solution is the best or most promising. Brainstorm all the criteria you can think of and choose the five that you believe are most relevant and important. Each criterion should address a single dimension of the problem. Put these five in the form of a question. For example, which solution is the most cost effective? Which solution is most humane? In which solution would the people who need the help voluntarily participate?

Criteria for grading step 4:

Relevance and applicability of the criteria

Ability of the criteria to be scaled

Step 5: *Evaluate* the five *solutions* according to the criteria developed in step 4. Construct a chart listing your solutions in a horizontal row at the top and the criteria for evaluation in a vertical column on the left. Each member of your group should rank the solutions numerically from 1 (best) to 5 (least acceptable) according to each of the criteria; enter the number in the appropriate cell on the chart. Then tally the total points for each solution on your chart and combine your individual rankings into a group evaluation.

Step 6: *Present your primary solution.* Write a three to four page essay describing the most promising or best solution (either the one that received the lowest score in step 5, a combination of the top vote getters, or perhaps some underlying solution). Develop and explain your solution. Include a description of your plan of action for carrying out the solution. Make sure that you relate your best solution back to the original story and your statement of the underlying problem. *Show* how it will solve that problem.

You might consider some of the following concerns: Who will be involved? What actions will be taken? When and where will the plan be carried out? How might obstacles be overcome? You should assume that your instructor is unfamiliar with the discussion of the problem and so be clear and concise, yet thorough in your written description.

Criteria for grading step 6:

> Relevance of your solution to the described scenario
>
> Strength and clarity of the arguments supporting your view
>
> Depth of your insight into the problem
>
> Effectiveness of your solution
>
> Creativity
>
> Awareness of difficulties in implementing the solution
>
> Impact of your solution
>
> Humaneness of your solution
>
> Good writing

Step 7: *Identify* either three possible negative *side effects* or three *objections* to your solution. Show either how the side effects will not occur or how they can be handled. Provide a reasonable response to the objections, showing how they may be overcome.

Step 8: Theater. On the final day of the group project, your group will be given ten minutes to act out a short play that demonstrates your chosen solution. Plan the theater ahead of time and bring to class whatever props you want to use in the play. Before the play, read your underlying problem to the class and present a *brief* (one paragraph) summary of your primary solution.

Criteria for grading step 8:

Relevance of the play to the underlying problem and primary solution

How well the play communicates the solution

Creativity

SCENARIOS: PROBLEM SOLVING IN ACTION

Scenario 1: Racial Conflict

In the warm summer of the year 2015 a group of forty youths carrying baseball bats and golf clubs jumped out of their electric cars as they drove past a low-income apartment complex inhabited by members of a minority group. Many of the minority kids who lived there ran away, but one young boy was caught and badly beaten, losing teeth and suffering a concussion.

Several other incidents followed in which the All-American Boys gang attacked and beat members of minority groups wherever they could find them. These groups, in return, formed gangs to defend themselves. In fact, members of the minority group were accused of attacking members of the majority group in similarly vicious fashion.

Townsville is a midwestern community of about 100,000. In the past the city was racially uniform, populated largely by people of the upper and middle class. Its main industries are medical technology and delivery of health care, high-tech computer manufacturing, and telecommunications. Until recently it had one of the lowest rates of crime in the country, an excellent health care system, low unemployment, and was recognized nationally as an outstanding city in which to live.

In the five years prior to the gang attacks, a fairly large number of people representing two different racial minorities moved into the city looking for work and economic opportunity. They were attracted by the city's good paying jobs and reputation for excellent schools and safety. About half of the immigrants are foreign born. The result has been a significant increase in racial tension, with gangs of youths beating up members of the other communities. Crime has increased, police have been assigned to the schools, school performance has deteriorated, and citizens are afraid to venture out at night. The city has also begun to develop segregated housing patterns based on race, ethnicity, and class.

When the police cracked down on marauding youth, members of the minority communities accused the police force, staffed wholly by members of the majority community, with harassment and discrimination in intervening in the racial conflicts. The police defended themselves by saying they were doing their best to control a bad, tense situation. All members of the police force have undergone sensitivity training in the last five years.

The mayor convened a blue-ribbon panel of persons representing various populations of the community, of which you are a member. Your task is to isolate the key problem and draw up a program for resolving it so as to restore peace, safety, harmony, opportunity, and prosperity to the community.

Scenario 2: Educational Challenges

In the year 2015 the State Board of Education was authorized by the legislature to institute high school graduation requirements in reading, writing, mathematics, social science, and science. This was in response to a perceived progressive deterioration in the ACT and SAT test scores of the high school juniors across the state and to complaints from business leaders that those applying for jobs in the state had a high degree of functional illiteracy in English and mathematical incompetence. The results of the first state-wide tests given to ninth graders shocked the community. In the large urban areas of the state, only about 45 percent of the ninth graders passed the four tests. The suburban areas did better, though the percentage of students passing still hovered at about 78 percent. Only in some of the affluent suburbs and in about a quarter of the rural areas did students consistently do better than 85 percent passing.

When these figures were analyzed, the educators discovered that the failure rate correlated with a number of other figures, including those of students receiving free school lunches, of students from single-parent working families, of students with special learning needs, and of recent immigrants from non-English speaking countries. It was also the case that schools that had integrated students with special, severe learning disabilities into their regular classes had lower passing rates. At the same time, schools with PTA organizations and heavy parental involvement in the schools reported markedly better results, regardless of their economic status.

In 2015 the schools in the urban areas have 65 percent minority enrollment, while those in the inner ring of suburbs have 35 percent minority enrollment. Proportions similar to those holding between urban and suburban apply to single-parent versus two-parent families and to those receiving and not receiving free school lunches. In the rural areas minority populations vary depending on location, with some school districts having a much higher percentage of minorities and foreign immigrants than others. This results from immigration over the years from nonwestern countries and migrant laborers now establishing residence. The minorities are both native English and non-English speakers.

The governor of the state has assembled a blue-ribbon commission, of which you are a part, to discuss ways of improving the test performance and the graduation skills of the students in the state. Your task is to isolate the fundamental problem and suggest measures to address it so as to improve the overall education in the state.

Scenario 3: Environmental Damage

In the second half of the twentieth century, the size of American forests, particularly in the East, increased dramatically; in some areas it approached the size found by the early European settlers. At the same time, however, the health of the eastern forests declined substantially. By the year 2020 some species such as the hickories, which generally don't begin to produce viable seedlings until they are 150 years old, are practically extinct. Butternut trees are succumbing to the butternut canker, oak trees to oak wilt, and pine trees to various infestations of bark beetles and diseases. The forests are filled with dead and dying trees, the food of insects and fungi. Hence, what looks healthy and thriving from a distance is in ecological ruin when you investigate up close.

The worst degradation occurs on the higher slopes of the forests, where the winds blowing over the industrial centers and tall smokestacks of power plants of the West and Midwest waft across the forests. Population growth and a robust economy in the midwestern and especially the western states have encouraged significant industrial growth, particularly in the petrochemical industry. This expansion has fueled an increased industrial and residential demand for electricity. At the same time, public resistance to nuclear power plants out of fear of a nuclear accident encouraged utility companies to build and maintain coal-burning power plants. Local pollution control regulations require that industries and power plants construct tall smokestacks to disperse the pollutants by the upper wind patterns away from local communities.

Chemical analysis of tree rings reveals increased absorption of toxic metals like barium, cadmium, zinc, lead, and copper. Many of the lakes in the region are empty of life because of their high sulfuric acid content.

The result has been a severe decline in animal and bird population in the eastern forests. Some species, such as the white-tailed deer, thrive, since the dying trees allow more sunlight to penetrate the forest, enabling low vegetation needed for forage to grow. Deer overpopulation, however, contributes to the further destruction of the forest, since they eat both bushes and young saplings. Further, the increased run-off that results when the trees can no longer hold the soil in place and when the deer have overgrazed certain areas pollutes the streams so that fish and other aquatic populations are in serious jeopardy.

Lumber companies have lobbied state and federal governments to allow them to harvest the dead and dying trees, arguing that they present a serious fire danger. They maintain that lumbering would also bring additional jobs and revenue to communities in the region. At the same time, environmentalists have lobbied against harvesting, responding that new forest roads and forestry practices would further debilitate the soils and increase erosion and discourage conservation-minded recreational use of the forests.

The President has appointed a blue-ribbon commission, of which you are a member, to identify the main problem and to suggest the best plan of addressing it, a plan that the President can get through a Congress controlled by members of the opposition party.

Notes

1. Alex F. Osborn, *Applied Imagination: Principles and Procedures of Creative Problem Solving* (Buffalo: Creative Education Foundation, 1993).
2. Here is the solution.

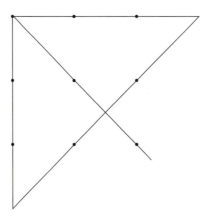

CHAPTER 10

Evaluation

Assessing the Strength of Inductive Arguments

At last we come to the major goal of critical thinking, namely, to be in a position to evaluate expressed opinions. We have learned how to discover and comprehend people's opinions when expressed as claims, to discover and analyze the reasoning behind opinions, and to synthesize them to resolve problems in creative ways. Now we investigate how to decide whether a person is justified in holding certain opinions or believing particular claims—the sixth and final step in our structure of critical thinking.

Source: BLONDIE. Reprinted with special permission of King Feature Syndicate, Inc.

What premise do both Dagwood and his boss Mr. Dithers accept? _____

What would each conclude from that same premise? _____

_____

_____

Do they conclude the same thing? Why or why not? _____

_____

_____

Which conclusion appears to be the most reasonable? Why do you say

that? _____

_____

This last question asks you to evaluate. We certainly are no strangers to evaluation. Often when we read a book or article or listen to a talk, we focus on evaluation. Frequently our first questions are these: Is that true? Why should I believe that? Sometimes we are skeptical about what the person says and may even have the opportunity to ask the person to "prove it."

But what basis do we use to make our evaluation? If speakers or writers agree with our position, we tend to think that what they say must be true, well argued, and worthy of attention. If they disagree with us, we tend quickly to reject what they say or tune them out without further exploration. A human response is to use our own opinions or beliefs as standards to test the adequacy of other views.

But possibly our own views are incorrect; perhaps they too need critical evaluation. Hence, it is risky to judge others' views solely on the grounds that they agree or fail to agree with our own views. We need to look for better reasons to accept or reject the views of others.

Critical thinkers adopt an open mind about other positions. They first try to understand and comprehend what is said; then they seek out the reasoning behind the position advanced. Only after they understand others' opinions and their basis do critical thinkers evaluate those opinions. They do not judge opinions without looking at the evidence for and against those opinions. They bring their experience, knowledge, understanding, and critical evaluation skills to bear on what they are asked to believe.

Chapters 10 through 12 aim to assist you in this difficult but important task of evaluation. They look at questions of truth, the reliability of sources, the cogency of arguments, and the validity of arguments in order to help you determine when you are justified in believing a claim. When you complete these chapters, you should have a better understanding of what makes an argument cogent or valid and of what fallacies or bad reasoning to avoid.

DETERMINING THE TRUTH OF STATEMENTS

People can legitimately differ over whether a claim is true or not and to what degree they believe it to be true or false. This is nowhere more evident than in the areas of politics, religion, and morals. That the latest crime bill will end narcotics crime, that current economic policies are expanding the gap in standards of living among segments of our society, that a creator-God exists, that a woman should have the right to terminate her pregnancy, that integrity of character is relevant to job performance—all these claims would be hotly debated in certain quarters. People appeal to their experience, authorities, and diverse arguments to come to different conclusions. But these are not the only areas where opinions are disputed. Indeed, there is hardly a subject about which differences in knowledge and viewpoint will not lead people to make different truth claims. Hence, while there may be unanimity about the truth of a few opinions, with many others disagreement (sometimes heated) reigns.

The ultimate task of critical thinking is to decide whether a statement or claim is true or false. In trying to decide, critical thinkers look at a variety of things. They

- Check their experience
- Review their background knowledge
- Ask others for their opinions
- Consult authorities
- Construct arguments
- Conduct research
- Review the research of others.

Some of our knowledge comes from *direct experience.* We have experiences and on this basis believe that some statements are true. For example, I know the statement "It is raining outside" is true because I look out my window and see drops of water on the driveway. Or again, I believe the statement "I ate an omelet for breakfast" is true because I saw the omelet, ate it, and recall doing so. I need not argue for the truth of this statement about my breakfast; my experience of eating the omelet is sufficient to establish its truth.

We must be careful here. From the fact that we experience something, it does not follow that the way we interpret or describe it necessarily is the way it really is. Consider, for example, the time when you drove down a road on a hot summer day, and in a dip in the road ahead you saw water. When you arrived at the dip there was no water; what you saw was an illusion produced by the sun and the heat on the dark pavement. In the omelet example, the statement that I ate an omelet for breakfast presupposes the accuracy of my senses and my memory, both of which are fallible. Similarly, the fact that we *do not* experience something does not mean that statements about what we have not experienced are not true. More is the case than we have experienced. Hence, though our experience is relevant to the truth of statements, it is neither necessary for a statement's truth (a statement can be true regardless of whether we have experienced it) nor always sufficient (our experience might be wrong). It will be sufficient when we have reason to think that our senses and memory are acting properly.

Another way of determining truth is to *consult your background knowledge.* Over the years you have acquired a store of information that provides a good data base from which to make judgments about whether claims are true or false. The better your background knowledge, the better positioned you are to decide the truth of new claims. For example, suppose you are asked, "What factors contributed to the Crusades?" Probably you have never been exposed to the question. So if asked whether it is true that inheritance customs in Europe contributed significantly to the Crusades, you might say that, given what you know, the truth value of this statement is unknown to you. At the same time, those who have studied medieval history probably would have known that the statement is true. This example illustrates the claim that people with richer or broader backgrounds are often in a better position to determine the truth or falsity of new statements they encounter.

Again, this background information may be mistaken; what you think you know may not be knowledge at all. However, it provides an important resource for assessing the truth of new claims.

Another option is to ask *friends, acquaintances, or authorities for their opinions.* Sometimes this provides a reliable source of information; at other times it proves unreliable. The reliability of the information depends in part on the experiences and knowledge of the persons consulted. Yesterday my neighbor asked me whom I might recommend to reshingle his roof. Some years ago he noticed that I had mine reshingled and wondered whether I would recommend that person. I might have replied, "B. P. is a good shingler because he did my roof well." Whether B. P. is a good shingler or not depends on many things, including whether B. P.'s work on my roof represents his work in general. My neighbor may want to consult others, including authorities like the Better Business Bureau, before he hires a roofer.

Research likewise extends our knowledge. We may conduct our own research, in which case what we learn is dependent on our own experience. Or we may consult others' research, in which case we rely on the opinions of others who often claim to be authorities. Thus, research piggy-backs on the other ways of determining truth.

Arguments also provide a way of determining truth. If we are interested in establishing the truth of a statement, we might infer it from other statements that we take to be true. In arguments we move from the more known to the less known. As we noted in Chapter 7, deductive arguments establish conclusions with certainty, while inductive arguments establish conclusions with varying degrees of probability. Chapter 12 takes up the evaluation of deductive arguments. This chapter concentrates on inductive reasoning.

COGENCY IN INDUCTIVE ARGUMENTS

In Chapter 7 we noted that an inductive argument is *cogent* when its premises

(1) are true,
(2) are relevant to the conclusion, and
(3) provide good reason to think that the conclusion is true.

In contrast to deductive arguments, the premises of inductive arguments do not necessitate, but only make probable, the conclusion. Inductive arguments yield probability, not certainty. Hence, we are justified in believing the concluding statement to be probably true when the argument is cogent, though it remains possible that despite the evidence the conclusion is false.

In the next four sections we explore how to evaluate the cogency of arguments from authority, generalizations, analogies, and causal inferences.

Arguments from Authority

Chapter 8 discussed the importance of determining the reliability of the authors of our sources. Sometimes we consider those authors to be authorities. Authorities play a significant, indeed necessary, role in our lives. To discover what needs to be done, to get things done, or to learn the truth, we rely on the word of authorities, for each of us has serious limits. None of us possesses all the knowledge required to make our machines, grow our crops, repair our vehicles, survey our property, defend ourselves in a court of law, invest in a stock, and build bridges.

When I am sick I visit my physician. He studies my symptoms, suggests the cause of my illness, and proposes some remedies. I could inquire about the basis of his statements and then proceed to investigate his claims. In the course of the investigation, I might seek a second opinion. But then I have traded one authority's opinion for another. To have a second opinion can sometimes be good, for authorities can be mistaken or unsure of their diagnosis. But most of the time I choose to accept my physician's assessment of my illness and prescriptions for its treatment. I find this to be the most effective and efficient way to handle my medical problems.

Though we need to rely on authorities, the difficult problem arises about how to identify *reliable* authorities. How can I find a reliable dentist, auto mechanic, lawyer, salesperson, beautician, politician, minister, teacher, realtor, or insurance salesperson? Looking in the Yellow Pages is one place to begin, but this does not provide a very reliable way to find a trustworthy authority. Anyone who has sufficient funds can advertise, name their company AAAWhatever, or place a fancy boxed ad to catch the consumer's attention. The Yellow Pages lists candidates to help me, but it fails to sort among them for reliable performance.

Six factors may be considered in your search for an authority whom you can trust.

- Is the authority properly qualified? What training has she or he had in the specialty? Has the person continued training to remain current with the latest information? To ascertain this, look for diplomas, certificates, or ask the person about his or her training.

Several years ago I took some students on a trip to visit archaeological sites in Mexico and Guatemala. In the course of our trip, one person so severely shattered his elbow that I had to take him to the hospital in Guatemala City. The surgeon called me to his office to discuss the case. When I entered his office, I quickly scanned the diplomas on the walls to ascertain where the surgeon was educated, how recently, and what his expertise was. I wanted some evidence of his qualifications before I would allow him to perform surgery on the injured person.

- Is the authority commenting on his or her area of expertise?

If the person is an authority on the cinema, is he or she commenting on the cinema or advertising some wine to be purchased?

- Does the person have something to gain personally from what he or she says?

A "yes" answer would not necessarily exclude someone from being a reliable authority. People properly develop an expertise in an area to make money. But you have to determine whether personal reward is the primary reason the authority makes the particular recommendation and whether this reward may affect the truthfulness of the claims made. For example, why is the baseball star promoting a brand of shoes with his name on them?

- What kinds of experiences have other people had with the alleged authority? Did the authority perform competently for them?

Here you might consult your friends, neighbors, the Better Business Bureau, and other individuals in the community.

- How long has the person been in that occupation or business?

On the whole, persons who have practiced their trade or profession successfully for a long time are more likely to be authorities. Presumably, they have had many different experiences and consequently have developed the expertise to cope with novel situations. However, this rule of thumb must be tempered, for people setting up new businesses might possess more up-to-date information or training and hence be more authoritative on what is necessary to solve your problem.

- What has the person accomplished in his or her field? Can you observe what he or she has created, made, or repaired? What is the quality of the craftsmanship or service rendered?

In certain fields it is appropriate to ask what people have done, published, or created to demonstrate their expertise. In other fields you might look for practical problem solving or creativity or for how they have performed the service they offer.

The **appeal to authority** generates an argument of the following sort.

Smith is an authority in her field.

Smith says that such and such is true.

Therefore such and such is probably true.

Appeals to authority are inductive arguments. We have noted that in inductive arguments we can accept the premises as true while still denying the conclusion. In appeals to authority, we could accept what the authority said, but since the authority could be wrong, even when speaking about his or her own field, the conclusion is at best probably true. There are degrees of probability, however, so that qualified people speaking in their field have a greater chance of speaking the truth than people who are less well qualified, who have, for example, weaker training and less experience.

Though at times this inductive argument from authority is cogent, at other times it contains a fallacy. A **fallacy** occurs when *an argument breaks a rule or where the premises fail to support the conclusion.* In constructing arguments, it is important to avoid fallacies. Fallacious arguments are useless to critical thinkers, though they might be persuasive to others.

The **Fallacy of Appeal to an Unqualified Authority** occurs when someone asks you to accept a statement as true or to take a certain action because someone who is an actual or alleged authority has said so, but the actual or alleged authority is commenting on a subject about which he or she is not qualified to speak. That person may not be an authority at all, or that person may be an authority in a specific area but not in the area on which he or she is commenting. In the last case, what the arguer is hoping is that you will extend or transfer that person's credibility from one realm to another so that you will accept the statement or take an action recommended (such as purchase a product).

For example, an advertisement for a particular brand of hair care product featuring three pictures of the model Cheryl Tiegs, ends with the statement: "Clairesse . . . because I love the look." The advertisement is signed, "Cheryl Tiegs." Here someone who knows something about modeling is asked to endorse a product that is tangently related to her area of expertise, while the advertiser hopes that her endorsement will persuade you to purchase the product. A similar expectation is set up when, in an entirely different ad, Cheryl Tiegs endorses an Olympus camera. "Cheryl Tiegs praises her favorite model [note the ambiguity of meaning]. Cheryl: Once I get going, I can talk about the Olympus OM-10 all day." The fact that she poses in front of cameras does not make her an authority on single lens reflex cameras, or even cameras in general.

Advertisers also like to use sports figures to market their products. A current favorite is the former basketball superstar Michael Jordan. In an ad for Ball Park Franks, Michael Jordan holds a half-eaten hot dog under the caption, "It's not really summer 'til you have your ball park. Put summer in play Michael's way. With big, juicy, nothing-else-like'em Ball Park Franks." Although he is surely an authority on playing professional basketball and perhaps even of playing professional baseball, he has no special expertise on the subject of hot dogs.

Sometimes the connection between the authority and the product is very strained. Several years ago Dewar's Whiskies ran a series of ads that featured ordinary people who plugged the Dewar brand. For example, "Dewar's Profiles: Ed Silvers. Home: Los Angeles, California. Age: 39. Profession: Music Publisher. Hobbies: Sailing, collecting antiques. Last Accomplishment: Bringing to life a large, dormant music publishing company. . . . Scotch: Dewar's 'White Label.' "The fact that Ed Silvers knows something about the music business and has succeeded in it does not make him an authority on scotch. That he drinks and recommends a specific brand provides no relevant reason for you to use it.

Sometimes the names of the authority are not used, only the title. For example, an advertisement for Mercury automobiles proclaims, "44 out of 50 airline pilots judge Mercury more comfortable to drive than a $31,000 Rolls Royce. The jury: 50 commercial airline pilots—professionals with acute sensitivity to motion, vibration, and noise." But though pilots would be authorities on piloting planes, they are not necessarily authorities especially suited or more qualified than others to judge whether one automobile excels over another in smoothness of ride, steadiness, ease of handling, and quietness. Of course, they are not unqualified either. The question you must raise is whether the fact that pilots and automobile drivers both "drive" motored vehicles subject to noise and vibration makes the pilots specially qualified to comment on certain characteristics of cars.

It is not always easy to discern whether the person is an authority in the area on which he or she is commenting. When a basketball player promotes a certain brand of shoe, a skier a certain brand of skis, a business traveler a brand of suitcase, a model a brand of make-up, we might think that these persons should know something about the things they use. But consider all the things you use. Does using something make you an authority about that item? Are you, by using it, an expert on its construction? Probably not. Special education or carefully tested experience is needed to make a person an authority. It is this added dimension that results in the specialized knowledge that you want to look for when an authority tells you that you should believe or do something because he or she says so.

One final point. Why do advertisers in particular use fallacious arguments when they probably know these arguments are fallacious? The answer is that there is a difference between cogency and *persuasiveness*. People who give arguments or evidence want to persuade you to think or act in a certain way. Advertisers want you to purchase their product; why else would they pay millions of dollars to sports stars or Hollywood personalities to endorse their products? For them it is persuasiveness, not cogency, that matters. It is up to you as a critical thinker to resist the persuasive appeal in order to assess the cogency of the argument. When you evaluate the reasons presented to you to do something, act in a particular way, or buy a product or service, you utilize the highest level of critical thinking skills: critical evaluation.

Exercise 1

First, identify the conclusion of each argument. Second, identify the authorities to whom the author appeals. Finally, using the criteria suggested in this section, tell which of the following arguments commit the Fallacy of Unqualified Authority and explain why they do.

A. 1. Ad with a picture of a Ford Taurus and the claim, TALK ABOUT A SAFE INVESTMENT. "It's important to believe my family's safe." Wesley Howard, loyal Ford owner. "It feels safe. It gives me peace of mind." Jay Seifer, former import owner. "I feel safe in this car." Ann Kimble, former import owner. "I feel like I'm getting a safe, solid, valuable ride." Dennis Bryant, former import owner. (Advertisement)

2. "I don't skimp on nutrition. That's why Tang is on my table."—says research psychologist Jennifer Macleod. When large corporations have people problems they turn to Jennifer Macleod. She's a private consultant with a Ph.D. in Research Psychology. (Advertisement)

3. A recent technique, just coming into widespread use, measures minute changes in the amount of oxygen in blood vessels in the brain. Known as functional magnetic resonance imaging, . . . it lights up areas that are active during some mental processes, such as seeing, calculating or remembering. . . . "These new imaging techniques provide a window into the brain," Dr. Joseph Coyle, a professor of psychiatry at Harvard medical school, said. . . . "For the first time, they permit us to document individual brain functions (and) can lead to drugs and other interventions." (Robert S. Boyd, "New Techniques Allow Scientists to 'Map' Brain," *St. Paul Pioneer Press,* November 9, 1997).

4. "French Colombard from Ernest and Julio Gallo is a richly rewarding experience. It will surely be one of the finest wines you have ever tasted." signed, Peter Ustino, film director. (Advertisement)

5. There's nothing upright about *Central Park West* star Lauren Hutton or the character she plays, Linda Fairchild Rush. Who else has what it takes to make us believe that "bohemian socialite" is not an impossible contradiction? Here, she wears a wool suit that fits a relaxed attitude without compromising professional style. Wool is a favorite. You can dress up or down; it's all in the way you wear it. (Advertisement)

6. I challenge you to get more lather with Zest Body Wash. Craig "Iron Head" Heyward, NFL Running Back. (Advertisement)

7. [Picture showing a woman holding flowers, standing in front of her home.] Beverly Hills: Insured by Foremost. "I depend on AARP Mobile Home Insurance Program for security I can afford and the service is excellent." Melba Beverly, Marietta, Ga. Give your mobile home the VIP treatment. In the flowing hills of Marietta, Georgia, Melba Beverly is all smiles. She enjoys the affordable security of AARP Mobil Home Insurance Program, provided by the Foremost Insurance Group. (Advertisement)

8. Our members know why they belong. Peter Max: Artist. Interests: Creating the universe. Passions: Creating new images, inventing color combinations and rising artwork for good. Lifestyle: Holistic living, Macrobiotic diet, Working out regularly, Yoga, Taking time to serve others and the planet. Sports Club/NY. The finest sports and fitness complex in the world. (Advertisement)

9. Photo with a woman holding a puppy. "She got her healthy start on Pedigree Puppy food long before she was even born." Dr. Fran Smith, Veterinarian & Top Breeder of Champion Labrador Retrievers. "This little girl is only 16 days old, but she's been getting the nutritional benefits of Pedigree Puppy for 11 weeks already. That's because I fed her mom Pedigree Puppy all through her pregnancy. I wouldn't raise my puppies on anything else." (Advertisement)

10. "The next century will be the golden age of sea power," predicts Admiral Donald Pillig, vice-chief of US Naval Operations. (*Christian Science Monitor,* December 2, 1997)

B. Return to the two case studies used in Chapter 1. Which of the individuals appealed to as witnesses or authorities in the respective cases are reliable and why?

Generalizations

A second kind of inductive argument is a generalization. In a generalization, the arguer infers a conclusion about all or a certain percentage of a group from information about a select sample. We discussed generalizations in detail in Chapter 7. Our concern here is to determine when a generalization is cogent and when it has committed a fallacy.

The basic rule for a generalization is this: *the stronger the sample, the more cogent the argument.* An argument commits the **Fallacy of Hasty Generalization** when it draws a conclusion from an inadequate sample. What we need to address is what makes a sample adequate and when the sample is so weak or inadequate that the generalization drawn from it is fallacious.

A good sample must satisfy several conditions. *First, it must be of an adequate size.* As we noted in Chapter 7, the larger the sample, the smaller the margin of sampling error. A sampling error is the difference between how frequently the characteristic occurs in the sample and how frequently it occurs in the group about which we make the generalization. For example, if a sample showed that 51 percent of Americans would vote for a Democratic candidate for president, the prediction is that the number who actually vote that way in the election will be within so many percentage points of this 51 percent. A sample of 100 yields a margin of error of +/− 11 percentage points (a range of 22 percent). A sample of 1,500 yields a margin of error of +/− 3 percentage points (a range of 6 percent). Whereas investigating a sample above 1,500 might not be cost effective (that is, the cost of increased sampling does not significantly reduce the margin of error), reducing samples below a certain size greatly increases the margin of error and thereby the chances of making a sampling error. At some point the sample is too small to adequately ground an inference, and an argument with too few samples may commit the Fallacy of Hasty Generalization.

Consider the following letter to a college newspaper, which we used as an exercise earlier in the book.

> To refute some of the claims made in last week's editorial I will present some of my own evaluations from my experiences on the college board plan. In evaluation, I looked for tastiness, appearance, and cost of the food, cleanliness, and politeness and friendliness of the kitchen staff. I found that the food tasted very good and appeared very attractive. The cooks are so concerned about the attractiveness of their food that they wipe off any soup that drips down the side of each cup before presenting it to someone . . . All in all, the college has a quality food service that is deserving of praise from our newspaper rather than scorn. (Neil Pauluk, letter, *Echo*, February 22, 1974)

The sample here is very small, namely, this one person's experience during one week between when the editorial was printed and the time he wrote his letter in reply. The generalization the author makes seems very hasty, based on an inadequate sample.

You might have noticed that I said that an argument with a small sample *may* commit the Fallacy of Hasty Generalization. There are cases where we may be safe in making a generalization based on a few instances. For example, if I am trying out a new drug on mice, and the first five mice I give it to die immediately from convulsions, it is probably safe to conclude that every mouse would die from convulsions if I administered the drug to them—and I need not risk my entire batch of test animals on a worthless experiment.

Sample size for small groups also presents problems. That is why, for example, surveys of small classes in school are not very helpful unless you get a complete response (in which case you no longer have a generalization but a complete enumeration). If you survey a class of ten students, for example, and get responses from seven, the margin of error is very great. Since you have no assurance that the answers from the seven represent those of the three who did not take or return the survey, it is difficult to draw reliable conclusions from such a sample.

As you can see, although there are figures that give us set ranges for margin of error, a more individual dimension also is present. How large is the group about which you are generalizing? What characteristics are being generalized? In each case the critical thinker has to ponder what would be a good sample size to justify making the generalization and evaluating it as cogent.

Sometimes the audience is not given enough information to know how good the sample is. Consider this advertisement.

> Discover the medically proven way to lose weight. In universities across the country, clinical studies prove four out of five people lost weight successfully with Dexatrim. In fact, no other weight-loss product has more published clinical and medical studies than Dexatrim to prove it works.

Before we run out to purchase Dexatrim to lose weight, as critical thinkers we would want more evidence. The advertisement lists no studies to enable the reader to follow up the claims made. The claims may be true, but the critical thinker in not in a position to know.

Second, every member of the population under study must be given an equal chance to be sampled. Hence, the sample must be **random.** Otherwise, the sample may be biased and not yield accurate results about the population.

A classic example was the *Chicago Tribune's* sample of potential voters in the 1948 presidential election. The newspaper sent poll takers into the suburbs in the afternoon to sample how people were voting. It then reported, in a famous erroneous headline, that Thomas Dewey won the presidential election, though in fact Harry Truman did. The problem was that the newspaper's sample was not random but biased: it favored suburban, nonworking women, who tended to vote Republican in the election.

A truly random sample is not easy to attain. Many popular polling methods fail this test. Standing outside the Student Center from 11 A.M. to 1 P.M. and stopping every tenth person is not a random sample of the entire college population, because it omits students who have classes or work at that time. Polls in shopping malls often have similar defects. On one hand, if the poll-takers are attempting to generalize about the entire population, they are sampling only those who shop in malls at the time they sample. On the other hand, if they are generalizing only about shoppers in malls during the hours they are polling, then by stopping every fifteenth shopper their poll may satisfy the criterion of randomness. In short, whether the sample is random enough depends in part on the population about which a person wants to generalize.

Similar problems arise with questionnaires mailed out, inserted into magazines, or stuffed in college post office boxes. Since only a certain percentage of those polled return the questionnaires, the resulting sample is not random. Those who have strong opinions about the matter, pro or con, have a greater tendency to take the time to respond, whereas those with weak or no opinions do not bother. Hence, the return, which is usually low on such polling techniques, often provides an unrepresentative sample from which to generalize.

Third, *the approach taken to the sample should be **unbiased***. For example, critical thinkers pay attention to *how* the questions are phrased. They look for a possible bias in the questionnaire that reveals the questioner's wishes or predispositions. Here is an example from a student survey on sexual attitudes. Can you determine the questionnaire's bias?

This questionnaire is designed to measure the way you feel about sexual behavior. It is not a test, so there are no right or wrong answers. Place a number beside each question as follows:
1. Strongly disagree 2. Disagree 3. Neither agree nor disagree 4. Agree 5. Strongly Agree

___ 1. I think adults have too much sexual freedom these days.

___ 2. I think that the increased sexual freedom seen in the past several years has done much to undermine the American family.

___ 3. I think that young people have been given too much information about sex.

___ 4. Sex education should be restricted to the home.

___ 5. Older people do not need to have sex.

___ 6. Sex education should be given only when people are ready for marriage.

___ 7. Premarital sex may be a sign of a decaying social order.

___ 8. Extramarital sex is never excusable.

___ 9. I think there is too much sexual freedom given to teenagers these days.

___ 10. I think there is not enough sexual restraint among young people.

___ 11. I think people indulge in sex too much.

___ 12. I think the only proper way to have sex is through intercourse.

___ 13. I think sex should be reserved for marriage.

Further, how clearly are the questions posed? Could the question be understood in a variety of ways? Will an answer to the question (for example, a yes or no) provide a clear response? Are the questions phrased so that the allowed responses could be ambiguous or vague, capable of being interpreted in a variety of ways? If ambiguity is present in either the question or the response, then the way the respondent understands the query might differ from how the poll taker understands the query. This ambiguity would invalidate the question asked.

Consider the following example from a soccer questionnaire polling parents' views of the coach's performance.

Did the coach emphasize winning?

Respondents might read *emphasize* as *overemphasize*. They might be concerned with certain attitudes or policies that the coach displayed in his or her drive to win—did the coach berate the players when they were losing, did the coach yell at or complain about the referees? Or the respondents might understand the question in terms of a comparison, comparing a coach's emphasis on winning with an emphasis on all the team members getting playing time. In this case, how readers respond depends on whether they think that their child got to play sufficiently. On one hand, if their child was not a very good player but played a lot, they may answer negatively, thinking that the coach preferred player involvement to winning; if their child did not get to play much, they might answer affirmatively. On the other hand, if their child was a very good player and got enough playing time, they may answer affirmatively; if their child did not play much, they may answer negatively, thinking that the coach preferred participation to winning.

Another way the sample may be biased involves the samplers themselves. Who asks the questions? Is the questioner in a position of power so that the person's mere presence biases the respondent's answer? For example, should physicians be put in charge of asking their clients questions to ascertain the clients' views of the clinic? Should professors be present when students fill out a classroom questionnaire on faculty performance? Moreover, if the questioning is oral, what kind of body language does the questioner use in asking the questions? Does it indicate what response the questioner wants the respondent to provide?

In short, the very act of sampling sometimes affects the sample. If it alters the sample significantly, then it biases the sample and the results are less trustworthy. To generalize from such results may cause us to commit the Fallacy of Hasty Generalization.

The key, then, to a good generalization is how the population is sampled. The larger the sample, the more random the selection process, the more carefully bias is avoided in the questions asked, the clearer and more definitive the questions asked, the better will be any generalization based on that sample. Any generalization that fails to meet any of these criteria in a significant way commits the Fallacy of Hasty Generalization.

At the same time, although we must be careful with our generalizations, we cannot abandon them. We cannot sample every instance. We cannot taste each grape in the store before buying it or check each gallon of milk to see whether it is spoiled. We must make decisions based on limited samples, and we must do so in ways that are time and cost effective. Critical thinking involving generalizations requires a balanced approach to the sample to create the most cogent generalizations possible, given the limited resources of time, energy, money, and information at our disposal.

Exercise 2

In the following generalizations, identify the conclusion. Then evaluate the samples for size, randomness, and bias. Which generalizations are cogent, and which are examples of hasty generalizations? Explain why in each case.

1. Pine floats. Maple floats. Oak floats. Elm floats. Therefore all wood floats.

2. In a survey of physicians, a major drug firm inquired whether the physicians used the firm's brand of pain reliever or that of its competition. The firm paid the physicians for their time in answering the survey and promised more surveys in the future. On the basis of the reports, the firm advertised that doctors recommend its brand of pain reliever twice as frequently as that of the leading competitive brand.

3. The first three cabinet appointments the president made graduated from Yale. The president must be biased toward his alma mater.

4. In a remarkable survey of children between the ages of 10 and 16, the Los Angeles polling firm of Fairbank, Maslin, Maulin and Associates learned that one-third of the kids "often" want to try what they see other people doing on television, while two-thirds said their peers are influenced by what they see on the tube. The survey shows that television has a more profound impact on the lives, values, ethics and morals of the young than perhaps even television's greatest critics thought. And the kids in the survey handed down a two-count indictment. The first was against the television industry. The second was against their parents. Sixty-five percent said programs like "The Simpsons" and "Married . . . With Children" encourage children to disrespect their parents. Sixty-two percent said sex portrayed on TV shows and in movies influences kids to have sex when they're too young. Eighty-two percent said TV should help teach children right from wrong. (Cal Thomas, "Children Take a Look at TV, and the Results Are a Turn-off," *Philadelphia Daily News*, March 6, 1995.)

5. When Joel couldn't remember his locker combination, he tried 15 before he tried 25. It didn't work. When he found out it was 25–15, he said that he thought about trying this, but remembered that from his experience the lower number always came first.

6. To assure quality, the inspector tested the twenty-fourth can in every two-dozen cartons of peaches. She found that each of the cans had been properly sealed and the fruit was safe. Based on her recommendation, the company passed the inspection.

7. A large insurance company wanted to assess customer satisfaction and so had its agents poll their clients about their customer satisfaction. In the interview the agents asked whether the client was satisfied with the agent's performance. The company was pleased to receive a report that showed well over 75 percent of respondents were satisfied with their agents and service.

8. In a recent telephone survey, the pollster asked over the phone whether the person was pro-life or pro-choice. Based on the sample, the survey reported that about 48 percent of Americans favored maintaining the present policy on abortion.

9. In the last 100 years, no president has been elected without winning Maine's electoral votes. As goes Maine, so goes the nation.

10. The Gallup survey, released by the National Academy of Social Insurance, found strong public support for Social Security but a lack of confidence in its future. The national survey was based on interviews with 1,002 adults in February and 1,000 adults in March. It has a margin of sampling error of plus or minus 3 percentage points. The National Academy of Social Insurance is an independent research and education organization that focuses on Social Security and related public and private programs.

According to the survey, 80 percent of adults voiced support for Social Security, but only 30 percent expected to receive benefits throughout their retirement. . . . Of those surveyed, 88 percent said that the government "routinely mismanages money" and 72 percent believed that Social Security "suffers from mismanagement and fraud." ("Few Have Confidence in Social Security," *St. Paul Pioneer Press*, May 17, 1994)

11. Just two weeks ago I was on the Coast Daylight Starlight train, completing the last leg of my trip out west on Amtrak. The air conditioning failed. A steam pipe exploded in the dining car. We were an hour late arriving in Oakland. The bus to San Francisco that is part of the train trip could not accommodate all the passengers—and it was the only bus that night. Amtrak has *not* improved train travel. (Maureen Cohen, letter, publication unknown.)

12. My sister was taken to General Hospital as an emergency patient a week or so ago. Upon arrival she was given immediate attention, and during her stay in the hospital everything possible was done for her in tests and treatments, all with a warm, personal relationship. The doctors and nurses surely deserve the new hospital now being built, because of the excellent care they give in this old and crowded building. (A. T. Henrici, letter, *Minneapolis Tribune*)

13. Anyone can win. I did! And I'll be back again this year." Terry Maanum. (Casino advertisement)

14. Minnesota Public Interest Research Group (MPIRG) recently conducted an energy poll on seven Minnesota campuses, including Augsburg. The results indicate a great willingness by students to conserve electricity rather than increase the amount of nuclear energy being produced.

    A total of 938 students were polled at Carleton, Hamline, Macalester, St. Catherine, University of Minnesota Duluth, University of Minnesota Minneapolis, and Augsburg. . . . "These results show that students are concerned about radioactive waste storage in Minnesota," said the MPIRG executive director. Ninety percent of Augsburg students feel that instead of increasing the supply of electricity, the supply should be reduced and consumers should be more efficient. In order to provide for Minnesota's overall electricity needs in the future, 72 percent of Augsburg students believe that alternative energy sources such as wind and solar should be the highest priority. For 21 percent more efficiency is the highest priority; and five percent rank nuclear power the highest. . . . Fifty-three percent of Augsburg students believe that nuclear waste will be a very serious problem for future generations.

    Overall, 97 percent of Minnesota students are willing to conserve more than they already do by turning off lights and other relatively easy means if it meant that nuclear storage was prohibited in Minnesota. (Rhonda Bock, "MPIRG Releases Results from Poll," *Echo*, November 8, 1991)

15. "Now some questions about paying for a new baseball stadium. Please tell me if you favor or oppose each of the following and how strongly you feel about it . . ."

	Favor Strongly	Favor Not Strongly	Oppose Not Strongly	Oppose Strongly	No Opinion
A sales tax on goods and services purchased in the metro area?	11%	10%	15%	62%	2%
A tax on liquor sold in the metro area?	33%	17%	12%	35%	3%
A tax on all hotel rooms in the metro area?	14%	18%	18%	45%	5%
An additional statewide tax on cigarettes?	39%	9%	10%	40%	2%
A ticket tax on events at a new stadium?	29%	21%	14%	30%	6%

Note: questions were rotated

Results are based on a Star Tribune Minnesota Poll conducted statewide Jan. 17–21 by phone with 699 randomly selected adults. Results were weighted for age, gender and education to make sure the sample reflected 1990 census proportions. Weighting accounted for household size and the number of phone lines going into a household. For results based on the sample, one can be 95 percent confident that error due to sampling will be no more than 3.7 percentage points, plus or minus. (Robert Whereatt, "Public Unmoved by Twins Proposal," *Minneapolis Star Tribune*, January 26, 1997)

Arguments from Analogy

In Chapter 7 we noted that arguments from analogy contend that since two things are alike in one or several ways, and since one of the analogues has a certain additional property, the other analogue must likewise possess that property. For example, because governments are like ships, and both must have strong people at the helm to make sure that they accomplish their mission, if the captain becomes incompetent and begins to run the ship aground on the shoals, the crew must remove the captain for dereliction of duty and install another captain. Similarly, should the president be morally incompetent and mishandle the affairs of state, the people must remove the president for dereliction of duty and install another in the office.

Arguments from analogy presume several things.

1. They presume that two things (*analogues*) are like each other. In our example, ships and governments are analogues.
2. They presume that all instances of the assumed analogue (ships) possess the same features (the captain will be removed for incompetent performance or dereliction of duty). We call this the *fundamental generalization*.

In the structure we used to show analogies,

$$\frac{A}{B} : \frac{C}{\therefore D}$$

A and B are analogues (in our example A stands for ships, B for governments); A and C are connected by the generalization that all As that have the property C (in our example C stands for the property of necessarily removing a captain derelict in duty). From these presumptions, the arguer concludes that since one analogue has a certain property, the other analogue will possess that property D (the head of state ought to be removed). The conclusion is D.

But how strong is an argument from analogy? It is only as strong as its two presumptions are true. First, the strength of the argument depends on how similar the two analogues are. The more the two things resemble each other, the more likely it is that they will possess similar properties. The more dissimilar they are, the less likely it is that they will have similar properties. In short, an argument from analogy is only as good as the compared analogues resemble each other. Thus, in our example, how similar are ships to governments? Are they generally alike, or do their dissimilarities outweigh their similarities such that we cannot draw a conclusion from one analogue to the other?

Second, an argument from analogy is only as strong as its fundamental generalization, namely, that things of a certain sort (like ships) have a certain property. The critical thinker might agree that this property is present in some cases, but might wonder whether the property will be present in most or all cases so that one can draw a conclusion based on that presence.

Arguments that either lack a close relationship between the two analogues or have a suspect generalization regarding the analogue and its properties are guilty of the **Fallacy of Faulty Analogy.** This fallacy contains a significant subjective element. Whereas one person might see a close relationship between the analogues, others might see a distant relationship, if any. Thus, to make analogies work, the arguer must convince the listener at the very beginning that the two analogues are enough alike to provide the basis for a cogent argument.

Exercise 3

For each of the following analogies, (1) identify the analogues, (2) identify the generalization covering the analogue and its characteristics, and (3) determine whether the analogy commits the Fallacy of Faulty Analogy and explain why or why not.

1. Follow the Ayds diet plan. That's what Judie Miskella of Arlington, VA. did and lost 66 pounds. And if it worked for Judie, it should work for you. (Advertisement)

2. I feel that fish have been neglected in the hunting controversy. The supposed cruel and inhuman treatment shown to four-legged creatures by hunters is, in my estimation, mild compared to that which the fisherman inflicts on his prey. The next time you bite into a fish sandwich, think of what it would be like to have a hook rammed through your mouth, then have your lungs pierced by a stringer or have someone run fingers into your lungs to hold you up to the admiration of others. (David Lucca, letter, *Minneapolis Tribune*, November 2, 1975. Reprinted by permission.)

3. Suppose you merely scolded your puppy, never punished him, let him go on making messes in the house, and occasionally locked him up in an

outbuilding but soon let him back into the house with a warning not to do it again. Then one day you notice that he is now a grown dog and still not housebroken—whereupon you whip out a gun and shoot him dead. Why that's the craziest way to raise a dog I ever heard of! Yes, but isn't that the way people raise their kids nowadays? (Robert A. Heinlein, *Starship Troopers*, 1959)

4. We are not like the giant soap manufacturer who produces millions of bars on a continuous assembly line with ingredients poured in one end, hardened, squeezed, and scrunched out the other. It takes more time and money to make our soap our way. Think about Neutrogena this way: wouldn't you rather have a little glass jar of jam grandma made than any kind you can buy? (Advertisement)

5. Picture showing a package of cigarettes on the back of a turtle. "You can't rush smooth flavor." (Advertisement)

6. Students enrolled in a Russian course at Eckerd College approached their first class with some apprehension about its difficulty. The professor entered the room, followed by his dog. Before saying a word to the students, he commanded the dog to sit, beg, lie down, roll over—all in Russian. The dog obeyed each command perfectly. "See how easy Russian is," the professor said. "Why, even a dog can learn it!"

7. Contemplate the whole of [nature] and every part of it: You will find it to be nothing but one great machine, subdivided into an infinite number of lesser machines, which again admit of subdivisions. All these various machines, and even their most minute parts, are adjusted to each other with accuracy. . . . The curious adapting of means to ends, throughout all nature, resembles exactly, though it much exceeds, the productions of human contrivance; of human design, thought, wisdom, and intelligence. Since therefore the effects resemble each other, we are led to infer, by all the rules of analogy, that the causes also resemble, and that the Author of Nature is somewhat similar to the mind of man, though possessed of much larger faculties. (David Hume, *Dialogues Concerning Natural Religion*)

8. "You go to an expert for medical advice. You should go to a professional travel agent for travel advice. Doctors and lawyers and architects. Because of their years of knowledge and practice, you can put your well-being into their hands. It's the same with travel agents. Especially your local ASTA agent. Where years of study and knowledge get you the most safety and comfort in travel, as well as the most for your dollars."

9. Coke is like family. You can never have enough. Coca Cola. Always.

10. I am a 33 year-old wife and mother. I am college-educated and work for a Fortune 100 company. My husband is not a participant in Promise Keepers. But it's about time we had someone praise leadership in the home. What is wrong with promoting faith, integrity and loving your wife? I consider my husband to be the head of my household, and that has never

infringed on my individuality. At work, I have a supervisor who makes a game plan, and then everyone pitches in to get the job done. My part is vital and my talents are unique. That is just like in my home—someone has to be in charge, and I'm glad it is my husband; it makes me and my child feel secure and loved. (Karen Beauvais, letter, *The Atlanta Constitution*, October 18, 1997)

Causal Arguments

The third kind of inductive argument we need to evaluate is the causal argument. The **causal argument** moves from certain evidence—effects—to suggest or hypothesize a cause of those effects. For example, my car engine misfires when I go uphill. The gas tank is full, but it has been 40,000 miles since my last tune-up. So I make an appointment with the mechanic to tune up my engine. My hypothesis is that dirty or worn out spark plugs are causing the misfiring.

In our daily life we need to form causal hypotheses; yet we must be very careful in concluding that what we hypothesize is really the cause of the effects we observe. In the example, it turned out that my car did not need a tune-up after all; the engine was misfiring because a spark plug wire had become disconnected. But my mistaken hypothesis cost me over $100. I had not investigated all the possibilities, so although I *correlated* the lack of a tune-up with my poorly performing engine, the lack of a tune-up was not the *cause* of the poor performance.

Hence, one must guard against the **Fallacy of False Cause.** This fallacy occurs when one takes two events as causally related when in fact they are either (1) merely correlated with each other or else (2) unrelated except that the one occurs before the other.

Let us focus first on correlation between events. When two events occur repeatedly together over a period of time, they may be causally related: the one brings about the other. But they also may be merely correlated with each other, such that although when one occurs so does the other, they do not occur because of each other. For example, an observer may notice that the price of a certain commodity rises in the year before the Democrats win a majority in Congress, and it falls in years before the Republicans win. This observer may be tempted to suggest that a causal relation holds between the price of the commodity and which party wins the election. In fact, the observer may even be tempted to use this hypothesis to predict the winner of the next election. However, the relation may be simply a coincidental correlation that fails to be borne out in the future. Arguments of this sort *confuse causation with correlation.*

The distinction between cause and correlation can have great significance. In recent years a national debate has raged on the issue of whether or not silicone breast implants caused illness and disease in women. Lawyers for the women affected argue that the breast implants caused the women's illnesses; lawyers for the sued companies argue that the illnesses and implants are merely correlated, that the illnesses could not be traced to the implants but was coincidental with them. Hundreds of millions of dollars and the survival of a major corporation ride on the outcome of the case. Juries and judges and a scientific panel have been called upon to decide whether the relationship is correlation or causation. So far, juries have concluded the relationship is causal and have awarded women damages; the scientific panel concluded that the illnesses and implants were only correlated, that there was no scientific evidence of a causal connection.

Although the correlation of two events may be mere coincidence, at other times the correlation may be connected with some third feature. For example, birds reproducing and leaves sprouting on trees occur regularly at the same time in spring. These events are not causally connected; leaves sprouting on trees do not cause birds to lay eggs. But neither is their correlative occurrence a coincidence. Both are connected to certain features of nature: climate and season cycles. That is, though they have a common cause, it would be a mistake to causally connect birds reproducing with leaves sprouting.

It is very easy to confuse causes with correlates. Causes help us to understand our world, while correlates contribute little. Hence, in attempting to understand events, critical thinkers look for causes to inform them about why something happened and carefully assess the evidence to see whether it is strong enough to suggest more than an affirmation of a mere correlation between events.

A second version of the Fallacy of False Cause focuses on the time dimension between two events. When one thing occurs after another has occurred, we sometimes conclude that the first caused the second to happen. When the two are not actually related causally, the argument commits the fallacy of "after this, therefore because of this" (at times you may see this referred to by its Latin phrasing, *post hoc, ergo propter hoc*).

For example, Frank may notice that after he changed from cologne A to cologne B, Susie started paying attention to him. He might then conclude that the change to the new cologne is what *caused* Susie to have an interest in him. But in fact, the two events may have no causal connection at all; it may be that she noticed him for the first time because when she recently dumped her old boyfriend, Frank was sitting across the table from her.

This version of the Fallacy of False Cause, which focuses on the time dimension of one thing following another, is the source of many of our superstitions. Something fortunate or unfortunate occurs after some other event, and we immediately conclude that they are causally related. For example, how many times have you played a game with a pair of dice, and the rolls were not going your way? So you blew on the dice, and, wonder of wonders, the number you needed came up. So what did you do the next time you rolled? My guess is that you blew on the dice again—and hence committed the fallacy! A quick look at the habits of many athletes—for example, batters when they come to the plate or basketball players when they step to the free-throw line—will confirm the suspicion that many athletes fall prey to this fallacy.

Sometimes it is not easy to decide whether two events are merely temporally connected or whether they are causally connected. On the day of a recent primary election in a major city, the newspaper mistakenly published the picture of one of the candidates in conjunction with an article on fraud. That candidate lost the election by fewer than 200 votes and in turn sued to force another election. He argued that he lost the election because the newspaper printed the wrong picture in connection with its report on fraud. The court was now in a difficult position, having to decide to what extent the candidate's picture connected the candidate with the fraud in the minds of the voters, and then whether this association, if it occurred at all, contributed to his defeat. The court in this case concluded that merely because the candidate lost the election after the mistaken photo was published was insufficient evidence that the photo and the article caused his defeat.

Or again, suppose that a football team hires a new coach, and the team has a losing season. Should the coach be fired? Would firing the coach be an instance of a false cause? Was the arrival of the coach merely an antecedent to the losing season, or was the coach part of the cause? Deciding the issue is vitally important to the coach, team, and fans.

Critical thinkers are wary of assertions of causal relations and will want more evidence to confirm that the relationship is more than mere coincidence. But how will they find this evidence? One way is to apply what is called the **Method of Difference.** To test whether two events are causally related, set up a test where everything is the same in two groups except for the causal condition for which you are testing. In the *test* group make sure that causal condition is present; in the *control* group see to it that causal condition is absent (or vice versa). If the effect you are looking for occurs in the test group but not in the control group (or vice versa), you have reason to think that the condition is truly causally related to the effect.

For example, suppose one wants to find out why it is that legs sprout from an insect in a certain place on its body. A researcher may set up a test with two groups of fruit flies and remove certain genes from the embryos of one group. If in one case the legs sprout from the head rather than bud from the body, whereas in the other case the fruit flies develop normally, the researcher may legitimately conclude that these specific genes control or regulate where the legs bud.

The method of difference, however, is not foolproof, for insuring that the control and test groups are identical is difficult. The less identical the two groups, the less certain it is that you have isolated the cause of the effect. Hence, scientists in particular are careful both about their experiments and the conclusions they draw from them. Critical thinkers likewise must be careful not to make unwarranted inferences when they see two events either correlated or succeeding each other.

In short, though we naturally look for causes, for this is how we explain our world, critical thinkers must resist the tendency to make the easy inference that one thing caused another. Careful study and investigation is often required, especially in cases whether the decision has significant importance. Being careless can have serious consequences.

Exercise 4

In the following arguments, (1) identify the effect(s) and the causal hypothesis. (2) Identify what, if anything, is fallacious about the argument and explain why it is or is not fallacious.

1. At a White House reception in 1910, the wife of the Russian Ambassador stepped outside the bounds of decent society by asking President Taft for a cigarette. Taft stepped outside the bounds of decent society by giving her one and even lighting it. Taft was not re-elected. (Advertisement)

2. "My dad's real big. Mom says it's 'cause he always ate raisins for snacks. So I eat raisins, too. Sure hope she's right." (Advertisement)

3. A marshmallow a day makes your blue eyes bluer. (Advertisement)

4. A gentleman sitting on a Los Angeles park bench was not swept up in the excitement of election year. He said, "I am 105 years old. I've never touched a politician or been touched by one in my whole life. I think I owe my longevity to that." (Source unknown)

5. "I don't know how to tell you this, Phil, but channel 4 comes in clear when you leave the room." *Cartoon*

6. We raised the salaries of the President and Congress and just take a good look at the "great" job the President has done. The public got the short end again and again. (Source unknown)

7. Damning rock music for its "appeal to the flesh," a Baptist church . . . has begun a campaign to put the torch to rock music records. About $2,200 worth of records were tossed into a bonfire this week after church officials in [Tallahassee] labeled the music immoral. The . . . associate pastor of the church said he had seen statistics which showed "of 1,000 girls who became pregnant out of wedlock, 984 committed fornication while rock music was being played." (Excerpted by permission of Associated Press.)

8. Be a winner in a Prinz Heinrich cap from Austria. Smart, stylish, made of sturdy navy blue loden wool. Whatever your sport, you'll be that much better in this handsome imported cap. (Advertisement)

9. Want him to be more of a man? Try being more of a woman. Emeraude by Coty. (Advertisement)

10. Picture showing a beautifully dressed woman smoking. "Come all the way up to Kool Filter Longs. Stylishly long, tastefully cool. Lady Be Cool." (Advertisement)

11. The United States built the greatest system of public education the world has ever known not at the federal level, not even at the State level, but at the level of the local school district. Until a few years ago, the people had direct control over their schools: how much to spend, what kind of courses to offer, whom to hire. Is it an accident that as this local control gave way to funding and control at the federal and state level, reading and other test scores have declined? The truth is, a good education depends far more on local control and accountability than on the amount of money spent. (Ronald Reagan)

12. Wear an Eva Gabor's "Great Going Wig" and you'll be going great! (Advertisement)

13. As for Ronald Campbell's untimely slam at the Cincinnati Bengals' new helmet (with tiger stripes on them), don't knock the stripes. They seem to be working! (Mark Shump, letter, *Sports Illustrated*, January 4, 1982, p. 103)

14. All of the in-depth political analysis of the past election has ignored one aspect both historical and astro-mystical. That is the brief and disappointing appearance of Haley's Comet this year. The approach of a comet is believed to coincide with the fall of kings.

   Historically we find earlier appearances of Haley's coincide with the fall of Jerusalem to Rome in 70 A.D., the invasion of Europe by the Turks in 1456, the death of King Edward VII in 1910 and the fall of King Harold II at the Battle of Hastings in 1066. It is particularly noteworthy that this year when Haley's Comet first went behind the sun, Jacques Duvalier and Ferdinand Marcos were both in power, and when it reappeared they were gone.

   So it should have been little surprise to find the reigning Independent-Republicans in the Minnesota House and their counterparts in the U.S. Senate eclipsed. Gov. Rudy Perpich, as a true man of the people, was spared a similar fate. (Phyllis Kahn, letter, *Minneapolis Star and Tribune*, November 18, 1986)

15. Since the end of the Gulf War, some veterans have reported suffering from a variety of problems, including mood changes, concentration problems, muscle pains, skin rashes and diarrhea. The conclusion of two studies of Gulf War veterans' health published in the New England Journal of Medicine concluded that the health of veterans of the Persian Gulf War has differed slightly from that of other groups of soldiers, but not in a way that suggests a "mystery illness" is afflicting them. One of the new studies found that a higher-than-expected number of Gulf War veterans died of accidents—car accidents, in particular,—in the two years following the war's end in 1991. Deaths from infection, cancer or diseases of major organ systems, however, were no higher among them than among their military compatriots who didn't go to war. ("2 Studies Explore Gulf Vet's Health," *Charlotte Observer*, November 13, 1996)

Critical Thinking in the Corporate World

You may think that critical thinking is only meant for college or university courses, that it has little application in the business or corporate world. If so, consider the true story of Scott Adams, the creator of the comic strip *Dilbert,* whose cartoon message highlights and pokes fun at the follies and weaknesses of corporate practices. Scott Adams wanted "to see if a group of executives would allow somebody who has very few credentials, except for good hair, to come into their meeting and get them to write a mission statement which is so impossibly complicated that it has no real content." To accomplish this outrageous experiment, he collaborated with Pierluigi Zappacosta, the co-founder and vice chairman of Logitech, the world's largest manufacturer of computer mice and related devices, and someone with apparently a large sense of humor. With Zappacosta's blessing Adams posed as a corporate consultant whose goal was to help Logitech executives write a new mission statement. It didn't matter that they already had one; Adams, donning a wig and assuming the alias of Ray Mébert, would help them redefine their mission statement, to "crisply define the goals" of

continued

Critical Thinking in the Corporate World *continued*

the New Ventures Group in the company.

In a memo distributed to a select group of Logitech's vice presidents and senior managers, Zappacosta described Mébert as a man with "special talents as a facilitator" and "a very original thinker" who had collaborated with big-name consultants.

Mébert came to Logitech with an entourage consisting of a photographer, videotaping crew, and personal assistant (*West Magazine* contributing editor Tia O'Brien, who wrote the story that appeared in the *San Jose Mercury News*), purportedly to help sell the mission statement they would devise to those who would implement it. In a conference room with eleven senior executives, nine men and two women, Mébert quickly established his credentials as a well-qualified management consultant. "I did the Harvard MBA thing, and then I went to Procter & Gamble where I worked on the Taste Bright Project," Mébert said. Taste Bright, he explained, was a top-secret effort to use the taste of soap to increase sales. He affirmed that "There actually are some people who admitted in focus groups that they would sometimes taste soap. We found that to get repeat business it was necessary to actually improve the smell as well as the taste of the soap." He continued listing his (false) credentials: he worked at Fortune Computer (a widely known, failed Silicon Valley business venture) and then founded Ray Mébert Associates. He claimed that Apple Computer recruited him to formulate strategy to market the Newton (a hand-held computer that also failed). None of the executives present questioned Adams's qualifications when he revealed his record of past failed accomplishments.

"If any of you recently read the Yankovitch and Meyer study about mission statements comparing companies that have mission statements with those that don't have them, it wasn't enough to just have a mission statement but rather the companies that had a high awareness among the employees about what the mission statement was, tended to have higher profits year after year." Although the Yankovitch and Meyer study was a pure fiction, no one questioned this assertion.

Mébert continued by presenting an analogy. A mission statement's mysterious role in generating higher profits is like a great broccoli soup recipe from your neighbor. "You wouldn't say, 'Well, this is a great soup, but I could take the broccoli out or take a little pepper out and it would still be great soup.' You never know exactly which part of the soup is the part that kind of made it work. In fact, it's that it all worked together that really makes it kind of work at all. So it is with mission statements."

Mébert proceeded to draw three overlapping circles on an easel. He labeled them Authority, Linguistics, and Message. He called the area where they overlapped the Buy-in Zone. Authority "is the reason for having the people in this room, the people who have credibility with the people who are actually going to be doing the day-to-day work." Linguistics: "Picking the wrong words is a mistake a lot of companies have made." Message: "You have to have the right message!"

With this structure in mind, Mébert began to develop the new mission statement. The previous statement, crafted six months earlier by some of the same executives now in the room, read, "The New Ventures mission is to provide Logitech with profitable growth and related new business areas."

"Doesn't that seem vague enough for you?" Mébert challenges. Not all of the executives were convinced, especially those who helped write that mission statement. Mébert told them that by "concentrating on the linguistics part of the exercise" he would help them produce a new, focused mission statement. He

concluded

began by asking the executives to suggest "specific words" that "describe where you are and where you want to be."

"Active," suggested one executive. Mébert wondered why they should use a two-syllable word when three syllables are available. "So really a pro-active kind of thing," he said, writing "Proactive" as the first word on the list. Another suggested "Education."

"Education, hmmm," Mébert pondered. "Seems like there's a better word for that. There's really an osmosis kind of thing here." He scribbled "Education-Osmosis" on the easel. "Is it a formal process with classes?" he asked, then added "Formal" next to "Osmosis."

"Relationships," "Breaking Paradigms," "Fertilizing," "Consumerization Process," "Vision Alignment." Within fifteen minutes Mébert collected about twenty-five terms for constructing the revised mission statement. He then explained the next step: "Essentializing is the key to the good mission statement. But you want to essentialize in a way in which when you're done, you've got something that will cause action." He indicated that they should cross out the less important terms on his list. Few of the executives, however, were willing to erase terms they suggested, so with only three terms crossed off, Mébert invited them to complete the sentence, "The New Venture Mission is . . ."

An hour after beginning, the executives had fashioned their new mission statement. "The New Ventures mission is to scout profitable growth opportunities in relationships, both internally and externally, in emerging, mission inclusive markets, and explore new paradigms and then filter and communicate and evangelize the findings." The executive team appeared satisfied with the results. But Mébert was not finished. A mission statement is worthless, he said, unless it is communicated to—and accepted by—employees. Remember the Buy-in Zone?

"Anybody play an instrument or do any composing?" Mébert asked. "Because what I've found is that some companies have created, like, a division song around the mission statement." One executive said he played the flute, the sax, and the keyboard; another affirmed that he wrote music. "So you'd be willing to take it on?" asked Mébert. "Yeah," the executive replied.

Only then did Mébert, pulling off his wig and drawing a sketch of Dilbert on his easel, reveal that he was not a corporate consultant at all but Scott Adams, the creator of Dilbert. The executives at first were startled by Adams's revelation. Then a couple of the executives started clapping, and the entire group burst into applause.

(*Source:* From Tia O'Brien, "Mission Impertinent," *San Jose Mercury News,* November 16, 1997)

Discussion Questions

A. What is the context in which Scott Adams impersonates the corporate consultant Ray Mébert? Note his goals and objectives and with whom he works. What helps Adams succeed in pulling off his hoax?

B. What roles do authorities play in this hoax?

1. What authorities are appealed to in this story and how do they function?

2. How reliable are the various authorities noted in this story? Has a fallacy been committed here? Explain.

3. Why is "Mébert's" appeal to authorities so successful in leading this group of executives to form a new mission statement?

C. "Mébert" focuses on linguistics as a key to forming a good mission statement.

    1. What is linguistics according to "Mébert"? Is this definition consistent with the traditional understanding of linguistics?

    2. What does "Mébert" see as the role of linguistics in crafting a mission statement?

    3. Has the New Ventures mission statement satisfied the role "Mébert" assigned to linguistics?

    4. Why are the executives apparently unaware of how language is functioning in their new mission statement?

D. "Mébert" introduces an analogy to help the executives understand the role and importance of a mission statement.

    1. What is the analogy "Mébert" creates?

    2. What conclusion does "Mébert" draw from this analogy?

    3. What conclusion do you think can be drawn from this analogy? Defend your view.

    4. Has the fallacy of faulty analogy been committed?

E. What dimensions of critical thinking play a role in this story?

    1. Think especially about what you learned about language and ambiguity in Chapter 5 and apply those insights to this case. (You may want to review Chapter 5.)

    2. How does the problem solving technique developed in Chapter 9 compare to that used by "Mébert"? What steps are not used by the group and to what problems do they lead?

F. The third circle in "Mébert's" diagram is labeled Message.

    1. What kind of message did the new mission statement send? Why do you say this?

    2. What is the message that Scott Adams wanted to send with his experiment? Why or why not was he successful?

    3. Why did the executives clap at the end of the presentation when "Mébert" revealed his true identity?

SUMMING-UP

In this chapter we have reaffirmed that inductive arguments should be cogent. An inductive argument is *cogent* when its premises are true, relevant to the conclusion, and provide good reason to think that the conclusion is true. Arguments that fail to support the conclusion either because they break a rule or are inadequate or irrelevant in some way are *fallacious*. We have looked at four common inductive fallacies in this chapter.

Appeals to Unqualified Authority occur when a person asks you to accept a statement as true or to take a certain action because a person who is an actual or alleged authority has said so, but the actual or alleged authority is commenting on a subject about which he or she is not qualified to speak.

Hasty Generalizations draw conclusions about all or a percentage of a specific group from an inadequate sample.

Faulty Analogies either lack a close relationship between the two analogues or make a suspect generalization about the analogue and its properties.

False Cause occurs when a person takes two events as causally related when in fact they are either merely correlated with each other or else unrelated except that the one occurs before the other occurs.

Each of these inductive fallacies focuses on the content of the argument; in each case the premises fail properly to support the conclusion. In the following chapter we will learn some additional fallacies of content.

ANSWERS TO THE EXERCISES

Answers to Exercise 1

1. C: Ford is a safe investment. We have no reason to think these persons are any more qualified than anyone else to judge automobiles.
3. C: These new imaging techniques provide a window into the brain. Dr. Coyle is probably a relevant authority.
5. C: You should wear wool. Lauren Hutton is probably not an authority on clothing fibers.
7. C: AARP Mobile Home Insurance Program provides affordable security. Melba Beverly is not a qualified authority on insurance.
9. C: Don't raise your puppies on anything but Pedigree Puppy food. Fran Smith is a veterinarian and a kennel owner and hence would have relevant knowledge about feeding animals.

Answers to Exercise 2

1. C: All wood floats. Inadequate sample of four instances. Iron wood does not float.
3. C: The president must be biased toward his alma mater. Inadequate sample size.
5. C: Lower numbers always come first in combination locks. Inadequate sample size, based on limited experience.
7. C: Well over 75 percent of respondents were satisfied with their agents and service. Probable bias in the survey, since it was asked by the agents themselves.
9. C: As Maine goes, so goes the nation. The causal relation between the electoral votes in Maine and the election of the president is very slim, given Maine's few votes. Hence a predictive generalization based on this information is risky.
11. C: Amtrak has not improved train travel. Inadequate sample size.
13. C: Anyone can win. Inadequate sample size.
15. C: In this poll, the results are given but no conclusion drawn. A properly conducted poll.

Answers to Exercise 3

1. (1) Judie Miskella and you. (2) Judie lost 66 pounds. (3) The argument depends on how similar you are to Judie in body type, age, weight, metabolism, reason for being overweight, and so on.

3. (1) Puppies and humans. (2) You do not train puppies by not punishing them and then, when they turn out bad, killing them. (3) The argument depends on how similar raising and disciplining humans is to raising and disciplining puppies.

5. (1) Cigarettes and turtles. (2) Turtles cannot be rushed in their movement. (3) The slowness of turtles is quite irrelevant to that of smoking.

7. (1) Machines and nature. (2) Machines have a marvelous mean-ends adjustment. (3) The argument depends on how similar nature is to machines. Nature operates on other than mere mechanical principles.

9. (1) Coca Cola and Family. (2) One never has family around enough. (3) Soft drinks and family are significantly different.

Answers to Exercise 4

1. Taft was not re-elected. The suggested causal hypothesis is that the populace's failure to condone men's helping women to smoke led to Taft's defeat. After this, therefore because of this.

3. Getting bluer eyes. Eating marshmallows every day makes your eyes bluer. Confused a possible (though unlikely) correlation with causation.

5. Channel 4 comes in clearly. Phil's leaving the room causes better TV reception of channel 4. Confused correlation with causation.

7. Pregnancy. Rock music helps teen girls get pregnant out of wedlock. Confused correlation with causation.

9. Being a man. Being a woman (and wearing Emeraude perfume) will cause a man to be a man. After this, therefore because of this.

11. Test scores declined. Federal and state control replacing local control over education caused the decline in test scores. Confused correlation with causation.

13. Winning. Wearing a helmet with tiger stripes caused the Bengal team to win. Confused correlation with causation.

15. Illnesses of various sorts. The question considered here is whether exposure to something in the Gulf War caused a variety of illnesses. It concerns whether there is a causal relation or a correlation between serving in the Gulf War and the presence of a variety of illnesses.

CHAPTER 11

Evaluation

Identifying More Fallacies of Content

The previous chapter introduced you to four fallacies of induction: appeal to irrelevant authority, hasty generalization, faulty analogy, and false cause. But there are many more fallacies of content. In fact, in this book we barely touch the surface on fallacies. One book lists over a hundred different kinds. All fallacies share the problem that, for one reason or another, the conclusion fails to follow from the premises.

To give you a flavor of the more common fallacies and to tie into some of the things we addressed in earlier chapters, this chapter considers a few additional major fallacies of content. These are called fallacies of content or informal fallacies to distinguish them from the fallacies of structure or form.

Fallacies of *form* are found in deductive arguments. In arguments with a fallacious form, the conclusion fails to follow from the premises not because of what the premises say but because of the structure of the argument. Any argument with a fallacious structure or form, regardless of the content of the premises and conclusion, is fallacious. For example, consider the argument:

Dogs are animals.

Cats are animals.

Therefore, cats are dogs.

The premises of this argument are true, but the premises do not establish the conclusion about cats because the argument has a fallacious form. Though dogs and cats are both animals, they do not share enough animal properties for cats to be dogs. We will briefly look at formal fallacies in deductive arguments in Chapter 12.

Fallacies of *content* occur where the conclusion fails to follow from the premises because of the content of the premises. What the premises say determine whether the premises are strong, clear, or relevant enough to establish the conclusion. Such fallacies are referred to as **fallacies of content** or **informal fallacies** (*informal* means *not pertaining to form*, that is, arguments whose fallaciousness does not depend on the form or structure of the argument). Their fallaciousness is not a matter of the truth or falsity of the premises; the premises could be true and the argument would still commit a fallacy. Rather, the fact that such arguments are fallacious has to do with the content of the premises and their relationship to the conclusion. The premises are either too ambiguous to support the conclusion (Fallacies of Ambiguity), irrelevant to the conclusion (Fallacies of Relevance), or make critical presumptions that prevent us from being able to draw a cogent or valid conclusion (Fallacies of Presumption). This chapter adds eleven more examples to those found in Chapter 10.

You will notice that our examples are generally drawn from real life. That is because people actually commit these fallacies; they are not mere textbook problems. Frequently such faulty arguments are used because they are persuasive; in one way or another they get the reader or listener to agree with the thesis proposed by the writer or speaker. Since this is especially characteristic of advertisements, we will consider a significant number of examples from that medium. Critical thinkers look beyond the persuasive power of the argument to evaluate whether the premises really support the conclusion. Being aware of these fallacies should assist you in assessing the real worth of persuasive arguments.

FALLACIES OF AMBIGUITY

Arguments that trade on ambiguity commit the **Fallacy of Ambiguity.** In these arguments the conclusion seems to follow from the premises, but a closer look reveals that this is only an illusion created by ambiguity of meaning (semantic ambiguity), ambiguity of use (syntactical ambiguity), or vagueness. Before you go on, you might want to return to Chapter 5 and review the sections on ambiguity.

1. Equivocation

Ambiguity of meaning (semantic ambiguity) occurs when the same term (or its synonyms) changes meaning in the course of the discussion. Such changes of meaning are called *equivocation.* When an argument trades on ambiguity of meaning, it commits the **Fallacy of Equivocation.** When an argument commits this fallacy, the conclusion does not follow from the premises because at some point in the argument the topic has changed, though because of grammatical similarity it might not appear so.

Consider the following example of equivocation.

Sharon's new boyfriend is a turkey.

Turkeys gobble.

Therefore, Sharon's new boyfriend is a fast eater.

The problem with this argument is obvious. The word *turkey* has two different meanings in the premises. In the first premise it refers to undesirable characteristics of persons—that the boyfriend is not very bright; he does not have it all together. In the second premise *turkey* refers to an animal. But for the argument to succeed, the word *turkey* must mean the same in both premises; otherwise, the topic has changed from persons to animals, and the conclusion does not follow.

The other change of meaning or equivocation is on *gobble*. In the second premise, *gobble* refers to a sound made by turkeys. In the conclusion, the word *gobble* is not used, but its synonym—*fast eater*—is given. But this synonym relates to a different meaning of *gobble—to eat one's food quickly*. This second example of an equivocation shows that the same word or symbol need not be used for the fallacy to occur; equivocation can occur when the synonym presents a different meaning of a word than the meaning used elsewhere in the argument.

When you accuse an argument of equivocation, you need to be able to *identify the word or words that have an ambiguity of meaning* and to *give their different meanings*. This enables you to show someone that the argument actually commits the Fallacy of Equivocation.

2. Amphiboly

Ambiguity of use (syntactic ambiguity) occurs when the grammar of the sentence is unclear. As we noted in Chapter 5, it might be due to such things as a misplaced or absent comma or a pronoun with an unclear referent. When we are led to draw an incorrect conclusion based on evidence presented in a syntactically ambiguous way, we have committed the **Fallacy of Amphiboly.**

To identify an amphiboly, look for ambiguity of use. For example, suppose someone said that environmentalists should not vote for Smith because in her stump speech she said, "One should save cans and waste paper." The implied conclusion that Smith is not an environmentalist (probably) is mistakenly drawn from the ambiguity of the term *waste.* If *waste* is a verb, then Smith probably is not an environmentalist, for she encourages us to waste paper. But if *waste* is an adjective modifying *paper,* then probably she is an environmentalist, for she encourages us to save both cans and waste paper. The use of *waste* can be ambiguous in this sentence.

Amphiboly can also occur where pronouns have unclear referents. For example, suppose a friend argued, "In the confrontation between the thief and the police officer, he was shot. This again shows why we should strengthen the ban on weapons." Whether the conclusion follows may depend on the referent of *he.* If *he* refers to the police officer, the premises are relevant to the conclusion; banning weapons may control their proliferation among thieves. If *he* refers to the thief, the conclusion probably does not follow from the premises because the premises do not inform us whether the thief had a weapon and the police officer was firing in self-defense.

Amphibolies are not all that common. But we include them here to emphasize the broader point that critical thinkers should always pay attention to grammar, whether their own or others. In their communication they should strive for grammatical clarity and accuracy so that their audience does not draw an incorrect conclusion from the information presented.

Exercise 1

For each of the following arguments, identify the conclusion. Then determine whether the fallacy committed is equivocation or amphiboly. If equivocation, determine which terms have an ambiguous meaning (are semantically ambiguous) and give the two meanings used. If amphiboly, identify the syntactic ambiguity (ambiguity of use) on which the argument trades. Some arguments may commit both fallacies.

1. The IRS official is correct: Filing a federal income tax return does not violate your rights. However, being *forced* to file does. Since taxes are revolting, why aren't you? (Todd J. Olson, letter, *Minnesota Daily*, May 5, 1982)

2. This is the season of harvest, so harvest some clothes at Hauglands. (Advertisement)

3. Before my daughter's graduation exercises began, I was reading the program. On the cover was a picture of a boy and girl in cap and gown, the school's name and the words "The Sixty-Second Annual Commencement." An elderly woman sitting next to me leaned over to comment, "My, but they're cutting down on graduation ceremonies. Sixty seconds is the shortest one I've ever attended."

4. Conrad

Conrad / By Bill Schorr

5. The lady has taste. Taste in the pretty things around her. Taste in her cigarette. Flavor-rich Eve. A rich yet gentle tobacco blend. Smooth. Satisfying. Made for the lady with taste. Smoke pretty Eve. (Advertisement)

6. Everyone needs a little comfort. Getting comfortable sometimes means getting away from it all. And then settling back with the smooth, easy taste of Southern Comfort. (Advertisement)

7. "Statistics show that in China a child is born every 47 seconds," reported a TV commentator. "Isn't it a wonder," remarked a viewer to her husband, "that they manage to space them so regularly." (Mina and Andre Guillois, *Les Femmes Marrantes*)

8. Dennis the Menace

Source: © 1987 DENNIS THE MENACE. Reprinted by permission of King Features.

9. For Better or For Worse

Source: FOR BETTER OR FOR WORSE. Reprinted by permission of United Features Syndicate, Inc.

10. Photograph of a woman in black fur, a black Rolls Royce, black oil derricks against the sky, and a label reading, "Johnnie Walker Black Label Scotch." Success is often measured by how deeply you are in the Black. [Advertisement]

11. Tiger

TIGER

Source: TIGER. Reprinted with special permission of King Features Syndicate, Inc.

12. Why are fire trucks red? Fire trucks are red because they have six tires and two drivers, which make 12, and 12 inches makes a ruler, and a ruler is Queen Elizabeth, and Queen Elizabeth is also a ship, and a ship floats on water, and there are fish in the water and there are fins on the fish, and the Finns fought the Russians, and the Russians are red, so fire engines are red because they are always rush'n.

13. Picture showing a man being intimate with a woman. "Gravity . . . The Force that Pulls You Closer. Gravity, fragrance for men." (Advertisement)

14. B.C.

Source: B.C. By permission of Johnny Hart and Creators Syndicate.

Source: BEETLE BAILEY. Reprinted with special permission of King Features Syndicate, Inc.

FALLACIES OF RELEVANCE

A second type of fallacy of content focuses specifically on whether the premises are relevant to the conclusion. In a good argument, the premises are relevant to the conclusion. In particular, the premises of deductive arguments are conclusion-specific; that is, given specific premises, only a specific conclusion follows. When the premises are irrelevant to the conclusion, the argument commits a **Fallacy of Relevance.** We will consider six different types of this fallacy.

3. *Appeal to Force or Fear*

Sometimes people argue for the truth of a conclusion based upon premises that appeal to force or fear. The **Fallacy of the Appeal to Force** occurs when a person argues that a statement is true or that you should do something because that person or others have the power to make bad things happen to you if you do not believe the statement or fail to perform the recommended action. The person supports the conclusion by making a threat against your own or another's safety or a threat to remove a privilege. For example, "I ought to pitch. Otherwise I am going to take the bat and ball and go home." The threat fails to provide good evidence for the claim that the person should pitch. A much better argument would appeal to the person's pitching skills as a reason why that person should be the pitcher.

The appeal to fear is the same fallacy but viewed from the perspective of the person to whom the argument is directed. The **Fallacy of the Appeal to Fear** occurs when persons adopt a specific truth or take a specific action based on fear that something bad will happen to them if they do not believe or act in a certain way. For example, mother to daughter: "You should eats lots of broccoli, or else you will get cancer." The mother is arguing that the daughter should include broccoli in her regular diet based upon an appeal to the daughter's fear about getting cancer.

Appeals to force or fear are fallacious because from the threat of force or fear any conclusion—even contradictory conclusions—can follow. A person might argue that you should come or that you should go, or that you should believe or not believe something, using the same threat of force. But premises are used to support a specific conclusion. If you can derive multiple or contradictory conclusions from the same set of premises, the argument fails in its task of establishing any specific position.

There are, of course, relevant appeals to fear. For example, "You should not drive over the speed limit on this road because the police strictly enforce the speed laws." This appeal provides a good, relevant reason in this instance for not speeding. Hence, since fear can at times provide a legitimate or relevant reason, you have to decide from the context when the appeal to fear or force is irrelevant and when it is relevant to the conclusion. When it is irrelevant, the argument commits the fallacy.

4. *Appeal to Pity*

The Fallacy of the Appeal to Pity is similar to the Appeal to Force in that the arguer uses an emotion to recommend the truth of the conclusion or to recommend that you take some action. In the **Fallacy of the Appeal to Pity,** the arguer appeals to pity.

Students sometimes use this type of argument: "I had two other tests to study for, and then I overslept. Please excuse me from doing today's assignment." Faced with such appeals, who can resist? Yet, although such arguments might be persuasive with teachers, they are generally fallacious, for as with the appeal to force, anything, including contradictory conclusions, can follow from invoking pity. Since such arguments do not support a specific conclusion, they are generally fallacious.

As with the Appeal to Fear, there are times when it is legitimate to appeal to the emotion of pity to support a conclusion. Persons may legitimately argue that you should help rescue them from a flood because the roof on which they are sitting is about to be inundated by rising water. Concern for their safety would be *directly relevant* to the action they are requesting you to take on their behalf. Hence, again, you need to decide from the context when the appeal to pity is irrelevant and when it is relevant to the conclusion. When it is irrelevant, the argument commits the fallacy.

5. *Ad Hominem*

The **Ad Hominem** fallacy (Latin, meaning *directed to or against the person*) is particularly pernicious because it directs its attention not to the issue but to the person him or herself. Consequently, the premises of these arguments are irrelevant to the conclusion. At the same time, such arguments are often persuasive because of our concern for character. Their persuasiveness accounts for their frequent use in political campaigns and debates.

The fallacy comes in several varieties. The **Abusive Ad Hominem** argument takes the form of saying that what someone says is false or not to be believed because that person has a bad character or set of habits. For example, "You should not trust Jones's testimony because he is an alcoholic." Now it might be true that Jones is an alcoholic, but at the same time in this case he might be telling the truth. If he came running to you and told you that your house was on fire, it would not be wise to dismiss his statement simply on the grounds that he is an alcoholic. He may, at this moment, be sober (or even inebriated) and have important news for you. You need to check out the truth of his claim.

The **Non-abusive Ad Hominem,** on the other hand, has the form of saying that what someone says is true or to be believed because that person is such a nice person. Consider an ad for Golden Sun Feeds showing a feed dealer umpiring a little league baseball game. "To think a half hour ago this Sunshine Guy brought you a load of feed. Now your Golden Sun dealer's calling them the way he sees 'em at the little league playoff game. Depending which team you're pulling for, the Sunshine Guy can be a saint or a bum. But when he teams up with you to work out the most profitable feeding programs for your livestock, there's no questioning his decisions on the choice of Golden Sun quality products." The appeal is to a civic minded person who is also a feed dealer; his civic mindedness is given as a reason for doing business with him.

A third version appeals not to the person's character but to the person's circumstances to support the claim that what that person is saying is true or false. This is called the **Circumstantial Ad Hominem.** For example, "You cannot accept Ms. Smith's testimony about keeping the system of tenure at the university. After all, she is a tenured professor and has a vested interest in keeping tenure." The fact that Ms. Smith is a tenured professor should not be used to dismiss her testimony regarding keeping the system of tenure at the university. What has to be assessed are the reasons she gives for keeping it. Her argument and not her position as a teacher is relevant to the truth of the conclusion.

Here is another example of the circumstantial *ad hominem* fallacy, this time in an advertisement for Shalimar perfume showing an intimate couple in Indian garb. "The inspiration for this classic fragrance came from the story of a man who loved a woman so deeply, that when she died, every fiber of his being was devoted to creating a monument to her memory. Twenty thousand men labored daily for twenty-two years to fashion marble into . . . the Taj Mahal. The garden where their love grew was called the Garden of Shalimar." The perfume is being recommended on its name alone, which is connected with an exotic garden in Agra, India. The name of a perfume provides no reason for determining its quality or for you to purchase the product.

6. *Appeal to Vanity*

The **Fallacy of Appeal to Vanity** (also called the **Appeal to Flattery**) occurs commonly in advertisements because it is particularly persuasive. The arguer contends that a particular statement is true or that you ought to take a particular action because of some quality that you, the reader or listener, possess. What is emphasized in the reasoning is the purchaser, not the qualities of the product. For example, consider an advertisement showing a wood stereo cabinet in a living room. "Magnavox stereo. When it's not playing beautiful music, it's still saying beautiful things about you. Whichever magnificent Magnavox stereo you select, it will speak eloquently of your good taste." The ad appeals not to the quality of the stereo, but to you and your taste as a reason for purchasing the product. Or again, in an advertisement for the Jaguar automobile. "Some people seek the sun. Then again, there are others who bask in it at will. If you're in the latter group, consider the XJ-S Convertible." Here the ad appeals to your uniqueness: you are special, and since this product is made for special people, you should purchase it.

The Appeal to Vanity is fallacious because it supports the conclusion not by appealing to evidence that is relevant to the conclusion (for example, the quality of the product) but by appealing to some feature about the person who is to believe the conclusion. But the features of the reader are quite irrelevant to the truth of the conclusion. When what is recommended is the product, one wants evidence of the quality or serviceability of the product, not an irrelevant appeal to the reader's "good taste."

7. *Appeal to Numbers*

The fallacy of the **Appeal to Numbers** is the opposite of the appeal to vanity. Whereas the appeal to vanity appeals to the reader's uniqueness, the appeal to numbers occurs when a statement is thought to be true because many people believe it. This is often called the **Bandwagon Fallacy.** For example, a student argued, "Many people today believe in angels. In a recent poll 64 percent reported they believed in angels, and 46 percent believed they had some experience of angels. This is the reason I believe that angels exist." The argument, however well intentioned, is fallacious: many people could be wrong in their beliefs. Not too many centuries ago most people believed that the sun went around the earth, but the fact that most believed this provides no evidence for how the solar system functions.

Appeals to numbers or mass appeal are irrelevant because the premise is not about the topic found in the conclusion but about the *beliefs* of those who consider the conclusion. But unless the conclusion is likewise about those beliefs, persons' beliefs are irrelevant in determining whether some opinion is or is not true.

At the same time, you should be aware of the persuasiveness of such arguments. The fact that everyone is doing it provides a powerful motivator for thinking that something is true or for purchasing a product. People—especially young people—do not like to be odd, unusual, or left out. Because they do not want to stand out from their peers, they often demand or purchase brand name clothing. Peer pressure successfully functions to get them to purchase socially accepted products. Recognizing the fallaciousness of appeals to numbers is a first step to convincing people that such arguments should be resisted.

8. *Fallacies of Time*

A final set of fallacies of relevance concerns time. People often use time as a reason for claiming that a statement is true or false, or that one ought or ought not to purchase a product. There are four versions of the fallacy of time.

Appeal to Tradition: The argument goes like this: because a belief is old, or because a product or company has been around for a long time, the belief must be true or the product of good quality. Consider the following ad for Simonize car wax. "1910: Simonize introduces the first car wax ever. 1920: Simonize is introduced to England. 1937: Simonize helps a lot of people through college. 1955: Simonize introduces the first one-step wax . . . Simonize. You've always heard how good it was." The advertisement introduces an appeal to a long tradition to get you to purchase Simonize car care products. But nothing is said about the contemporary quality, let alone the past quality, of the product.

Appeal to Novelty: the argument contends that because a belief or a product is new, the belief must be true or the product of good quality. Consider this Volkswagen advertisement. "NEW. What does it mean? It's probably the most powerful word in advertising. . . . In the case of an automobile, it's starting from scratch and totally redesigning just about every single part to best fill your needs. . . . Which is exactly what we did with our Volkswagen. Five years ago, we set out to design the car of the future. . . . To do that properly, we had to start from ground zero, taking everything into consideration. . . . You see, if you're in the market for a new car, we think your hard-earned money deserves more than just the word NEW with an exclamation point after it. It deserves new, period." The car company is pushing novelty as a reason for purchasing its car.

Stagnation: because a belief is old or a product or company has been around for a long time, the belief must be false or the product or company out-of-date. Perhaps someone has told you that you should not take a course in ancient philosophy or literature because people back then were unscientific; by now their ideas are out-of-date. But though it is true that such thinkers preceded the era of modern science, it does not follow that their ideas are worthless. There may be some very good and true ideas in ancient philosophy and literature that are worth considering despite the fact that they were written 2,500 years ago.

No Precedent: because a belief is new or a product is new, the belief must be false or the product suspect in quality. Those who resist change often appeal to this reasoning: it has never been done that way before, so we should not do it now. But the fact that something has not been done a certain way before provides no good reason to reject the claim that the project may now be worth an attempt.

You can easily see from this list of four types why arguments that appeal strictly to considerations of time are fallacious. The matter of time alone is generally irrelevant to the truth of the conclusion, for from time alone it does not follow that the statement is true or false or that the product has or lacks quality. Statements that have been around for a long time can be true or false; new claims likewise can be true or false. Products or companies that have lasted over the years are not necessarily good now; likewise new products can be good or bad, regardless of being new. It is not time itself that determines the truth or falsity of claims (unless they are about time) or the quality of a product or company.

Exercise 2

For each of the following arguments, (1) identify the conclusion, (2) identify the fallacy, and (3) tell why it is fallacious.

1. You're not John Doe. Why drive his car? A car isn't just something you drive. It's something you wear. The Mazda MX-3 is a new sports coupe for those of us who'd never be seen driving a beige cardigan. Instead of making a car that everyone would like, Mazda engineers made a car that a few people will love. (Advertisement)

2. More and more Americans are coming out of the fog to realize that we have an unfit president, a man clearly holding a position far beyond his

wisdom and his skill. In his movie career, Reagan played many roles and played them competently. He played gun fighters and fighter pilots and professional athletes, but he wasn't really any of these things. Then he got to play President. He did well at first. When Americans saw him on the screen he looked, spoke, and acted like a president. Congress was afraid of him because the people loved his act. The press was afraid of him because the people loved his act. One problem with Hollywood is that the sequel seldom matches the original. In Reagan's first term his luck held. In the second term (the sequel) his luck ran out. (Ron Palossari, "Dear Ron," *Echo*, March 6, 1987. Reprinted by permission.)

3. You take out Table 22's order, bring the ice water for Tables 19 and 21, prepare the desserts for Table 17, drop off the check for Table 11. You rush out to take Table 19's order, and as you're headed for Table 21, Table 22 needs more coffee. Meanwhile, the manager has just seated a party of eight in your section, and Table 17 is ready for the check. . . . A restaurant nightmare, the kind waiters and waitresses experience all the time. . . . I don't know how much waiters and waitresses make these days, but it probably isn't enough. There are few jobs that take so much out of you emotionally as well as physically. There may be none so stressful. . . . So the next time you're in a restaurant or cocktail lounge, be good to those who wait on you. They want to provide good service as much as you want to receive it. And chances are, their job is a lot tougher than yours. . . . (Excerpted by permission from Pete Temple, "Waiting on Tables can be a Nightmare." *This week*, June 15, 1987.)

4.

Source: *Good Housekeeping*. April 1982. p. 178. © 1982 Good Housekeeping. Reprinted by permission of Orlando Busino.

5. Taste the flavor of times long gone. In Heartland Natural Cereal. Your first taste of Heartland Natural Cereal will seem strangely familiar. As if you've tasted it sometime, someplace, long ago. As if, somehow, it's part of your past. Because it is. Pet Incorporated has reached back, beyond today's complicated, artificial times, to bring back a taste rich in the natural goodness Americans enjoyed long ago. (Advertisement)

6. A newborn goes from Nature's perfect surroundings right into diapers. So 1,760 hospitals use Pampers. Now your baby's on his own—but he needs more love and care than ever. No wonder so many hospitals think Pampers are the best all-around way to diaper babies. And so many mothers think Pampers are the best diaper to surround a baby with. (Advertisement)

7. They say a woman thrives on change. That's why you're always looking for something new to do. Something new to wear. And something different for dinner. It's a good day for Stouffer's. (Advertisement)

8. With the month of May we have Poppy Day coming up the 19th. As an auxiliary member of the V.F.W. and a poppy seller who has taken many nasty rebuffs from the people I asked to buy, I want to make one thing clear. The money collected is used only to help the poor boys who went and gave of themselves so we could keep our freedom. Many of them came back only in part. Who cares? The many auxiliaries and posts care. We sell the poppies to help the forgotten ones crowded in hospitals and institutions. If you can come away and not feel you want to help, then don't put anything in that poppy can when the girl thrusts it toward you, but don't belittle us who are standing in the cold and rain trying to help in our small way. (Jeanette Fitch, letter, *Minneapolis Star and Tribune*)

9. At Ste. Pierre Smirnoff Fls., we've been making vodka for 150 years. Tava is the only liqueur which bears our name. (Advertisement)

10. Of all the people in all the world, if you don't deserve one, who does? You, of all people. You've probably been told that to own a fur is to be pampered and self-indulgent. And so stoic little you have resisted. But your time has come. Because if you're seeking lots of attention in this world, you have to love yourself first. And show it. And what better way than in fur. Come on, you've been a good girl too long. Unpampered. Unspoiled. And perhaps even unnoticed. So own up. You've always wanted to own one. This winter get all wrapped up in yourself. In fur. You deserve it. You'll love yourself in fur. (Advertisement)

11. Why [vote for] Bill Bednarczyk? The present City Treasurer is 76 years old—eleven years past retirement age for most workers. He is drawing a full pension from the Minneapolis Fire Retirement Fund in addition to his salary as Treasurer. . . . Whatever his past accomplishments for the city, most people feel he should retire. (Political pamphlet of the Bednarczyk Volunteer Committee)

12. It comes to some as a rich, lingering moment and maybe it can to you. Because when you put on a piece of real gold jewelry, it is a different feeling. Real gold jewelry goes beyond fashion. You don't wear it just to complement an outfit, you wear it because it's personal—because it expresses you. Real gold jewelry always means Karat Gold Jewelry. Nothing else feels like real gold. (Advertisement)

13. During Watergate, President Nixon argued that he did not have to make the White House Tapes, which he considered his personal documents, available to Congress, on the grounds that no other Presidents had been required to do so.

14. We senior citizens who play golf were pretty shaken when we heard that the all-course senior ticket for the city's public golf courses had been raised from $250 to $290 for the coming year. Why penalize the seniors on fixed incomes so severely all in one year? It is unfair to us who have only a few years left to play. (W. A. Wicks, letter, *Minneapolis Star Tribune*. Reprinted by permission.)

15. Photograph showing clipping from a newspaper. "2 Children Killed Inside Clothes Dryer. Two small children left alone by their mother when she went to work died Thursday while playing inside a clothes dryer that began running, Miami police said." The cost of having a corporate day-care program is nothing compared to the cost of not having one. Licensed day-care centers and homes have room for only 6 million of the 24 million children needing day-care today. By 1990, that figure will grow to 30 million. Find out how to start a day-care program. (Advertisement)

16. How good it is with Winston's finer flavor. It's America's largest-selling long cigarette. That's how good it is! (Advertisement)

17. We didn't make them for the masses. We didn't make them for the average jock. We didn't make them for athletes who settle for second best. Get serious. Twinlab Sports Drinks. Serious nutrition for serious athletes. (Advertisement)

18. You may lose 10 lbs. in 10 days with the delicious Grapefruit Juice Diet! The revolutionary grapefruit diet that everyone is talking about. THIS STARTLING DIET REALLY WORKS! TV personalities, movie people, and fashion models (men, too) are raving about this diet. A copy of this new and startling successful Diet Plan can be obtained by sending only $1.00 to Waist Watchers. (Advertisement)

19. Photo showing a woman entering a room, and all at the circular table stare at her. AN UNRELIABLE WATCH CAN MAKE YOU UNRELIABLE. Your watch has done you in again. And everybody's fed up with your excuses. To insure your dignity, not to mention your job, you need an Accutron watch. (Advertisement)

20. Is the Lynx a nuisance? If a marauder, a killer, is not a nuisance, just what in your opinion is? Evidence showed that this Lynx has killed at least two deer; how many more is hard to provide but very easy to guess. Had he killed

only to satisfy his hunger, he would have eaten the one before killing the other, and one deer would have been enough for a cat of that size to satisfy him for two weeks. But he killed another one and perhaps many more. For what? it must be for blood thirst, or was it for "ego boosting" of the Lynx.

These people who trap predators don't kill for "ego boosting" but because they have a heart for the innocent deer and sheep, who need protection. Trappers kill only the beasts that kill the poor animals that have no protection. You never saw a lamb or deer do any harm to others.

Why don't you open your heart for our animals that are needed for our own existence, instead of for some needless beasts? Did you ever see the killing of a wolf or lynx? It's the most brutal way imaginable. They snatch the young from their mothers and sometimes I wonder if they even bother to kill them, but just start tearing them apart and eating them while still alive, and beasts like that get protection from people that are supposed to be "humane." Now you tell me if a predator is a "nuisance." (E. Buschmann, letter, *The Country Echo*)

21. Readers inclined to take this gospel [that alien spacemen are responsible for ancient buildings and events] with a grain of salt as large as Lot's wife will fly in the face of some 14 million other readers who have harkened to the intriguing theories of a 38-year-old Swiss hotelier, iconoclast, school dropout and ex-convict named Erich von Däniken. . . . Lecture audiences lap up the von Däniken gospel while orthodox critics argue that his theories are as full of holes as his native Swiss cheese. They claim he was psychically marked as a child when he saw Allied airmen climb out "like creatures from another world" from their force-landed bomber in Switzerland. They cite his three and a half years in prison for embezzlement, forgery and fraud—including heisting money from his Boy Scout troop. They say he wears elevator shoes. . . . (S. K. Oberbeck, "Deus ex Machina," *Newsweek*, October 8, 1973, p. 104)

22. Ah yes, the "thirties" were the days of simple tastes and simple pleasures. They were the days of affluence and abundance. They were the days when bad news didn't seem to travel as fast as it does today. And the family contented itself to sit around the living room listening to the radio together. And of course the most popular face of the "thirties" was Shirley Temple. She brightened up the silver screen and became "America's Sweetheart."

Try as we can, we will never bring back the good old days. But we can revive some of the simple little pleasures from the past. So now Ideal proudly introduces the new Shirley Temple doll. Her head, arms and legs are moveable to create different poses. Her dimples, sunshine smile and golden curls all helped to make her the 'most loved little girl in the world.' Yes, the 'dimpled darling of the thirties' is back again to shower joy and tears on a whole new generation of admirers. (Advertisement)

23. This paper has been sent to you for good Luck. The original is in New England. The Luck has been sent to you. You will receive good luck within four days of receiving this letter, provided you in turn send it on. This is

no Joke. Send copies to people you think need good Luck. Do not keep this letter. It must leave your hands within 96 hours.

A R.A.F. officer received $470,000. Constantine Dias received the chain in 1953. He asked his secretary to make twenty copies and send them out. A few days later he won a lottery of two million dollars. Joe Elliot received $40,000 and lost it because he broke the chain. While in the Philippines, Gene Welch lost his wife six days after receiving this letter. He had failed to recirculate the letter. However, before her death, he received $7.75 million. Carlo Dadditt received the letter and forgot it had to leave his hands within 96 hours. He lost his job; later after finding the letter again, he mailed twenty copies. A few days later he got a better job. (Chain letter)

24. Hägar the Horrible

Hägar the Horrible / By Dik Browne

Source: HÄGAR THE HORRIBLE. Reprinted with special permission of King Features Syndicate, Inc.

25. Smokers Joining Merit Bandwagon. Low tar MERIT attracts increasing number of former high tar smokers. It's clear: MERIT taste is changing attitudes toward low tar smoking. [Advertisement]

26. Surely the professor jests when he says that he agrees with Senator Pococurante's view of opera in Voltaire's "Candide." The professor is a choice example of that more tiresome of beings, the jaded and dyspeptic critic who likes nothing and is in reality a frustrated, nonproducing would-be artist. The joke is on him, ultimately, as Voltaire rather clearly implies. (Letter, *Minnesota Daily*)

27. Been looking for that great, ungainly pen your father had in 1927? Big Red writes again. Too many good things get lost in the shuffle. It's time to get back to fundamental values. It's time for virtue to triumph. So we're bringing back the giant of a pen that roared through the Twenties and Thirties writing checks, letters, autographs, great novels, jazz and mash notes. Yes, Big Red writes again. (Advertisement)

28.

Help us get to the heart of the problem.

29. The BMW 3.0Si. For those who deny themselves nothing. (Advertisement)

30. Changes such as the DH are equal to altering the Ten Commandments. Restore baseball to a nine-player game. (Thomas Zocco, letter, *Sporting News,* April 4, 1983)

31. Senior advisor, speaking to the president: "The Secretary of State has a plan to stop the bickering with your Cabinet. He'll simply fire a warning nuclear shot over the White House." (Cartoon, Ralph Dunagin, *Minneapolis Tribune,* December 24, 1981)

32. Picture of old man and boy. "For four generations we've been making medicines as if people's lives depended on them." Lilly Pharmaceuticals. (Advertisement)

33. 20,679 Physicians say Luckies are less irritating. (Advertisement)

34. Honeywell Pentax ES—a camera for the busy, demanding and talented two percent. If you're successful in your business or profession, the drive to excel and the demand for perfection that helped you get there are the same qualities that can make you a fine photographer. And now photography can be an exceptionally satisfying way to express your creativity and sensitivity without spending a lot of the one thing you're shortest of—time. At about $600, the Honeywell Pentax ES was not designed for mass appeal. (Advertisement)

35. Revolutionaries . . . have never earned a decent wage by legitimate work in which they provided a needed service or product. The reason is they are just too lazy to work at a productive job. . . . [R]evolutionaries are nothing new. They are the same lazy, shiftless visionaries and petty criminals who are always around, only lately they have had more publicity, protection, and attention than ever before. If the college creeps had to pay their own way, if the window smashers had to work at day labor to pay for the windows, and the flag burners were run through boot camp, our revolution would disappear. (Edward Brown, Jr., letter, *Newsweek*, June 1, 1970, p. 12)

36. The Gallup Poll stated that 49 percent were for abortion, 45 percent opposed. It is clear that it is the immoral people who are for abortion. Broken down into age, single, married, education, etc., the figures showed that twice as many single people are for abortion as opposed. This tells us that they are engaged in sexual activity and want abortion to be legal. Also, college graduates were 2 to 1 for abortion. This tells me how colleges are decaying. When you take these percentages off the total, it doesn't leave many decent, sensible people for abortion. (Ron Stevens, letter, *Minneapolis Tribune*)

37. Because you enjoy going first class. In Toledo, Spain or at home, life's more satisfying when you're enjoying the best. That's Passport. Ask for Passport—go first class. (Advertisement)

38. I'm convinced that Madalyn O'Hair is nothing but another moronic Martha Mitchell. She continuously beats her little pink gums, but nothing ever seems to come out. I feel she mocks Christianity because she's just plain jealous. The reason she thinks Christians haven't done anything is because her own moron species keep butting in. All the atheists have done is tell lies about the Bible, organize crime, plot political assassinations, rape, steal, etc. In short, they're making earth hell. (Steve Nichols, letter, *Campus Life*)

39. If not for yourself, for your image. Old Grand-Dad. Head of the Bourbon Family. (Advertisement)

40. New technology. New designs. New standards. New thinking. Add in a great warranty and you have a whole new Hundai. (Advertisement)

FALLACIES OF PRESUMPTION

A third kind of fallacy has to do with presumptions, that is, with taking things for granted in the argument that should not be taken for granted. In Chapter 4 we noted that many arguments make implicit assumptions, and that this is an important and often necessary feature of reasoning. We cannot explicitly say everything that needs to be said; we have neither time nor space for this. But when assumptions become presumptions that so bias the premises that the argument is not cogent or sound, a **Fallacy of Presumption** is committed. Let us look at three of these fallacies.

9. False Dichotomy

The Fallacy of False Dichotomy occurs in an argument of the following sort.

1. You have only two options, A and B.
2. Option B is undesirable (or false).
3. Therefore, you must choose option A (option A is true).

If the premises of this argument are true, if in fact there are only two options and you cannot have one option, you necessarily are left with the other option. In Chapter 12 we show that this presents a valid deductive argument form. The **Fallacy of False Dichotomy** occurs when the arguer presumes in the first premise that there are only two real options, whereas more than two exist in reality. If the options are more than two, the conclusion does not follow.

1. You have option A, B, or C.
2. Option B is undesirable (or false).

It no longer follows that you must choose option A, for you have more options than A, namely, you have either A or C. Consider the Amtrak example on the next page.

The argument here is

1. Either you go to the city by car (and have a long, tortuous drive) or you go by Amtrak.
2. You don't want a very long and tortuous drive.
3. Therefore, you should go by Amtrak.

But there are other options. You could fly (and probably get there much faster). The Amtrak ad assumes that the reader has only two options to get to the city, when another realistic option exists.

10. Begging the Question

Arguers commit the **Fallacy of Begging the Question** when in one way or another they assume what they have to prove. Sometimes this assumption is obvious—for example, the author may simply repeat the conclusion using other language. Consider this argument:

> Voluntary euthanasia is justified because dying people ought to have the right to decide whether to live or die.

Here the conclusion essentially repeats the premise, so that what has *not* been defended is why voluntary euthanasia is justified. This version of the fallacy occurs frequently in dorm or lunchroom discussions. When the arguing gets tough, arguers may simply repeat what they have said, thereby trying to

bolster the truth of their claim. Repeating what is said may be persuasive in the end, but simply repeating the assertion in so many ways provides no evidence for its truth. The argument begs the question in that the conclusion remains undefended and hence is fallacious.

In more challenging versions of this fallacy, the place where the argument has begged the question may be more carefully hidden. In one version a person argues in a circle; that is, the arguer contends that the conclusion is true because it follows validly from true premises. When the person is asked why one of the premises is true, the person defends that premise by appealing to the conclusion. For example:

> (1) Our company produces the highest quality product in the industry. We know this because (2) we sell more of it than our competitor, and (2) the reason we sell more of it than our competitor is that (1) we produce the highest quality product in the industry.

If you carefully follow this reasoning through, you can see that the author has begged the question by arguing in a circle. The conclusion—our company produces the highest quality product—is used to support the premise—we sell more than our competitor—which in turn provides evidence for the claim that we produce the highest quality product in the industry. This becomes very apparent if you diagram this argument: $1 \rightarrow 2 \rightarrow 1$. Arguments that beg the question are suspect because they fail to provide *independent* evidence for the conclusion.

11. Complex Question

A third example occurs in a slightly different context, namely, of arguing not directly but indirectly for a conclusion by means of a question. We noted earlier in this book that questions generally do not make assertions; in a question the person generally seeks information. When so used, questions cannot serve as premises in arguments. At the same time, questions can be so phrased that they make a claim that in turn plays a role in supporting a conclusion. This occurs in the **Fallacy of Complex Questions.** A Complex Question occurs when the question is so phrased that it assumes that you have already agreed to a specific claim, which then provides the basis for further argument. For example, the question "When did you stop beating your roommate?" is complex, for it assumes that you have beaten your roommate in the past; the issue now concerns when you stopped the practice.

Or consider an ad that pictures a motorcycle with all its special parts labeled and a price tag of $3,999. The text reads "Will that be cash or charge?" The question is complex, because it assumes that you will purchase the motorcycle, and all that needs deciding now is whether you will pay for it with cash or a charge card.

This fallacy frequently occurs in business transactions. Managers instruct store clerks not to ask customers whether they want a certain product, but to assume that they want it and to ask customers how they want to pay for it, whether they want it in a bag or box, or whether they want to take it now or put it as layaway. In each case, the clerk wants the customers to assume that they will buy the product so that the only remaining decision is how to pay, wrap, or take it away. The assumption is hidden in the question, and that is what makes this form of discourse persuasive.

Exercise 3

In each of the arguments, (1) identify the conclusion where there is one, and (2) identify the fallacy committed.

1. Tiger

TIGER by Bud Blake

Source: TIGER. Reprinted with special permission of King Features Syndicate, Inc.

2. I've heard enough to make me decide one of two things: quit or smoke Brand X. I smoke Brand X. (Advertisement)

3. "What are you going to do with the extra energy you'll feel wearing SHEER ENERGY?" (Advertisement for pantyhose)

4. It's us. Or rust. Bring your new car to us soon after you buy it and we'll totally rustproof it. Or don't bring your new car to us. And expect to have the body start rusting to pieces from the inside out in a couple of years. Because no car is really rustproofed at the factory. Us. Or rust. It's your choice. (Advertisement)

5. Is Early Times really necessary in your Pussycats? Anything else, and you might wind up with an alleycat. (Advertisement)

6. Which of these highly intelligent Minolta SLRs is right for you? (Advertisement)

7. When asked what makes his team strong yearly, the coach thought the school's tradition was the answer. He backed this by pointing out that when counting all sports, his school is the winningest school in conference history. (*Roseville Suburban Sun*)

8. Citizens can either remain living with the hatred racial conflict brings and not increase taxes and spending, or one can live in a more peaceful environment with a decrease in racial conflict and have to pay a little more. When analyzing the two options, the obvious choice should be the one that eliminates racial conflict in having to spend a little more money. (Student paper)

9. Photo showing four Number One drivers made by the same golf equipment manufacturer. "Which *one* for you?" (Advertisement)

10. Garfield

Garfield ®   by Jim Davis

Source: GARFIELD, © 1987 Paws, Inc. Reprinted with permission of Universal Press Syndicate. All rights reserved.

11. Funky Winkerbean: Well, Les, that big clod, Bull Bushka, has been picking on you for a full week now!

 Les: Yeah! I hate to do it, but I guess there's only one course of action open to me! Who do I see about dropping out of school?
 Source: FUNKEY WINKERBEAN. Reprinted with special permission of North America Syndicates, Inc.

12. The President is a very shrewd politician. If he weren't, he would not be President.

13. Isn't it time you started thinking about number 1: (yourself)?

14. There has never been a sports superstar like [Michael Jordan]. . . . [There is] room to debate who actually was pro football's ultimate ballcarrier. But there is no room for debate with Jordan, because he has left us no room. (Bryan Burwell, "There's No Air Apparent," *Sporting News,* November 3, 1997, p. 9)

15. We don't want to confuse anyone out there. Some people do get what they pay for. Others get much more. Maybe they know something the rest of us don't. Or maybe they simply drive a Chevy Cavalier. It's loaded with gadgets you usually get in more expensive cars. (Advertisement)

Exercise 4

Create a portfolio of fallacies that provides examples from ten of the fifteen major fallacies noted in this chapter and in Chapter 10. The examples can come from advertisements, letters to the editor, editorials, cartoons, articles, books, radio, and television. Include in your portfolio either the original piece or a facsimile of it. Indicate separately (1) the argument in the editorial, advertisement, and so on that you are considering. (2) Name the fallacy committed.

(3) Convince the reader that the argument commits this fallacy (arguments are innocent until proven guilty). (4) Document your source.

Collaborative Learning Exercise

Bring a copy of the examples you are going to use in your portfolio, without your notations, and give the copy to your partner. Have your partner find the conclusion of the arguments and the fallacy your examples commit. Compare answers, and where you and your partner disagree about either the conclusion or the fallacy, come up with a reasoned defense of an agreed-upon position about the fallacy committed.

SUMMING-UP

In this chapter we have considered eleven additional fallacies.

This list of fallacies touches on the more common examples; there are many others. Though learning these examples is important, the larger point is that critical thinkers pay attention to the language of the argument. Chapters 4 and 5 stressed the role of language in comprehending what others say. This chapter makes the same point, though now in the context of arguing. If you pay careful attention to the language, you will be on your way to identifying whether the premises are ambiguous, irrelevant to the conclusion, or by making crucial presuppositions that fail to adequately support the conclusion. Paying attention to language often is no simple task, but it is the first step in freeing you from the persuasive power of arguments that should not be persuasive.

Fallacy of Equivocation: we draw an incorrect conclusion based on ambiguity of meaning.

Fallacy of Amphiboly: we draw an incorrect conclusion based on evidence presented in a syntactically ambiguous way.

Fallacy of the Appeal to Force: the arguer uses the threat of force to establish the truth of a conclusion.

Fallacy of the Appeal to Pity: the arguer uses pity to establish the truth of the conclusion.

Ad Hominem Fallacy: the arguer contends that what a person says is true or false based on that person's character or circumstances and not on evidence relevant to the conclusion.

Fallacy of Appeal to Vanity: the arguer appeals to some quality of the reader or listener to establish the truth of the conclusion.

Fallacy of the Appeal to Numbers: the arguer contends that a statement is true because many people believe it.

Fallacy of Appeal to Time: the arguer appeals to time alone to establish the truth of the conclusion.

Fallacy of False Dichotomy: the arguer presumes that the premise contains only two options, whereas there are really more than two.

Fallacy of Begging the Question: arguers assume what they are trying to prove.

Fallacy of Complex Questions: a question is so phrased that it assumes a person has already agreed to a specific claim, which then provides the basis for further argument.

One final, important point. The fact that an argument is fallacious does not imply that the conclusion of the argument is false. The conclusion may still be true; it is just that the premises fail to establish that truth. For example,

All cows give purple milk.

Whatever moos gives purple milk.

Therefore, all cows moo.

This argument is unsound; it has both false premises and breaks a rule (what we will call being invalid in Chapter 12). Yet the conclusion is true: cows do moo. It is just that we know this fact about cows based on other information (probably a generalization or as an item of common knowledge) but not based on the premises of the argument. So when critical thinkers discover a fallacy, they do not immediately reject the conclusion, for the conclusion may still be true. They realize that the conclusion is not supported by these particular premises, though perhaps people can present other good reasons for accepting the conclusion. Fallacious reasoning leaves the matter undecided.

ANSWERS TO THE EXERCISES

Answers to Exercise 1

1. Conclusion: you should be revolting. Amphiboly on *revolting:* in the premise an adjective; in the conclusion a verb. Equivocation on *revolting:* disgusting or rebelling.
3. Conclusion: This is the shortest graduation ceremony I have attended. Equivocation on *sixty-second:* the number of the commencement or how long in seconds.
5. Conclusion: Smoke pretty Eve. Equivocation on *taste:* flavor vs. aesthetic culture.
7. Conclusion: They manage to space their children so regularly. Equivocation: is *every* exact or an average.
9. Conclusion: Michael left the leaves. Equivocation on *leaves:* items on a tree vs. items not moved.
11. Conclusion: The Kellys will have difficulty fitting the new family in. Amphiboly on *Kelly house:* the house the Kellys owned or where the Kellys live.
13. Conclusion: Use Gravity fragrance for men. Equivocation on *gravity:* a physical force or the cologne.
15. Conclusion: He tastes the salt. Amphiboly: does *it* refer to the salt or the food?

Answers to Exercise 2

1. Conclusion: You should drive the new Mazda MX-3. Appeal to flattery.
3. Conclusion: Be good to those who wait on you in restaurants. Appeal to pity.
5. Conclusion: Eat Heartland cereal. Appeal to the past (tradition).
7. Conclusion: Purchase Stouffer's dinners. Appeal to time (novelty).
9. Conclusion: Purchase Tava liqueur. Appeal to the past (tradition).
11. Conclusion: Vote for Bill Bednarczyk. Ad hominem.
13. Conclusion: Nixon does not have to make White House Tapes available to Congress. Appeal to time (no precedent).
15. Conclusion: Find out how to start a day-care program. Appeal to fear.
17. Conclusion: Drink Twinlab Sports Drinks. Appeal to flattery.

19. Conclusion: You need an Accutron watch. Appeal to fear.
21. Conclusion: Von Däniken's book is suspect. Ad hominem.
23. Conclusion: Send copies of this letter on to others. Appeal to fear. Also hasty generalization.
25. Conclusion: Smoke Merit. Appeal to numbers.
27. Conclusion: Purchase Big Red pens. Appeal to time (tradition).
29. Conclusion: Purchase the BMW 3.0Si. Appeal to flattery.
31. Conclusion: The President's Cabinet should stop bickering. Appeal to force.
33. Conclusion: Smoke Lucky Strike cigarettes. Appeal to numbers.
35. Conclusion: Revolutionaries have never earned a decent wage by legitimate work in which they provided a needed service or product. Ad hominem.
37. Conclusion: Drink Passport Scotch. Appeal to flattery.
39. Conclusion: Drink Old Grand-Dad Bourbon. Appeal to flattery.

Answers to Exercise 3

1. Begging the Question (circular reasoning). Technically this is not an argument because of the questions.
3. Complex Question.
5. Conclusion: Early Times is necessary with your Pussycats. False dichotomy.
7. Conclusion: Our team is strong every year. Begging the Question (circular reasoning).
9. Complex question.
11. Conclusion: I'm going to drop out of school. False dichotomy.
13. Complex question.
15. Conclusion: Drive a Chevy Cavalier. False dichotomy.

Evaluation

Assessing the Validity of Deductive Arguments

The prison inmate in this cartoon makes an unusual confession to the priest. He argues that since all dogs go to heaven and since he is extremely allergic to dogs, he had to commit a crime to avoid accompanying the dogs to heaven. Supposing he is correct about dogs and his allergies, did he really have to commit a crime? Without disputing the truth of the premises, what do you think?

VALIDITY IN DEDUCTIVE ARGUMENTS

In Chapters 10 and 11 we learned how to evaluate the cogency of arguments in terms of their content. We studied standard cases of inductive reasoning—appeals

313

to authority, generalizations, analogies, and causal inferences—and then considered a select number of other fallacies of content in both inductive and deductive reasoning.

This final chapter continues the emphasis on the skills needed for evaluative reasoning. Here we focus on good and bad deductive reasoning. In Chapter 6 we saw that if the premises of a deductive argument are true and the argument breaks no rules (is valid), the conclusion *must* be true; the conclusion follows with certainty from the premises. The reason for this concerns the argument's form or structure, not its specific content. What matters is how the argument is constructed or put together. In fact, no matter what the content, so long as the statements are meaningful and the deductive argument has a valid form, if the premises are true, the conclusion is true.

Deductive arguments whose form or structure does not violate rules of good reasoning are **valid arguments.** Deductive arguments whose form or structure violates rules of good reasoning are **invalid arguments.** They commit what are termed **formal fallacies** because something is amiss with their form or structure. Critical thinkers avoid invalid arguments because they fail to establish the truth of the conclusion. Our task is to learn how to identify and distinguish some valid and invalid forms of deductive reasoning.

An argument that both has true premises and is valid is called a **sound** argument. The following argument is sound, for its premises are true and it violates no rule of sound reasoning.

> Premise: If the Earth were the same distance from the Sun as Mercury, organic life as we know it would not exist on Earth.
> Premise: Organic life exists on Earth.
> Conclusion: The Earth is not the same distance from the Sun as Mercury.

This means that in evaluating deductive arguments we look at two things. One is the truth of the premises. For any argument, we want to know whether the premises are true. The defense of the premises of deductive arguments occurs in the way described in Chapter 10, where we saw that we can determine the truth of premises based upon such things as our experience, authority, or other arguments. We also want to know whether the argument is valid. In this chapter we consider validity.

Logic is the study of arguments and how to evaluate them. To master logic takes substantial time and practice. Since this is an introductory text, we do not attempt such an endeavor here. Many good logic texts are available that can help you succeed in mastering logic. Rather, this chapter introduces you to some basic argument forms or structures that you frequently encounter and helps you to distinguish valid from invalid arguments. If successful, this chapter can whet your appetite for further study of formal reasoning.

ARGUMENT FORMS

As the argument diagrams in Chapter 6 revealed, arguments come in many forms. Yet many of the forms we actually use can be traced back to combinations of a few fundamental forms. In what follows we concentrate on some of these so that you can learn to recognize a few common valid and invalid argument forms.

Valid Conditional Argument Forms

Many of our arguments use the if-then form. For example,

- If the Republicans capture the Congress, we can expect a cutback in social programs. The Republicans did capture Congress, so the cutback is around the corner.
- If I pass my biology test, I will get an academic scholarship, and if I get an academic scholarship, I will be able to stay in school. Hence, if I pass my biology test, I will be able to stay in school.

Whether these if-then or conditional arguments are valid depends on their form or structure. Before we look at their structure, some new vocabulary will be helpful.

- Statements that have an if-then structure are called **conditionals.** As we noted earlier in this book, in a conditional the *if* part of the statement cannot be separated from the *then* part; together they make one statement or claim.
- The claim that follows *if* is called the **antecedent.**

- The claim that follows *then* (whether the word *then* is stated or implicit) is the **consequent.**
- We say that the antecedent **implies** the consequent, which means that the antecedent cannot be true and the consequent false.

In the conditional "If the Republicans capture the Congress, we can expect a cutback in social programs," "the Republicans capture the Congress" is the antecedent, and "we can expect a cutback in social programs" is the consequent. When we say that the antecedent implies the consequent, we mean that the statement "the Republicans capture the Congress" cannot be true while the statement "we can expect a cutback in social programs" is false.

1. Affirming the Antecedent

The first kind of valid conditional argument form has the following structure. [p and q are variables that stand for statements.]

If p is true, then q is true. p is true. Therefore, q is true.

We call this argument form **Affirming the Antecedent.** When we say that the antecedent implies the consequent and that the antecedent is true (that is, we affirm the antecedent), we can conclude that the consequent is true. In the schema, saying that "p is true" affirms the antecedent of the conditional statement. Any argument of this form (provided that p and q remain constant in the argument) is valid.

Our argument about Republicans exemplified this form. The antecedent was "the Republicans capture Congress"; the consequent was "we can expect a cut back in social programs." In our argument we said that since the antecedent implies the consequent, and since the antecedent is true, so is the consequent. The argument, then, is valid.

Note that the order in which the antecedent and the consequent are given is irrelevant. We could just as well argue

p is true. If p is true, then q is true. Therefore, q is true.

John is growing a mustache. If he grows a mustache, he will be more attractive to coeds. Therefore, John will be more attractive to coeds.

or

q is true because p is true, and if p is true then q is true.

Samantha will make varsity because she is the only goalie trying out for the team, and if she is the only goalie trying out for the team, she will make varsity.

Here is another example of this valid argument form but using between the antecedent and the consequent another connector that functions like *if.*

Whenever great earthquakes occur in the San Andreas fault, significant damage to structures occurs. A great earthquake occurred in Los Angeles several years ago along the San Andreas fault. Consequently, great damage to structures must have occurred.

Sometimes the conditional is masked by a statement that says more than is apparent. For example,

Since he entered the room with dirty shoes, he is the culprit who left the footprints in the living room.

Since is a premise indicator; the premise is "he entered the room with dirty feet." The argument assumes the conditional "if he entered the room with dirty shoes, he is the culprit who left the footprints in the living room." That is, when given one premise and a conclusion, you can often find the *assumed premise* by inserting a conditional with the given premise as the antecedent and the conclusion as the consequent. This technique, about which we will say more later, you can use frequently when reconstructing and evaluating arguments.

2. Denying the Consequent

A second valid conditional argument form has the following structure.

If p is true, then q is true. q is false. Therefore, p is false.

We call this argument form **Denying the Consequent.** By saying that the antecedent implies the consequent, and that the consequent is false, we can infer that the antecedent is false (that is, the opposite or denial of the antecedent is true). By saying that q is false we deny the consequent. Any argument of this form (provided that p and q remain constant in the argument) is valid.

We can modify a previous argument to illustrate this form.

> If the Republicans capture Congress, we can expect a cutback in social programs.
> We cannot expect such a cutback, so the Republicans did not capture Congress.

The antecedent is "the Republicans capture Congress"; the consequent is "we can expect a cutback in social programs." We said that since the antecedent implies the consequent, and since the consequent is not true, the antecedent is not true.

To repeat a previous point, the particular order in which the premises and conclusion occur is irrelevant to the validity of the argument. The fundamental structure is what matters. Likewise, you can use words that function like *if* with the same result.

Here are some additional examples.

> If I could just get around this tractor-trailer, we could make it to school on time. Since we didn't make it to school on time, you know that I couldn't pass the tractor-trailer.

> Whenever I try to get my paper done at the last minute, the computer fails. I was lucky this time; the computer finally was working. [Can you supply the conclusion?]

3. Hypothetical Syllogism

We will look at one final valid form using conditionals. [There are other forms that we will not consider.] The **Hypothetical Syllogism** connects two conditional statements in order to conclude to a third conditional statement. In this argument the component conditional statements must exactly exemplify the form we give (though the order of the premises and conclusion does not matter).

> If p is true, then q is true. If q is true, then r is true. Therefore, if p is true, then r is true.

or

> If q is true, then r is true. If p is true, then q is true. Therefore, if p is true, then r is true.

For example:

> If Celeste is Cherie's only sister, and if Cherie's only sister is engaged to Ralph, then Celeste is engaged to Ralph.

> If Arlyn gains back all the weight he lost, his racquetball game will suffer. If Arlyn must have his ice cream every evening before bed, he will gain back all the weight he lost. So if Arlyn must have his ice cream every evening before bed, his racquetball game will suffer.

Note that in contrast to the first two argument forms, both premises are conditional statements and the conclusion of the hypothetical syllogism is itself a conditional. An arguer who uses this form validly concludes to a conditional from two other conditionals.

Invalid Conditional Argument Forms

Each of the valid forms just discussed is associated with a form that is *invalid*. Failure to recognize the difference between different argument forms leads to the failure to distinguish between valid and invalid arguments. In an invalid argument, even though the premises are true, the conclusion *does not follow* from those premises (though the conclusion still might be true for reasons other than found in the premises). We will concentrate on fallacies connected with the first two valid argument forms.

4. Fallacy of Affirming the Consequent

The first of these invalid forms is called the **Fallacy of Affirming the Consequent.** This fallacy occurs when the consequent of a conditional statement is affirmed. Since the antecedent implies the consequent, the arguer then proceeds to affirm the antecedent. This argument has the following form.

> If p is true, then q is true. q is true. Therefore, p is true.

Any argument of this form is fallacious because it has an invalid form. The form is invalid because q might be true for reasons that have nothing to do with p. For example:

> If I drop an egg, it will break. This egg is broken. Therefore, I dropped it.

Suppose it is true that *if* I drop an egg, it will break. Yet finding a broken egg does not tell me that the egg was dropped. Its breakage could result from a number of causes: hitting it with a knife, bouncing it off someone's head, or cooking it with too high heat. That is, the egg may be broken for reasons that have nothing to do with my dropping it, and hence I cannot conclude from the presence of a broken egg that it was dropped. Any argument, therefore, that adopts this form will be invalid: the conclusion neither follows from nor is established by the premises.

Here is an example that some beginners in science think is a good argument.

> If the hypothesis is true, the experiment will work. The experiment worked, so the hypothesis is true.

In this argument because the consequent is affirmed in the premise, the antecedent is believed to be true. This exemplifies our invalid argument form. The argument is fallacious because since the experiment might have worked for reasons that have nothing to do with the truth of the hypothesis, we cannot conclude anything about the hypothesis from the fact that the experiment worked.

5. Fallacy of Denying the Antecedent

Another related invalid form is called the **Fallacy of Denying the Antecedent.** This fallacy occurs when the antecedent of a conditional statement is denied. Since the antecedent implies the consequent, the arguer then proceeds to deny the consequent. This argument has the following form.

> If p is true, then q is true. p is not true. Therefore, q is not true.

For example,

> If the dam breaks, the town will be flooded. The dam did not break, so the town is safe.

Is the town safe? Not necessarily. It could be flooded from sources other than the dam breaking; for example, heavy rain could overload the storm sewers, which in turn will back up into the streets and flood the town. Hence, the conclusion does not necessarily follow from the premises.

Disjunctive Arguments

There is one final argument form to introduce: the disjunctive argument. In a valid disjunctive argument one premise asserts two options, while a second premise affirms that one of these options is unacceptable (false, impossible, unavailable, not wanted). Consequently, the other option must be true. The statement "p or q" is termed a **disjunct**, and an argument that uses a disjunct as one of its premises is a **Disjunctive Argument.** The *valid* form of the argument is

> p is true or q is true. p is unacceptable (false, impossible, unavailable, unwanted). Therefore, q is acceptable (true, possible, available, wanted).

For example, when you go to a restaurant, the waitress generally will offer you a soup or a salad. You might not want soup today. If what she said was true, she must bring you a salad.

> You may have soup or you may have a salad. You don't want soup, so I will bring you a salad.

Note how the disjunctive argument differs from the conditional. In the disjunctive argument, the statements are connected by *or,* whereas in the conditional they are connected by *if-then.* One thing they have in common, however, is that the disjunct and the conditional make one complete, compound statement; they cannot be separated into their component statements. That is, when the waitress offers you soup or salad, she is not offering you soup and she is not offering you salad. She is offering you one or the other. The two disjuncts are part of a single statement.

There is a form of the disjunctive argument that is *invalid.* The form is

> p is true or q is true. p is acceptable (true, possible, available, wanted). Therefore, q is unacceptable (false, impossible, unavailable, unwanted).

For example,

> Either Marvin is my friend or Bob is. Marvin is my friend. Therefore Bob is not my friend.

What makes this argument form fallacious and hence guilty of the **Fallacy of False Disjunction** is that it is possible that both of the disjuncts are true. That is, it is possibly true that both Marvin and Bob are my friends. The *or* is being used in a *weak sense* in that it allows one or the other or both possibilities.

Perhaps your mother has asked you if you wanted cake or ice cream for dessert. If you are wise (and hungry), you ask her for both. Depending on your mother's mood, she may give you both. In giving you both she is within her "argument rights." That is, if she responds to the disjunction of cake or ice cream by giving you both, her initial offer of one or the other remains legitimate because she was using the weak sense of *or.*

The trick with disjuncts is to discern whether the *or* is being used in a *strong* (it gives you only one of two options; you cannot have both) or a *weak* sense (you can have either one or both options). Your generous mother undoubtedly uses the weak sense of *or* when she offers you cake or ice cream for desert. But the waitress in the restaurant is not so generous; when she offers you soup or salad, she is using *or* in the strong sense: you can have one but not both. When critical thinkers consider disjuncts, they are careful to discern when the *or* is being used in the strong sense and when it is being used in the weak sense. This can make a difference, particularly in legal documents.

For example, consider the following argument.

> My house is covered for either wind damage or hail damage. My house received damage from both. Therefore, the insurance company will cover all the damage.

This is probably true, but its truth depends on the sense of *or* in the policy. If *or* is being used in the weak sense, my house is covered for both; but if *or* is being used in the strong sense, my house is not covered for both. When you are making important decisions, it is important to discern which sense of *or* is being employed. For example, if your employer says that you may apply for the position of supervisor or for a transfer to another plant, you will want to find out whether the employer is using *or* in the strong or the weak sense. If the employer is using *or* in the strong sense, *or* limits your options to only one; if the employer using it in the weak sense, *or* allows you to apply for both.

Exercise 1

This exercise is to help you learn the forms we discussed and distinguish valid from invalid arguments. For each of the following arguments, (1) circle the logical indicators, (2) identify the form used, and (3) determine whether the argument is valid or invalid.

1. If p is true, then q is true. q is true. Therefore, p is true.

2. If p is true, then q is true. p is false. Therefore, q is false.

3. Either p is true or q is true. p is false. Consequently, q is true.

4. If p is true, then q is true. If q is true, then r is true. Thus, if p is true, then r is true.

5. When p is true, then q is true. q is true. Hence, p is true.

6. Either p is true or q is true. Since p is true, q is false.

7. q is false because if p is true then q is true, and p is false.

8. Since p is true and if p is true then q is true, then q is true.

9. p is false. q is true, for either p is true or q is true.

10. If q is true, then r is true. Since if p is true then q is true, if p is true then r is true.

11. If p is true, then r is true, for if q is true then r is true, and if p is true, then q is true.

12. q is false because p implies q and p is false.

13. p is false because q is false and p implies q.

14. If p is true then q is true, and if p is true then r is true, so if q is true then r is true.

15. If q follows from p, and p is true, q must be true.

16. Because you have p, and since either p or q is true, q is false.

17. When you have p you have q, and when you have q you have r, so when you have p you have r.

18. Since you do not have q, then you do not have p, for if you have p you have q.

19. Since you do not have p, then you do not have q, for if you have p you have q.

20. Use disjunctive reasoning to solve the following puzzle. You have seven pennies, one of which is a fake. You can only tell it is a fake by weighing it and noting that it weighs more than the others. How would you determine which penny was fake by making only two weighings with a balance scale?

INCOMPLETE ARGUMENTS

Earlier in the book we discussed the fact that arguers make unstated or implicit assumptions. When we communicate, we do not have the time nor is it appropriate to state everything relevant. These assumptions we may expect the listeners or readers to pick out by themselves. We may omit a *premise.* For example, a student may argue

> Since the choir has to sing this evening, the teacher should postpone the paper for another day.

This argument presents one premise—the choir has to sing this evening—and the conclusion—the teacher should postpone the paper for another day. Since every informative deductive argument requires at least two premises, we need to supply the missing premise. We can do this by first finding the conclusion and then the premise. From these two we then construct a conditional statement that connects or links the two—if the choir has to sing this evening, the teacher should postpone the paper for another day. This conditional statement will express the arguer's unstated premise. When we supply the premise, we do so in a way that makes the argument valid.

Task: Consider the following argument and find the assumption the grocer makes.

"If you can learn by watching,
he'd have my job by now."

Source: MARMADUKE. Reprinted with permission of United Features Syndicate, Inc.

Sometimes the arguer supplies the premises but leaves the audience to draw the *conclusion.* This is an important persuasive rhetorical technique, often used in advertising. Advertisers know that if they can get prospective customers to draw the conclusion for themselves, this creates or reinforces the customers' desire to purchase the product, for the customers themselves have drawn the conclusion.

To fill in the conclusion, you need to evaluate the given premises and then decide on the proper form to create a conclusion that will make the argument valid. We try to make the argument valid because we want to give the benefit of the doubt to the arguer. For example, a candidate for office might argue

A vote for my opponent is a vote for higher taxes, and you don't want higher taxes.

The candidate leaves the conclusion—don't vote for my opponent—for the members of the audience to make, hoping that by their making it they will create or strengthen a resolve to vote for the candidate.

Filling in unstated assumptions is an important part of both argument reconstruction and evaluation. Most arguments in real life lack at least one premise; some lack the conclusion. So as you evaluate arguments, remember that premises or conclusions may be missing and that to fully understand what the person argues, you need to fill in these premises yourself from the information that is supplied and from your knowledge of proper argument forms.

Exercise 2

In the following arguments, first identify the conclusion and the premises. Then figure out the missing premise or the missing conclusion.

1. Since their all-star first baseman has not agreed to terms, the team will be looking to trade for a new infielder.

2. Cheryl won't be going to the Caribbean for spring break because she could not get a good enough paying job during the fall term.

3. I told you last week that either you pay your back rent or you move out. So now you must move out by Thursday.

4. Why am I here? Because last week I told you that either you pay your back rent or you must move out, and I haven't received a check in the mail.

5. Charlene cannot be older than her cousin, since her cousin is already in college and Charlene is only a junior in high school.

6. If you fight against that army, you will have to fight alone, and if you fight alone you will lose.

7. Shawn didn't get hired because when he filled out his resume, he was not entirely truthful.

8. He threatened that either I left the house or he would leave. So he is gone.

9. When the bills kept piling up I knew we were in serious trouble, for when bills keep piling up, you know you don't have enough money to survive.

10. Either Julius Caesar was killed on the Ides of March or that was his birthday. But Shakespeare would not have written about Caesar's birthday.

COMPLEX ARGUMENTS

Very often the conclusion of one argument becomes the premise of another argument, and so on, creating a complex argument. We noted these complex argument structures in Chapter 6, where, for example, we diagrammed serial arguments. In such arguments a premise leads to a conclusion, which in turn functions as a premise for another conclusion. $1 \rightarrow 2 \rightarrow 3$. Number 2 is a conclusion that follows from 1; in turn 2 functions as a premise to support conclusion 3.

In practice, such arguments need to be rewritten in order to find the unstated assumptions needed to make the argument fit the forms noted earlier. Consider the following serial argument given by Plato in the *Crito*.

The Laws replied, "Well then, since (1) you were brought into the world and nurtured and educated by us, (2) can you deny in the first place that you are our child and slave, as your fathers were before you?

And if (2) this is true, (3) you are not on equal terms with us; nor (4) can you think that you have a right to do to us (the laws) what we are doing to you."

We might rewrite this argument as follows, supplying the missing premises in order to make the argument valid.

1 + [If you were brought into the world and nurtured and educated by us, you are our child]

↓

2 + [If you are our child, you are not on equal terms with us]   2 + [If you are our child, you don't have the right to do to us what you are doing]

↓   ↓

3   4

Where arguments are complex, you need to evaluate each argument for its validity. In this argument, 1 → 2 must be evaluated, as must 2 → 3 and 2 → 4. Each of these arguments is an example of Affirming the Antecedent and hence valid. The remainder of the evaluation will deal with the truth of the individual premises, both of the given premises and of those assumed. The entire argument will be valid or sound if each of its component arguments is valid or sound. [This may be a good place to review your ability to diagram arguments.]

We will not pursue in more detail the analysis of complex arguments because this process requires developing more sophisticated reasoning skills. Exercises 3 and 4 contain some arguments of this sort to give you the opportunity to try your hand at this complex reasoning process.

Exercise 3

For each of the following arguments, (1) circle the logical indicators. (2) Diagram the argument. (3) Identify the form or structure of each argument, comparing it with the types discussed in this chapter. (4) Then determine whether the argument(s) is valid or invalid.

1. If capital punishment deterred violent crimes, it would be justified. Since it does not deter violent crimes, it isn't justified.

2. If capital punishment deters violent crimes, it is justified. It must deter violent crimes since it is justified.

3. Since capital punishment deters violent crimes, it is justified.

4. Capital punishment would be justified if it deterred violent crimes. But it doesn't deter violent crimes. You can draw the conclusion.

5. Either it is snowing or sleet is falling. Because there is no sleet, it must be snowing.

6. Where there is smoke there's fire. I don't smell any smoke, so the fire must be out.

7. If time means money, you'll save on USAir. Everyone wants to save time. Fly the USA on USAir. (Advertisement)

8. If T. J. told the truth, then his buddy lied. If T. J.'s buddy lied, T. J. is innocent. It follows that if T. J. told the truth, T. J. is innocent.

9. If you'd like to win a free vacation on your next business trip, Marriott has your ticket! So come to Marriott Hotels. (Advertisement)

10. If you're the kind of person who wants to get extra miles without spending extra money, change to Mobil Super 10W-40. Buy Mobil Oil for your next oil change. (Advertisement)

11. One bum to another. "I, for one, am glad the dollar's out of trouble, because if the dollar's in trouble, then the dime is certainly in trouble." (Dana Fradon, *The New Yorker Magazine*, 1971)

12. This chair is made of either walnut or mahogany. It is not made of mahogany, for it is made of walnut.

13. If everyone wore one of these tee shirts, the world would look a lot better. Buy a shirt. Save the earth. (Advertisement)

14. I think I have a very good chance of getting married because I am almost a straight A student. (5th grader)

15. Either you let me pitch or I'll take my bat and ball and go home. You won't let me pitch? See you later.

16. I told her that if she did not have enough money left when she arrived at Grandma's, she should call. She must have enough money left for she didn't call.

17. There is no better way to introduce your children to instant photography than with The Button, Poleroid's fun camera. The Button doesn't require hours of practice to master. You just aim and shoot. (Advertisement)

18. It's either us or rust! (Advertisement)

19. My mother always said, "If you want to marry a dentist, you better use Lavoris mouthwash." So instead of using some mild minty stuff . . . or something that smells like a bottle of medicine. . . I used Lavoris. And you know what? Mother was right. Take it from a dentist's wife: for really clean, really fresh mouth and breath, more dentists (including my husband) use refreshing Lavoris than any other mouthwash. (Advertisement)

20. When my sons are grown up, I would ask, O my friends, to punish them; and I would have you trouble them, as I have troubled you, if they seem to care about riches, or anything more, than about virtue; or if they pretend to be something when they are really nothing then reprove them, as I have reproved you, for not caring about that for which they ought to care, and thinking that they are something when they are really nothing. And if

you do this, both I and my sons will have received justice at your hands. (Plato, *Apology*)

Exercise 4

These are examples of more complex arguments, where statements in the argument are missing, where the conclusion of one is the premise for another, or where the argument needs reconstructing. Follow the directions for Exercise 3. You will need to rewrite the arguments to diagram and analyze them for validity.

1. Ultra Fine's precision plastic point and vivid Flair ink make your writing ultra-easy to read. That's a good enough reason to own one. The way it looks is a good enough reason to give one. (Advertisement)

2. So why not issue an apology to African-Americans, accompanied by reparations or some other form of compensation? "That's exactly why [certain Congressmen] don't want to talk about an apology, because the next step is to talk about reparations," [according to] Ron Walters, a political science professor. (George E. Curry, Editor's Note: 'A Better Way to Apologize,' *Emerge,* September 1997, p. 8)

3. Thanks to Hitachi's exclusive new Super Bright Lens technology, the world's brightest large screen TV picture belongs to Hitachi UltraVision. So does the ultimate in picture clarity with another exclusive, Magic Focus, the world's first and only automatic convergence adjustment feature. Then there's Dolby Pro Logic sound with twin built-in center channel speakers for audio as dramatic as the UltraVision picture. So who's the brightest of them all? The person who chooses Hitachi UltraVision, the best large screen TV in the world. (Advertisement)

4. If you run a business, you probably don't like the idea of paying more than you need to for employee health coverage. That's why Blue Cross and Blue Shield of Minnesota developed a new way of determining rates for our small group plans of 5 to 50 employees. . . . So why pay more than you need for health care coverage? Call a Blue Cross and Blue Shield Marketing Representative today. (Advertisement)

5. I find it pretty sad that [people advocate that] we should move out of the way of tailgaters speeding down the road. That encourages this very unsafe practice. I have had people tell me they tailgate just to get the person in front of them to go faster or get out of their way. If we continue to bow down to such overly aggressive and dangerous behavior, then driving will turn into a free-for-all, with the survival of the most aggressive driver. (Nancy Saville, letter, *U.S. News & World Report,* December 9, 1996, p. 8)

SUMMING-UP

The aim of this chapter is two-fold: to introduce you to valid and invalid argument forms that you encounter in your daily reasoning and to make you aware of how arguments can be strung together. Since many of the arguments we construct or encounter are deductive, it is important to develop the skills needed to assess deductive reasoning, particularly if you will be in an occupation that requires evaluation of reasoning. This chapter, however, presents only a sample of the variety of deductive argument forms. Here is a chart to help you review them.

Valid Argument Forms
    Affirming the Antecedent   Denying the Consequent
    Hypothetical Syllogism   Disjunctive Argument

Invalid Argument Forms
    Affirming the Consequent   Denying the Antecedent
    False Disjunction

By now you have observed several things.

- Critical thinkers carefully attend to the structure of deductive arguments.

Varying structures call for varying assessment. Whereas "If the dog is hungry, he will come home; the dog is hungry, so he will come home" is valid, the argument "If the dog is hungry, he will come home; the dog is not hungry, so he will not come home" is invalid. The arguments look very much alike, but their form or structure varies in ways that affect their validity.

- Critical thinkers know the difference between valid and invalid argument forms and evaluate arguments according to these forms.

After working with this introduction, perhaps you will take the time and have the interest to pursue the discovery of other argument forms in more detail, perhaps by taking a logic course. Taking such a course is especially important for people who are going into professions that require entrance reasoning tests (medicine, law) or that specialize in argumentation (communications, philosophy, politics, and the natural and social sciences).
    Finally,

- Critical thinkers use deductive reasoning to supply missing or assumed premises.

The argument about the dog may be presented with one of its premises missing. For example, "The dog is hungry, so he will come home." Critical thinkers realize that what is missing in the argument is the conditional statement that links the premise with the conclusion: "If the dog is hungry, he will come home." Learning the valid argument forms assists you in discovering what is assumed. And once you find the assumptions, you are in a better position overall to evaluate the argument.

LOOKING AHEAD

Although this book has come to its end, for you the task of critical thinking has just begun. The skills you developed will be in constant demand throughout your life. You will be asked to believe many claims and often take actions on those beliefs: buy a specific product, vote for a candidate for office, travel somewhere for a vacation, marry a special friend, take one job rather than another, pursue a profession, or choose a place to educate your children. To find out whether those claims are true and justified, your first tasks will be to learn what is said and to comprehend it. This involves putting the claims into your own language so that you can test your comprehension of them. Once you have comprehended the claims, you need to ask why they are true. Through analysis you will gather and identify the evidence and arguments relevant to deciding their truth. After analysis you may have the opportunity to work with the claims and their arguments by developing your own position in creative ways to solve the problems you confront. You will also have the opportunity to assess the truth of the proposed claims in light of the evidence provided. In each of these tasks, you will be functioning at the various levels of critical thinking we developed in Chapter 2.

Having worked through this book, you have learned the basic information and skills needed to be a critical thinker. Your challenge is to develop these skills through lifelong learning and practice.

ANSWERS TO THE EXERCISES

Answers to Exercise 1

1. Affirming the consequent. Invalid
3. Disjunctive argument. Valid
5. Affirming the consequent. Invalid
7. Denying the antecedent. Invalid
9. Disjunctive argument. Valid
11. Hypothetical syllogism. Valid
13. Denying the consequent. Valid
15. Affirming the antecedent. Valid
17. Hypothetical syllogism. Valid
19. Denying the antecedent. Invalid

Answers to Exercise 2

1. P: Their all-star firstbaseman has not agreed to terms.
   C: The team will be looking to trade for a new infielder.
   A: If their all-star firstbaseman has not agreed to terms, the team will be looking to trade for a new infielder.
3. P: Either you pay your back rent or you move out.
   C: You must move out by Thursday.
   A: You didn't pay your back rent.
5. P: Her cousin is already in college and Charlene is only a junior in high school.
   C: Charlene must not be older than her cousin.
   A: If her cousin is already in college and Charlene is only a junior in high school, Charlene must not be older than her cousin.
7. P: Shawn was not entirely truthful on his resume.
   C: Shawn did not get hired.
   A: If one is not entirely truthful on one's resume, one won't get hired.

9. P: When the bills keep piling up, you know you don't have enough money to survive.
C: When the bills kept piling up, I knew we were in serious trouble.
A: When you don't have enough money to survive, you know you are in serious trouble.

Answers to Exercise 3

1. (1) If capital punishment deterred violent crimes, it would be justified. Since (2) it does not deter violent crimes, (3) it isn't justified.
   Since: premise indicator

   1 + 2

   ↓

   3

   Denying the Antecedent. Invalid

3. Since (1) capital punishment deters violent crimes, (2) it is justified.
   Since: premise indicator

   1 + [assumed premise: If capital punishment deters violent crimes, it is justified.]

   ↓

   2

   Affirming the Antecedent. Valid

5. (1) Either it is snowing or sleet is falling. Because (2) there is no sleet, (3) it must be snowing.
   Because: premise indicator

   1 + 2

   ↓

   3

   Disjunctive argument. Valid

7. (1) If time means money, you'll save on USAir. (2) Everyone wants to save time. (3) Fly the USA on USAir.

   1 + 2

   ↓

   3

   Affirming the Antecedent. Valid

9. (1) If you'd like to win a free vacation on your next business trip, Marriott has your ticket! So (2) come to Marriott.
   So: conclusion indicator

   1

   ↓

   2

Affirming the Antecedent. Valid

11. One bum to another, (1) "I, for one, am glad the dollar's out of trouble, because (2) if the dollar's in trouble, then the dime is certainly in trouble."
Because: premise indicator

2

↓

1

Denying the Consequent. Valid

13. (1) If everyone wore one of these tee-shirts, the world would look a lot better. (2) Buy a shirt. (3) Save the earth.

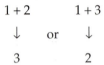

The argument is ambiguous. It is either Affirming the Antecedent (Valid) or Affirming the Consequent (Invalid).

15. (1) Either you let me pitch or I'll take my bat and ball and go home. (2) You won't let me pitch? (3) See you later.

1 + 2

↓

3

Disjunctive argument. Valid

17. (1) There is no better way to introduce your children to instant photography than with The Button, Poleroid's fun camera. (2) The Button doesn't require hours of practice to master; you just aim and shoot.

2 + [assumed: If the Button doesn't require hours of practice to master, there is no better way to introduce your children to instant photography than with The Button.]

↓

1

Affirming the Antecedent. Valid

19. My mother always said, (1) "If you want to marry a dentist, you better use Lavoris mouthwash." So instead of using some mild minty stuff . . . or something that smells like a bottle of medicine . . . (2) I used Lavoris. And you know what? (3) Mother was right. Take it from a dentist's wife: for really clean, really fresh mouth and breath, more dentists (including my husband) use refreshing Lavoris than any other mouthwash.

1 + 2

↓

3

Affirming the Consequent. Invalid

Answers to Exercise 4

331

CHAPTER *12*
*Assessing the Validity
of Deductive
Arguments*

1. (1) Ultra Fine's precision plastic point and vivid Flair ink make your writing ultra-easy to read. That's a good enough reason to (2) own one. (3) The way it looks is a good enough reason to (4) give one.
good enough reason to: conclusion indicator
two arguments:

1 + [assumed premise: If it makes your writing ultra-easy to read you should own one.]

↓

2

Second argument:

3 + [assumed premise: If it looks good, you should give one.]

+

4

Affirming the Antecedent. Valid

3. (1) Thanks to Hitachi's exclusive new Super Bright Lens technology, the world's brightest large screen TV picture belongs to Hitachi UltraVision. (2) So does the ultimate in picture clarity with another exclusive, Magic Focus, the world's first and only automatic convergence adjustment feature. (3) Then there's Dolby Pro Logic sound with twin built-in center channel speakers for audio as dramatic as the UltraVision picture. So who's the brightest of them all? (4) The person who chooses Hitachi UltraVision, the best large screen TV in the world.
So: conclusion indicator.

1 + 2 + 3 + [Assumed premise: if a TV has these features, you would be the brightest person to choose it.]

↓

4

Affirming the Antecedent: Valid

5. (1) I find it pretty sad that [people advocate that] we should move out of the way of tailgaters speeding down the road. (2) That encourages this very unsafe practice. (3) I have had people tell me they tailgate just to get the person in front of them to go faster or get out of their way. (4) If we continue to bow down to such overly aggressive and dangerous behavior, then driving will turn into a free-for-all, with the survival of the most aggressive driver.
The argument goes
(4)
(5) Assumed: If driving turns into a free-for-all, that encourages this very unsafe practice.
(6) Therefore, if we continue to bow to such overly aggressive and dangerous behavior, it will encourage this very unsafe practice.
(7) We don't want to encourage this very unsafe practice.
(1) We should not advocate moving out of the way of tailgaters speeding down the road.

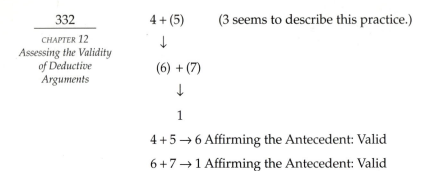

$$4 + (5) \qquad \text{(3 seems to describe this practice.)}$$

$$\downarrow$$

$$(6) + (7)$$

$$\downarrow$$

$$1$$

$4 + 5 \rightarrow 6$ Affirming the Antecedent: Valid

$6 + 7 \rightarrow 1$ Affirming the Antecedent: Valid

Credits

Chapter 1: Page 2: Wayne Wangstad, *St. Paul Pioneer Press,* August 22, 1995. Reprinted by permission.

Chapter 3: Page 33: Excerpted from Christopher John Farley, "If It Was a Bomb, Then Whodunit?" *Time,* August 12, 1996, p. 26. (1996 Time, Inc. Reprinted by permission. Page 33: From "Banned Freon Now Favorite of Smugglers," *Charlotte Observer,* August 13, 1996. Reprinted with permission of Knight-Ridder/Tribune Information Services. Page 34: Elisabeth Salina Amorini, letter, *U.S. News & World Report,* August 5, 1996, p. 11. Reprinted by permission. Page 35: Morton Sobell, retired electrical engineer, letter, *New York Times,* August 10, 1997. Reprinted by permission. Page 37: Bill Sharp, letter, *U.S. News & World Report,* January 27, 1997. Reprinted by permission. Page 37: Philip Guercio, letter, *U.S. News & World Report,* January 27, 1997, p. 7. Reprinted by permission. Page 37: Excerpted from Diane Ganzer, letter, *St. Paul Pioneer Press,* August 13, 1996. Reprinted by permission. Page 38: Rosemary Falls, "Look-Obsession Hurts Our Girls," *Waco Tribune Herald,* August 11, 1996. Ms Falls is a teacher and columnist. Page 41: Excerpts from Celia Moore, "Pensions Made Woman-Friendly," *Ms.,* July/August, 1997, p. 34. Reprinted by permission of Ms. Magazine, (c) 1997. Page 41: Letter from Harlan Smith, economics professor emeritus, University of Minnesota, letter, *St. Paul Pioneer Press,* January 25, 1997. Reprinted by permission. Page 42: Adapted by permission from Eugene Murphy and John King, "Icy Message from the Antarctic," *Nature,* September 4, 1997, p.20. Copyright, 1997, Macmillan Magazines, Limited. Page 42: Excerpted from "A Monument, or an Oilfield," *New York Times,* September 18, 1997, p.A34. Copyright, 1997, by The New York Times. Reprinted by permission. Page 42:Excerpted from "Birds Do It, Bees Do It," *The Economist,* August 30, 1997, pp.59-60. Copyright 1997, The Economist Newspaper Group, Inc. Reprinted with permission. Further Reproduction prohibited. *www.economist.com.* Page 44: Former First Lady, Rosalynn Carter, Vice Chair, The Carter Center, and Honorary Chair, Last Acts: Care and Caring at the End of Life, "All of Us Must Face Hard Facts of Death," *Atlanta Constitution,* July 2, 1997. Reprinted by permission. Page 47: Excerpted from Joe Klein, "Pretty Close to Awful," *Newsweek,* September 16, 1996, p. 51. Copyright 1996, Newsweek, Inc. All rights reserved. Reprinted by permission. Page 50: Molly Ivins, "You Don't Have to Rely on the Brokaw/ Jennings/Rather Cersions," *TV Guide,* December 3, 1985. By permission of Molly Ivans and Creatos Syndicates. Page 53: Excerpted by permission of author from E. Gordon Gee, "Coast of College Education Remains One of America's Great Bargains Despite Tuition Increases," *The Phoenix Gazette,* August 19, 1996. Page 54: Excerpted from Sheryl Gay Stolberg, "A Revolution in AIDS Drugs Excludes the Tiniest Patients," *New York Times,* September 8, 1997, p. A14. Copyright 1997 by the *New York Times.* Reprinted by permission. Page 54: Excerpted from James A. Lovell and Brian Kyhos, "Continue Our Quest in Space," *Denver Post,* August 10, 1996. Page 55: Excerpted by permission from Martin Olav Sabo, "Is Constitutional Change Needed to Slay Deficit Dragon?" *St. Paul Pioneer Press,* February 5, 1997. Page 56: Excerpted with permission from Donald M. Hunten, "Pipelines to the Planets," *Nature,* September 11, 1997. Pp. 125-6. Copyright 1997, Macmillan Magazines, Limited. Page 62: Walter G. Perry, letter, *St. Paul Pioneer Press,* September 4, 1996, p. 4. Reprinted by permission of Walter Gordon Perry. Page 62: Excerpted by permission of the author from Thomas Sowell, "Yes, Blacks Can Make It on Their Own," Time, September 8, 1997, p. 62. Page 62: Excerpted from "Let Private Partners Assist National Parks," *St. Paul Pioneer Press,* August 20, 1996. Reprinted by permission. Page 63: Excerpted from George Dohrmann, "Turnovers Tell Tennessee's Tale," *St. Paul Pioneer Press,* September 18, 1997. Reprinted by permission. Page 63: William F. O'Keefe, "Spend Road Taxes on America's Roads," *Tallahassee Democrat,* September 2, 1996. Reprinted with permission of Knight-Ridder/Tribune Information Services. Page 65: Excerpted from Sasha Nemecek, "Frankly, My Dear, I Don't Want a Dam: How Dams Affect Biodiversity," *Scientific American,* August, 1997, pp. 20, 22. Reprinted with permission. Copyright 1997 by Scientific American, Inc. All rights reserved.

Chapter 4: Page 85: Claire Rudolf Murphy and Hane G. Haigh, "Gold Rush Women," *Alaska,* October, 1997, p. 49, which was excerpted from the authors' book *Gold Rush Women* (Anchorage: Alaska Northwest Books, 1997.) Page 85: Maitland Sharpe, "Taking a Stand," *Outdoor Ethics Newsletter,* 12, no. 2 (Winter 1993), p. 7. Reprinted by permission of the Isaak Walton League of America. Page 103: Excerpted by permission of Les Palmer from "Expensive Meat," *Alaska,* April 1997, p. 54.

Chapter 5: Page 126: Reprinted by permission of the author from Charles W. Gusewelle, "The Weight of Remembrance Extends the Half-Life of a Life of Regret," *The Kansas City Star*, August 24, 1996. Page 129: Excerpted from Tim Giago, "Congress Should View Indian Nations as Sovereign Peers," *St. Paul Pioneer Press*, June 23, 1997. Reprinted by permission of the Giago Book Publishing L.L.C., 2218 Jackson Blvd., Suite 9, Rapid City, SD 57702. Page 130: Excerpted from Debra O'Connor, "Sending More Cops to the Suburbs May Be Misguided," *St. Paul Pioneer Press*, February 19, 1995. Reprinted by permission. Page 130: Excerpted from Martin Dyckman, "Breaking the Camel's Back," *St. Petersburg Times*, August 15, 1993. Copyright St. Petersburg Times, 1993. Reprinted by permission. Page 131: Excerpted from Darrell Caraway, letter, *Motor Trend*, January 1997, p. 12. Reprinted by permission. Page 132: Stephanie Palmquist, "Home, Shmome," *Echo*, October 10, 1997. Reprinted by permission. Page 133: Excerpted from Barbara Kantrowitz, "The Messiah of Waco," *Newsweek*, March 15, 1993, p. 56. Copyright 1993 Newsweek, Inc. All rights reserved. Reprinted by permission. Page 133: Tracey Glumich, "In Search for Identity," *Echo*, September 26, 2997. Reprinted by permission. Page 134: "Unembarrassable," an interview with Martin Amis, in "How the World Sees Us," *New York Times Magazine*, June 8, 1997, pp. 44-5. Copyright 1997 by the New York Times. Reprinted by permission. Page 135: Excerpted from Tom Powers, "Tonya Flashes Her Fascinating Facets to Media," *St. Paul Pioneer Press*, February 19, 1994. Reprinted by permission. Page 137: Excerpted from Matt Mirmak, "Political Correctness Hindrance to Liberal Arts," *Echo*, April 26, 1991. Reprinted by permission.

Chapter 6: Page 144: Excerpted from Tim Giago, "Congress Should View Indian Nations as Sovereign Peers," *St. Paul Pioneer Press*, June 23, 1997. Reprinted by permission of the Giago Book Publishing L.L.C., 2218 Jackson Blvd., Suite 9, Rapid City, SD 57702. Page 146: Excerpted from S.K. Oberbeck, "Dues ex Machina," *Newsweek*, October 8, 1973, p. 104. Copyright 1973 Newsweek, Inc. All rights reserved. Reprinted by permission. Page 155: Excerpted by permission of Sky Publishing from "A Dust-Choked Spiral," *Sky and Telescope*, November, 1997, p. 57. Page 168: Excerpted (with numbers added) from William Vickrey and James A. Mirrlees, "Making Honesty Pay," *Scientific American*, January, 1997, p. 18. Statement numbers added. Reprintedt with permission. Copyright 1997 by Scientific American, Inc. All rights reserved.

Chapter 7: Page 178: Excerpted by permission of the author from Cora Holmes, "Another Ghost at Chemofski," *Alaska*, October, 1997, pp. 40-41. Cora Holmes is the author of *Good-bye, Boise, Hello, Alaska* and *Dear Cora*,both published by Reinman Publications. Page 183: Gary Dawson, "New Speed Limits Being Enforced," *St. Paul Pioneer Press*, July 30, 1997. Reprinted by permission. Page 189: Excerpted by permission of Kalmbach Publishing Co., "Neanderthal Origins," *Earth*, October, 1997, p. 11. Page 199: Excerpted from Matt Clark, "The Calcium Craze," *Newsweek*, January 27, 1986, p. 50. Copyright 1986, Newsweek, Inc. All rights reserved. Reprinted by permission. Page 201: Excerpted by permission of C. Everett Koop, Surgeon-General of U.S., 1981-1989, "Let's Get Serious about Deterring Youth from Starting to Smoke," *Lexington Herald-Leader*, September 8, 1996. Page 205: Martin Dyckman, "Breaking the Camel's Back," *St. Petersburg Times*, August 15, 1993. Copyright, St. Petersbur Times, 1993. Reprinted by permission.

Chapter 8: Page 229: Bob Herbert, "After Collapse, Cities Emerging From Rubble," *Lexington Herald-Leader*, October 7, 1996. Reprinted with permission of Knight-Ridder/Tribune Information Services. Page 230: Arthur Caplan, "Spanking Experts Say It's Not Necessary," *Grand Forks Herald*, October 28, 1996. Reprinted with permission of Knight-Ridder/Tribune Information Services.

Chapter 10: Page 267: Robert S. Boyd, "New Techniques Allow Scientists to `Map' Brain," *St. Paul Pioneer Press*, November 9, 1997. Reprinted by permission. Page 272: Cal Thomas, "Children Take a Look at TV, and the Results Are a Turn-off," *Philadelphia Daily News*,March 6, 1995. Reprinted with permission of Knight-Ridder/Tribune Information Services. Page 272: Excerpted by permission of Associated Press from "Few Have Confidence in Social Security," *St. Paul Pioneer Press*, May 17, 1994. Page 273: Rhonda Bock, " MPIRG Releases Results from Poll," *Echo*, November 8, 1991. Reprinted by permission. Page 276: Anecdote contributed by Richard Bredenberg in "Campus Comedy." Reprinted with permission from the April 1981 *Reader's Digest*, p. 49. Copyright 1981 by The Reader's Digest Assn., Inc. Page 277: Karen Beauvaus, letter, *The Atlanta Constitution*, October 18, 1997. Reprinted by permission. Page 281: "2 Studies Explore Gulf Vet's Health," *Charlotte Observer*, November 13, 1996. Reprinted with permission of Knight-Ridder/Tribune Information Services.

Chapter 11: Page 290: Anecdote contributed by Lois Garman, "Cap and Gone." Reprinted with permission from the May 1979 *Reader's Digest*, p. 200. Copyright 1979 by The Reader's Digest Assn., Inc. Page 301: S. K. Oberbeck, "Deus ex Machina," *Newsweek*, October 8, 1973, p. 104. Copyright 1973, Newsweek, Inc. All rights reserved. Reprinted by permission.

Chapter 12: Page 326: Nancy Saville, letter, *U.S. News & World Report*, December 9, 1996, p. 8. Excerpted by permission.

Index

Places in the text where the word listed is defined are indicated by page numbers in bold type.

335